OECD Development Pathways

Multi-dimensional Review of Kazakhstan

VOLUME I. INITIAL ASSESSMENT

OECD

dev
DEVELOPMENT CENTRE

This work is published under the responsibility of the Secretary-General of the OECD. The opinions expressed and arguments employed herein do not necessarily reflect those of the OECD, its Development Centre or of their member countries.

This document and any map included herein are without prejudice to the status of or sovereignty over any territory, to the delimitation of international frontiers and boundaries and to the name of any territory, city or area.

Please cite this publication as:
OECD (2016), *Multi-dimensional Review of Kazakhstan: Volume 1. Initial Assessment*, OECD Development Pathways, OECD Publishing, Paris.
http://dx.doi.org/10.1787/9789264246768-en

ISBN 978-92-64-24675-1 (print)
ISBN 978-92-64-24676-8 (PDF)

Series: OECD Development Pathways
ISSN 2308-734X (print)
ISSN 2308-7358 (online)

The statistical data for Israel are supplied by and under the responsibility of the relevant Israeli authorities. The use of such data by the OECD is without prejudice to the status of the Golan Heights, East Jerusalem and Israeli settlements in the West Bank under the terms of international law.

Photo credits: Cover © design by the OECD Development Centre.

Corrigenda to OECD publications may be found on line at: *www.oecd.org/publishing/corrigenda*.

Foreword

Economic growth matters, but is just one facet of development. Policy makers are required to reconcile economic, social and environmental objectives to ensure that their country's development path is sustainable and that the lives of its citizens improve.

OECD Development Pathways is a series that looks at development from the perspective of the multiple objectives it involves, beyond an exclusive focus on growth. The OECD launched Multi-dimensional Country Reviews (MDCRs) in 2012. This new tool aims to assist countries in achieving inclusive, sustainable and equitable growth that can improve the well-being of citizens. The reviews identify and analyse the major constraints to development and provide concrete policy recommendations. MDCRs take a cross-cutting rather than a sectoral perspective, allowing for the discussion of policy interactions. The MDCR methodology is based on quantitative economic analysis, as well as qualitative approaches including foresight and participatory workshops that involve actors from the private and public sectors, civil society, and academia.

This report is the first volume to be produced in the context of the MDCR of Kazakhstan. The first three MDCRs, undertaken in Myanmar, the Philippines and Uruguay, allowed for the methodology to be tested and further improved. Kazakhstan is one of three countries to engage in an MDCR as part of the second wave. The other two are Côte d'Ivoire and Peru. The MDCR of Kazakhstan is the first review to be implemented as part of the 2015-16 Country Programme signed between Kazakhstan and the OECD.

This review comes at a time when Kazakhstan faces new challenges in transforming its model of development to sustain inclusive growth and progress in the well-being of its citizens. While the recommendations are intended primarily to support public action by the national authorities of Kazakhstan, the findings are also useful for academics, the private sector, and civil society.

The MDCRs are implemented in three distinct phases: diagnosis, in-depth analysis of the main constraints to development, and support to implementation. The phased approach allows for a progressive learning process and culminates in a final synthesis report to inform reforms in Kazakhstan. This diagnostic report is the outcome of the first phase of the MDCR of Kazakhstan. It delivers an overarching assessment of development in Kazakhstan and identifies the main constraints to sustainable and equitable development.

Acknowledgements

Multi-dimensional Country Reviews are the result of a collaborative effort of the OECD and the country under review. Work on the first phase of the MDCR of Kazakhstan was carried out jointly by the OECD Development Centre, the OECD Economics Department and the OECD Statistics Directorate, with support from the Ministry of National Economy of Kazakhstan. The review was initiated with an OECD mission to Astana in December 2014. The editorial cut-off date for this manuscript is 31 July 2015. Amendments to relevant sections were made following the change in exchange rate regime in August 2015.

The review was produced under the guidance of Mario Pezzini, Director of the OECD Development Centre, Martine Durand, OECD Chief Statistician, and Catherine Mann, OECD Chief Economist, and the leadership of Jan Rieländer, head of the MDCR Unit at the Development Centre. The review was co-ordinated by Juan Ramón de Laiglesia (OECD Development Centre) and drafted by Juan Ramón de Laiglesia (OECD Development Centre), Koon Hui Tee (OECD Development Centre), Carine Viac (OECD Statistics Directorate), Martin Wermelinger (OECD Development Centre), and Sanne Zwart (OECD Economics Department). Deirdre Culley (OECD Development Centre) managed the workshop "Kazakhstan: Vision and Challenges" held in Astana on 9 December 2014 and provided significant inputs to the report. The review also benefited from the contributions made by Vararat Atisophon, Céline Colin, Sinead Dwyer, and Natasha Tereshchenko, as well as from administrative support provided by Myriam Andrieux and Georgina Regnier, and logistics support provided by Saltanat Janenova (Graduate School of Public Policy, Nazarbayev University).

The team is grateful for insightful comments provided by Amandine Aubry, Carl Dahlman, Nicola Harrington and Lahra Liberti from the Development Centre and Pierre Beynet from the Economics Department, as well as Andrew McQueen (OECD Education Directorate), Jibran Punthakey (OECD General Secretariat), Azhar Umbetova, Dastan Umirbayev (both from the Ministry of National Economy) and participants in the workshop held in Astana on 16 and 17 July to discuss the diagnostic. Sara Alpysbayeva, Zhanna Kapsalyamova and Batzhan Akmoldina from the Economic Research Institute provided valuable inputs and insights. Useful inputs were also received from Krzysztof Michalak (OECD Environment Directorate), Jean-François Lengellé (Global Relations Secretariat), and Aktoty Aitzhanova (National Analytical Centre). The Economic Research Institute hosted the workshop "Kazakhstan: Vision and Challenges".

The Multi-dimensional Country Review of Kazakhstan was made possible by the financial contribution of the Ministry of National Economy of Kazakhstan. The review has benefited from the support of Erbolat Dossayev, Minister of National Economy of the Republic of Kazakhstan, and his staff. Madina Abylkassymova (Vice-Minister of National Economy) and her team have been a valuable counterpart throughout the process, both technically and analytically. The contributions of Zhandos Rustembaev, Azhar Umbetova and Dastan Umirbayev, were particularly valuable to ensure continuous interaction between the OECD team and the administration of the Republic of Kazakhstan. Other ministerial departments and agencies also provided useful contributions, namely, the Civil Service and Anti-Corruption Agency, the Committee on Statistics of the Republic of Kazakhstan, the Ministry of Agriculture, the Ministry of Education and Science and its Information-Analytical Center, the Ministry of Healthcare and Social Development, the Ministry of Internal Affairs, the Ministry of Investment and Development, the Ministry of Finance, and the National Bank of Kazakhstan. The team is also grateful for inputs received from the Baiterek Holding Co., the *Damu* Entrepreneurship Development Fund, the Development Bank of Kazakhstan, the Federation of Trade Unions of the Republic of Kazakhstan, the International Bureau of Human Rights, Kasipkor, Kazagro, Kazakhstan Temir Zholy, National Analytical Centre, the National Chamber of Entrepreneurs, Nazarbayev University, Samruk-Kazyna Holding Co., the Asian Development Bank, the Eurasian Development Bank, the World Bank, the United Nations Economic Commission for Asia and the Pacific and the United Nations Development Programme.

The team is grateful to Stephen Jessel for editing the manuscript and for the OECD Development Centre's Communications and Publications Unit, especially Aida Buendía, Delphine Grandrieux, Vanda Legrandgérard and Elizabeth Nash for their support in editing, laying out and producing the report.

Table of contents

Tables

Figures

Acronyms and abbreviations

ADB	Asian Development Bank
BCP	Becas Chile Programme (Scholarship Chile Programme)
BTI	Bertelsmann Stiftung Transformation Index
CAGR	Compound Annual Growth Rate
CAPEX	Capital Expenditure
CEPII	Centre d'Etudes Prospectives et d'Informations Internationales
CIS	Commonwealth of Independent States
CPI	Corruption Perception Index
DAMU	"DAMU" Entrepreneurship Development Fund
DH	District Heating
EBRD	European Bank for Reconstruction and Development
EEU	Eurasian Economic Union
EGDI	United Nations E-Government Development Index
EITI	Extractive Industries Transparency Initiative
ESCAP	United Nations Economic and Social Commission for Asia and the Pacific
EU	European Union
FDI	Foreign Direct Investment
GCR	Global Competitiveness Report
GDP	Gross Domestic Product
GHG	Greenhouse Gas
GNI	Gross National Income
HIV	Human Immunodeficiency Virus
HOB	Heat-Only Boiler
HR	Human Resources
IBP	International Budget Partnership
ICT	Information and Communications Technology
ILO	International Labour Organization
IMF	International Monetary Fund
IPR	Intellectual Property Rights
ISCED	International Standard Classification of Education
ISIC	International Standard Industrial Classification
IT	Information Technology

LITS	Life in Transition Survey
LPI	Logistical Performance Index
LULUCF	Land Use, Land-Use Change and Forestry
MDCR	Multi-dimensional Country Review
MLS	Minimum Living Standard
MTEF	Medium-term Expenditure Framework
NAP	National Action Plan for Development of Functional Literacy for School Children
NBK	National Bank of Kazakhstan
NEET	Not in Employment, Education, or Training
NF	National Fund
NIS	Nazarbayev Intellectual Schools
NU	Nazarbayev University
O&M	Operations and Maintenance
OBI	Open Budget Index
OECD	Organisation for Economic Co-operation and Development
OGD	Open Government Data
OPEX	Total Operating Costs
PISA	Programme for International Student Assessment
PM10	Particulate Matter up to 10 micrometers in size
PPL	Public Procurement Law
PPP	Purchasing Power Parity
R&D	Research and Development
RCA	Revealed Comparative Advantage
SAI	Supreme Audit Institution
SEZ	Special Economic Zone
SGBP	State Guaranteed Benefit Package
SIGI	Social Institutions and Gender Index
SITC	Standard International Trade Classification
SMEs	Small and Medium-Sized Enterprises
SOE	State-Owned Enterprise
SPAIID	State Programme on Accelerated Industrial and Innovative Development
SSSAP	State Sponsored Study Abroad Programme
TB	Tuberculosis
TFP	Total Factor Productivity
TSA	Targeted Social Assistance
TVET	Technical and Vocational Education and Training
UGS	Ungraded Schools
UNCITRAL	United Nations Commission on International Trade Law

UNCTAD	United Nations Conference on Trade and Development
UNDP	United Nations Development Programme
UNECE	United Nations Economic Commission for Europe
UNT	Unified National Test
USSR	Union of Soviet Socialist Republics
WEF	World Economic Forum
WHO	World Health Organization
WIPO	World Intellectual Property Organization
WJP	World Justice Project

Editorial

Improvements in living standards and the quality of life that are associated with development involve multiple processes of structural transformation in the economy. Kazakhstan has been engaged in a process of deep transformation in the last decades, from a planned to a market-based economy and from a Soviet republic to a unitary, multi-ethnic sovereign state. It has achieved stability and fast economic growth based on its natural wealth. In turn, in Kazakhstan economic growth produced improvements in citizens' material conditions and reduced income inequality.

Maintaining the momentum of socio-economic development will require continued structural transformation. Oil, gas and mining played an important role in igniting growth at the beginning of the century, and Kazakhstan weathered the great recession thanks to prudent management of natural resource income. However, significantly lower oil prices and the weaker economic performance of China and the Russian Federation call for structural transformation if Kazakhstan is to sustain its growth path. Sustainable growth underpinned by productivity gains can be reaped by broadening the base of domestic activities, by shifting labour and capital from low to high productivity sectors, and by moving up the value chain. More broadly-based growth will increase inclusiveness, and productivity increases will underpin further wage growth and widen the demand for higher skills. To achieve balanced development, Kazakhstan must also turn its attention to dimensions beyond economic growth, to the environment and to non-income dimensions of well-being, where progress has not kept pace with income growth.

Kazakhstan faces significant challenges in bringing about these transformations. The report identifies seven key constraints. Natural resource wealth presents great opportunities but natural-resource dependency exposes the economy to external risks and can crowd out growth in other sectors. The concentration of economic clout in the hands of the state and of a few private actors, and the fragility and underdevelopment of the financial sector, also limit prospects for economic diversification. In the environmental arena, regulation has so far proved insufficient to overcome the legacy of natural resource exploitation, with consequences for well-being in Kazakhstan and for climate change globally. Implementation capacity for certain government functions is still limited. Despite government efforts, corruption still affects multiple state functions, undermining trust in the state, the business environment, meritocracy, and entrepreneurial spirit. Finally, the skills system has achieved an increase in years of schooling for the labour force, but has failed so far to equip it appropriately for a number of sectors.

Kazakhstan has embarked on an ambitious reform agenda. It intends to strengthen competitiveness and increase the effectiveness of public institutions to achieve better environmental outcomes and sustainable and inclusive economic growth. Kazakhstan is working with the OECD to advance this reform agenda through a Country Programme that includes 19 policy reviews and possible adherence to 29 OECD legal instruments. This report documents the first phase of the *Multi-dimensional Review of Kazakhstan*, the first policy review undertaken in the context of the Country Programme. The Multi-dimensional Review brings together expertise from across the OECD and uses a multiplicity of perspectives and analytical tools to provide a multidimensional diagnostic of Kazakhstan's development dynamics and of what it will take to achieve Kazakhstan's development goals.

Mario Pezzini	Martine Durand	Catherine Mann
Director	OECD Chief Statistician	OECD Chief Economist
OECD Development Centre	Director of the Statistics Directorate	Head of the Economics Department

FACTS AND FIGURES OF KAZAKHSTAN

(Numbers in parentheses refer to the OECD average)

THE LAND, PEOPLE AND ELECTORAL CYCLE			
Population (million)[e]	17.5	Official language	Kazakh, Russian[1]
Under 15 (%)[e]	27.8 (18)	Form of government	Constitutional republic
		Last presidential election	April 2015
Population density (per km²)[e]	6.4 (37)		
Land area (thousand km²)	2 724.9		
THE ECONOMY			
GDP, current prices (billion USD)[e]	222.4	In % of GDP	
Latest 5-year average real GDP growth[e]	7.7 (0.6)	Exports of goods and services[d,e]	38.8 (49.2)
GDP per capita, PPP (thousand USD)[e]	23.1 (37.2)	Imports of goods and services[d,e]	26.7 (46.0)
Inflation rate[e]	6.7 (0.6)	Main exports[e] (% of total merchandise exports)	
General government total expenditure[e] (% of GDP)	22.1 (41.9)	Crude oil	68.5
General government revenue[e] (% of GDP)	23.8 (38.0)	Iron and steel	4
		GDP shares (%)[d]	
		Agriculture, forestry and fishing	4.6 (2.5)
		Industry, including construction	34.5 (26.6)
		Services	54.2 (70.7)
WELL-BEING			
Consumption possibilities			
GDP per capita (thousand USD)	13.6	Proportion of population under national minimum income standard[d] (%)	2.8
Income inequality (Gini coefficient)	28 (31)		
Work			
Labour force participation (% of 15 to 64 year old)	78.5 (71.1)	Unemployment rate[e] (%)[b]	5.0 (8)
Employment-to-population ratio (15 and over, %)	68.7	Youth unemployment rate[d] (ages 15 to 24, %)	3.9 (17.3)
Housing			
Households with improved sanitation facilities[c] (%)	97.5	Satisfaction with the availability of affordable housing[e] (% satisfied)	37.1 (45.7)
Environment			
Fine particulate matter concentration (urban-population PM10, µg per m³)	47	Perceived water quality[e] (% of respondents satisfied with water quality)	52 (68.0)
Education			
Expected years of schooling	15	PISA score (2012)	
Enrolment rates[e]		Reading	393 (496)
Primary (Net)	98.7	Mathematics	432 (494)
Secondary (Gross)	106.6	Science	425 (501)
Tertiary (Gross)	48.4 (70)		
Health			
Life expectancy[e]	71.6 (80)	Satisfaction with personal health	69.6 (75.6)
Vulnerability			
Homicide rate[c] (per 100 000)	7.8	Perceived safety[e] (% felling safe working at night)	53.0 (60.3)
Social connections		*Empowerment*	
Population stating they have someone to count on in case of need[e] (%)	76 (79.8)	Perceived corruption[e] (%)	66
Life evaluation			
Life satisfaction[e] (average on 1-10 scale)	6.0		
THE ENVIRONMENT			
CO_2 emissions[b] (kg per 2005 PPP USD of GDP)	0.78	Forest area[c] (% of land area)	1.2
Renewables[c] (% of total primary electricity supply)	8.38		

Notes: 1) According to the Constitution of Kazakhstan, Kazakh is the state language of Kazakhstan, while Russian is used officially on equal grounds in state institutions and local administrations.

a) Data for 2010

b) Data for 2011

c) Data for 2012

d) Data for 2013

e) Data for 2014

Sources: Committee on Statistics (2015), Ministry of National Economy of the Republic of Kazakhstan, *www.stat.gov.kz/* last accessed August 2015; Committee on Statistics (2014), *Kazakhstan in Figures*, Ministry of National Economy of the Republic of Kazakhstan, Astana; World Bank (2015) World Development Indicators (database), *http://data.worldbank.org/*, Washington DC; IMF (2015), World Economic Outlook Database, International Monetary Fund, April 2015 edition, Washington DC; Gallup (2015), Gallup World Poll (database), Gallup Organisation; OECD (2015), Better life index 2015 (database), Paris; OECD (2015), OECD Labour Force Statistics Database, Paris; OECD (2014), PISA 2012 Results in Focus: What 15-year-olds know and what they can do with what they know, OECD, Paris.

Administrative regions of Kazakhstan

Executive summary

Kazakhstan's economy and society have undergone deep transformations since the country declared independence in 1991. The transition period was unstable and disruptive, with a 31% contraction of real gross domestic product (GDP) by 1995, hyperinflation, and the destruction of 1.6 million jobs during the 1990s. Kazakhstan's growth performance since recovering in 2000 has been impressive, averaging almost 8% per annum in real terms and leading to the creation of 2.3 million jobs. The period since independence was also marked by significant social transformation evidenced by massive migration flows during the 1990s and the evolution of social policy.

In 2012 Kazakhstan set the overarching objective of becoming one of the 30 most developed countries in the world by 2050. Under this overarching objective, the Kazakhstan 2050 Strategy sets priorities for economic, social and political development in the medium term.

This report is the first volume of the Multi-dimensional Country Review (MDCR) of Kazakhstan. It describes the driving forces of development in Kazakhstan and identifies the major constraints to equitable and sustainable progress in growth and well-being.

Main findings

After deteriorating during the early years after independence, living standards have improved, although outcomes remain below par in several non-monetary dimensions. The improvement has been notable in material conditions. Growth in incomes and the creation of salaried jobs have contributed to a dramatic fall in poverty, while inequality remained low. In dimensions of well-being where public services provision plays an important role, Kazakhstan performs well in measures that assess quantity but underperforms in measures of quality and effectiveness. For example, basic education is quasi-universal but average quality and learning outcomes are below par. Health outcomes also remain poor whether measured by life expectancy, mortality rates or the prevalence of major infectious diseases.

Extractive industries play an important role in the economy of Kazakhstan, as they generate 16% of GDP. The oil and gas sector contributed half of real GDP growth between 2000 and 2005. It still looms large in the economy. When related activities are included, the oil and gas sector generates as much as 30% of GDP, almost a third of budget revenues and close to two-thirds of exports.

Flows linked to oil and gas revenues are managed prudently, avoiding the main symptoms of Dutch disease. Most oil-related public revenues are channelled to a National Fund with limited transfers to and from the national budget. However, large oil-related flows have challenged macroeconomic and financial stability in the past, mainly through large exchange rate devaluations and instability in the banking sector.

Kazakhstan is vulnerable to external shocks through its dependency on natural resources and its geographic position. Fluctuations in raw material prices, the economic performance of its main trade partners (in order of importance, the European Union, the People's Republic of China and the Russian Federation) and geopolitical tensions have important effects on economic performance. Kazakhstan is landlocked, which makes it dependent on its neighbours for the efficiency of logistics networks. Ties with the Russian Federation are strong and further sustained by the creation of the Eurasian Economic Union in January 2015.

Sources of growth beyond natural resource sectors remain underexploited. With labour force participation at almost 80% and unemployment at 4%, there is little scope for activating workers. However, there is scope for increasing productivity by shifting labour to more productive sectors, especially away from agriculture (which represents 24% of employment but 5% of GDP). There is also scope to increase investment which, at 23% of GDP, is lower than in comparable countries.

Diversification has progressed modestly but faces multiple obstacles. Manufacturing and knowledge-intensive services have experienced growth in employment and productivity since 2011 but remain small. The market structure limits competition and contestability, and there is ample room to lower regulatory burdens and improve the business climate.

Key constraints to development

Natural-resource dependency exposes the economy to external risks and can hamper growth in other sectors. Natural wealth offers great opportunities. However, the importance of extractive sectors has led to a configuration of the economy that is not conducive to the development of other sectors.

The concentration of economic clout in the hands of the state and of a small number of private actors constrains investment and dynamism. Public and state-owned entities still account for 30% to 40% of GDP. Strong price controls in a number of markets, discretionary intervention by state actors and limited competition distort price signals and limit opportunities for new entry and innovation. A privatisation programme is being implemented and legislation adopted in 2015 constrains the sectors of intervention of state-owned firms.

The financial sector remains fragile and underdeveloped. Non-performing loans accounted for 26% of the total loan portfolio in December 2014 before falling to 10% in June 2015. Banks are the main source of external funding for firms, yet lending to the private sector remains low. The financial sector operates in a difficult environment, characterised by weak rule of law, dollarisation and until recently a challenging exchange rate regime.

The effectiveness of environmental regulation is insufficient to overturn a legacy of overexploitation of natural capital and has consequences for environmental well-being. The energy intensity of the economy is high, as is the rate of greenhouse gas emissions. Adverse environmental outcomes are a major concern due to the inherent value of the environment but also because they challenge the sustainability of the current development model.

Widespread corruption hinders the business environment and undermines meritocracy and entrepreneurial spirit. It affects key state functions including the delivery of public service and public procurement. The government has identified control of corruption as one of its key priorities and has undertaken several anti-corruption measures as well as key institutional reforms.

There is limited implementation capacity for certain government functions. Outcomes in the quality of service provision are mediocre. Some constraints are sector-specific, such as the legacy of underinvestment in primary healthcare or the difficulties in human resource management in the education sector. Others are cross-cutting, including integrity issues, and difficulties in co-ordination across agencies and in managing efficiency differentials across administrations.

The skills system has so far failed to generate appropriately equipped labour in sufficient quantity in the labour market for a number of sectors, which limits their growth potential. Skills formation is focused on the education system. A more integrated approach to skills formation and acquisition and human resources management, going beyond formal education, would link skills formation with the importance of small and medium enterprises, the development of opportunities, and the attraction and retention of talent.

Multi-dimensional Review of Kazakhstan
Volume 1. Initial Assessment

Chapter 1

Overview: Realising Kazakhstan's development vision

Kazakhstan's economy and society have undergone deep transformations since the country declared independence in 1991. The country has adopted an ambitious vision for the year 2050 with the overarching goal of joining the group of the 30 most developed countries. This report is the first output of the Multi-dimensional review (MDCR) of Kazakhstan. The goal of the MDCR of Kazakhstan is to support Kazakhstan in achieving its development objectives by identifying the key constraints to development, providing actionable policy recommendations and supporting the implementation of these recommendations. This chapter contextualises the work of the MDCR by discussing the deep determinants of socio-economic development in Kazakhstan in terms of economic growth and well-being. It goes on to summarise the key findings of the remaining chapters. Finally, it discusses the key development constraints identified in the first phase of the MDCR.

This document is the first report prepared in the context of the Multi-dimensional Country Review (MDCR) of Kazakhstan. The MDCR is undertaken to support Kazakhstan in achieving economic and social development objectives and improving the well-being of its citizens. The MDCR of Kazakhstan is being implemented in three phases, each leading to the production of a report.

This first report aims to identify the binding constraints to achieving sustainable and equitable improvements in well-being and economic growth. The second phase will further analyse the key constraints identified in this report in order to formulate policy recommendations that can be integrated into the development strategy of Kazakhstan. The final phase of the MDCR will provide support to the implementation of these recommendations.

The analysis relies on benchmarking the performance of Kazakhstan against two reference points. The first is a set of comparator countries, selected in consultation with Kazakhstan on the basis of their similarities to Kazakhstan in terms of economic structure and endowments and their history of development. The second is a synthetic benchmark constructed to indicate how the average country would perform across a number of dimensions if it had Kazakhstan's income per capita.

This introduction highlights the main findings and summarises the key issues and constraints of the first report. It sets out with a discussion of economic developments since independence. It then broadly follows the four thematic chapters of the report by analysing well-being, growth, competitiveness and governance. After an overview of the main determinants which shape the perimeter of future of growth, it concludes by summarising the key constraints that will be the focus of the second stage of the MDCR.

Kazakhstan has undergone deep transformations since independence

Kazakhstan's society and economy have undergone deep transformations since the country declared independence in 1991. The unstable and disruptive transition period between independence and the turn of the century was ultimately succeeded by a period of high economic growth. Although the country experienced a brief but severe crisis during 2008-09, it recovered quickly and has experienced slower, but more balanced, economic growth since. During this second period, Kazakhstan has intensified its engagement in the global arena.

The country established national economic institutions and started the transition from a centrally planned to a market economy at independence, and the related disruption and economic instability led to a deep recession between 1992 and 1994 and to hyperinflation. Between 1990 and 1995, GDP fell by 36% and inflation rates peaked at 3 060% in 1992. While the country was recovering, it was hit by the fallout of the Russian financial crisis of 1998. The deep disturbance in the economy led to the destruction of 1.6 million jobs during the 1990s.

Since recovering in 2000, Kazakhstan's growth performance has been impressive, averaging almost 8% per annum in real terms between 2000 and 2013 despite a considerable slowdown during the crisis. This growth acceleration has to a large extent been driven by the oil and gas sector, since production, which expanded dramatically between 1998 and 2007, and prices were high in most years of the period. During this period of high growth, income poverty fell dramatically from 47% to 2% of the population as unemployment fell to 5% in 2013.

The trends since independence have led to a transformation of the economy away from agriculture and towards extractive industries. The share of industry in value added rose from 20% in 1990 to a maximum of 33% in 2010, largely driven by the growth of the oil, gas and mining sectors from 8% of value added in 1998 to 20% in 2010. Employment has also shifted from agriculture, the share of which fell from 35% to 24% between 2001 and 2014, and towards services, which provide 56% of jobs, and construction, the share of which rose from 4% to 8% over the decade.

The period since independence was also marked by significant social transformation. During the transition period, massive emigration of ethnic Russians, Germans and Slavs led the population of Kazakhstan to fall from 16.5 million in 1991 to 14.9 million in 2000. At the same time, Kazakhstan welcomed significant numbers of ethnic Kazakh immigrants (*oralmans*), profoundly transforming the composition of society. During the same period fertility plummeted, falling from 3.16 births per woman in 1987 to 1.76 in 1999, while out-of-marriage births increased from 13% to 26%, signalling an evolution in cultural norms. During the 2000s, the downward trend of fertility was reversed, but the rate stabilised at 2.5, largely below pre-independence levels. Similarly, marriage patterns recovered partially while age at marriage continued on an upward trend.

Since independence, Kazakhstan has been engaged in a process of state-building and construction of a national identity strongly influenced by Kazakh symbolism and values. The inflow of ethnic Kazakh migrants and the increasing importance of the Kazakh language were important components of this process. During the bonanza of the 2000s, state-building progressed steadily with a strong focus on technocratic management and greater balance between the preponderance of Kazakh culture and language and the construction of a civic Kazakhstani identity.

State-owned companies and large conglomerates dominate the business landscape in Kazakhstan. Privatisation in Kazakhstan began as early as 1991. In spite of the rapid privatisation of small scale assets and businesses, by 1996, only 35% of gross domestic product (GDP) came from the private sector. Public and state-owned entities still account for 30% to 40% of GDP at present. Moreover, the first wave of privatisations gave rise to large firms headed by powerful businessmen who extended their range of operations into diversified holding companies.

Structural determinants of growth

The economic history of Kazakhstan since independence has been marked by strong external forces which also shape current growth perspectives. Kazakhstan's oil production accelerated from 1998, with crude prices at historical lows (below USD 20) and increased as prices were multiplied by seven in ten years before their fall in the midst of the 2007/08 financial crisis. The future will also be marked by the evolving significance of its geographical position and by key structural factors. Being landlocked makes Kazakhstan dependent on its neighbours for the efficiency of logistics networks. However, growth in the People's Republic of China since 1990 and significant regional and transcontinental projects such as the Eurasian Customs Union and the New Silk Road offer new opportunities for Kazakhstan's development.

Geopolitical factors can heavily influence future economic developments in Kazakhstan. Trade ties with the Russian Federation are strong and further sustained by the creation of the Eurasian Economic Union (EEU) in January 2015. The creation of the EEU has the potential to boost regional trade but also further exposes Kazakhstan to economic developments in Russia. Price competitiveness suffered from the depreciation of the Russian ruble, leading to an expansion of the band in which the tenge (KZT) was allowed to fluctuate. Moreover, around 50% of Kazakhstan's exports are sold to European Union (EU) countries, most of which pass through Russia and are likely to be affected by trade disputes between Russia and the EU. To the east, trade with China has been flourishing, with non-oil exports expanding by around 20% per annum, and Chinese growth in the 2000s played an important role in sustaining high prices for primary exports. However, the slowdown in China's growth is reducing prices and demand for natural resources, with lower export growth for Kazakhstan as a result.

Kazakhstan faces a unique demographic situation which is likely to pose a challenge to performance in a number of well-being dimensions in the medium term. The dependency ratio is expected to rise from 46% to between 55% and 60% by 2020 and then remain at such levels for a significant period of time (up to 2100 according to UN population estimates). This is the result of the massive population movements of the early 1990s. The smaller cohorts born during those years will arrive on the labour market at the same time as the baby boom generation of the post-World War II era retires, causing an increase in dependency ratios. However, as newer, larger generations reach working age, they will compensate for the gradual ageing of the population which will stabilise the dependency ratio. The rapid increase in the share of older people among dependents in the late 2010s will pose a challenge given the relatively undistinguished outcomes in the health sector.

Whether future growth will enhance the role of the major growth poles of Astana and Almaty or be more diversified will have a significant bearing on the sector composition of growth and the evolution of the large regional inequalities that exist. The low levels of labour productivity in agriculture, paired with low levels of internal migration and of urbanisation, make it likely that rural to urban migration will accelerate if there are significant improvements in productivity in agriculture, or in the urban manufacturing and services sectors. The creation of other growth poles in secondary cities would help diversify the economy but such choices may be linked to the level of sophistication of the industries developed.

Human capital is the source of key competitive advantages in Kazakhstan, as the labour force has significantly more schooling than a number of comparator countries. With 15 years of education, the average worker in Kazakhstan is more educated than in benchmark countries (Chapter 2). Whether the choice is made to seek the implantation of a large set of manufacturing industries to counter deindustrialisation or to find high-tech niches to better exploit the human capital base or to expand service provision (in financial services and more) for the region and beyond, the quality and adaption of human capital will be a critical element in the success of the development strategy.

Kazakhstan's vision, objectives and strategy for 2050

Building on the success of the past 15 years, in 2012 Kazakhstan set the overarching objective of becoming one of the 30 most developed countries in the world by 2050. Kazakhstan's recent growth performance means it is well placed to reach this goal. Under this overarching objective, the Kazakhstan 2050 Strategy sets priorities for economic, social and political development (see Box 1.1).

Box 1.1. **Kazakhstan's vision for 2050**

In December 2012, President Nursultan Nazarbayev presented the vision of Kazakhstan for 2050 and the strategy which is to serve as the foundation of Kazakhstan's development strategy architecture. In January 2014, the president presented the plan to achieve the objectives for 2050 in a subsequent speech entitled "Kazakhstan's way – 2050: Common Aim, Common Interests, Common Future".

The vision for 2050 is that of "a society based on a strong state, a developed economy with universal labour opportunities" where citizens "represent a society of educated, free people speaking three languages. They are citizens of the world. They travel. They are open to new knowledge. They are industrious. They are patriots of their country". "[The] Kazakhstan of 2050 is ... a state with a strong economy, with everything devoted for a person. With a strong education, a great healthcare. With peace and serenity. With citizens who are free and equal, and the authority is fair. With supremacy of the law".

The "main goal is to join the group of 30 most developed countries" by 2050. The meaning of "developed" in this overarching goal is indefinite but eminently multi-dimensional as what characterise a developed country are fundamentally "new qualities in the life of people".

This objective is associated with multiple targets, some of which are quantified, related to economic performance (including targets for annual GDP growth and GDP per capita), to the structure of the economy, and to social sectors – from urbanisation to life expectancy, safety, peace and stability. President Nazarbayev's January 2014 speech highlighted the rates of investment, scientific research, productivity, share of small and medium enterprises (SMEs) in the economy and standards of living of OECD countries as the "natural benchmark for Kazakhstan" in realising the vision for 2050.

In the 2012 speech, President Nazarbayev listed seven primary objectives:

- Further developing and strengthening statehood
- Transitioning to new principles of economic policy
- Comprehensive support for entrepreneurship will be a leading force of the national economy
- Forming the new social model
- Creating modern and efficient education and healthcare systems
- Increasing the accountability, efficiency and functionality of the state apparatus
- Establishing adequate international and military policy that is responsive to new challenges

Sources: Linn (2014), Nazarbayev (2012), Nazarbayev (2014).

Success in achieving Kazakhstan's vision for 2050 will be judged not only on the basis of GDP per capita but also on the basis of citizens' well-being and the transformation of the economy and society. As part of the first phase of the MDCR, the OECD organised a workshop in Astana, to explore the collective view of Kazakhstan in the future of a set of participants from a variety of sectors (government ministries, research institutes, the private sector, and academia). The themes that emerged reflected the dimensions outlined in Kazakhstan's long-term vision. Besides economic outcomes (economic modernisation, trade diversification, income, infrastructure, technology, and agriculture), the workshop identified dimensions relating to social development (education, population, health and healthy lifestyles, social inclusion), sustainability (through the green economy) and institutional development (efficiency of government institutions, culture).

Kazakhstan takes a strategic and hierarchical approach to development planning that translates long-term objectives into sectoral and local plans. The long-term strategic vision is at the top of this hierarchy. This is understood to be the Kazakhstan 2050 vision and strategy, although elements of the previous strategy (Kazakhstan 2030) remain in force. The second level is represented by ten-year strategic development plans, of which the current one was approved under the Kazakhstan 2030 strategy and runs until 2020. The ten-year strategic development plans include quantitative targets and progress is assessed at the mid-point and the end of each implementation period. The third level is represented by sectoral programmes, of which a small number are given priority and classified as state programmes.

Box 1.2. **Multi-dimensional Country Review workshop: "Kazakhstan: Vision and Challenges"**

The OECD Multi-dimensional Country Review (MDCR) methodology includes a series of participatory workshops designed to facilitate an exchange of information and ideas between the research team and local stakeholders. The workshops also provide context for the treatment of specific issues and ensure that the eventual recommendations are both relevant and actionable. Their design relies on strategic foresight methodologies that emphasise participatory processes and contend that the future is shaped by present preferences and choices. In this way, the research team can optimally learn from participants' different perspectives, as well as their aspirations for their country.

The first MDCR workshop for Kazakhstan was held in Astana on 9 December 2014 with support from the Ministry of National Economy. The workshop drew together almost 40 participants from government ministries, research institutes, the private sector and academia around the theme *Kazakhstan: Vision and Challenges*.

The first session focused on Kazakhstan's developmental objectives and vision for the future. In small groups, participants prepared a story about a citizen's life and lifestyle in 2050 when Kazakhstan is one of the ten most developed countries in the world (see the Annex for the story summaries). The main themes emerging from the different stories reflect those outlined in Kazakhstan's long-term visions, notably the Kazakhstan 2030 and 2050 Strategies: economic modernisation, most notably in terms of agriculture and diversification, as well as sustainability and the environment. Most groups also mentioned access to healthcare and culture, and citizens enjoying a healthy lifestyle, while modern technology, connectivity and infrastructure featured prominently in some of the stories.

The second session reflected on the importance of context and the external environment for Kazakhstan's development. Oil dependency and climate change were identified as major vulnerabilities. Participants also emphasised geopolitical risks related to the crisis in Ukraine, regional terrorism and drug trafficking. On the other hand, integration into global markets and institutions were noted as major opportunities.

The workshop identified several challenges for Kazakhstan in realising its developmental objectives. Access to high-quality education and healthcare emerged as major constraints, and participants highlighted in particular the lack of good training and proper remuneration in related professions, the existence of corruption and the major existing differences between regions. Participants also emphasised the dearth of healthy lifestyles and the potential health impacts on the population. National reliance on resource extraction, lack of business culture, difficulties in arranging financing, and insufficient research and development (R&D) were seen as hampering progress towards a more diversified and sustainable economy. The cost of green technologies and the related lack of trust in their efficiency and uncertainty around investment returns further impede sustainable development. Finally, improving institutional quality and eradicating corruption would help considerably in reaching Kazakhstan's 2050 objectives.

The long-term strategy of Kazakhstan also includes a strong drive towards a greener economy. In 2013, Kazakhstan adopted the *Concept for Transition of the Republic of Kazakhstan to Green Economy*. This policy document sets objectives in several sectors for 2020, 2030 and 2050 (water resources, agriculture, energy efficiency, power, air pollution, and water management). While this policy document was adopted after the presentation of the long-term strategy Kazakhstan 2050, it will be implemented through the incorporation of its provisions into strategic and sectoral programmes and is therefore a key instrument of long-term strategy.

Summary and main findings

Well-being in Kazakhstan has improved significantly since the year 2000

Well-being encompasses many dimensions, from material conditions to the multiple aspects of quality of life. This report draws on the "How's life" framework for the measurement of well-being established for the OECD and adapted for emerging economies to match the breadth covered by the vision.

After deteriorating during the early years after independence, living standards have improved although outcomes remain below par in various dimensions of quality of life. Material conditions improved, with a dramatic fall in poverty driven by growth in incomes and in particular the creation of salaried jobs, as well as wage policies. Subjective satisfaction with quality of life has also increased since 2005 and income inequality has fallen from already low levels (the Gini coefficient falling to 0.28). Nevertheless, marked inequalities persist between regions and between urban and rural populations. Most market-driven well-being outcomes have improved, as have quantity indicators such as school enrolment or access to health. However, the quality of public services remains low relative to comparable countries and outcomes in education and health in particular remain below what would be expected from a country with the level of per capita income of Kazakhstan. Subjective assessments of overall living standards have also improved, in contrast with perceptions of certain dimensions of well-being such as housing or health, which are poorer than those of comparator countries.

In dimensions of well-being where public service provision plays an important role, Kazakhstan performs well in indicators that assess inputs and quantity, but underperforms in measures of quality and effectiveness. In education, basic education has become quasi-universal, but the average quality remains poor. Learning outcomes, such as those measured by the Programme for International Student Assessment (PISA), are below par. Notwithstanding recent progress in key indicators such as maternal and child mortality and in the provision of healthcare by a national health system, with a set of guaranteed benefits provided free, health outcomes also remain poor whether measured by life expectancy, mortality rates, the prevalence of major infectious diseases such as tuberculosis or the severity of certain public health problems.

A transformation of the social model is under way but still faces a number of hurdles

The social protection model is evolving towards a less protective model that rewards individual responsibility. The pension system transitioned from pay-as-you-go to a fully funded defined contribution system from 1998. Currently, social security is organised in a three-pillar system with guaranteed benefits, mandatory and voluntary pillars. Income support has evolved away from social assistance, with means-tested income support losing funding in favour of more generous categorical allowances covering specific categories regardless of income for disabled persons and families with children, and survivor allowances among others. A health system reform is under consideration which would move from a budget-financed national health system to a contribution-based system.

The income support system currently plays a minor role in lowering inequality. The tax and transfer policies reduce inequality by 7% in Kazakhstan, compared to 29% in OECD countries. The fall in inequality during the 2000s can be largely attributed to the evolution of market incomes, as the creation of salaried jobs accelerated, absorbing unemployment, and wage policy sustained widely distributed growth in incomes.

Greater efficiency in delivering social protection and social services will be fundamental to avoiding inequality of opportunity. Inter-regional inequality remains high, in income as well as in several other dimensions of well-being, notably health. Given the high level of out-of-pocket payments for health services relative to comparator countries, there is a risk of unequal treatment. The education system is multi-tiered with wide variations in quality. While generally, socio-economic status is found to matter less for learning outcomes in Kazakhstan than in the majority of countries participating in PISA, the performance of the education system in terms of equity depends critically on meritocratic criteria for access to elite schools, which is apparently challenged by corruption.

Extractive industries, in particular the oil and gas sector, play an important role in the economic fortunes of Kazakhstan

The oil and gas sector was the driving force of the economic acceleration at the beginning of the century but appears somewhat less important for economic growth now. Between 2000 and 2005, the oil and gas sector contributed half of GDP growth. The take-off in growth was spurred by the combination of a dramatic increase in oil production in 1998, a large devaluation of the tenge in 1999 and rising oil prices. However, oil production has levelled off since 2007 and the non-oil economy has become the driver of the economy since the mid-2000s.

Extractive industries still make up a large share of value added and the majority of exports and foreign investment, a sign that conditions are not sufficient for diversifying the economy. The oil and gas sector generates around 30% of GDP, almost a third of budget revenues and close to two thirds of exports. Exports are highly concentrated with the five top exports (all of them from extractive industries) commanding 70% of total exports. Extractive sectors also command the majority of foreign direct investment (FDI) flows (over 50% over 2010-14 down from 70% to 80% before 2008).

By and large, flows linked to oil revenues have been managed prudently, avoiding the main symptoms of Dutch disease. Most oil-related public revenues (9.9% of GDP or total public revenues from the oil sector of 11.4% of GDP in 2012-14) are channelled to the National Fund and sterilised. Transfers to and from the national budget are limited, which to a large extent isolates public finances from the volatility of oil-related revenues. As a result, Kazakhstan has been in a good position to deal with transient shocks, including through one of the largest stimulus packages (relative to GDP) implemented in response to the crisis in 2009.

Large oil-related inflows have nonetheless challenged macroeconomic and financial stability in the past, mainly through the exchange rate and the financial sector. Monetary policy is aimed at maintaining price stability. Until the switch to a feely floating currency in August 2015, tight management of the exchange rate limited short-term exchange rate volatility, but this led occasionally to large devaluations of 18% against the US dollar in February 2009 and again in February 2014. The transition to a floating exchange rate will mitigate the uncertainties regarding the timing and scale of potential devaluations which weighed on the business climate. This transition may however, lead to volatile exchange rates and challenge financial sector stability in the short run. Rapid oil-based growth also triggered major inflows to the banking system, which caused a real estate bubble and ultimately a banking crisis. Its aftermath has not yet been fully resolved, as non-performing loans still accounted for 26% of total banking sector loans at the end of 2014 before falling to 10% by mid-2015.

The economy's reliance on natural resources remains high and is a major source of exposure to external risks, in particular in the current geopolitical situation. The bulk of foreign direct investment (FDI) in the recent past has been related to the extraction of national resources. Moreover, the dominant share of raw materials in exports makes the country vulnerable to external shocks and signals a missed opportunity to move up the value chain.

The weight of extractive industries also imposes significant environmental risks that need to be tackled more effectively. The energy intensity of the economy is high, as is the rate of greenhouse gas emissions. Past growth patterns have created significant environmental challenges that challenge the sustainability of the current growth model, the achievement of goals in economic policy and well-being. Scarce water resources and mounting industrial waste will require better management if agriculture is to grow at a reasonable pace, while air pollution in major urban centres is likely to challenge both health objectives and the attraction of international talent.

Sources of growth in non-oil sectors remain underexploited

Labour productivity growth has been steady, but there are signs of exhaustion in the driving forces. Average labour productivity grew by 50% between 2003 and 2013. The main contributor to GDP growth in the 2000s was growth in total factor productivity, which has slowed since the crisis. This development could foreshadow a middle-income trap. Non-resource goods and services became less competitive internationally during the commodity price boom as prices increased rapidly. Wages also rose rapidly and are now broadly in line with productivity. To maintain price competitiveness – essential for future diversification – wage growth should not overtake growth in productivity.

Labour utilisation is high, but there is significant scope to increase productivity by shifting labour to more productive sectors. Labour force participation, at almost 80%, is comparable to that of advanced economies and unemployment is low at 4%, indicating little scope for activating workers. However, employment is concentrated in the least productive sectors, especially agriculture, which employs 24% of the workforce but produces only 5% of GDP. Shifting labour to more productive sectors could raise GDP per capita by some 30%, but closing the gap in GDP per capita with OECD countries would require a further increase of more than 100%.

A sustainable increase in productivity requires raising investment. Investment as a share of GDP is low at 23% and has fallen since 2010. As capital stocks are a fraction of those in advanced economies, maintaining, let alone improving, competitiveness requires a boost to public, private and foreign investment. Insufficient access to external financing is a bottleneck for private sector development.

Diversification has progressed modestly but faces multiple obstacles

Growth since 2010 has benefited from positive developments in manufacturing and knowledge-intensive services, but the size of manufacturing remains small. It employs about 5% of the labour force and generates 11% of GDP, figures which are low compared to both emerging economies and advanced resource-rich countries. Since 2011, manufacturing and knowledge-intensive services such as information and communications technology (ICT), finance and professional services have increased both in size of employment and labour productivity. Labour productivity has grown dramatically in transport equipment manufacturing and in chemicals and pharmaceuticals. However, growth increases in labour productivity in the largest sectors in terms of GDP contributions supported the bulk of the recovery since 2010.

The macroeconomic consequences of rapid, natural resource-fuelled growth challenge diversification. Increased domestic spending thanks to high oil-related revenues prompted growth in the services sector which was faster than in the manufacturing sector during the 2000s, making certain non-oil sectors less attractive. High volatility in the real exchange rate makes investment in tradeable sectors more risky and may overwhelm microeconomic policy interventions aimed at incentivising diversification.

Ineffective implementation of industrial policy programmes may hamper enhanced competitiveness and diversification in the future. The 2050 strategy includes priorities for diversification to be implemented via industrial policy programmes. In the past, industrial policy has had limited success. However, it was insufficient to make the country more resilient to external shocks at the end of the 2000s as many of the projects implemented under the umbrella of industrial policy did not meet their objectives.

The market structure of the economy is dominated by state entities and by large conglomerates, limiting competition and contestability. The sovereign wealth fund Samruk-Kazyna, established to enhance the competitiveness and sustainability of the national economy, controlled assets amounting to roughly half of GDP in 2013. State entities account for 30% to 40% of GDP. The first wave of privatisations created large market players that have strong incentives to resist market entry and reform. A new wave of privatisation has been announced but its successful implementation is subject to challenges of transparency and hampered by the underdeveloped local capital market.

More generally, Kazakhstan has ample room to lower regulatory burdens and improve the business climate. Interest in competing in certain markets may be reduced because of the sometimes non-transparent and unpredictable regulatory burdens and price controls. While Kazakhstan scores well in a number of areas of the business climate, there is room for improvement in arranging construction permits, trading across borders and getting electricity. Moreover, corruption is perceived to be widespread.

The financial sector risks becoming a bottleneck for private sector growth. Bank lending is low and limits firms' access to finance, with only 19% of firms having a bank loan and credit line although banks are the main source of external finance for firms. The local stock and bond markets are underdeveloped, limiting alternative sources of funds for firms.

Despite high levels of educational attainment, there seems to be a skills mismatch in certain sectors in Kazakhstan. The average number of years of schooling in the workforce is, at well over ten years, almost as high as that of OECD countries. Nevertheless, firms, especially larger manufacturing firms, single out skills as one obstacle to further growth. It remains to be seen whether an implemented strategy to enhance the quality of education and to better align the supply of skills with evolving needs will be successfully implemented.

Corruption and limited state capacity still permeate public action

The perception is that widespread corruption affects key processes in public governance such as public procurement. Expert assessments led by international bodies coincide with businesses' and citizens' perceptions that corruption is widespread. Two out of three Kazakhstanis agree that corruption is extensive and mention corruption as the key constraint on doing business. Public procurement commands 43% of government expenditure and is viewed as particularly corrupt, which limits its usefulness to further government strategy in a number of areas, including environmental standards.

The delivery capacity of the public administration remains low, and many efforts are directed at this area. Capacity constraints are evidenced by mediocre outcomes in key public services of health, education and utilities, especially in terms of the quality of public service delivery. They also arise in the limited inefficiency of implementation of certain strategic plans that have had much lower impact than expected. Reforms continue both in governance inputs, in particular to professionalise and improve meritocracy in the civil service, and processes, including results-based budgeting and the adoption of e-government tools to increase transparency.

Key constraints to development

Kazakhstan has set a number of ambitious long-term goals in the Kazakhstan 2050 strategy and key policy documents such as the *Concept on Transition of the Republic of Kazakhstan to Green Economy*. Against this backdrop, this report assesses performance on a wide array of outcome dimensions and highlights the drivers of under-par performance. On the basis of this analysis, the report identifies seven constraints to development in Kazakhstan which limit potential progress in equitable and sustainable growth today or in the future. The constraints identified often cut across sectoral lines and therefore have a major impact on the dynamics of the economy.

Natural-resource dependency exposes the economy to external risks and can hamper growth in other sectors in the future. The weight of natural-resource sectors in the economy makes it difficult to diversify. Kazakhstan has succeeded in avoiding the most immediate consequences of its vast natural-resource wealth for the exchange rate and the volatility of public revenues. Natural-resource revenues offer great opportunities, by allowing the state to maintain low tax rates and to channel funds for long-term investment or countercyclical expenditure. However, the importance of the natural-resource sector as a driver of economic growth and a source of public revenue as well as foreign exchange has led to a configuration of the economy that serves the major actors of the natural-resource sectors while not being conducive to the development of other sectors. The challenge for Kazakhstan is to make the best use possible of its natural wealth to build a more diversified and resilient economy for the long term.

The concentration of economic clout in the hands of the state and of a small number of private actors constrains investment and dynamism. The conjunction of strong price controls in a number of markets, discretionary intervention by state actors and limited competition in key markets leads to distorted price signals and limited opportunities for new entry and innovation. Corruption is perceived to be widespread and to affect critical governance functions such as public procurement, which is likely to reduce market contestability. A more detailed analysis of the regulatory functions of the state in key markets would shed light on the potential of competition to unlock growth in non-oil sectors and on the mechanisms that limit market contestability.

The financial sector remains fragile and underdeveloped. Despite efforts on the part of the National Bank of Kazakhstan (NBK) to address the aftermath of the banking crisis of 2008, the share of non-performing loans remains a concern. Non-performing loans accounted to 26% of the total loan portfolio in December 2014 before falling to 10% at the end of June 2015. The banking sector is the main source of external finance for firms, which consistently rank access to finance as a constraint on growth. Indeed, domestic credit to the private sector in Kazakhstan, at around 40%, is well below international benchmarks. An underdeveloped financial sector limits potential investment. Significant new capital investment could also serve to modernise machinery and technology, with positive impacts on labour productivity and the environmental impact of economic growth. The financial sector operates in a relatively difficult environment, characterised by weak rule of law, dollarisation and a challenging exchange rate regime. The transition to a free-floating exchange rate in August 2015 can potentially strengthen inflation targeting but will be challenging for the financial sector given the still extensive dollarisation. The financial sector requires regulation that is adapted to this environment – yet allows for the emergence of diverse institutions and vehicles, including non-bank financial intermediaries, microcredit lenders, and other market actors able to respond to different needs.

The effectiveness of environmental regulation is insufficient to overturn a legacy of overexploitation of natural capital and has consequences for environmental well-being. Adverse environmental outcomes are a major concern: because of the inherent value of clean air and water, but also because they challenge the sustainability of the current development model, with its heavy reliance on extractive industries, as well as certain features of the vision for the Kazakhstani economy in 2050. The planned increases in agricultural output and productivity will be particularly challenging given issues of water scarcity and quality. The challenging environmental outcomes in water and air quality, as well as in energy intensity and the emission of greenhouse gases, have multiple causes, including mismanagement of natural resources in the past. They are also symptomatic of failings in the quality of environmental regulation and its implementation. Better incentives and institutions for environmental protection and the management of natural capital can potentially open pathways for enhancing growth both in environmental services and in other sectors, for example through compliance with more demanding quality standards that open opportunities for international trade.

Widespread corruption and perceptions of corruption affecting multiple state functions are a constraint on doing business and undermine meritocracy and entrepreneurial spirit. The government has identified control of corruption as one of its key priorities and has undertaken several anti-corruption measures as well as key institutional reforms. The challenge is significant, in particular because corrupt practices not only affect key government functions such as public procurement, but are also present in public service delivery and in private market interactions between firms or with the public. Governance issues play a significant role in collaboration between Kazakhstan and the OECD and in the Kazakhstan Country Programme in particular.

There is limited implementation capacity for certain government functions. Weak government capacity limits the effectiveness of the planning machinery in delivering results. While some constraints are sector-specific, such as the legacy of underinvestment in primary healthcare or the difficulties in human resource management in the education sector, others are broader. They include difficulties in co-ordination across agencies or in managing differences in the efficiency of different national and regional administrations, as well as integrity issues. Past industrial policies, for example, did not achieve their goals or were not fully implemented. These are particularly critical in view of the other key constraints identified.

The skills system has so far failed to generate appropriately equipped labour in sufficient quantity in the labour market for a number of sectors, which limits their growth potential. Skills formation is focused on the education system and has only recently addressed the issues of skills mismatches, in particular with new developments in vocational education. A more integrated approach to skills formation and acquisition and human resources management, going beyond formal education, would link skills formation with the importance of SMEs and the development of opportunities, the absence of which is likely to lead to the continued growth in the urban informal sector. A skills strategy would also incorporate the necessary elements for the attraction and retention of talent and provide a partial answer to the consequences of the unbalanced pattern of international migration in Kazakhstan.

References

Linn, J. F. (2014), "Kazakhstan 2050: Exploring an ambitious vision", *Global Journal of Emerging Market Economies*, Vol. 6, No. 3.

Nazarbayev, N. (2014), "Kazakhstan's Way – 2050: Common aim, common interests, common future", Address of the President of Kazakhstan to the nation.

Nazarbayev, N. (2012), "Strategy 'Kazakhstan-2050'" New political course of the established state, speech delivered in Astana, 12 December 2012.

ANNEX 1.A1

Citizen stories of the MDCR workshop

Citizen story 1: Jeanibek the organic farmer

In Kazakhstan in 2050, I imagine the life of a 50 year-old organic farmer, Jeanibek, who lives in a village with his wife and four children. His wife is a rural doctor, and all his children have benefited from good access to high-quality education. Jeanibek's eldest son has decided to help the family business by going to work on innovative agriculture systems at a local research institute. His two other children are at university. Jeanibek was able to avail himself of good financing opportunities to modernise his business and introduce green technologies, such as wind and solar energy, thanks to a government subsidy and a competitive banking sector. Jeanibek now exports his organic produce, and has expanded his business to employ eight people. He respects the law and legislation in his daily activities, and pays his employees a decent wage. In his spare time he enjoys going to the theatre with his wife and also practises sport. They both travel several times a year to take time off in their secondary residence in the middle of Kazakhstan by the lake, which is conveniently connected by high speed train to their local station.

Citizen story 2: Temerlan the doctor

In Kazakhstan in 2050, I imagine Temerlan, with his family and four children. He is 24 years of age and a doctor; a high-prestige profession. On the morning of 9 December 2050, he looks out of the window: there is snow – very white snow because the environment is healthy since Kazakhstan replaced coal with natural gas. In 2050, culture and the education are well-developed, the economy is thriving, highly diversified, and a favourable business climate allows for the setting up of businesses with ease. The quality of life is very high for Temerlan and his family, with good wages, flexible working hours, high levels of social protection, and low levels of criminality. Emigration has slowed down dramatically, and fears of brain drain have dissipated.

Citizen story 3: Green modern technology

In Kazakhstan in 2050, I will be 60 years old with a wife and two children in college. I imagine my life will be embedded in useful technologies, work, and leisure. Let me describe a typical day to you. In the morning I wake up at 7a.m. with a special device and a "voice" which tells me the weather, my temperature, and my agenda for the day. I go to the kitchen: the refrigerator "speaks" and tells me how many fresh products I have left in it. I get ready for work and take an electric bus there. My wife works from home: she is a lecturer at the university and gives interactive lectures and tutoring through the internet. Just before I get to work my parents call me on Skype; they are in the United States, spending their holidays in a resort. My job is to design cars working with renewable energies. There are many employees from different countries in my workplace, and we often socialise after work. At the end of the day, I go to the fitness room located on the top floor of my office premises. After working out I go home to discuss and organise an upcoming skiing trip with my wife. We decide to stay in Kazakhstan and go skiing outside Almaty, as it is connected via high speed train.

Citizen story 4: Aslan the organic farmer

In Kazakhstan in 2050, I imagine a modern, efficient agricultural sector, which employs 60% of the population. With the development of large territorial expanses thanks to government policy and investment, Kazakhstani agricultural products are exported all over the world to feed the growing global population. I imagine a farmer, Aslan, who is 50 years old and has two children. One is an art student, and the other has followed his father's footsteps and also works in agriculture. In 2050, working in agriculture is a high-prestige profession. Public services are highly developed, including housing and access to healthcare. Aslan runs a highly sustainable farm, with innovative technologies that generate energy and save water, and he even owns his own recycling plant as a side business. Aslan is also careful to operate sustainable crop rotations and diversified agriculture: this season he is growing soy beans.

Multi-dimensional Review of Kazakhstan
Volume 1. Initial Assessment

Chapter 2

How's life in Kazakhstan?

Over the last decade, life in Kazakhstan has improved significantly, profiting from robust economic growth. But what exactly does having a good life mean? This chapter uses the OECD well-being framework to assess well-being outcomes in Kazakhstan, in relation to a set of identified benchmark countries.

The diagnosis shows that material conditions have improved for Kazakhstanis over the last decade. Income and living standards have increased markedly since the year 2000 as gross national income (GNI) per capita doubled and poverty fell dramatically. These outcomes have been largely driven by growth in market incomes and in particular by the creation of salaried jobs and wage policies. As incomes have grown equitably, outcomes determined by the market are largely positive, with the exception of housing, which remains a significant gap in material well-being.

Despite improvements and significant progress in other areas, the performance of Kazakhstan in the dimensions of quality of life remains low relative to comparator countries. Levels of empowerment and participation are still low in the country, potentially hindered by the high prevalence of corruption. Additionally, health outcomes remain a challenge, and may remain so, unless a strong impetus is given by the government to improving environmental conditions and the capacity to deliver higher quality public services. Indeed, all the indicators related to environment are below what could be expected and are not likely to go in the right direction unless decisive action is taken to limit the adverse impact of natural resource-intensive growth and to accelerate structural transformation. In addition, quantitative educational indicators have overall improved but qualitative outcomes are still lagging.

This chapter assesses well-being in Kazakhstan, with particular emphasis on developments since the turn of the century. To do so, the chapter relies on the OECD framework for measuring well-being (OECD, 2013a), which has been adapted better to reflect the realities of non-OECD countries (Boarini, Kolev and McGregor, 2014). The first section of this chapter highlights the dimensions of well-being in which Kazakhstan outperforms or underperforms relative to international benchmarks. The second section assesses material conditions while the third section considers the quality of life in the country. For each of ten dimensions, Kazakhstan's position is measured in relation to benchmark countries, as well as over time, where possible. Where it is relevant, this section also examines the distribution of well-being outcomes according to gender, socio-economic status, region, ethnicity and age inequalities. For dimensions that are particularly salient, the chapter goes beyond describing the evolution of key indicators to provide an account of ongoing policy efforts.

Life in Kazakhstan has improved significantly over the last decade

Rapid and inclusive economic growth has driven improvements in well-being

The economic performance of Kazakhstan since the year 2000 has been impressive. The transition from a centrally-planned Soviet Republic to an independent market-based economy generated significant economic turbulence during the 1990s, as did the consequences of the Russian crisis in 1998. Since 2000, however, Kazakhstan's economy has grown strongly, driven by the increase in prices of its leading exports – mainly oil, metals and grain, allowing the country to record double-digit growth rates.

Economic growth has had a positive impact on Kazakhstanis' well-being. The OECD measures well-being on the basis of a framework that focuses on two pillars: material conditions and quality of life (see Box 2.1). In Kazakhstan both have shown improvement. Economic growth has made possible the improvement of people's material conditions. Income has grown dramatically, with gross national income (GNI) per capita more than doubling between 2000 and 2013 in purchasing power parity (PPP) terms and two Kazakhstanis out of three are now satisfied with their standard of living. Economic growth has also stimulated the labour market, reducing unemployment rates from double digits to 5% and vulnerable employment rates (own-account workers and unpaid family workers as a share of total employment) from 40% to 29%. Overall, quality of life has also benefited from economic development. Expenditure on education (in percentage of gross domestic product [GDP]) has increased more than four-fold over the last decade (moving from 0.7% in 2010 of GDP to 3.1% in 2012), allowing access to education to become universal with significant progress in access to pre-primary education. Health status has also improved with an increase of seven years in life expectancy, accompanied by a decline in maternal and infant mortality ratios.

Figure 2.1. **Income has grown dramatically in Kazakhstan since the year 2000**

GNI per capita in 2011 International USD

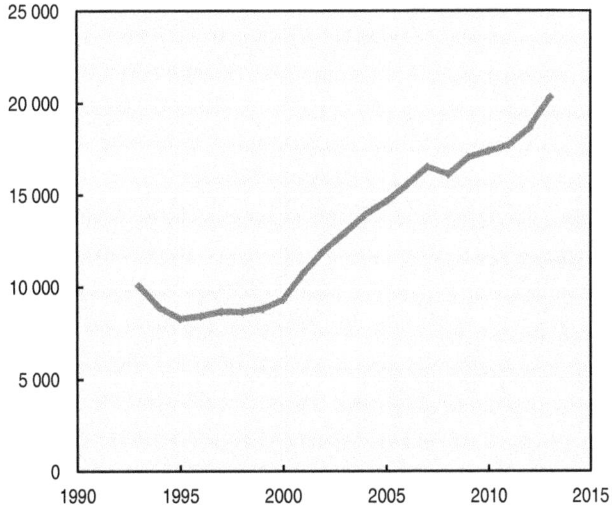

Source: World Bank (2015), *International Comparison Program Database, http://icp.worldbank.org/.*

StatLink http://dx.doi.org/10.1787/888933288973

Figure 2.2. **Satisfaction with living conditions is also on the rise**

Percentage of people saying they are satisfied with their living conditions, 2006-14

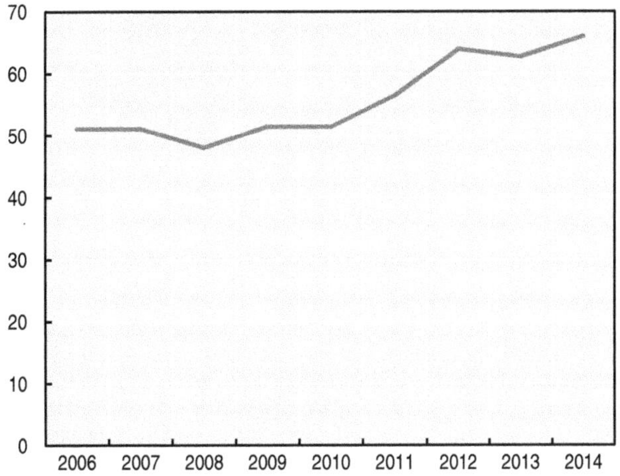

Source: Gallup (2014), *Gallup World Poll* (database).

StatLink http://dx.doi.org/10.1787/888933288982

Material conditions are adequate, but the quality of life remains low in many respects

Despite significant progress since 2000, most well-being outcomes are below what could be expected from a comparable country at the same level of economic development. Figure 2.3 shows measures of performance for Kazakhstan on the different dimensions of the well-being framework compared to a regression-based synthetic benchmark with the same level of GDP per capita. All indicators are normalised so that indicators above the reference line reflect better performance than the benchmark and indicators below the reference line reflect worse performance than the benchmark. The benchmarking tool gives an overview of the country's relative performance along the ten well-being dimensions by comparing

Figure 2.3. **Current and expected well-being outcomes for Kazakhstan: Worldwide comparison**

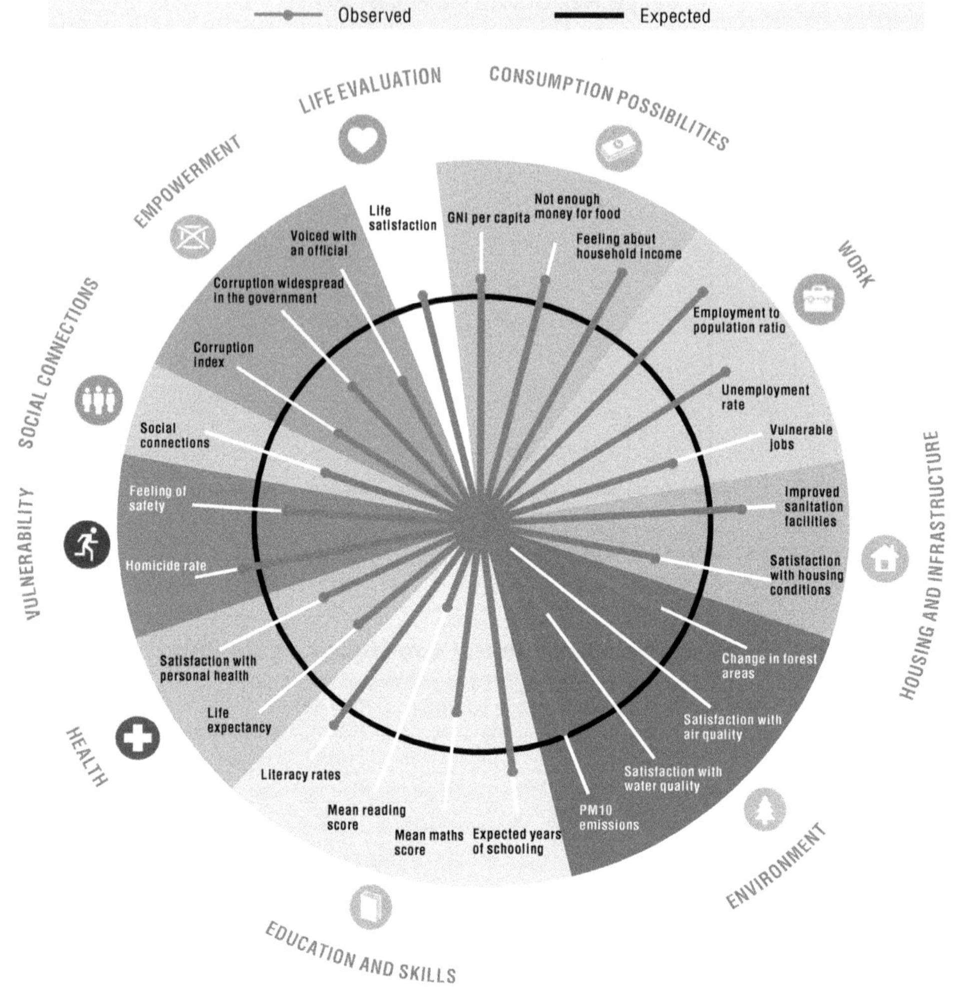

Note: For the variable "corruption widespread in the government", the share of respondents answering "yes" and those refusing to answer have been summed. The figure is based on running bivariate regressions where the indicator is the dependent variable and GDP per capita is the independent variable. The expected value of each indicator is then computed by taking the coefficient of the bivariate regression and applying it to the actual GDP per capita of the country. The country's observed results are then compared to the expected value for each indicator. In a second step, the difference between the fitted values and the observed values is standardised by the standard deviation of the indicator. Standardising the size of the gap highlights specific dimensions in which the performance of the country is particularly notable.

Source: OECD calculations based on Gallup (2014), *Gallup World Poll* (database); UNDP (United Nations Development Programme) (2014), *International Human Development Indicators* (database), United Nations Development Programme, *http://hdr.undp.org/en/data*; UIS (UNESCO Institute for Statistics) (2013), *UIS Data Centre* (database), United Nations Educational, Scientific and Cultural Organisation, *http://data.uis.unesco.org/* (accessed 15 January 2014); World Bank (2014a), *World Development Indicators* (database), Washington, DC, *http://data.worldbank.org*; OECD (2014a) *PISA 2012 Results: What Students Know and Can Do – Student Performance in Mathematics, Reading and Science.*

StatLink http://dx.doi.org/10.1787/888933288998

absolute and fitted values of 25 indicators. Kazakhstan is compared to all countries with more than 1 million inhabitants and covered in each indicator (according to data availability).

Consumption possibilities and most of the job indicators are better than expected while most quality of life dimensions are under the level expected on the basis of GDP per capita. Life evaluation is in line with what could be expected. However, Kazakhstan is performing worse than expected in the dimensions of health, social connections, empowerment and participation, and environmental conditions. To a lesser extent this is also the case for education and skills

Box 2.1. **The OECD framework for measuring well-being in developing countries**

Well-being is multi-dimensional, and as such, can be a difficult concept to define in itself as it covers many areas of people's lives. However, the core concept is relatively intuitive: well-being encompasses the aspects of life which are considered as essential to meet one's needs, to pursue one's goals and to feel satisfied with life. Based on the various national initiatives undertaken in several countries and based on several years of collaboration with experts and representatives from national governments, the OECD developed a framework for measuring well-being in OECD countries (OECD, 2011a). Taking stock of the literature on measuring development outcomes and embracing the realities of non-OECD countries, this analytical tool has been tailored to measure well-being issues in non-OECD countries. The dimensions of the OECD well-being framework have been redefined in ways that better match the availabilities of data and the priorities and critical concerns of these countries (Boarini, Kolev and McGregor, 2014).

This adjusted framework, like the "How's life?" framework, measures well-being outcomes according to two broad pillars. The first pillar, material conditions, comprises consumption possibilities, work, housing conditions and infrastructure dimensions. The second pillar, quality of life, comprises health status, education and skills, social connections, empowerment and participation, vulnerability and subjective well-being (Figure 2.4). These ten listed dimensions are used to measure current well-being and are complemented with another set of indicators to measure the sustainability of well-being into the future. The framework emphasises the importance of well-being sustainability based on the preservation of natural, human, economic and social capital stocks that are essential for ensuring well-being for future generations.

Figure 2.4. **OECD well-being framework for developing countries comparison**

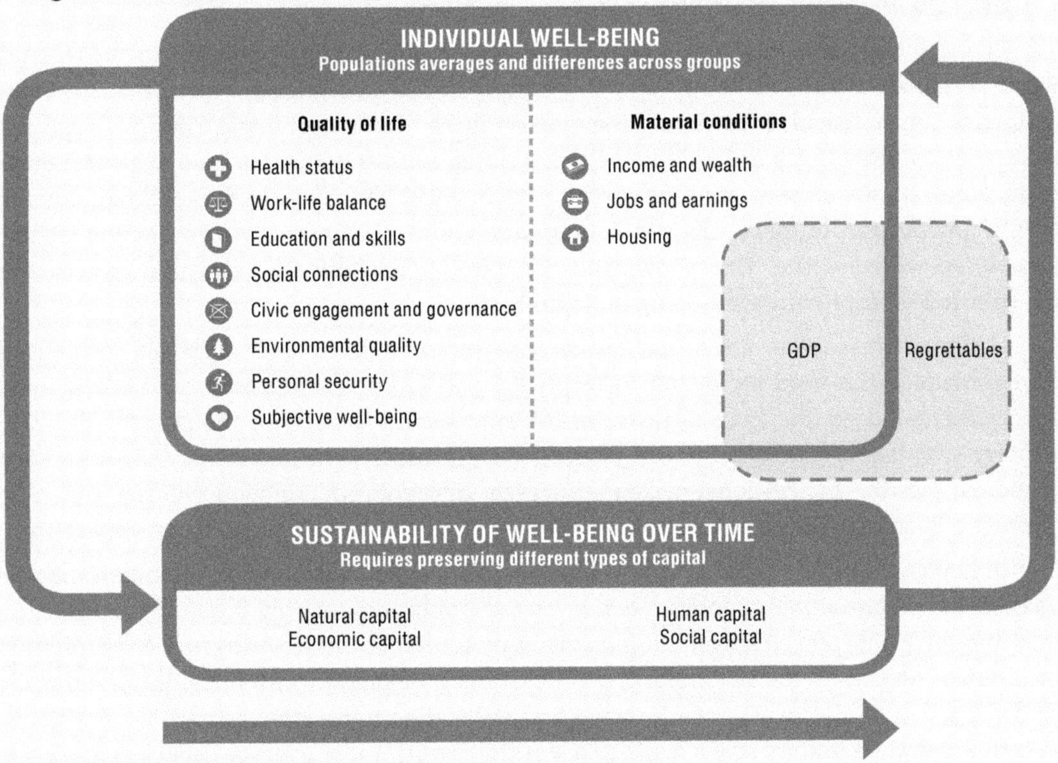

The OECD well-being framework is informed by a number of analytical principles. First, it is concerned with the well-being of individuals rather than with aggregate economic conditions. Second, it focuses on well-being outputs rather than inputs, recognising that outcomes may be uncorrelated with the resources devoted to achieve them. Third, it emphasises the need to measure the distribution of well-being outcomes

Box 2.1. **The OECD framework for measuring well-being in developing countries** *(cont.)*

to identify inequalities across and within population groups. Finally, it considers both objective and subjective indicators, as people's own evaluations and feelings about their lives matter as well as the objective conditions in which they live (OECD, 2011a).

Sources: OECD (2011a); Boarini, Kolev and McGregor (2014).

where qualitative indicators (i.e. internationally comparable scores in the Programme for International Student Assessment, PISA) are below expected values. Finally, for the dimensions of vulnerability and housing, the different indicators used paint a more nuanced picture.

In the domains where Kazakhstan underperforms, such as environment and health, there has been progress according to objective measures but at slower pace than economic growth. This is the case for life expectancy, which increased from 63 years in 2000 to 68 in 2012,[1] especially to the advantage of women who live almost ten years longer than men. It is also the case of PM10 emissions (emissions of particulate matter up to ten micrometres in size which cause respiratory diseases in high concentrations) which fell by 15% between 2005 and 2013.[2] However in both cases, the synthetic benchmark improved faster, as a result of improvements in the majority of countries and the expected improvement in well-being linked to GDP growth. Moreover, subjective indicators have deteriorated: 53% of respondents were satisfied with the quality of air in 2014 compared to 56% in 2006.

Drivers and obstacles affecting progress in well-being

Economic growth has been the driving force behind improvements in well-being. Some dimensions of well-being tend to be more closely correlated with income across countries, in particular consumption possibilities, housing, infrastructure and life evaluation, while others are only loosely correlated with income, such as environmental conditions, empowerment or vulnerability (OECD, 2013b). By and large, the dimensions in which Kazakhstan outperforms the benchmark are those where performance is closely associated with income. This shows that, despite its limitations, economic growth has contributed to improving well-being in Kazakhstan.

Underperformance in areas that are typically not correlated with aggregate incomes is symptomatic of the need for greater focus on the non-income dimensions of well-being and development. Indeed, the focus of Kazakhstan's strategic framework for the period – the 2030 Strategy – was largely in accordance with an overarching focus on political stability and accelerating economic growth.[3] International evidence suggests that economic growth will not suffice to improve outcomes in areas such as environmental quality, which require specific public action.

In housing, education and health, where public service provision plays an important role, Kazakhstan performs well on indicators that assess inputs and quantity, but underperforms on measures of quality and effectiveness. In housing, performance in access to improved sanitation facilities is better than the benchmark, while citizens' satisfaction with housing conditions is below it. Likewise, in the area of education and skills, the improvement in school enrolment at primary and secondary levels leads to a workforce with more average schooling than the benchmark and almost universal adult literacy. However, when compared to other countries participating in PISA, the learning outcomes of 15-year old Kazakhstani students are significantly below the benchmark. The mean score in reading, at 393, was far below the OECD average of 496, a difference equivalent to almost two and a half years of schooling (OECD, 2014a). Similarly, in the area of health, Kazakhstan is endowed with nearly twice as many hospital beds and physicians relative to population as comparable countries, yet outcome indicators, be they objective (life expectancy) or subjective (satisfaction with personal health) are below the benchmark.

Environmental concerns also loom large in the medium to long term given Kazakhstan's greenhouse gas emissions as well as its exposure to water scarcity. As discussed elsewhere in this report (see Chapter 3), Kazakhstan is among the largest emitters of carbon dioxide per capita, while also being a major exporter of fossil fuels. The country will therefore be affected both directly and through derived demand by efforts to reduce global emissions. At the same time, certain environmental issues, including drought are likely to be exacerbated by climate change (OECD, 2015a). The combination of Kazakhstan's water scarcity and the importance of agricultural development in the medium-term plans will pose significant challenges in the future.

Women and men have similar well-being outcomes

Gender inequality is generally low in Kazakhstan but labour market outcomes exhibit differences between men and women. On a selected list of well-being indicators, gender inequalities appear relatively limited in the country (Figure 2.5) with Kazakhstan ranking 43rd out of 142 countries in the Gender Gap Index 2014 (World Economic Forum, 2014). Even if they remain limited, inequalities are most prominent in the material conditions dimensions as women under-perform men in terms of income and participation to the labour market. As to labour force participation, there is a ten percentage points difference between men and women (68% vs 78%) but this remains in line with the OECD average. The gender pay gap exists but it remains relatively low, below 10%, whereas this ratio can be much higher in some OECD countries.

Figure 2.5. **Gender disparities in Kazakhstan: Selected indicators**

Gender gap (in standard deviations of the cross-country distribution)

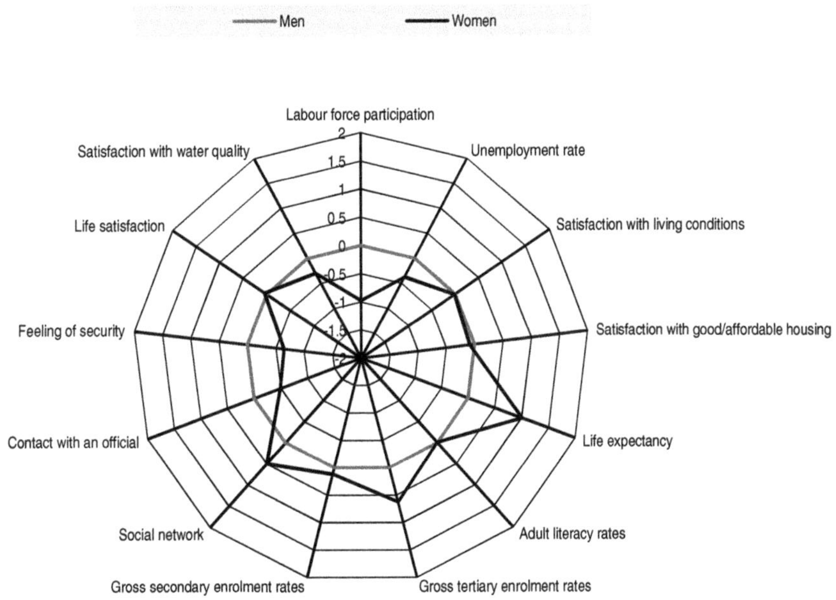

Note: Female performances on the well-being indicators are expressed in comparison to male performances on the same indicators. The gender gap is assessed in standard deviations.

Sources: OECD calculations based on Gallup (2014), *Gallup World Poll* (database); UNDP (United Nations Development Programme) (2014), *International Human Development Indicators* (database), United Nations Development Programme, *http://hdr.undp.org/en/data*; UIS (UNESCO Institute for Statistics) (2013), *UIS Data Centre* (database), United Nations Educational, Scientific and Cultural Organisation, *http://data.uis.unesco.org/* (accessed 15 January 2014); World Bank (2014), *World Development Indicators* (database), Washington, DC, *http://data.worldbank.org*; Committee of Statistics in Republic of Kazakhstan, 2014.

StatLink http://dx.doi.org/10.1787/888933289009

In the dimensions related to the quality of life, women tend to perform better than men. This is particularly marked in the dimension of health where women live on average ten years longer than men. In respect of education, literacy as well as access to primary and secondary education are universal for both sexes while enrolment rates in tertiary education appear higher for women (37% versus 53%). In the other dimensions, there is no significant difference between men and women in Kazakhstan as shown in the figure below.

Social institutions are fairly egalitarian in Kazakhstan, except in the realm of civil rights where women are less present than men. Recently, Kazakhstan adopted several gender equality laws, including a new "Law on Equal Opportunities for Men and Women" that prohibits discrimination based on gender. In addition, the president of Kazakhstan identified gender as an important policy priority of the nation's strategic 2020 and 2050 Development Plans, with the ambitious target of reaching gender equality by 2016. Supporting this analysis, the 2014 OECD Development Centre's Social Institutions and Gender Index (SIGI) (OECD, 2014b) reports that Kazakhstan is classified with a low level of discrimination against women whereas its neighbourhood and/or benchmark countries (i.e. Azerbaijan, Indonesia or the People's Republic of China) generally report medium levels of discrimination against women (OECD, 2014b). It is in the domain of civil rights and empowerment where the women tend to be the most discriminated against: fewer than 25% of parliamentary seats were held by women in 2013 and women are less keen to contact officials or public institutions when they need to (12% of women contacted an official in 2014 compared to 16% of men).

Material conditions: Incomes, living standards and employment have increased since 2000, while the quality of jobs and housing remain sources of concern

Income and living standards have increased, fairly evenly, over the last decade

Income and living standard indicators have increased sharply in Kazakhstan since 2000. Gross National Income (GNI) per capita, measured in PPP terms (constant international dollars of 2011), doubled in Kazakhstan over the last decade from USD 9 336 in 2000 to USD 19 441 in 2013, the highest increase among the benchmark countries, behind China and Azerbaijan. However, GNI level per capita remains quite low in Kazakhstan compared to the benchmark countries.

Figure 2.6. **Income levels and their evolution since 2000**

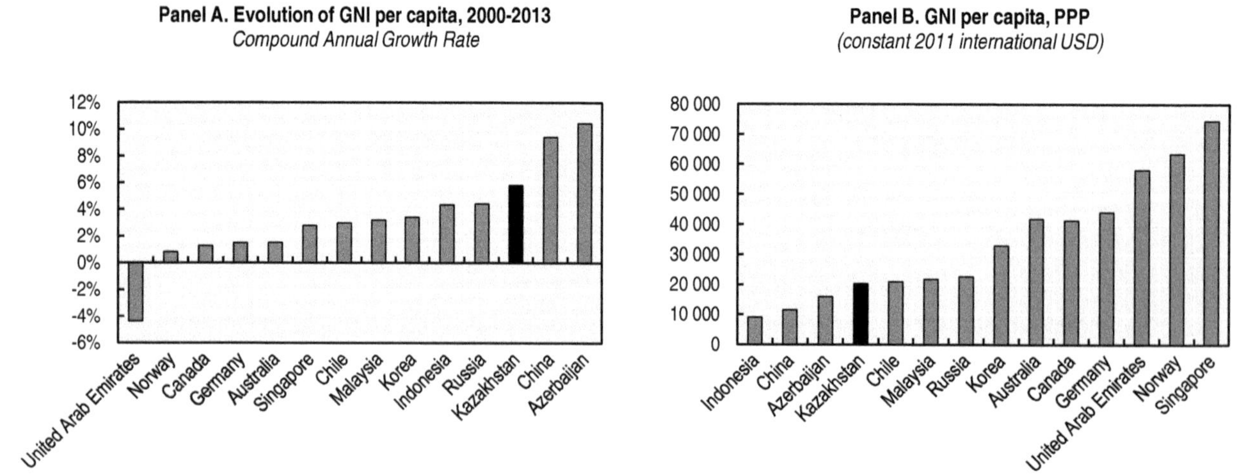

Source: World Bank (2015), *International Comparison Program Database*, World Bank.

StatLink http://dx.doi.org/10.1787/888933289019

Figure 2.7. **Poverty has fallen dramatically in Kazakhstan since the year 2000**

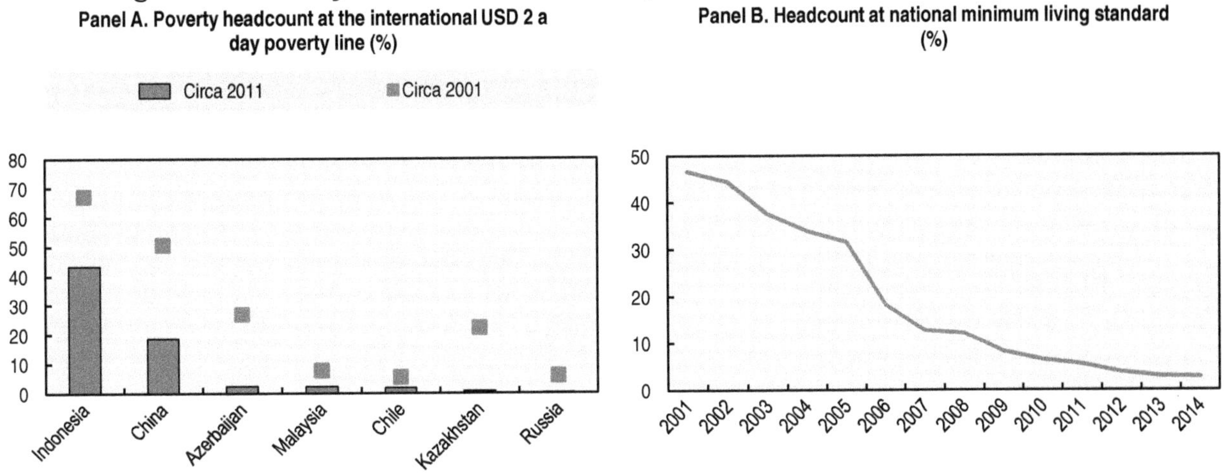

Note: Panel A: data are for 2001-08 for Azerbaijan, 2000-11 for Chile, 2002-11 for China, 2002-11 for Indonesia, 2001-10 for Kazakhstan, 2004-09 for Malaysia, 2001-09 for the Russian Federation.

Sources: Panel A: World Bank (2014a), *World Development Indicators* (database), Washington DC, *http://data.worldbank.org*. Panel B: Committee on Statistics, Republic of Kazakhstan, *http://stat.gov.kz*.

StatLink http://dx.doi.org/10.1787/888933289020

Poverty has fallen dramatically in Kazakhstan since 2000. Poverty at the international line of USD 2 per day has virtually been eradicated in Kazakhstan. Among comparator countries, only Azerbaijan has achieved a comparable performance. On the basis of Kazakhstan's national *subsistence minimum* (see Box 2.2), which was higher than the international line for the whole period,[4] the share of households with income below the reference line fell from 46.7% in 2001 to 5.5% in 2011 and 2.8% in 2014. Poverty was a major issue in Kazakhstan following independence. Poverty rates increased dramatically during the deep recession in the 1990s, a trend that was reversed in the 2000s with the return of economic growth. Poverty reduction accelerated in 2006 and was maintained, albeit at a slower pace, through the crisis in the latter part of the 2000s.

Relative poverty also fell in Kazakhstan during the 2000s, and has reached low levels relative to benchmark countries. Given the low levels of absolute poverty, meant to measure the share of the population whose subsistence is threatened, it is relevant to examine the evolution of relative poverty, which measures social inclusion (Garroway and de Laiglesia, 2012). The relative poverty[5] headcount is calculated as the share of the population with consumption expenditure below 60% of the median. Unlike most similar episodes of rapid growth, relative poverty fell in Kazakhstan during the 2000s, led by the increase in productive employment and the fall in inequality. Relative poverty in Kazakhstan in 2010 was lower than in most OECD countries, although the figures are not strictly comparable as they are based on different welfare metrics (per capita consumption expenditure for Kazakhstan and adult-equivalent disposable income for OECD countries).

Income inequality fell in Kazakhstan during the 2000s as a result of the progressive distribution of the proceeds from growth. The Gini coefficient, a measure of inequality, fell from 0.36 in 2001 to 0.28 in 2013. It is therefore on a par with the lowest inequality countries among the benchmark countries. Although the Gini coefficients for Kazakhstan are not fully comparable to those for OECD countries because of methodological differences[6] only the most equal of OECD countries (Belgium, the Czech Republic, Denmark, Finland, Norway, and Sweden) have more equal distributions of income.

Box 2.2. **Poverty measurement and social policy in Kazakhstan**

Official poverty figures in Kazakhstan are derived from the minimum living standard (MLS). The MLS plays a major role in Kazakhstan's social policy, because it serves as the basis for setting the value of social transfers and as a reference for setting minimum wages

The MLS reflects the cost of a consumption basket. The reference consumption basket includes a food basket composed of 43 items. The cost of this food basket is then taken to be 60% of the minimum living standard per capita. The food basket is set according to nutrition criteria for 11 socio-demographic groups (by age and gender). The MLS is calculated for the Republic of Kazakhstan and for individual regions. While the food consumption basket is unchanged across regions, MLSs for individual regions incorporate the differential evolution of food prices. Unlike most countries, Kazakhstan uses income used for consumption by households as the welfare metric for distributional statistics, including poverty and inequality (Brysseva, n.d.).

The methodology for setting the food basket and its price was updated in 2006 as part of the requirement of a national plan to further social reforms. Remarkably, while the real value of the minimum standard had remained largely stable between 1997 and 2005 at around 4 000 KZT (in year 2000 KZT), it has since progressed steadily and gained 50% in real terms between 2006 and 2013.

Beyond measurement, the MLS has multiple roles in social policy in Kazakhstan. The eligibility lines for targeted social assistance transfers are set at multiples of the MLS as are, in some cases, the benefits. For example, Targeted Social Assistance, the main anti-poverty programme, is provided to those with per capita incomes below 40% of the MLS and the basic pension is set at 50% of the MLS.

The official poverty line is set at 40% of the MLS or at the food poverty line for certain uses – in particular to correspond to the threshold for targeted social assistance and therefore make provisions for the expected budgetary cost of social programmes. International analyses of the poverty line of Kazakhstan (World Bank, 2004; ILO, 2012) have found poverty lines close or below the MLS when estimating poverty lines on the basis of survey data and caloric requirements. The MLS therefore appears to be a reasonable poverty line for Kazakhstan (while 40% of the MLS seems too low to reflect living costs).

The MLS also sets a lower limit for the minimum wage, which is set every year, and according to the Labour Code must not be less than the MLS excluding additional payments and mark-ups, compensation and social payments, bonus or incentive payments.

Source: ILO (2012), Ministry of Healthcare and Social Development.

Income inequality fell in Kazakhstan during the 2000s as the pattern of growth was progressive throughout the period. Figure 2.9 shows a growth incidence curve for 2001-10 based on consumption expenditure data. The negative slope of the curve indicates that growth in the incomes of the poor was significantly faster than for the richer segments of the population. The use of consumption data can exaggerate this pattern as it does not capture other uses of income (in particular savings) that are more likely to be common among the better off.

Growth led to lower inequality largely through the increase in labour incomes for households across the range of the income distribution. Between 2001 and 2009, the share of labour income in households' monetary income increased from 65.9% to 80.4% (Committee on Statistics, 2015). The recovery of employment from the year 2000 played an important role, as did the government wage policy to sustain a rise in wages and policies even during the second part of the decade, despite the slowdown in growth[7] (Kudebayeva and Barrientos, 2013).

Figure 2.8. **Inequality is relatively low in Kazakhstan**
Gini coefficient

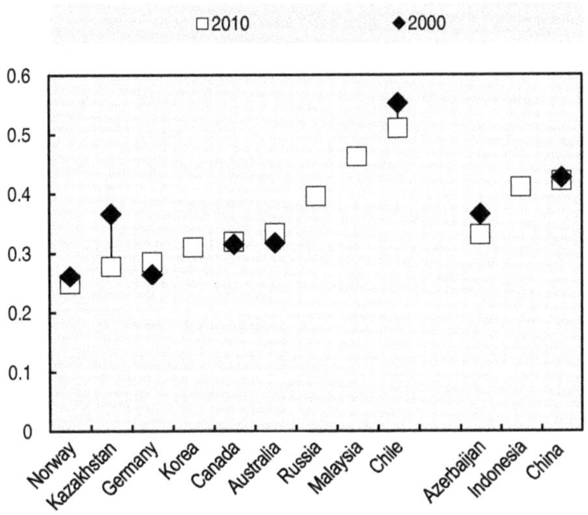

Notes: Data for Azerbaijan, Indonesia and China refer to consumption expenditure rather than income. Data are for the years 2000 and 2012 when available or closest data available. Data are for 2001 and 2012 for Kazakhstan, 2000 and 2011 for Canada, 2009 for Malaysia, 2000 and 2011 for Chile, 2001 and 2008 for Azerbaijan, 2010 for Indonesia.

Source: OECD Income Distribution Database for OECD countries and Russia; World Bank (2014a), *World Development Indicators* database for Malaysia, Azerbaijan, and China; Statistics Indonesia (Susenas) for Indonesia (reported in OECD [2015b]); Committee for Statistics for Kazakhstan.

StatLink http://dx.doi.org/10.1787/888933289032

Figure 2.9. **Growth has been progressive in Kazakhstan**
Growth incidence curve, annualised growth rates (2001-10)

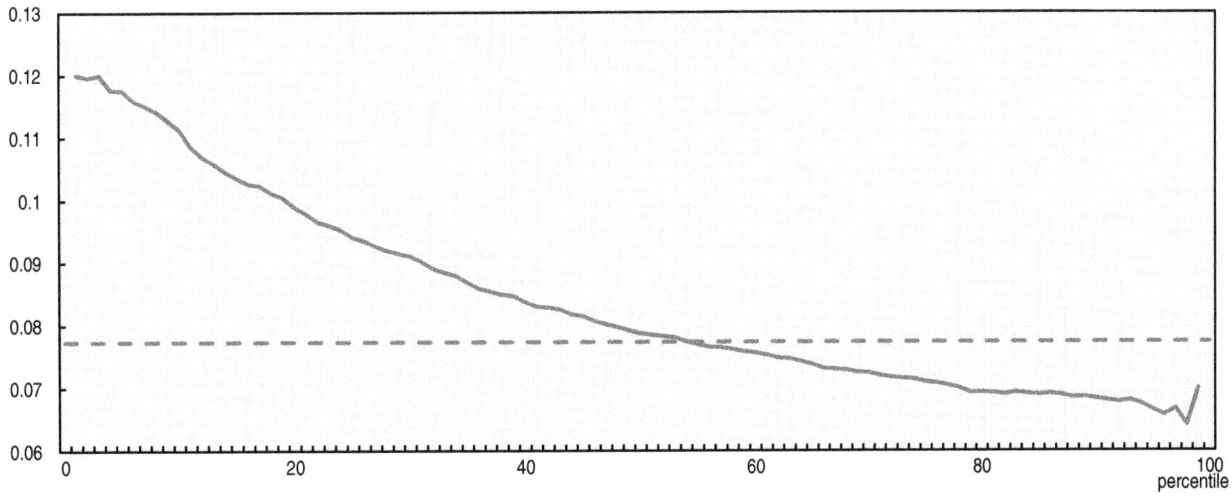

Note: Sample figures have been adjusted to match average Household Consumption Expenditure per capita from National Accounts data.

Source: Authors' calculations based on World Bank (2014) PovcalNet: the on-line tool for poverty measurement developed by the Development Research Group of the World Bank, accessed 7 Nov 2014, *http://iresearch.worldbank.org/PovcalNet/*.

StatLink http://dx.doi.org/10.1787/888933289049

Kazakhstan has put in place a set of public transfers to tackle hardship and poverty. Social assistance is composed of a number of poverty-targeted benefits, a set of categorical benefits to cover vulnerable groups and a set of universal benefits. The former include targeted social assistance (TSA), designed to assist the poorest households (with per capita income under 40% of the minimum standard), a state allowance for children under 18 and a housing allowance. Categorical benefits, which benefit specific groups without a means-test, include disability benefit (state basic disability allowance), loss of breadwinner allowance and special benefits for families with many children and for children with disabilities as well as benefits for war veterans and Chernobyl victims. Universal benefits include one-off allowances for each birth, a universal benefit for children under one year of age and a benefit for parents caring for children with disabilities.

Tax and social policies make a noticeable but small contribution to bringing about a low degree of income inequality in Kazakhstan. Since 2000, expenditure on social protection has grown in Kazakhstan. Within the social sector, which commands just over 51% of the budget, the trend during the 2000s was towards an increase in the weight of education at the expense of transfers, while health expenditure has grown steadily. Expenditure on social support and welfare fell during the 2000s from 6% to 4% of GDP. From 2002 to 2013, direct taxes and public transfers contributed to lowering the Gini coefficient by respectively one and two points or 7% of the value of inequality in market income. By comparison, for a set of 12 OECD countries, it is estimated that taxes and benefits contribute on average to lowering the Gini coefficient by 11.4 points or 29% of market income inequality (OECD, 2011b).

Public transfers contribute to lowering income poverty, especially allowances for persons with disabilities and those unable to work, while targeted transfers play a relatively small role. The lowest three income deciles receive over 50% of all public transfers, and the first decile receives 29% (Mun et al. 2015). However, analyses based on household survey data find that most households at the lower end of the income distribution do not receive

Figure 2.10. **Taxes and transfers play a limited role in reducing inequality in Kazakhstan**

Gini coefficients for market income and disposable income

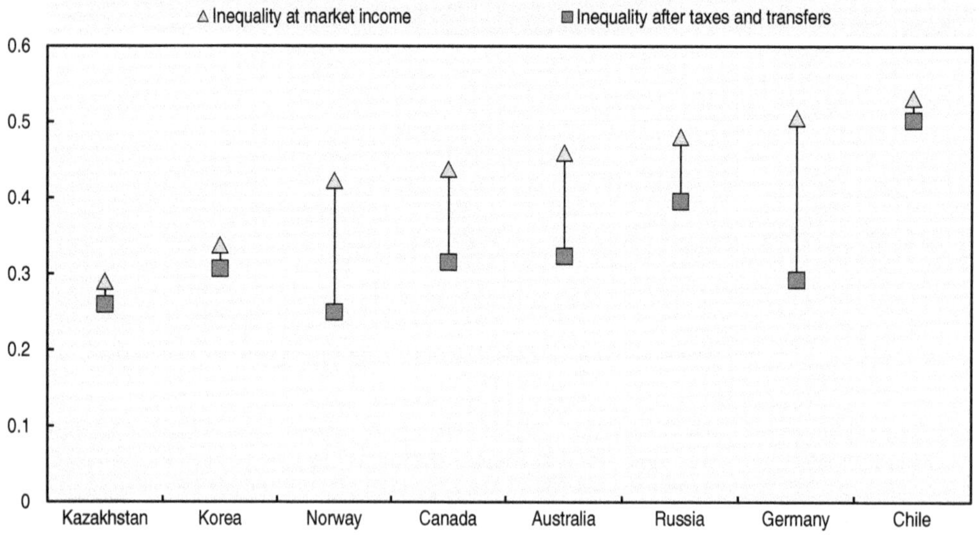

Notes: Market income for Kazakhstan includes all pension income. Gini coefficients are calculated on the basis of household per adult equivalent income using the square root equivalence scale. Data are for 2013 for Kazakhstan, 2012 for Korea and Australia, 2010 for Russia and 2011 for other countries.

Source: Mun et al. (2015), "Social spending, taxes and income redistribution in Kazakhstan" for Kazakhstan, OECD (2015c) *OECD Income Distribution Database* for OECD countries.

StatLink http://dx.doi.org/10.1787/888933289059

means-tested social assistance even though their market income is under the eligibility threshold. Income from transfers counts against the means test for poverty-targeted transfers, which leads to a relatively low prevalence of multiple transfer receipts amongst poor households. On the other hand, coverage of certain vulnerable groups by categorical transfers (heads of household out of the labour force, households with disabled members) is much better (Babajanian, Hagen-Zanker and Salomon, 2015). These groups are better covered by social assistance (62% of households whose head is out of the labour force receive some form of social assistance, as do almost 100% of households with a disabled member). Moreover categorical transfers are more generous than means-tested transfers and reach lower income quintiles disproportionally, thereby making a significant dent on poverty.[8]

The progressive pattern of growth and the fall in poverty has led to the emergence of a middle class in Kazakhstan. Figure 2.11, drawn on the basis of distribution data for disposable income per capita shows the recent increase in the size of the middle class, defined as the share of the population with disposable income above USD 10 (2005 international dollars) a day, a threshold that is commonly used in the literature to mark the lower boundary of the middle class (Kharas, 2010; Ferreira et al., 2013). In 2013, almost two thirds of the population fell in this category. The sustained growth of the middle class will be an important element in diversifying the economy as it favours the emergence of groups with entrepreneurial capacity, lower vulnerability and demand for greater variety in consumer goods and services.

Figure 2.11. **The emergence of the middle class in Kazakhstan**

Size of income groups as share of the population, selected years

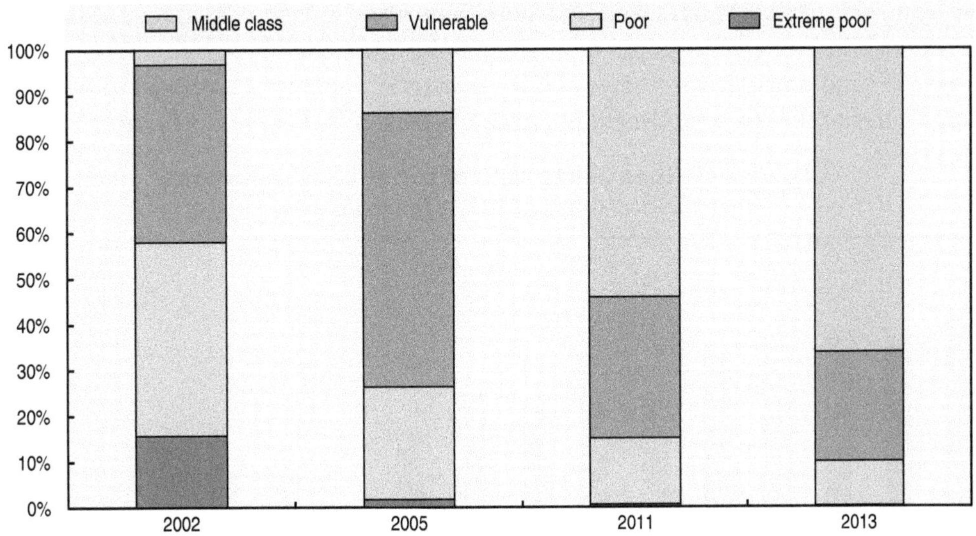

Notes: The groups are defined on the basis of daily per capita disposable income as follows: extreme poor if income is below 40% of the minimum living standard (MLS), poor if between 40% and 100% of the MLS, vulnerable if between the MLS and USD 10 (PPP), middle class if between USD 10 and USD 100 in purchasing power parity (PPP), rich if above USD 100 PPP per day. The rich group is not shown as the size of the group in sample surveys is very small and not representative of that group.

Source: Juatova, Mun and Kapsalyamova (2015), "Economic Assessment of Socio-economic Classes in Kazakhstan".

StatLink http://dx.doi.org/10.1787/888933289062

The middle class in Kazakhstan has yet to play a major role in driving and sustaining economic growth. The characterisation of the middle class carried out by Juatova, Mun and Kapsalyamova (2015) shows that the ownership of assets (housing and transport) is much higher among the middle class than the vulnerable or poor classes. An analysis of consumption behaviour across income groups suggests that rather than increase expenditures on durable goods, the middle classes spend more on personal services and other non-essential goods. Juatova, Mun and Kapsalyamova (2015) do find a significant positive relationship between disposable income and the elasticity of expenditure in durable goods, but only at significantly higher levels of income than the threshold for the middle class (USD 36 PPP per day for 2013 data).

Territorial inequality among regions (*oblasts*) in Kazakhstan is high compared to OECD standards. In 2014, GDP per capita in Atyrau (USD 39 072), was more than three times the national average (USD 12 496) and in Almaty city (USD 29 286) it was twice the national average. At the bottom of the scale South Kazakhstan's GDP per capita (USD 4 775) was almost one-third of the national average. These marked variations yield a Gini coefficient of 0.37 among Kazakhstan's regions, almost twice the national average value (Figure 2.12). Even when comparing inequality to Chile, Mexico and the Slovak Republic, which represent the most unequal countries in the OECD, inequality is high. Compared to other large OECD countries such as Canada and the United States, regional inequality is twice as high. Among the comparator countries for which data is available, only in Russia is regional inequality higher than in Kazakhstan.

The divide between urban and rural areas is very substantial in Kazakhstan. In 2013, rural poverty rates, at 4.9%, are almost four times higher than urban poverty rates (1.3%). Not only are incomes and consumption expenditures higher in urban areas, but rural households also tend to be larger (they have on average four members in rural areas compared to 3.1 in urban areas). Moreover, social services in rural areas are weaker so that public transfers reach urban households more than rural households. Indeed, despite rural areas representing 46% of the population and having much higher poverty rates, only about a quarter of rural households receive social assistance transfers, compared to over 40% in the large cities of Astana and Almaty (Babajanian, Hagen-Zanker and Salomon, 2015).

Figure 2.12. **Inequality in Territorial Level 2 regions**

Gini index of GDP per capita, latest available data

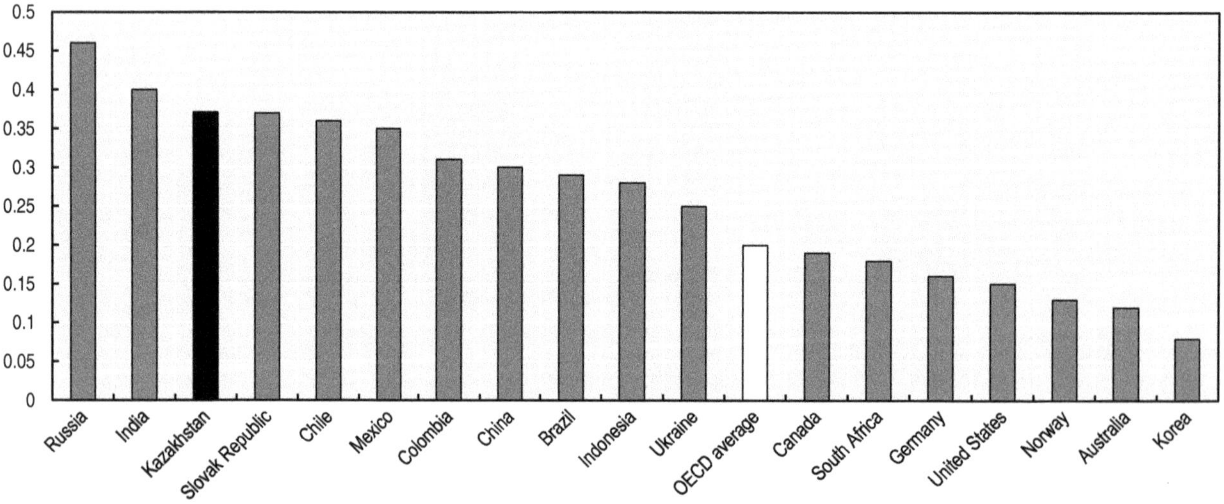

Notes: Data are for 2010 for comparator countries, 2014 for Kazakhstan. For analytical purposes, regions are classified by OECD as the administrative tiers of sub-national government. Large regions, also referred to as Territorial Level 2 (TL2) regions correspond to the first tier, and correspond to *oblasts* in Kazakhstan.

Source: OECD (2014c), *OECD Territorial Reviews: Colombia 2014*, *http://dx.doi.org/10.1787/9789264224551-en*; Data for Kazakhstan are authors' calculations based on 2014 estimates of regional product per capita provided by the Committee on Statistics of the Republic of Kazakhstan.

StatLink http://dx.doi.org/10.1787/888933289078

Improvements in individual income levels have been accompanied by an increase of subjective evaluation of living standards. In 2014, two-thirds of the persons interviewed reported being satisfied with their standards of living (Figure 2.13), a relatively low rate compared to the benchmark countries, almost ten percentage points below the average and far below the rates recorded in Europe. However, this rate has steadily increased by more than 35% over the last seven years, one of the highest increases among the comparison countries from the former Soviet Union (Figure 2.13). These levels of satisfaction increased even during the global financial crisis whereas most of the OECD countries recorded a bearish move during this period.

Figure 2.13. **Satisfaction with conditions of living is relatively low in Kazakhstan but has improved over the last years**

Percentage of people saying they are satisfied with their living conditions, 2014 or latest available year

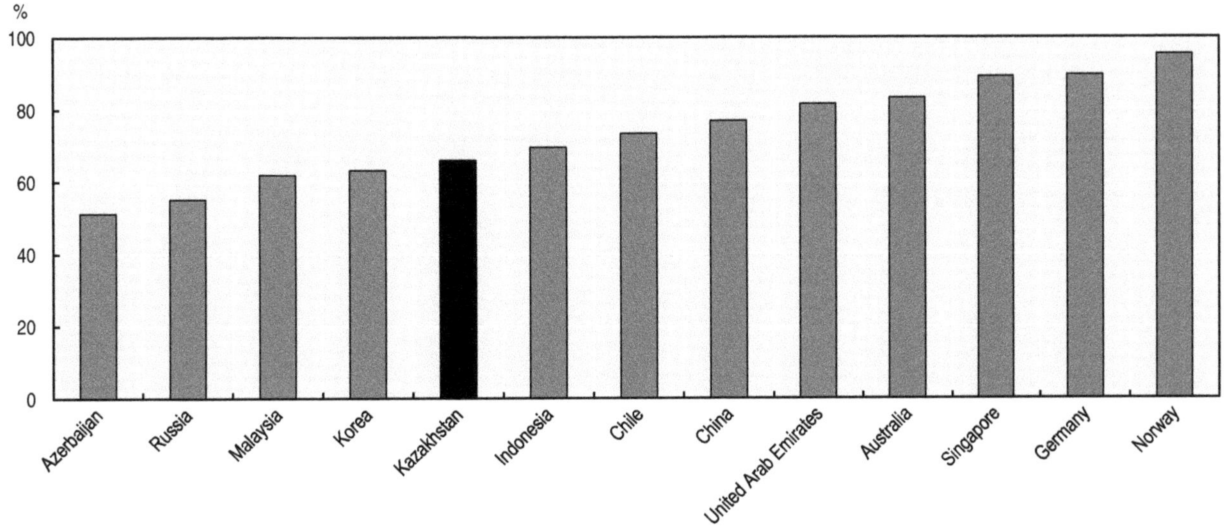

Note: The graph "Satisfaction with standards of living" shows the percentage of the sampled population who answer positively to the question "Are you satisfied or dissatisfied with your standard of living and with all the things you can do and buy?". Data are for 2014 with the exception of Chile (2013).

Source: Gallup (2014), *Gallup World Poll* (database).

StatLink http://dx.doi.org/10.1787/888933289084

The economy has overcome the job shortages of the 1990s but has yet to generate better quality jobs

Economic growth since 2000 has generated 2.3 million jobs, recovering the ground lost during the post-independence transition phase but job creation has lost steam since 2013. The deep disturbance in the economy, including in economic relations with neighbouring countries at independence, led to the destruction of 1.6 million jobs during the 1990s. With the pick-up in growth, employment has performed well, and unemployment fell from 13.5% in 1999 to 5.2% in 2013. Moreover, even the slowdown during the crisis of 2007-09 did not lead to further increases in unemployment. However, after rapid job creation during the early 2000s, the employment content of rapid growth led by the oil sector between 2001 and 2006 was relatively modest. Moreover, with the slowdown of the economy in 2013 and 2014, employment growth rates have fallen below 1%.

Low unemployment and high participation rates show that the economy has been good at generating jobs. The labour force participation rate in Kazakhstan is 77.3% for men and 66.7% for women above 15 years old.[9] The labour force participation for the age group 15-64, at 78.5%, is above the average of the OECD labour force participation rate (71.1% for people aged 15-64). The employment-to-population rate in Kazakhstan is therefore, at 68%, higher than in OECD countries and also higher than in almost all comparator countries.[10] This positive outcome is partly a reflection of the favourable demographic situation that is likely to be challenged as the ageing of the population accelerates in the coming decade.

Youth unemployment is also particularly low but NEET (youth Not in Employment, Education, or Training) rates are high in certain regions. Youth unemployment is lower than overall unemployment. It stood at 3.9% in 2013 for the 15-24 group (and 5.5% for the 15 to 28 age group used in national youth statistics). Despite low levels of youth unemployment in the country, NEET rates are high in certain regions, in particular in the southern regions of the country. In South Kazakhstan, Kyzylorda and Karaganda regions, a significant proportion of young people are disconnected from the labour market in spite of not being in education and in spite of low youth unemployment rates.

Figure 2.14. **Economic growth has led to massive job creation**

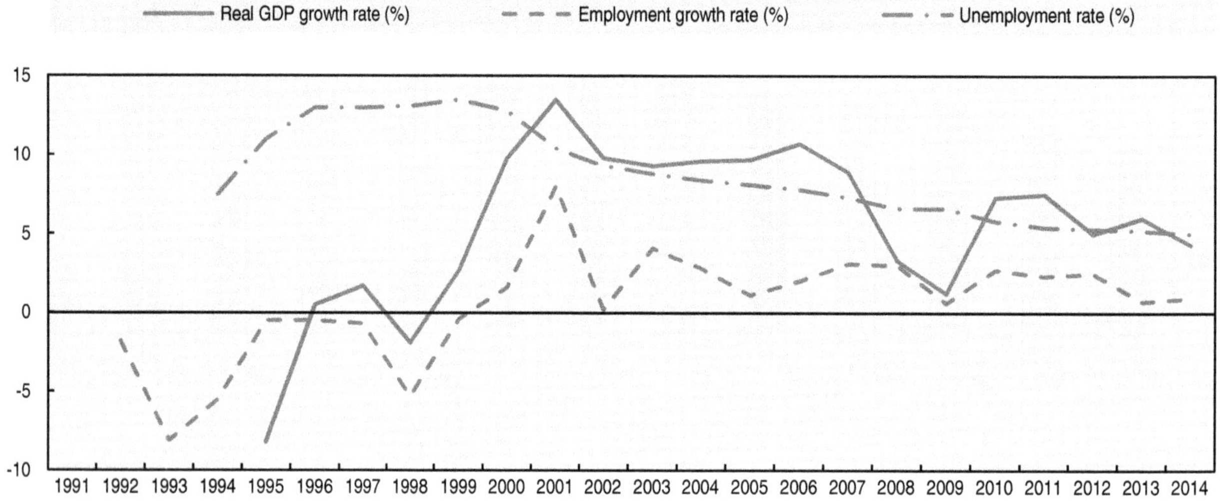

Source: Elaborated on the basis of Committee on Statistics, Kazakhstan.

StatLink http://dx.doi.org/10.1787/888933289097

Figure 2.15. **Youth unemployment is low but hides regional disparities in attachment to the labour market by young people**

Q4 2014 data

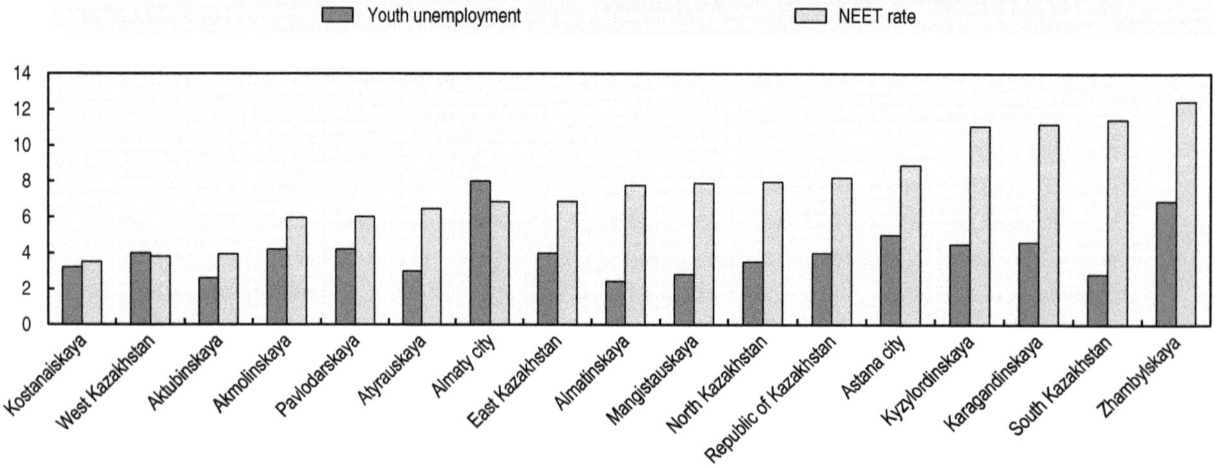

Source: Committee for Statistics, Kazakhstan, *www.stat.gov.kz*.

StatLink http://dx.doi.org/10.1787/888933289106

Job quality remains an issue for a large number of workers concentrated in several sectors and regions. The absolute number of self-employed has remained stable between 2.6 million and 2.8 million since 2000. Over half (56%) are concentrated in agriculture, forestry and fisheries, and their share is increasing in the trade and construction sectors. Moreover, almost half of the self-employed are concentrated in the southern regions of the country: South Kazakhstan, Zhambyl and Almaty region are home to 48% of the self-employed. In agriculture, despite the increase in salaried work, there is significant underemployment, as evidenced by the much shorter weekly hours worked (33 versus 40 to 41 hours in most other sectors and 39 for the national average).

In 2013, informal employment in Kazakhstan affected 24.3% of workers despite recent falls in its degree. This level of informality is not particularly high given the level of development of the country and the sector composition of the economy. Informal employment includes those self-employed workers whose enterprises are informal and all contributing family workers, but also employees who are undeclared, not covered by labour law or do not receive basic labour and employment-linked social rights. While comparable data are not available for most comparator countries, informality outside of agriculture was 72% in Indonesia and 32.6% in China in 2010 compared to 18% in Kazakhstan. The self-employed in agriculture, including contributing family workers, make up most of informal employment[11] (62% in 2009, according to Rutkowski [2011]). Non-agricultural informal employment on the other hand is composed in almost equal parts of wage workers without social benefits or contracts and of self-employed workers. While informal jobs tend to be low-paid and exhibit higher turnover, a small but non-negligible upper tier or informal employment among professionals and skilled workers exists.

Informal self-employment played a buffer role for some socio-demographic groups during the slowdown at the end of the 2000s. Informality increased among women from ethnic minorities (groups of ethnic origin other than European or Kazakh) in 2009, before returning to a downward trend (Mussurov and Arabsheibani, 2013). The over-representation of the young among informal workers suggests, on the other hand, that informal employment provides not only employment of last resort but also a stepping stone for entering the labour market. Indeed, those with less advanced educational attainment (secondary education and less) are over-represented in informal employment while younger groups tend to have higher educational achievements.

Self-employment has dropped since 2001, largely because of shifts in employment from agriculture to services and the growth of certain sectors such as education. The proportion of salaried workers in total employment increased from 58% to 69% between 2001 and 2013. Self-employment is less widespread in the services sector in Kazakhstan than in those of middle-income economies in other regions (78% of services workers are employees). As a result, the shift from agriculture to services has served to cut the proportion of self-employment in the economy. At the same time, the rate of self-employment fell in most sectors, including agriculture. Both structural transformation and the increased reliance on salaried work within sectors had similar weight in the overall change. The single greatest factor within a sector was the marked increase (60% over 12 years) in employment in the education sector, which is almost entirely composed of salaried workers.

Wage growth has been impressive, with real average wages growing at 7.9% a year between 2001 and 2014, driven in part by wage policies. While market forces have certainly played a role, government policy to sustain wages has been effective. Both minimum wages and public sector wages have played a role. Minimum wages in Kazakhstan are low and, at

16.5% of average wages in 2014, considered to be largely non-binding. However, the wage bargaining system in Kazakhstan is based on the negotiation of sector-level increases that are passed on to the wage structure on the basis of occupation multipliers. Indeed, an examination of the rates of growth of average and minimum wages (Figure 2.16) shows that average wages have tracked minimum wage growth quite closely over the period.

Figure 2.16. **Minimum wages are low but play a role in the wage determination process**

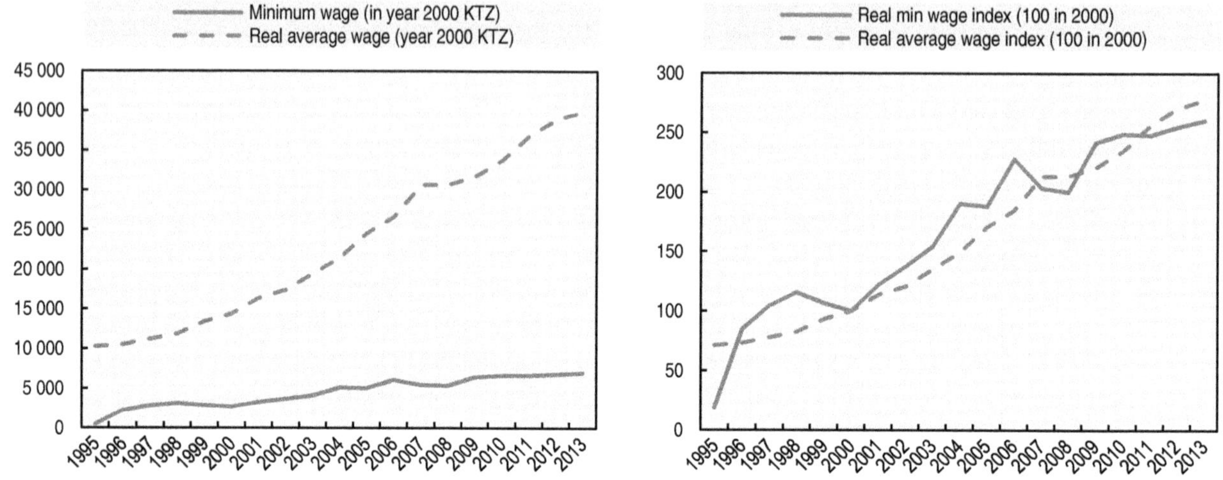

Source: Calculations based on Committee on Statistics data, *www.stat.gov.kz*.

StatLink http://dx.doi.org/10.1787/888933289114

The wage distribution in Kazakhstan is fairly unequal, with 28% of salaried workers receiving low pay. Low pay is defined by the OECD and the International Labour Organization (ILO) as pay below two-thirds of median earnings. That rate is at the upper end relative to comparator countries and especially to OECD countries. Moreover, in certain sectors, the great majority of workers receive low pay. The rate of low pay is 90% in agriculture and 83% in the education sector. Conversely, high wages are concentrated in a few activities, in particular mining, financial activities and professional and technical jobs (ERI, 2014a). Kazakhstan defines low pay as earnings below KZT 30 000 which describes the situation of 8.7% of salaried workers.

Self-employment and informal work represent pockets of low-paid, low-quality jobs. According to official statistics, 8.1% of the employed population (708 790 workers) were in unproductive self-employment in 2014, characterised by having an inactive enterprise or working as self-employed with income below the Minimum Living Standard. Figure 2.18 shows that the self-employed and the informally employed together constitute the bulk of those earning below the poverty line. The concentration of low employment incomes among the self-employed explains the apparent dichotomy between an equal overall income distribution and an unequal wage distribution.[12]

The sector of employment plays a more important role than education in the determination of wages, which is indicative of limited mobility in the labour market. The sectors with the highest-paid workers also have the largest within-sector wage gaps (air transport, oil and gas, finance and insurance). The wage premium in the mining sector, for example, at 96% (for a male worker) is almost twice as large as the average premium a university graduate receives over a worker with secondary education (Keskeyev and Kapsalyamova, 2015). The fact that the premium for working in the extractive sector is larger than the higher education premium in other sectors is likely to distort education incentives.

Figure 2.17. **The proportion of low-paying jobs in Kazakhstan is high**

Proportion of employees with earnings below 2/3rds of those of the median full-time worker (%)

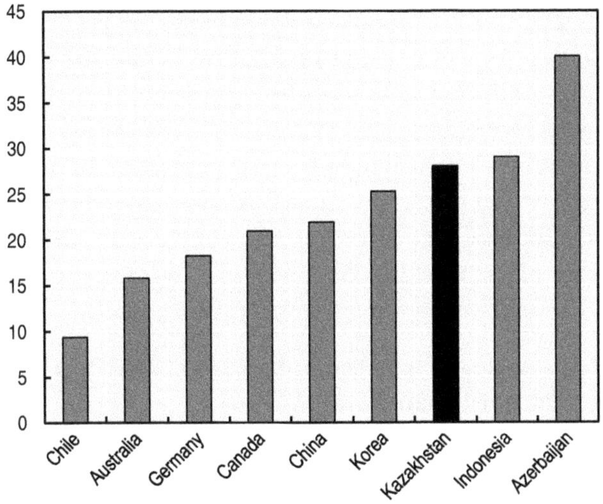

Note: Data for China, Indonesia and Azerbaijan are from the ILO Global Wage Database and measure the share of employees with hourly earnings below 2/3rds of median hourly earnings.

Source: OECD *Employment and Labour Market Statistics* (database), ERI (2014a), "Development Perspectives of Labour Market and Formation of Effective Labour Policies of the Republic of Kazakhstan" and *ILOSTAT* database.

StatLink http://dx.doi.org/10.1787/888933289125

Figure 2.18. **The self-employed and informal employees receive much lower wages**

Share of employed by labour market status and income (in KZT thousand)

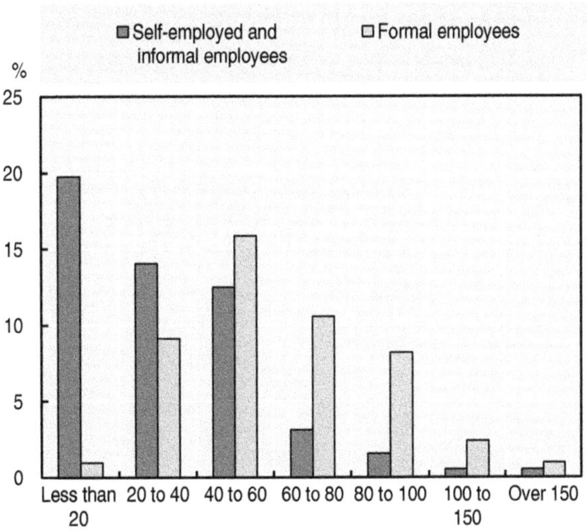

Source: Mun et al. (2015), "Social spending, taxes and income redistribution in Kazakhstan".

StatLink http://dx.doi.org/10.1787/888933289130

Labour market policies are attempting to deal with regional imbalances in labour and skills demand, but have limited reach. The flagship labour policy programme "Employment roadmap 2020" includes a number of active policies to provide training, job matching and facilitating regional mobility of workers. However, labour programmes have limited reach: only 2.5% of the self-employed and 21% of the unemployed participated in the programme during the first ten months of 2014.

Labour market imbalances are exacerbated by migration as skilled migrants leave the country while less skilled migrants arrive. Kazakhstan has significant migration flows, although they have stabilised following the large flows of the 1990s. Nevertheless, the stock of emigrants amounts to 24% of the population, while the country is home to 20% of immigrants. A quarter of immigrants have less than complete secondary education. On the other hand, the migratory balance for those with professional and technical education has been negative in recent years. Although the absolute number of educated workers who leave is not very large (10 000 professional and technically educated persons over three years compared to a population of 3 million with technical education), the geographic pattern of migration, in particular the concentration of immigration in particular in the south of the country, can lead to significant local imbalances.

The people of Kazakhstan live generally in decent housing but express relatively low levels of satisfaction with their housing

Kazakhstan has achieved almost universal access to basic sanitary facilities but access to improved water sources remains an issue in some rural areas. Access to basic sanitary facilities is an accepted indicator of housing quality as it allows international comparison and can be complemented by other subjective indicators. In 2012, fewer than 3% of the households in Kazakhstan did not have access to improved sanitation facilities which include indoor flushing toilets and the presence of a bathroom (World Bank, 2014a) (Figure 2.20 – Panel A). This rate, however, had not improved significantly for Kazakhstan from 2006 to 2012.[13] The percentage of rural population with access to electricity is also high, reaching 100% in 2012 (up from 97.5% in 2010 [World Bank, 2014a]). However, because of the vastness of the territory and the scattered population, access to water remains an issue for some households living in rural areas. Nearly 15% of rural households do not have access to improved water sources, a proportion that has slightly increased from 2001 contrary to the general trend (Figure 2.20 – Panel B).

Figure 2.19. **Migration in Kazakhstan poses challenges for increasing the skills of the labour force**

International migration flows (2009-13) by level of education

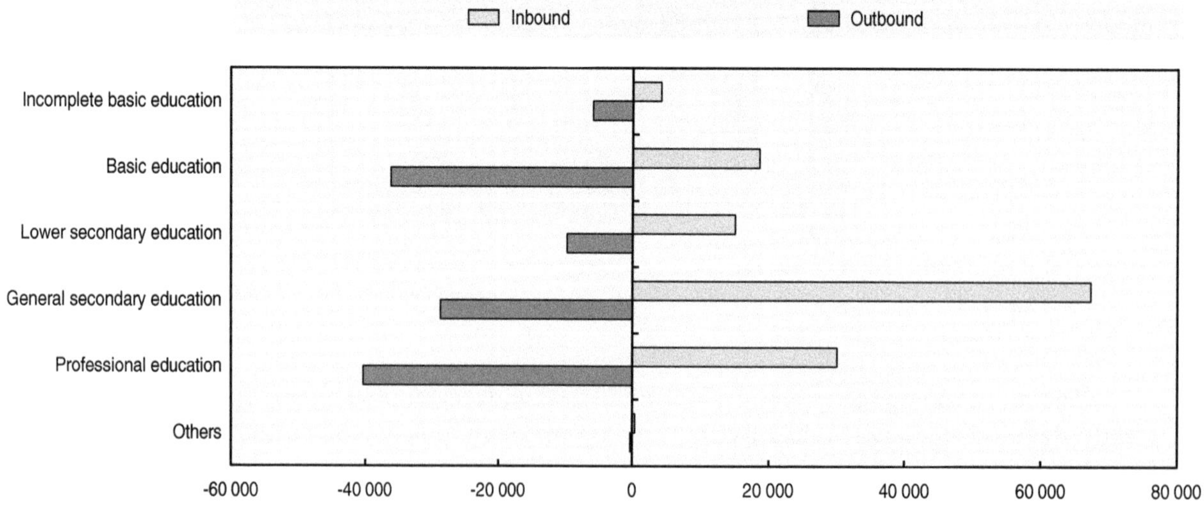

Source: ERI (2014b), "Migration in the Republic of Kazakhstan".

StatLink http://dx.doi.org/10.1787/888933289145

Figure 2.20. **Almost all the Kazakhstani population live in dwellings with private access to an indoor flushing toilet but access to water in rural areas could be improved**

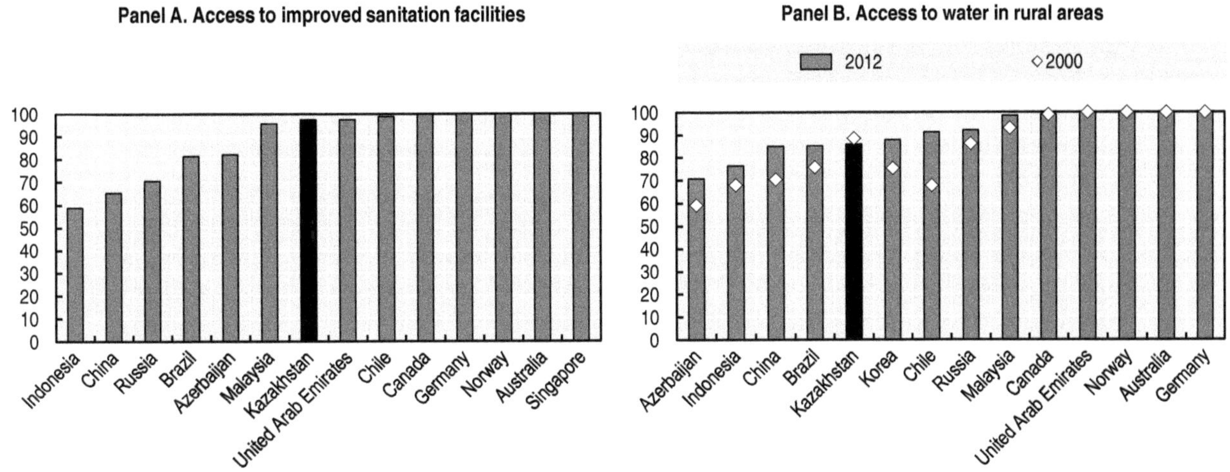

Note: Panel A - Data are for 2012 with the exception of Korea for which data are not available. Panel B – Data are not available for Singapore.

Source: World Bank (2014a), *World Development Indicators* (database), Washington DC, *http://data.worldbank.org*.

StatLink *http://dx.doi.org/10.1787/888933289151*

Rising prices in the housing market, combined with high interest rates and shortage of housing, negatively affect the overall satisfaction of the population with the availability of good affordable housing. In 2014 more than one-third of the population of Kazakhstan reported financial hardship getting adequate housing for themselves or their families, one of the lowest ratios among the benchmark countries but in line with those of the Russian Federation. A similar proportion of people reports not being satisfied with the availability of good affordable housing in their local area (Figure 2.21). Even if salaries are higher, housing is particularly expensive in Astana and Almaty where households have to spend twice as much on housing as in the rest of the country (respectively KZT 48 000 and KZT 55 000 per year). These reported levels of satisfaction on housing confirm the housing problem prevailing in the country, in which the real estate market has gone through several phases (Box 2.3).

Figure 2.21. **Levels of satisfaction with the availability of housing**

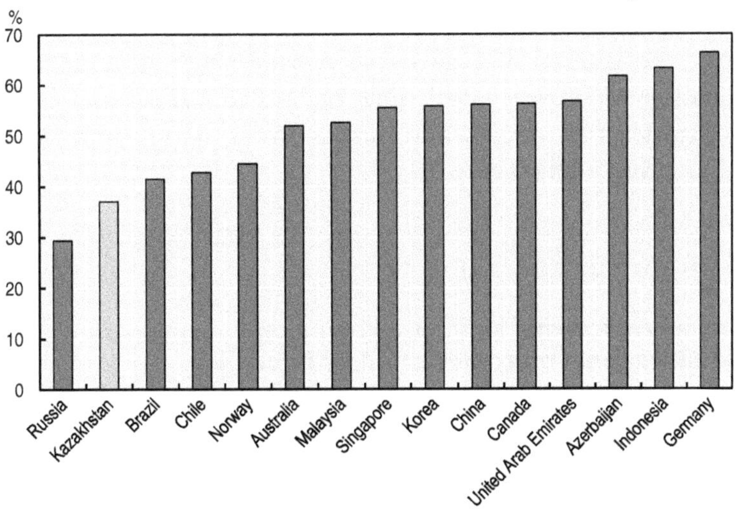

Note: Data for the "levels of satisfaction" graph are for 2014 with the exception of Chile, China, Malaysia and the United Arab Emirates (2013). It shows the percentage of people replying 'satisfied" to the question: "In the city or area where you live, are you satisfied or dissatisfied with the availability of good, affordable housing?"

Source: Gallup (2014), *Gallup World Poll* (database).

StatLink *http://dx.doi.org/10.1787/888933289162*

Box 2.3. Evolution of the housing market from 2000s to nowadays

In the early 2000s, the housing market in Kazakhstan faced an economic boom, while the introduction of mortgages stimulated high real estate demand and developers drove up housing prices. Until 2008, Kazakhstani real estate was among the most attractive investments in Central Asia with massive capital inflows from the banking sector which ultimately fuelled a real estate bubble in the major cities and led to a banking crisis (see Chapter 3).

Since 2008, prices have resumed their upward march, and Kazakhstanis borrow again to buy their houses but at high interest rates. Similarly to other Central Asian countries, mortgage rates have increased to 13-15% in Kazakhstan, preventing a large share of the population from entering the market. In addition, the country faces a severe housing shortage. According to some experts, at least 150 000 people need housing in the country and the waiting list is growing (Central Asia Online, 2012).

Under the umbrella of its "Affordable Housing-2020 initiative", the government has implemented some affordable housing initiatives and accelerated housing construction. The government of Kazakhstan has adopted successively a number of programmes on housing construction development since the mid-2000s (2005-07 and 2008-10 housing programmes). The latest one, named "Affordable Housing-2020 initiative", seeks to reduce the deficit of housing and to promote access to home ownership. Ease in home ownership will be facilitated through an increase in the offer of social housing for rent, lease-purchase or ownership. Local authorities, and companies with some forms of state participation, are now developing new rental housing for all levels of population, including the most vulnerable individuals (population with the lowest revenues, orphaned children, public employees), and proposing attractive housing loans through a system of points. Housing will also be allocated to young families if they acquire a sufficient number of points based on social criteria (20 points for the first child, 30 points for each subsequent child, 10 points for each disabled or chronically ill family member, 10 points if the spouse belongs to the category of orphans and 10 points for children left without parental care). The aim of this new programme is to increase housing in Kazakhstan from 6 million to 10 million square metres by 2020 (Prime Minister of Kazakhstan website). With such an ambitious housing programme, construction growth rate is now highest in Kazakhstan compared to other neighbouring countries with Astana and Almaty Cities, Atyrau and Mangistau Regions leading the housing construction growth.

The quality of life remains low in many respects despite progress in key education and health outcomes

Public efforts on education and skills are paying off but qualitative educational outcomes could be improved

Following ambitious plans for reforming education, Kazakhstan has achieved some remarkable progress in the educational system, where basic education is almost universal. Education and skills are fundamental to well-being: in addition to its intrinsic value, education has a strong positive impact on material conditions and on the quality of life. Individuals with higher education are generally wealthier, healthier and are more integrated in society (OECD, 2011a). Kazakhstan has invested much in improving the capacity and the learning conditions in its primary and secondary schools (OECD, 2014d), and the overall educational picture is impressive. Over the past decade, school enrolment ratios have increased at all educational levels. In 2013, almost all children of a given class age were enrolled in primary and secondary education with ratios approaching, or above, 100% (Figure 2.22). Gender parity is also high for both enrolled and achieved rates. In addition, the expected number of years of schooling a child of school entrance age can expect to receive has increased by 2.3 years from 12.7 to 15 since 2000, one of the highest increases behind China and Singapore (UNDP, 2014). Finally, Kazakhstan also reports also a universal adult literacy rate (UIS, 2014; 2009 Census Data, Committee on Statistics, Kazakhstan).

Figure 2.22. **Enrolment rates for pre-primary, primary and secondary levels are still below average**

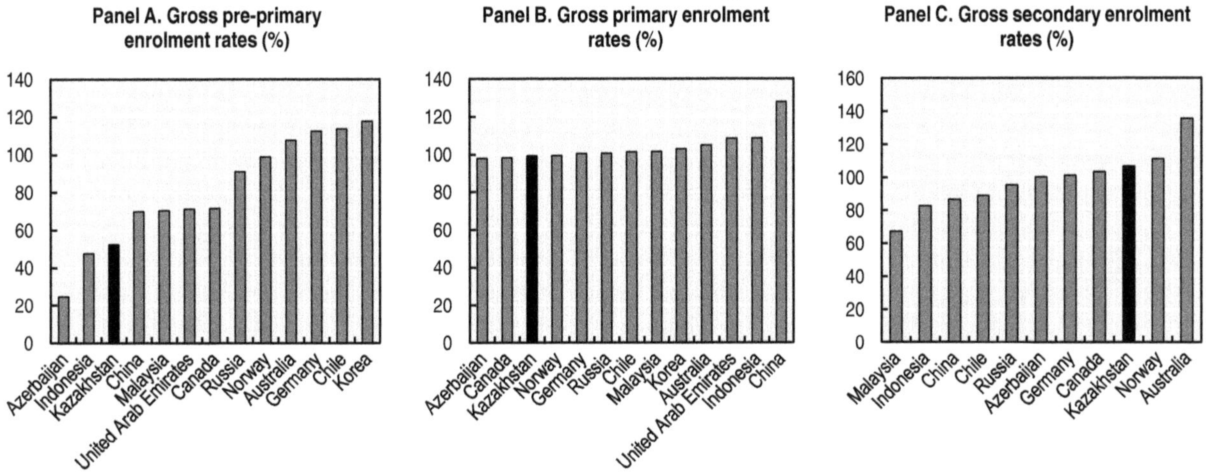

Note: Gross enrolment rates are the total enrolment rates in education, regardless of age, expressed as a percentage of the population of official education age. Gross Enrolment Rates can exceed 100% because of the inclusion of over-aged and under-aged students because of early or late school entrance and grade repetition. Data for pre-primary school enrolment rates are for 2012 apart from Canada, Malaysia, Korea (2011) and Kazakhstan (2014). Data for primary school enrolment rates are for 2012, apart from Malaysia (2005), Canada (2011) and Kazakhstan (2010). Data for secondary enrolment rates are for 2012, apart from Canada, China, Malaysia (2011), and Kazakhstan (2014); data are not available for Brazil, Korea, Singapore and United Arab Emirates for gross secondary enrolment rates.

Sources: UIS (2014), *UIS Data Center* (database), *http://data.uis.unesco.org/* (accessed 10 February 2015), Ministry of Education and Science of the Republic of Kazakhstan (2014a) and Committee for Statistics, written contribution received on 24 February 2015.

StatLink *http://dx.doi.org/10.1787/888933289174*

At the tertiary level, the enrolment rate has steadily increased but the level does not meet international standards. In 2014, the gross enrolment rate for tertiary education (International Standard Classification of Education [ISCED] 5 or 6) had reached 48.4% of a class age, representing 477 387 students admitted in 126 higher education institutions in the country. To enter universities, students pass a single national entry test, called the Unified National Test (UNT) which allows the best performing students to choose their preferred institutions. The UNT covers a wide range of secondary school graduates (79% in 2011), and plays an important selection role. However, its multiple-choice format and narrow scope along with its overwhelming importance for the careers of students and teachers skew incentives and learning outcomes (OECD, 2014d).

The creation of the Bolashak International Scholarships has contributed to the economic development of Kazakhstan and its international recognition. The most talented students can also benefit from the Bolashak scholarship programme through which young skilled students are financially supported to study abroad in leading institutions on the condition that they return to work in Kazakhstan for the benefit of the national economy (Box 2.4). Thanks to this programme, the share of tertiary students studying abroad represents almost 5% of the total number of students, with additionally 2% who are trained abroad at their own expense or through other international grants (see Chapter 4), a share which is ten times higher than those from the Russian Federation. Continuing international co-operation for tertiary education, and promoting this initiative, is one the main priorities of the 2011-2020 State Programme. The country joined the Bologna Process[14] to facilitate such factors as international recognition and mobility. Other countries have created similar initiatives to foster the development of a workforce with advanced international education (Box 2.4).

Box 2.4. **The Bolashak International Scholarship: International comparisons**

Created in 1993, the Bolashak Scholarship of the president of the Republic of Kazakhstan is given to the most qualified students to allow them to study abroad in leading educational institutions. Since its launch, 11 126 scholarships have been awarded in the country (Ministry of Education and Science, Kazakhstan). Up to 3 000 scholarships are awarded annually for recipients to study abroad in more than 33 countries. In 2014, 1 894 students were enrolled to study abroad mainly in the United Kingdom and Ireland (47%), in the United States and Canada (35%), in Europe (12%), in Asia and Oceania (3%) and in the Russian Federation (3%) (Ministry of Education and Science, Kazakhstan). The recent integration of e-services in the Bolashak programmes increased the participation of students coming from rural areas. Upon graduation, the scholarship requires that all recipients work for five years in Kazakhstan.

Other countries across the world have undertaken similar efforts for decades, and their experience provides useful points of comparison. In Asia, Korea was one of the first pioneers to promote the internationalisation of its students. More recently, China established the State Sponsored Study Abroad Programme (SSSAP) to develop China's exchanges with other countries in the field of education and to allow Chinese scholars to study abroad. In Chile, the Becas Chile Programme (BCP) has seen rapid success since its launch in 2005 when 172 young Chileans received scholarships to study abroad. Today, this programme provides scholarships to 6 000 students per year to study abroad. This programme offers 11 scholarship types and deliberate efforts have been made to expand the participation of people from less advantaged backgrounds (OECD/World Bank, 2010). Looking at the lessons learnt from other international scholarship programmes could help Kazakhstan to improve its own system in the future.

For pre-primary education, there is still room for improvement but the recent reforms are already paying off. Compared to the benchmark countries, gross enrolment rates in pre-primary schools (for children aged between one and six) remain low (52.3%% in 2014,[15] Ministry of Education, 2014a), far below the average of 80% for the benchmark group of countries (Figure 2.23 – Panel C). Among PISA participating countries (65 in total), Kazakhstan records one of the lowest percentage of students who attended pre-primary education (ISCED 0) while the positive impacts of pre-school attendance to secondary school outcomes have been proved (OECD, 2014a). The government has invested substantial resources to expand pre-primary education and has initiated a series of reforms (in 2011, the Balapan State Programme was launched to expand pre-primary education to increase participation of children with pre-school education to 77% in 2015 and to 100% by 2020). The latest available data show a 12.6 percentage points progression in the pre-primary enrolment ratio between 2010 and 2013 (Committee for Statistics, 2015).

Figure 2.23. **Mathematics and science achievements are at the bottom of the scale while reading achievements are the lowest across the benchmark countries**

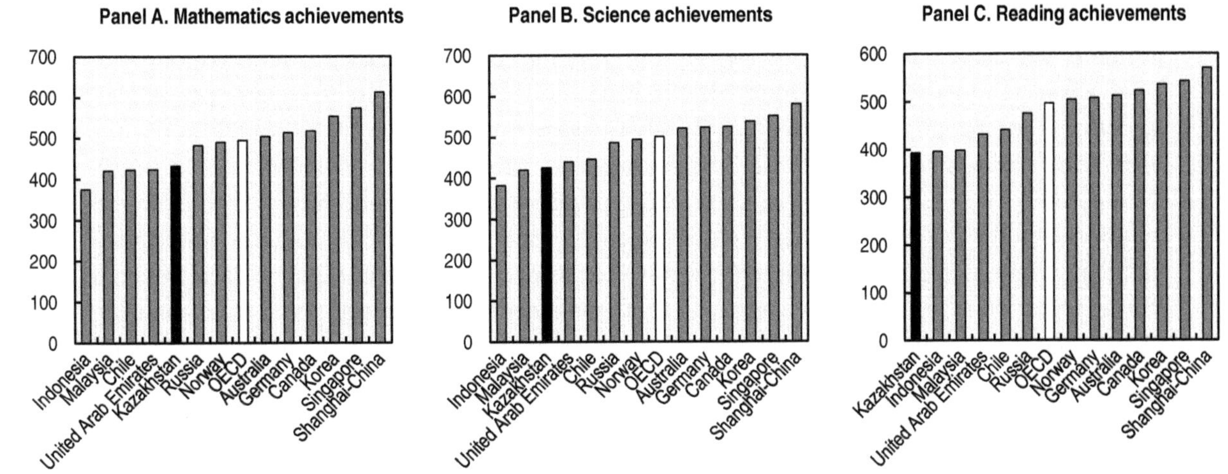

Source: OECD (2014a), *OECD PISA 2012 Database.*

StatLink http://dx.doi.org/10.1787/888933289185

Aside from quantitative indicators, the quality of education is relatively low. Despite being fairly equal, the average outcomes in education are relatively poor for Kazakhstan. The OECD PISA measures the cognitive skills of 15 years-olds worldwide in the areas of reading, mathematics and science. In 2012, out of 65 countries, Kazakhstan was ranked 49th in mathematics, 52nd in science and 63rd in reading (OECD, 2014a). Compared to the benchmark countries, Kazakhstan ranks the lowest in reading while it ranks slightly better in science and mathematics (Figure 2.23).

Reading performances are the most worrisome and have not improved over the last few years. Compared to 2009, Kazakhstan's PISA 2012 scores on reading improved only marginally. In addition, overall performances remain low, with some groups of students actually performing worse in 2012 (Inoue and Gortazar, 2014). These scores in reading lag by the equivalent of almost two years of schooling behind the OECD average. Reading skills are lower among students studying in Kazakh language schools (rather than Russian language schools) and among students coming from families with low socio-economic status where Kazakh is the language spoken at home.

While several reasons are put forward to explain the relatively poor learning outcomes in Kazakhstan, the lack of well-qualified teachers is often stressed. The lack of schooling infrastructures and material resources, the out-dated curriculum, the relatively low public expenditures on education, the mismatch between the educational programmes and the labour market needs are some of the reasons put forward to explain low education outcomes. The shortage of well-trained teachers, especially in rural areas is also often highlighted as one of the main issues in the schooling system of Kazakhstan. The 297 293 teachers (Ministry of Education of the Republic of Kazakhstan, 2014a) working in the country suffer from a low-status image and from a low salary (approx. 60% of the national average wage) with poor incentive pay structure. Despite recent salary increases, the pay of a teacher remains one of the lowest across the country. Most these weaknesses in the teaching system prevail also in the tertiary education system, damaging the quality of teaching and learning (OECD, 2007). The low salaries of the staff probably play a role in the existing levels of corruption in the educational system.

In addition, the country faces the risk of a two-tier education system with potential social inequity issues. The schooling system in Kazakhstan is singular: it is made up of public schools, public "ungraded" schools (UGS), public "specialised" schools, public "correctional schools" for pupils with special needs, and private schools (OECD, 2014d). Among the specialised schools, the prestigious "Nazarbayev Intellectual Schools" (NIS), one per region, accommodate about 10 000 gifted pupils. The government uses the NIS network to try out new educational practices that will be disseminated throughout the system (OECD, 2014d). The country gives high priority to these NISs for gifted children and, during the workshop organised by the OECD (see Annex 1.A1), most of the participants highlighted the importance of having their own children selected to enter such a special school. The lack of data prevents this report from assessing the process to enter these school communities and from measuring the degree to which children from economically disadvantaged families have access to them.

In the schooling system of Kazakhstan, the "ungraded" schools appear as the least favoured. Unlike the NIS schools, the "ungraded" schools, which represent 43.2% of the total number of schools, suffer from low financial, material and human resources, especially in rural areas, and teachers have to assemble students of different educational levels in one class (OECD, 2014d). PISA results show that pupils who studied in these small "ungraded" schools tend to record lower performances than others (OECD, 2014d). In addition, children with special needs and disabilities go to "correctional schools" (OECD, 2014d) and appear to be disadvantaged compared to other students in relation to access to and quality of good education. At the tertiary level, there are also significant inequities in access to university and to student financial support (OECD, 2007).

The government has set an ambitious policy roadmap to improve educational outcomes, translated into various programmes and initiatives. Education is identified as one of the main priorities of the "Kazakhstan 2030" Strategy and, within such a context, the government has set up a State Programme of Education Development in the Republic of Kazakhstan for 2011-2020 to develop a highly-educated labour force and improve the educational system. Even if it remains below the OECD average, public spending on education, expressed as a share of GDP, has increased significantly over the last few years (3.4% in 2012) to meet the government's stated objectives (UNDP, 2014). Among the different measures and strategic plans derived from this high-level roadmap, the five-year National Action Plan for Development of Functional Literacy for School Children (NAP), launched in 2012 to strengthen literacy skills, the extension of the Balapan State Programme to increase pre-primary school enrolment to 100%, and a transition from a 11 to 12-year educational model are worth mentioning. For teachers, new centres of excellence for pedagogical skills have been established in the NIS network and a three-tier system to train teachers was introduced to help them to upgrade their qualifications. The country has also undertaken major efforts to reduce the mismatch between the educated workforce and the current needs of industry, particularly in the area of vocational training (see Chapter 4).

Despite this ambitious reform plan, Kazakhstanis seem to acknowledge the weaknesses in the education system. In 2013, only half of those interviewed reported being satisfied with the national educational system, a share far below the OECD average but in line with neighbouring countries (Gallup, 2014).

From a policy perspective, there is still room for improvement in increasing public spending in education and eliminating corruption. Public spending on education has greatly increased over the last decade; from 0.7% of GDP in 2000 to 4.1% in 2014 (Ministry of Education and Science, 2014). However, this level of expenditure remains below the standards of the benchmark countries, twice as low as the proportion spent in Norway or Brazil for instance (UNESCO, 2012) and well below the OECD public expenditure in education (5.6% in 2011). Kazakhstan is also the country which spends the least per pupil on education in Europe and Central Asia (World Bank, 2014a). The gap in public spending is particularly marked for primary and secondary education, as Kazakhstan spends 11% of GDP per capita per student, compared to an OECD average of 25% (Pons et al., 2015). In addition, despite recent efforts, education continues to be highly corrupt (Bertelsmann Stiftung Transformation Index [BTI], 2014). According to the financial police, corruption cases in the education system make up 16% of the overall number of corruption crimes in Kazakhstan. The ministry of education has lamented that parents or students can be pushed into paying bribes to ensure enrolment in tertiary education where access is not universal, or to guarantee graduation at the tertiary level (see also Chapter 5) and has put in place anti-corruption measures specific to the field of education, especially in higher education. Beyond the corruption problem, this may have strong consequences on labour productivity and on the level of skills people can use when they are employed.

Despite recent progress, health outcomes still remain poor

The health care system in Kazakhstan has the hallmarks of a transition country currently undertaking profound reforms. Developing policy making in health is centralised within the large ministry of health care and social development whereas the 14 regions administer health services and health care facilities. Public expenditure on health is mainly spent on health services coverage under the State Guaranteed Benefit Package (SGBP) and on transfers to local budgets for *oblasts*. Some of them can be quite financially powerful but there are significant variations in power and revenue across *oblasts* (Figure 2.26). As a legacy of the Soviet period, the Kazakhstani health system is characterised by an excessive emphasis on hospital infrastructure whereas primary health care, disease prevention and health promotion have been neglected (Katsaga et al., 2012). The geographical features of the country, the lack of financial, physical and human resources, the legacy of Soviet-era policies and the complex institutional arrangements between the national and local authorities are among the challenges that remain to be overcome to improve health outcomes significantly.

Key indicators demonstrate that health outcomes are still low in Kazakhstan. Despite rapid economic growth and large increases in total expenditures on health, key health indicators have not improved significantly. The average overall life expectancy at birth was estimated at 71.62 in 2014: the lowest among the benchmark countries and also lower than the average regional life expectancy which is estimated at 76 (Committee on Statistics, Kazakhstan, 2015; WHO, 2014) (Figure 2.24). Compared to the benchmark countries, Kazakhstan has one of the largest gender gaps in life expectancy with almost ten years' difference between men (67.2) and women (75.9) (Committee on Statistics, Kazakhstan, 2015). Leaving aside lifestyle behaviours, this is typical of many post-Soviet countries, which experienced large increases in male mortality rates in the period following the break-up of the Soviet Union.

Over the recent years, maternal and infant mortality rates have decreased significantly, allowing the country to achieve Millennium Development Goals (MDGs). According to latest available data,[16] the 2014 maternal mortality ratio was estimated at 11.7 deaths per 100 000 births, a rate that has been divided by more than 4 since the 2000s (Committee on Statistics, Kazakhstan, 2015).[17] There is a similar trend for infant mortality ratio, which decreased from 18.8 deaths per 100 000 births in 2000 to 9.72 deaths in 2014 (Committee on Statistics, Kazakhstan, 2015).[18] Based on these national data sources, the country has achieved

Figure 2.24. **Kazakhstan reports one of the lowest health outcomes with respect to life expectancy and adult mortality ratios**

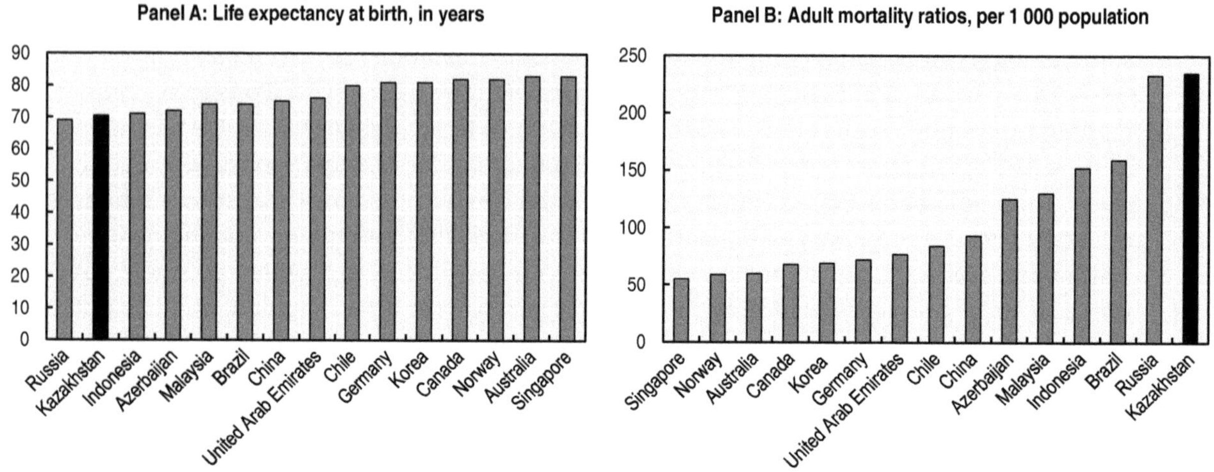

Note: Data are for 2012 with the exception of Kazakhstan where life expectancy data are from 2013.

Source: WHO (2014) database and Ministry of Health and Social Development in Kazakhstan.

StatLink http://dx.doi.org/10.1787/888933289192

its targeted objectives regarding maternal and infant mortality ratios as they were laid out in the Strategic Plan for Development of Kazakhstan until 2020 and the MDGs. However, these ratios are still higher than those in the region, explaining partially the low life expectancy. In addition, regional disparities are considerable and some regions, such as Mangystau and Zhambyl *oblasts*, still display high maternal mortality rates (respectively 21.2 and 18.1).

However, adult mortality ratios remain relatively high in Kazakhstan. Adult mortality ratios (i.e. the probability of dying between 15 and 60 years per 1 000 population) in Kazakhstan are estimated at 324 and 147 for men and women respectively, compared to 179 and 80 in the region (WHO, 2014) (Figure 2.24). Among the benchmark countries, the Kazakhstani average adult mortality ratio is in line with the Russian Federation but more than four times higher than those recorded in Singapore, Norway or Australia.

Tuberculosis (TB), blood-borne infectious diseases and cancers are of increasing public health concerns. Non-communicable diseases, such as cancers, cardiovascular diseases, upper respiratory diseases and other tobacco and alcohol-related diseases, dominate the diseases burden. Kazakhstan scores the highest rank for upper respiratory diseases (WorldLifeExpectancy, 2013). Over the last few years, cancer cases have increased, mainly in industrial regions. In terms of communicable diseases, tuberculosis and other infectious diseases have high prevalence rates in Kazakhstan. Tuberculosis, with 135.6 registered patients per 100 000 population in 2013, is considered to be an established disease in the country where the rate is much higher than that observed in the rest of the region (56 per 100 000 population) (WHO, 2014). According to WHO data, Kazakhstan leads in terms of the incidence of registered tuberculosis, and is one of 18 priority countries for TB in the WHO European Region. In respect of blood-borne diseases, human immunodeficiency virus (HIV) cases are multiplying in the country: from 345 affected persons in 2000 to 1 994 in 2013, 56% of them being men (Committee on Statistics, Kazakhstan, 2015). The prevalence of HIV cases is four times higher in urban than in rural areas (Committee on Statistics, Kazakhstan, 2015).

Finally, the rates of injury and suicide are also high in Kazakhstan compared to the rest of the world. Kazakhstan ranks second for injuries and third for suicide rates (WorldLifeExpectancy, 2013). In 2011 more than 30 deaths per 100 000 population were caused by suicide (20.54 in 2013 and 17.62 in 2014, [Committee on Statistics, 2015]), which can be related to some extent to the relatively low score of Kazakhstan in subjective well-being (WorldLifeExpectancy, 2013). The suicide rate in Kazakhstan, higher than Russia's, is almost three times higher than the OECD average suicide rate which is estimated at 12.4 (OECD, 2014e) and this issue is particularly challenging for teenagers who are the most liable to commit suicides.

These relatively poor health outcomes are echoed in the self-reported health status and subjective perceptions regarding health care systems. In 2012, the latest available data, almost 70% of Kazakhstanis reported being in good health, a figure higher than in Russia but lower than the rest of the benchmark countries where this rate is generally above 80% (Figure 2.25 – Panel B). In addition, Kazakhstanis are critical of the quality of the health care system. Fewer than 40% are satisfied with the availability of high-quality health care, a share which is below the average of 66% among the benchmark countries and which has decreased since 2006 (Figure 2.25 – Panel A).

Figure 2.25. **Kazakhstanis report low self-reported health status and are critical of the national health care system**

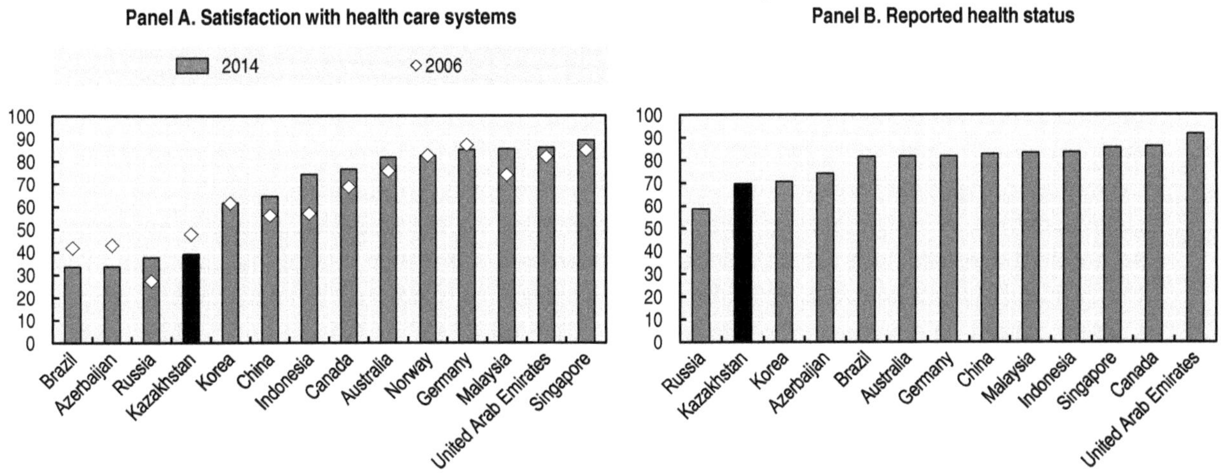

Note: Panel A - The graph "Satisfaction with health care systems" shows the proportion of respondents who replied "satisfied" to the question: "In the city or area where you live, are you satisfied or dissatisfied with the availability of quality health care?". Data are from 2014, with the exception of China and United Arab Emirates (2013), and from 2006, with the exception of Australia, Brazil, Canada, China and Germany (2007). Panel B - The graph "reported health status" shows the proportion of respondents who replied "satisfied" to the question "Are you satisfied or dissatisfied with your personal health?" The latest available data are from 2012, with the exception of Australia, Canada, Korea and United Arab Emirates (2011). Data are not available for Norway.

Source: Gallup (2014), *Gallup World Poll* (database).

StatLink http://dx.doi.org/10.1787/888933289206

Despite recent improvements, regional inequities in heath financing, health care utilisation and health outcomes remain substantial. People living in the cities of Almaty and Astana have better access to health services than those living in more remote areas. In terms of human resources, rural and remote areas continue to suffer from a shortage of well-qualified health personnel and health specialists. For instance, the available number of doctors varies at the top from 46 per 10 000 people in urban centres to 11 per 10 000 in rural areas (Ministry of Healthcare and Social Development, 2014). In addition, public health spending per capita shows significant variation across regions, reinforcing the existing social inequities (Figure 2.26 – Panel A). As a consequence, health outcomes present significant variations across regions. Maternal mortality varies from 4.1 per 100 000 in Karaganda or 5.1 per 100 000 births in Almaty City to more than 25 deaths per 100 000 births in Atyrau and Akmola *oblasts*.

Figure 2.26. **Per capita health expenditure (local and Republican budgets), life expectancy and TB morbidity by *oblast***

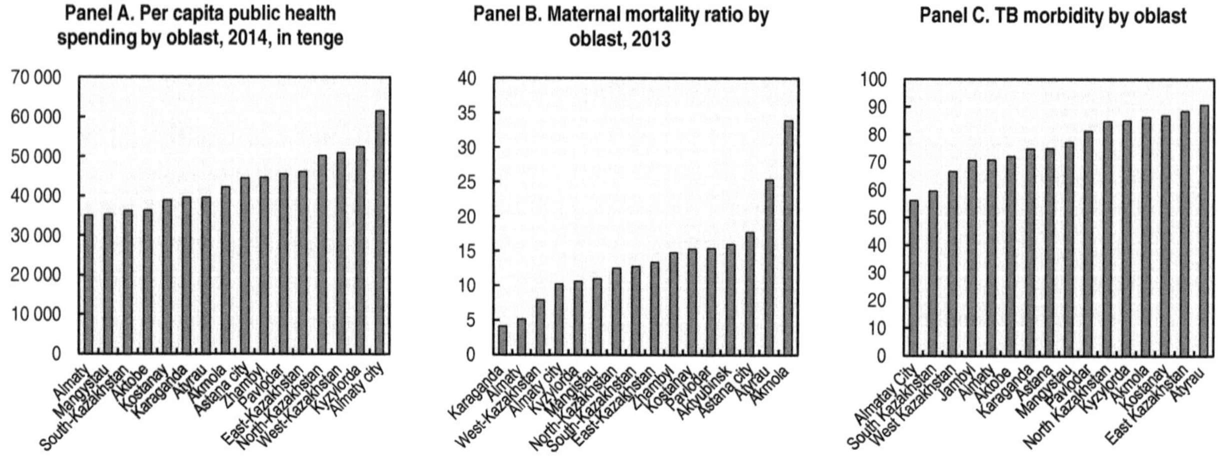

Source: Written contribution from the Ministry of Healthcare and Social Development.

StatLink http://dx.doi.org/10.1787/888933289211

In addition, the country has to deal with the legacy of environmental catastrophes and problems which may have significant impacts on public health in the long run. In the case of environmental catastrophe, 200 000 Kazakhs were exposed to direct and indirect radiation exposure from nuclear testing in the Semipalatinsk area over four decades, until the site was closed down in 1991. The health impacts of these tests on the increased number of cancers and related diseases have become evident in recent years (Katsaga et al., 2012). In addition, the draining of the Aral Sea in 1960s has left the remaining water and the surrounding land highly polluted. The country also has to deal with extensive air pollution and problems of contaminated water which may be detrimental for health outcomes (Katsaga et al., 2012).

With the State Health Care Development Programme for 2011-2015 "Salamatty Kazakhstan" and the former National Programme for Health care Reform and Development 2005-2010, the government has recognised health as one of the country's major priorities and has started implementing several policies to improve health outcomes. The vision of the Strategic Plan for 2014-2018 on health and social development is to reach an effective health care system satisfying the needs of the population with two main strategic dimensions. The first is to improve health outcomes and decrease mortality rates for Kazakhstanis. Some effective measures have been taken to improve epidemiological tuberculosis incidence rates and maternal and infant mortality ratios but much more still needs to be achieved. Improving access to primary health care services and their quality is at the forefront of the ministry's priorities to improve significantly health outcomes. In the second strategic dimension the government intends to improve the quality and the efficiency of the health care system. The development of an integrated and high-tech health care system is under way. In addition, the construction of mobile medical complexes should aim to increase health service offer in remote areas.

Social connections are weak in Kazakhstan compared to benchmark countries

One Kazakhstani in five reported not having someone to count on in 2014, the highest proportion among the benchmark countries. This is a disturbing proportion which can negatively affect individual and social well-being. Indeed, people with extensive and supportive social networks tend to have better health with a longer life expectancy and are more likely to be employed (OECD, 2013a). Also, at a societal level, social connections can play a role in creating common values and influence a range of outcomes such as democratic participation, crime levels and even economic growth (OECD, 2013a). Across OECD countries, around 90% of people report having someone to count on in time of need (OECD, 2013a). In 2014, this proportion was estimated at 76% for Kazakhstan, a decreasing proportion compared to 2013 when 87% of people said they had someone to turn to in case of need (Gallup, 2014).

Education, age, gender and ethnic origins influence social network support in Kazakhstan. As in most countries, education plays a role in social connections. This is the case with Kazakhstan where 75% of less well educated people report having someone to count on compared with 83% for people with tertiary education (Gallup, 2014). In addition, people's social support networks tend to weaken as they get older until late in their working life, but they increase again over the age of 65. This "U-shaped" pattern is also true in Kazakhstan and may reflect the supportive role played by parents in the case of the young, and by grown-up children and their spouses in the cases of elderly people (OECD, 2011a). Finally, in Kazakhstan, gender and ethnic origins also seem to play a role in social connections. Of the ethnic Russian women living in Kazakhstan 86% report having someone to count on in case of need, whereas only 70% of the men from other ethnic origins (non-Russian or Kazakh) report having someone to count on (Gallup, 2014).

Figure 2.27. **Perceived social network support in Kazakhstan is the lowest among benchmark countries whereas the stock of social capital is relatively high**

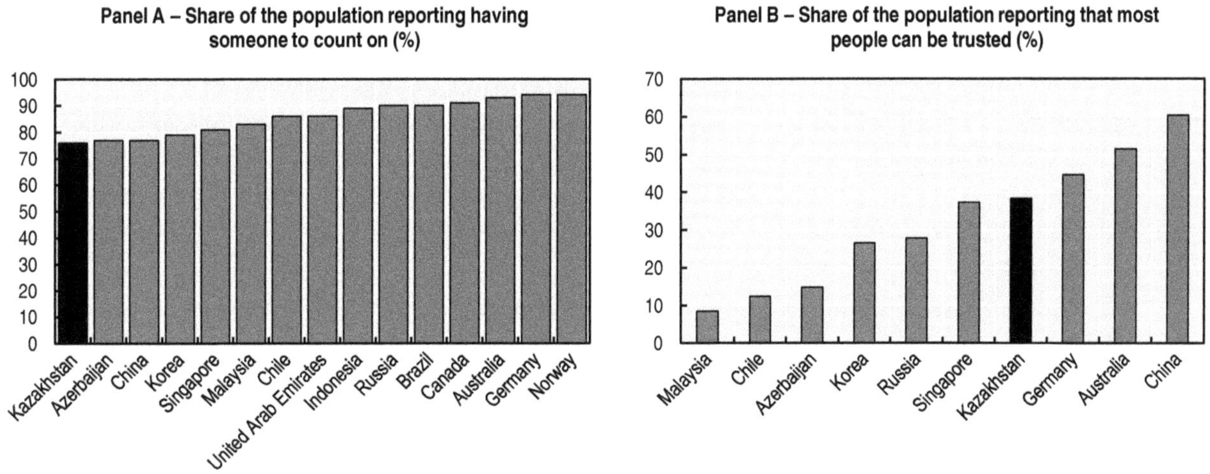

Note: Panel A - Data for the "Perceived social network" graph are for 2014, except for Australia, Canada, Chile, China, Korea, Malaysia (2013), and show the percentage of people replying "yes" to the question: "if you were in trouble, do you have relatives or friends you can count on help whenever you need them, or not?". Panel B - This graph shows the percentage of those replying "most people can be trusted" to the question "Generally speaking, would you say that most people can be trusted or that you need to be very careful in dealing with people?" Data are for 2012 with the exception of Chile, Kazakhstan, Malaysia (2011) and Korea (2010).

Sources: Gallup (2014), *Gallup World Poll* (database) and *World Values Survey* (2014), *Wave 6* (online database).

StatLink http://dx.doi.org/10.1787/888933289223

The level of "social trust" has significantly improved since the breakup of the Soviet Union. The measure of "social trust" can also supplement the analysis of social connections. This indicator captures the percentage of people saying that, generally speaking, most people can be trusted. Scholars have argued that social trust had broken down in post-Soviet societies, potentially leading to a cultural trauma (Sztompka, 1999). For instance, in a 1996 survey, 71% of Russian respondents thought they could not trust others. In 2001, a new survey was conducted which showed that only 18% of the Kazakhstanis agreed that the majority of the people can be trusted (Sapsford and Abbott, 2006), in line with the average of other Commonwealth of Independent States (CIS) countries. In 2012, this score improved quite dramatically with 38% of Kazakhstanis expressing trust in others (Word Values Survey, 2014). This proportion is in line with the OECD average (OECD, 2014e) and above the proportions reported in Azerbaijan and Russian Federation (Figure 2.27). The strong economic recovery, which benefited the population fairly evenly, may have helped increase the stock of social capital in the country. Indeed, there is some evidence suggesting that social trust can be eroded by economic inequality (OECD/ECLAC, 2014).

The prevalence of corruption may hinder empowerment while the participation of civil society in governance remains limited

Empowerment refers to the ability of citizens to participate in, negotiate with, influence, and hold accountable formal or informal institutions that affect people's lives. Greater levels of empowerment and participation may reflect higher levels of social integration and cohesion and the willingness of the population to have a voice in the systems of governance and in the legitimacy and accountability of public institutions. Indicators assessing levels of corruption and trust in institutions and local governments are useful in giving a broad picture on empowerment levels in a country. The last chapter of this report on governance offers a useful complement to this section (Chapter 5).

Corruption is still pervasive in Kazakhstan. Empowerment in the country is partially hindered by the prevalence of a corruption in formal institutions that is detrimental to the accountability of these institutions. Transparency International, which monitors corruption and produces the Corruption Perception Index[19] (CPI) measuring the perceived levels of public sector corruption from 0 (highly corrupt) to 100 (very clean), considers Kazakhstan as a highly corrupt country with a score of 26 (Transparency International, 2014). This score ranks the country 126th out of 175 and is in line with those from neighbouring countries but shows the weak performance of the country compared to other benchmark countries (Figure 2.28 – Panel A). In addition, Kazakhstan's score has remained stable over the last few years.

The notion of corruption seems to be taboo in Kazakhstan. The CPI results can be compared with the perception of corruption in the country as measured by the Gallup World Poll. According to this latter study, two Kazakhstanis out of three say that they believe corruption is widespread in the government and in business (Gallup, 2014). This percentage is surprisingly low compared to other benchmark countries which are considered as less corrupt but have a higher share of respondents criticising the prevalence of corruption within their national governments (i.e. Brazil, Chile, Indonesia, and Korea) (Figure 2.28 – Panel A). This pattern may be due to an unwillingness to respond to this type of question. In Kazakhstan, one person out of five refused to answer questions related to corruption in business and in government in 2014, a proportion which was even higher in previous years, rising to 35% in 2008 (Figure 2.28 – Panel B). This proportion is much larger in Kazakhstan than in other benchmark countries but is similar to the recorded shares in the neighbourhood countries (i.e. Russian Federation and Azerbaijan) and Singapore. To add together the share of respondents who report that corruption is widespread within their national governments and the share of respondents refusing to answer that question, perceived levels of corruption are among the highest in Kazakhstan, just behind Indonesia and the Russian Federation (Figure 2.28 – Panel B). As part of current efforts in the fight against corruption (discussed in Chapter 5 in this volume), anti-corruption education is to be included in curricula and dissemination of anti-corruption initiatives scaled up to change the behaviour of the population with respect to corruption.

Figure 2.28. **Subjective indicators regarding corruption within the government are very high**

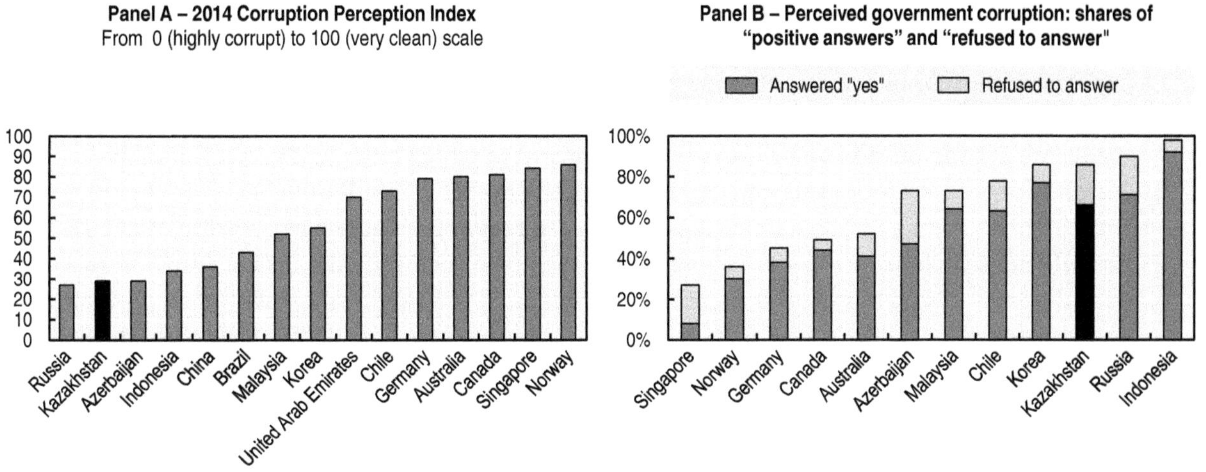

Note: Data for the Corruption Perception Index are for 2014. Data for "Perceived government corruption" graph are for 2014, with the exception of Chile and Malaysia (2013), and show the percentages of respondents replying "Yes" and not answering to the question: "Is corruption widespread throughout the government in this country, or not?" Data are not available for China and the United Arab Emirates.

Source: Transparency International (2014), *Corruption Perception Index* (database) and Gallup Organisation (2014), *Gallup World Monitor* (database).

StatLink http://dx.doi.org/10.1787/888933289235

A similar trend appears when the levels of trust with public institutions are examined. Trust in government is one of the most important foundations upon which the legitimacy and sustainability of political systems are built (OECD/ECLAC, 2014). Kazakhstan presents a level of confidence in government slightly above the average of the benchmark countries, with almost 60% of people saying they trust national government (higher than the OECD average estimated at 41%). However, 14% of people still refused to answer this question, the highest share among the benchmark countries. The confidence in national courts is lower than in governments (43% in 2014) and the proportion of people not answering the question is still the highest of the benchmark countries, behind Azerbaijan. The judicial system is criticised for being corrupt and weak in respect of law enforcement (Business Anti-corruption Portal, 2015).

The government has made considerable efforts to fight corruption and restore confidence in the country. Kazakhstan was one of the first former Soviet countries to adopt a law on fighting corruption in 1998, which defines the framework, principles and methods of fighting corruption. Chapter 5 of the report details the different reforms undertaken by the government to combat corruption.

However, corruption is still rampant in the various public and private circles of the country and is often perceived as part of local culture. The Office of the Prosecutor General of Kazakhstan considers that corruption in Kazakhstan has "become systemic" and operates at all levels of officials (Prosecutor General's Office, prokuror.gov.kz, 11 March). Developing a comprehensive, consistent and politically neutral roadmap will help alleviate corruption which would include addressing key corruption risk areas, strengthening judicial independence and government accountability (OECD, 2014f). The involvement of civil society in anti-corruption activities is also critical to creating low tolerance for corruption in society (OECD, 2014f). Indeed, corruption in Kazakhstan is often perceived as part of local traditions and culture which can partially explain a certain tolerance of people for corruption (Prosecutor General's Office, prokuror.gov.kz, 11 March).

Finally, the participation of civil society in various types of political activities is still very limited. Depending on the countries, forms of political participation can vary substantially in influencing and negotiating in public institutions. In Kazakhstan, only 14% of the population had contacted a politician, government or local government official over the last year, a rate which is lower than in the Western countries of the benchmark countries (Gallup, 2014). Public consultation on rule-making, the extent to which citizens are consulted in the design of regulatory proposals and can influence the drafting, is still unusual. Even if public consultations on regulations are accessible via the respective ministry's website, they are not sufficiently user-centred, nor pro-active (OECD, 2014f). For instance, online consultation with the public lacks an explicit call for comments, clear timelines, consultation periods and guidance, as well as a single online consultation platform listing all draft regulations (OECD, 2014f). The proportion of Kazakhstanis who reported having voiced an opinion to an official may also give insight into the willingness of civil society to participate in political activities. In 2013, the latest available data, only 14% people had voiced an opinion to an official in Kazakhstan, a share lower than the benchmark average and lower than expected considering Kazakhstan's economic development (Gallup, 2014).

The environment faces multiple challenges linked to past experiences and to the current economic model

Kazakhstan faces considerable and diverse environmental challenges, linked with difficult climate conditions, a history of environmental mismanagement under Soviet rule and the reliance of the economy on extractive industries. Because of its geographical situation, the country is highly exposed to several types of natural hazards, including earthquakes, floods, droughts, landsides and mudflows (UNESCO, 2013), and must deal with difficult climate conditions. In addition, the country has inherited some significant environmental disasters with which it still has to deal, such as the drastic contraction of Aral Sea, the threat of the former nuclear weapons tested at the Semipalatinsk site to the health of many Kazakhstanis, and the extensive exploitation of natural resources. Finally, the current development path of the country involves new challenges regarding the efficiency of energy use, the issues of waste management, the shortage of water resources and the increase in air pollution. Challenges include high GHG (greenhouse gas) emissions, significant water management problems from desertification to water pollution and extreme cases such as the Aral sea disaster, challenges in the management of industrial waste from current and past activities, especially from mining and heavy industry (UNECE, 2008).

Environmental outcomes affect health and well-being both directly through exposure to environmental risks and access to environmental services, and indirectly through their effect on the economy and the contribution to global phenomena such as climate change. This chapter is chiefly concerned with direct effects, while indirect effects are examined in Chapter 3. Of main concern are exposure to environmental pollution and environmental risks and access to environmental services such as clean water, sanitation, green spaces and biodiversity. People's lives are strongly affected by the quality of the physical environment in which they live. The impact of environmental pollutants, hazardous substances and noise on people's health is significant. In addition, quality of life can be negatively affected by poor environmental assets and services, such as scarcity or poor quality of water, or low access to sanitation services and waste disposal.

Air pollution has significant health and environmental impacts, particularly in urban and highly industrialised areas. The estimated health costs from air pollution are significant, mounting to 2 800 premature deaths and over USD 1.3 billion in health costs annually (World

Bank and Ministry of Environment and Water Resources of the Republic of Kazakhstan, 2013). Other authors find similarly high figures: Kenessariyev et al. (2013) estimate excess mortality of 4 075 for 11 cities. Figures 2.29 and 2.30 show the concentration of particulate matter pollution in Kazakhstan on the basis of data sources allowing international comparisons. Overall levels of small particulate matter concentration (PM2.5) appear modest (Panel A in Figure 2.29) in comparison to other countries, but it should be stressed that these are estimates on the basis of different observations and that they cover the whole country. Indeed, as evidenced by Panel B, almost the entire urban population of Kazakhstan is estimated to be exposed to levels above WHO guidelines. Similarly PM10 concentrations in cities (Figure 2.30), while below those of comparator countries, are above the WHO limit for annual exposure (40 µg/m³).

Figure 2.29. **Particulate matter pollution is high in cities in Kazakhstan**

PM2.5

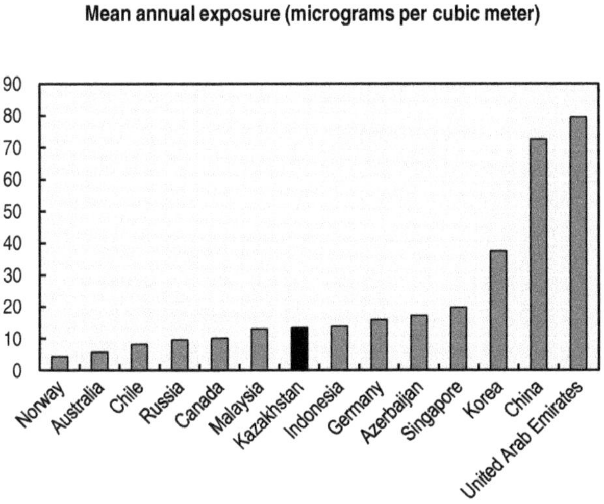

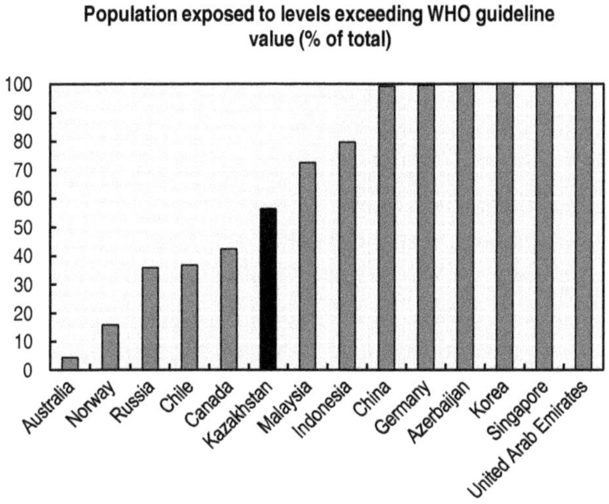

Source: Brauer, M. et al. (2012), "Exposure Assessment for Estimation of the Global Burden of Disease Attributable to Outdoor Air Pollution," *Environmental Science & Technology* 46, *http://pubs.acs.org/doi/abs/10.1021/es2025752*. Data provided through World Bank (2014a), *World Development Indicators*.

StatLink http://dx.doi.org/10.1787/888933289249

Figure 2.30. **PM10 in cities is also high in Kazakhstan**

Urban-population weighted PM10 (2011) micrograms per cubic metre

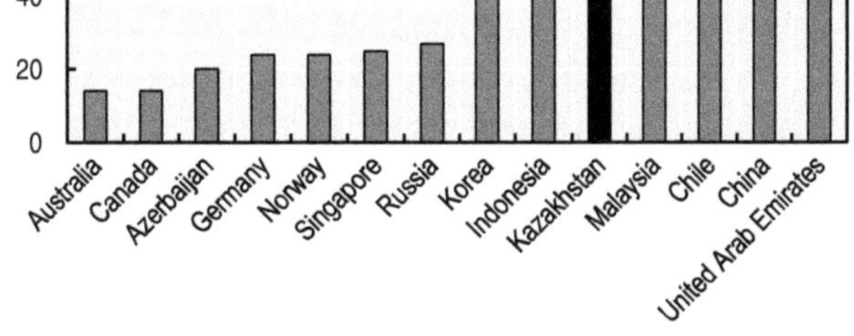

Note: Urban-population weighted average of PM10 concentration in cities with more than 100 000 inhabitants.

Source: World Bank (2014a), *World Development Indicators*.

StatLink http://dx.doi.org/10.1787/888933289257

Air pollution comes from a combination of sources and incentives to reduce each source may not suffice. In Kazakhstan stationary sources (industrial and energy plants) generate a significant share of air pollution, in particular because of the use of fossil fuels, and especially coal, for energy production. While total emissions from stationary sources have been on a downward trend, pricing policies keep the pump price of petrol and diesel low, which, given increases in income, is likely to lead to significant increases in pollution from vehicles.

Water pollution is also a major worry. The proportion of waste water discharges that are treated remains insufficient and fell during the decade to 20%. Moreover, between 2000 and 2009 waste water discharges without treatment increased fivefold in Kazakhstan (OECD, 2012). Water management remains a larger issue than its effects on individual wellbeing, however. Agriculture uses 55% of water in Kazakhstan and unsustainable irrigation has led to falls in soil fertility as a result of increased erosion and salinity as well as such visible disasters as the depletion of the Aral Sea (see Chapter 3).

Kazakhstan also faces significant challenges in dealing with waste and industrial pollution that are directly linked to the weight of extractive industries in the economy. The mining sector continues to generate high volumes of tailings (materials left over after the valuable fraction is extracted). UNECE (2008) estimated that 95% of total mined ore was discarded. These tailings typically contain a number of pollutants that if left untreated can pass into the soil or water. Kazakhstan, in particular, has large amounts of sulphur which are not marketable because of relatively low demand. When stored in open air, sulphur is believed to have negative impacts on the environment (OECD, 2012). Contamination from past military and industrial activities, including uranium mining and nuclear tests, makes the issues related to industrial pollution management particularly acute.

Land degradation and deforestation have progressed, albeit slowly, during the 2000s. Kazakhstan's ecosystem is naturally fragile and prone to desertification, and that has been exacerbated by unsustainable irrigation in the past (UNECE, 2008). Deforestation has progressed, increasing by 0.17% annually during the 2000s, in contrast with a number of comparator countries where significant reforestation has taken place (such as China, Norway or Chile). Degradation has major impacts on livelihoods and on agricultural potential, with one third of agricultural land degraded or at risk and over 10 million hectares of arable land abandoned (Government of the Republic of Kazakhstan, 2013).

In Kazakhstan, subjective assessments of environmental conditions rank both water and air quality low. Only one Kazakhstani in two was satisfied with air quality in 2014, the lowest figure among the benchmark countries. The perception is similar for the subjective assessment of water quality (Figure 2.31).

The recently adopted Concept for transition of the Republic of Kazakhstan to Green Economy states the ambitions for 2030 and 2050. It is structured around six main pillars: effective use of water resources use, high-yield agriculture, energy efficiency, electric power industry, air pollution reduction and waste management. Addressing environmental issues is critical to reducing the significant health costs environmental degradation imposes. Beyond direct costs, a number of risks are directly linked to the reliance of the economy on extractive industries and prevailing practices there. Moreover, better environmental outcomes may be necessary to access more environment-conscious markets. Therefore a more sustainable and environmentally-friendly growth path will not only be the result, but also a driver, of structural transformation, on top of addressing a significant obstacle to well-being.

Figure 2.31. **Satisfaction with water and air quality – 2014 or latest available year**

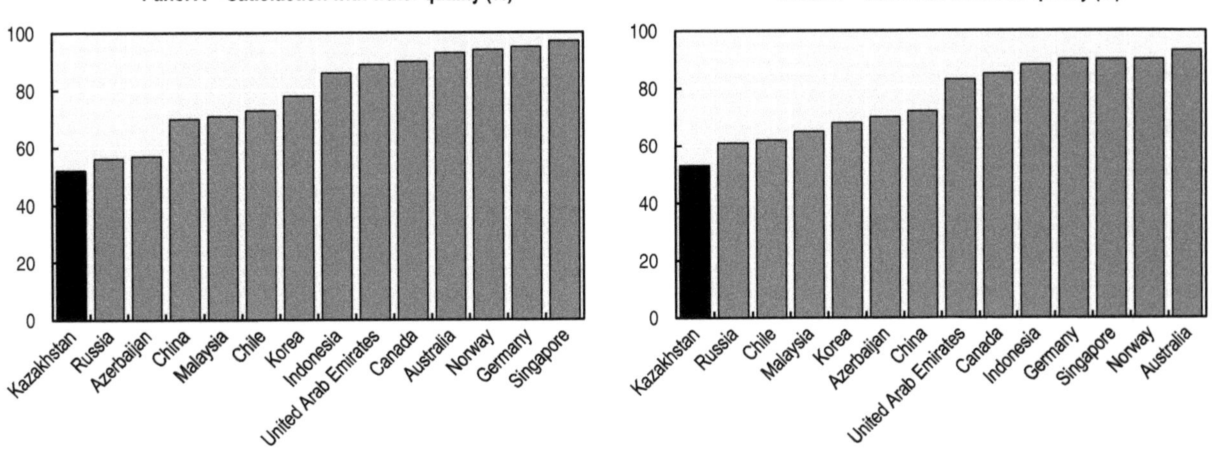

Note: Panel A: the graph represents the share of respondents who answered positively to the question "are you satisfied with water quality?" - Panel B: the graph represents the share of respondents who answered positively to the question "are you satisfied with air quality?" For both graphs, data are for 2014 with the exception of Australia, Canada, Chile, China, Korea, Malaysia, United Arab Emirates (2013).

Source: Gallup Organisation (2014), *Gallup World Monitor* (database).

StatLink http://dx.doi.org/10.1787/888933289263

Violent crime is declining while other forms of crime are increasing

Personal security includes a wide range of threats to people's lives from war and other violent conflict, to terrorism, natural hazards and occupational injuries. One of the most common threats to people's safety is crime, which is one of the main focuses in the OECD well-being framework. In addition, crime, including the fear of crime, has a direct impact on subjective well-being, through the increase in worry and anxiety.

Homicide rates, the most extreme form of contact crime, have halved over the last decade. The homicide rate in Kazakhstan is high compared to the benchmark countries but is relatively low compared to the rest of the world, with less than nine homicides reported per 100 000 inhabitants in 2012, the latest year for which data are available. In addition, this rate has decreased significantly over the last decade, moving down from 16 to 8.8 homicides per 100 000 people. This rate gives a number of 1 263 intentional homicides (UNODC, 2012).

Over the same period of time, however, other forms of crime - mainly crime against private property – have sharply increased. In 2014, the Committee on Statistics recorded almost 341 291 crimes for the country, one fourth of them (28.2%) being registered either in Almaty or Astana cities (Committee on Statistics, Kazakhstan, 2015). This is a very sharp increase compared to 2010 when the registered level of crime was 2.6 times lower (131 896 – Figure 2.32). This 2014 figure represents also an 18.6% increase compared to 2012. In Kazakhstan, 79.5% of these crimes are classified as crimes against private property, including robberies (Committee on Statistics, Kazakhstan, 2014). The implementation of a new course on "restoring order" to improve law enforcement in the field of registered crimes may partially explain the increase in the number of reported crimes in 2013 but the General Prosecutor's Office acknowledges the objective increase in the level of crime over the country. Recently, the committee for crime statistics of the General Prosecutor's Office reported that the crime rate fell by 5.2% in 2014 compared to 2013 (Prosecutor General's Office, 2014). According to the office, good co-ordination across different state bodies on prevention crime activities made it possible to reduce the rate of theft and disorderly conduct.

Figure 2.32. **Reported crimes in Kazakhstan and reports of being victims of crime follow the same upward trend**

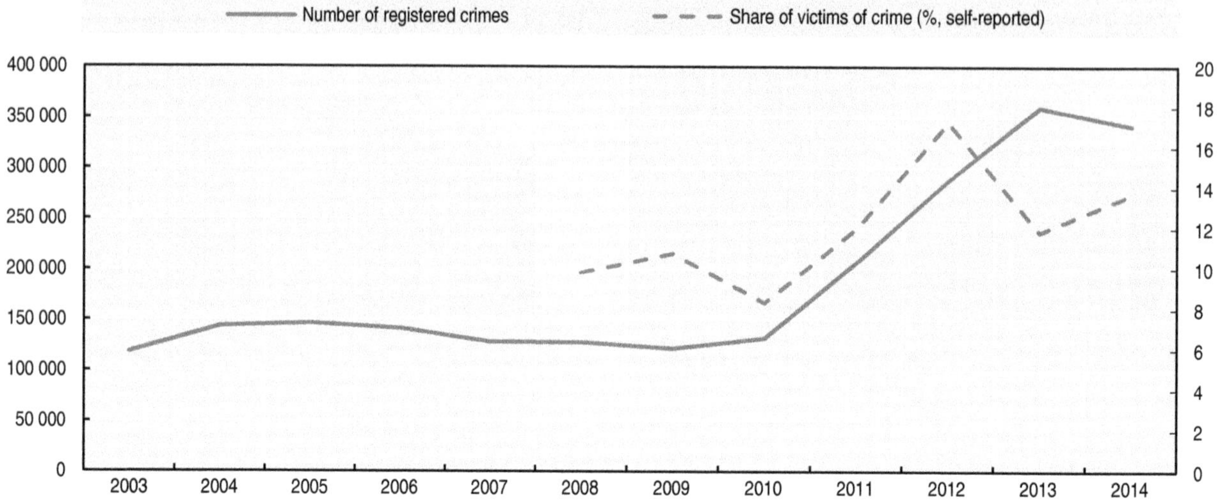

Note: This graph represents the number of registered crimes from the Committee of legal statistics and special registrations of the General Office of Public Prosecutor (left axis) and the self-reported perception on being a victim (right axis). The right axis represents the share of respondents who answered positively to the question "Within the last 12 months, have you had money or property stolen from you or another household member?" Data are from 2003-2013 for the number of crimes and from 2008 to 2014 for the self-perceived victimisation.

Source: Committee on Statistics, Kazakhstan *www.stat.gov.kz/* (accessed on 10 February 2015) and Gallup Organisation (2014), *Gallup World Monitor* (database).

StatLink http://dx.doi.org/10.1787/888933289275

The increase in reported crime against private property is echoed by the proportion of people reporting they have been victims of crime (Figure 2.32). The proportion of the population who reported having had money or property stolen has followed the same upward move in Kazakhstan, moving from an 8% share in 2010 to a 14% share in 2014. More women than men reported they had suffered from crime without any other relevant age or ethnic factor.

Figure 2.33. **Perceived safety has remained stable in Kazakhstan over the last four years**

2010 and 2014 or latest available data

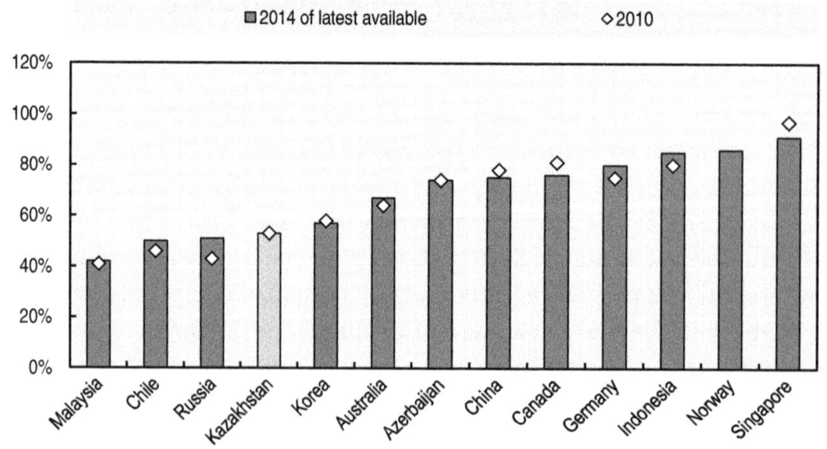

Note: This graph refers to the number of people responding "yes" to the question "Do you feel safe walking alone at night in the city or area where you live?" Data are for 2014 with the exception of Norway and Singapore (2013).

Source: Gallup (2014), *Gallup World Poll* (database).

StatLink http://dx.doi.org/10.1787/888933289285

Despite the increase level of crime all over the country, the fear of crime remains stable. In 2014, a small majority of Kazakhstanis (53%) reported they felt safe walking alone at night in the city or areas where they live (Gallup 2014 – Figure 2.33). This figure may reflect the latest efforts by the government to reduce the number of reported crimes. However, since 2006 when the survey first took place, the figure has remained quite stable without replicating the increase in non-violent crimes. As with most countries in the world, women are more concerned than men with this problem of perceived security (Gallup, 2014).

Life satisfaction is slightly below average and is recovering after falling during the economic crisis

The perception of life satisfaction has improved since 2009 but it remains slightly below other countries. The way people evaluate their own life outcomes provides essential information that cannot be obtained by objective measures alone. In the absence of official statistics, the best available indicator for measuring how people evaluate their life is based on the Cantril Ladder, which asks people to rate their current life from the best to the worst possible on a scale from 0 to 10. In 2014, Kazakhstan's life satisfaction (6.0) places the country slightly below the average of benchmark countries but in line with other countries in the region (Figure 2.34 – Panel A) and in line with its income level. Life satisfaction has been affected by the global financial crisis, as in almost all OECD countries but has increased by 0.6 points since 2009, reflecting the increase in GDP per capita over the same period of time (Figure 2.34 – Panel B). Indeed, Kazakhstan's GDP growth rates increased from 1.2% in 2009 to 7.3% and 7.5% in 2010 and 2011, respectively. Official data estimate that 76% of the population in 2014 are satisfied with their lives, an increase of two percentage points compared to 2013[20] (Committee on Statistics, Kazakhstan, 2015).

Figure 2.34. **A steady increase in life satisfaction but still lower than the benchmark average**

2014 or latest available year

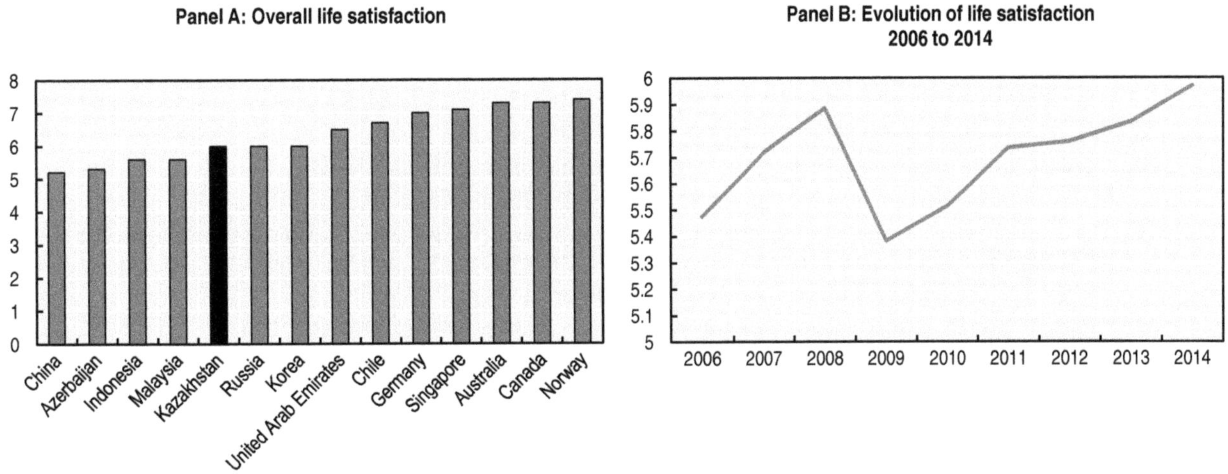

Note: The Cantril Ladder relates to the question: "Please imagine a ladder with steps numbered from 0 at the bottom to 10 at the top. Suppose we say that the top of the ladder represents the best possible life for you, and the bottom of the ladder represents the worst possible life for you. On which step of the ladder would you say you personally feel you stand at this time, assuming that the higher the step the better you feel about your life, and the lower the step the worse you feel about it? Which step comes closest to the way you feel?". Data for the graph "Overall life satisfaction" are for 2014 except for Chile and China (2013).

Source: Gallup (2014), *Gallup World Poll* (database).

StatLink http://dx.doi.org/10.1787/888933289296

In Kazakhstan, there is a variation of almost one point between different education levels. As in most countries, low levels of education are associated with lower levels of life satisfaction (OECD, 2013a). This is also the case for Kazakhstan where people who did not complete secondary school reported a score of 5.6 on life satisfaction compared to people with a tertiary degree who reported a score of 6.5 on life satisfaction (Gallup, 2014).

Notes

1. World Health Organization, accessed April 2015.
2. PM10 emissions were 55 micrograms per cubic metre in 2005, falling to 47 micrograms per cubic metre in 2013 (World Bank, 2014a).
3. The 2030 Strategy highlighted seven priorities: i) national security, ii) internal stability, iii) establishment of an open market economy with high levels of foreign investment and domestic savings, iv) health, education and well-being of Kazakhstani citizens, v) the development of energy resources, vi) transport and communications infrastructure and vii) building an efficient modern public administration.
4. The Minimum Living Standard (see Box 2.3) increased during the period. It rose from KZT 4 007 per month or USD 3.8 a day (2011 international USD in PPP terms) to KZT 17 789 KZT per month or USD 6.3 per day (in 2011 international USD) in 2013.
5. A relative poverty line is one that is set as a share of median (or average) income or consumption expenditure in contrast to an absolute poverty line set on the basis of the price of a fixed basket of goods and services.
6. The Gini coefficient for Kazakhstan is not strictly comparable to those of OECD countries because it reflects inequality between per capita household incomes, while the figures for OECD countries reflect inequality per adult equivalent. Since household sizes are larger for poorer households in Kazakhstan, the estimates in Figure 2.8 are in fact higher than they would be if fully comparable methodology was used.
7. Kudebayeva and Barrientos (2013) carried out a Blinder-Oaxaca decomposition and found that while the gap between the incomes of the poor and the non-poor in 2001 was explained by both household characteristics and working status and the returns to these characteristics, by 2009 returns played a much smaller role.
8. Babajanian, Hagen-Zanker and Salomon (2015) estimate that social transfers reduce the poverty headcount by 2.5 points.
9. Data used for comparison are from KILM 8th edition (ILO, 2014). Data for Kazakhstan relate to men and women over 15 years old. The corresponding rates for the 15 to 64 age group as estimated by the ILO are 75.1% for women and 82.4% for men.
10. Norway is an exception, because as female labour force participation is extremely high, the employment-to-population rate is 75.5% for people aged 15 to 64.
11. The Committee on Statistics of the Republic of Kazakhstan does not estimate informal employment by economic activity; the corresponding data are from secondary sources and may not exactly correspond to totals estimated by official sources.
12. Figure 16 shows individual rather than household incomes; therefore the 21% of the employed population with less than KZT 20 000 do not necessarily belong to poor households and are therefore not necessarily working poor as this term is usually defined on the basis of per capita household income.
13. The international indicator used to measure access to improved sanitation is used in Figure 2.20. This indicator measures access to facilities that hygienically separate human excreta from human contact and is the indicator used globally to track progress against the corresponding target in the Millennium Development Goals (MDG) (Goal 7). Kazakhstan's national MDG uses a higher standard (connection to a central or improved sewage system). Performance against this higher standard is lower (51.5% in 2012) but there has been significant progress since 2006 (almost six percentage points).
14. The Bologna Process is a series of ministerial meetings and agreements between European countries designed to ensure comparability in the standards and quality of higher education qualifications. One of the goals is to create a European Higher Education Area (EHEA) where degree programmes

and qualifications awarded in one country are recognised in another country. On a voluntary basis, Kazakhstan signed the Bologna Declaration in 2010 and joined the Bologna Process in March 2011.

15. Statistical data on pre-primary gross enrolment rates vary between data provided by the Committee on Statistics of the Ministry of National Economy of the Republic of Kazakhstan and those provided by Ministry of Education and Science of the Republic of Kazakhstan. The main methodological difference relies on the total number of population of children aged between one and six which differs between the two institutions. The Ministry of Education and Science usually communicates on the total number of children as of 1st of October 1st, while the Committee on Statistics uses data as collected on January (total for Kazakhstan) and on April (with a regional breakdown).
16. The Ministry of Health care and Social Development of the Republic of Kazakhstan and the World Health Organization (WHO) use different methodologies to measure maternal and infant mortality ratios. The WHO generates its estimates based on a series of sources, including civil registrations, civil censuses, various surveys and advanced statistical models whereas the Ministry of Health care uses mainly civil registrations and follows a different calculation formula. A UN Inter-agency Panel on Child Mortality Estimation conducted a mission in 2013 to assess the reliability of national statistical data and acknowledged the continued efforts by the government to improve the collection of statistical data on child mortality (Ministry of Health, Kazakhstan).
17. According to WHO, the 2013 maternal mortality ratio is estimated at 26 deaths per 100 000 births (WHO, 2014).
18. According to WHO, the 2013 infant mortality ratio is estimated at 14.6 deaths per 100 000 births (WHO, 2014).
19. The Corruption Perception Index is a composite index based on a combination of surveys and assessments of corruption.
20. The Committee on Statistics of Kazakhstan collects yearly data on life satisfaction based on the "Quality of Life" Survey. This survey captures life satisfaction from the following question "Are you satisfied with your life in general?" with "Yes", "No" and "Hard to say" as possible answers. This question was asked of 12 000 households, representing a 0.3% sample of the general population.

References

Babajanian, B., J. Hagen-Zanker and H. Salomon (2015), *Analysis of Social Transfers for Children and their Families in Kazakhstan*, UNICEF in the Republic of Kazakhstan.

Bertelsmann Stiftung Tranformation Index (BTI) (2014) *Kazakhstan Country Report*, Bertelsmann Stiftung, Gûttersloh.

Boarini, R., A. Kolev and A. McGregor (2014), "Measuring well-being and progress in countries at different stages of development: Towards a more universal conceptual framework", *OECD Development Centre Working Paper* No. 325, OECD Publishing, Paris, *http://dx.doi.org/10.1787/5jxss4hv2d8n-en*.

Brauer, M. et al. (2012), "Exposure assessment for estimation of the global burden of disease attributable to outdoor air pollution", *Environmental Science & Technology* 46, *http://pubs.acs.org/doi/abs/10.1021/es2025752*.

Brysseva, V. (n.d.), "Analysis of Poverty Measurement Methods in the Commonwealth of Independent States", Interstate Statistical Committee (CISSTAT).

Business Anti-Corruption Portal, *http://business-anti-corruption.com/country-profiles/europe-central-asia/kazakhstan/initiatives/public-anti-corruption-initiatives.aspx* (accessed on 27 February 2015).

Central Asia Online (2012), "Central Asia seeks to provide affordable housing", 9 April 2012, *http://centralasiaonline.com/en_GB/articles/caii/features/main/2012/04/09/feature-01* (accessed 3 March 2015).

Committee on Statistics (2015), Official statistical information provided by the Committee on Statistics of the Republic of Kazakhstan, available at *www.stat.gov.kz/* (accessed July 2015).

ERI (2014a) ,"Development Perspectives of Labour Market and Formation of Effective Labour Policies of the Republic of Kazakhstan", presentation given to OECD mission in Astana, Economic Research Institute, December.

ERI (2014b), "Migration in the Republic of Kazakhstan", presentation given to OECD mission in Astana, Economic Research Institute, December.

Ferreira, F. H. G. et al. (2013), *Economic Mobility and the Rise of the Latin American Middle Class*, World Bank, Washington DC, doi: 10.1596/978-0-8213-9634-6.

Gallup (2014), *Gallup World Poll* (database).

Garroway, C. and J.R. de Laiglesia (2012), "On the relevance of relative poverty for developing countries", *OECD Development Centre Working Paper* No. 314, OECD Publishing, Paris, *http://dx.doi.org/10.1787/5k92n2x6pts3-en*.

Government of the Republic of Kazakhstan (2013), "Concept for transition of the Republic of Kazakhstan to Green Economy", approved by decree of the President of the Republic of Kazakhstan dated 30 May 2013, No. 577.

ILO (2015), *ILOSTAT Database*, accessed July 2015, *www.ilo.org/ilostat*. International Labour Organization, Geneva.

ILO (2014), *Key Indicators of the Labour Market*, 8th Edition, International Labour Organization, Geneva.

ILO (2012), *The Methodologies of the Subsistence Minimum Determination in Kazakhstan: The Ways and Approaches to Improve*, International Labour Organization Decent Work Technical Support Team and Country Office for Eastern Europe and Central Asia, Moscow.

Inoue, K. and L. Gortazar (2014), "Strengthening Kazakhstan's education systems: An analysis of PISA 2009 and 2012", World Bank Group, Washington, DC. *http://documents.worldbank.org/curated/en/2012/01/20464344/strengthening-kazakhstans-education-systems-analysis-pisa-2009-2012* (accessed on 31 March 2015).

Katsaga, A., et al. (2012), *Kazakhstan: Health system review, Health Systems in Transition, 2012*, 14(4):1–154. *http://euro.who.int/__data/assets/pdf_file/0007/161557/e96451.pdf?ua=1*.

Kenessariyev, U. et al. (2013), "Human health cost of air pollution in Kazakhstan", *Journal of Environmental Protection*, Vol. 4, pp. 869-879.

Keskeyev, S. and Zh. Kapsalyamova (2015), "Skills and sector premiums in Kazakhstan", Background paper prepared for this report.

Kharas, H. (2010), "The emerging middle class in developing countries", *OECD Development Centre Working Paper* No. 285, OECD Publishing, Paris, *http://dx.doi.org/10.1787/5kmmp8lncrns-en*.

Kudebayeva, A. and A. Barrientos (2013), "A decade of poverty reduction in Kazakhstan 2000-2009: Growth and/or redistribution?", *Brooks World Poverty Institute Working Paper* No. 187.

Juatova, S., D. Mun and Zh. Kapsalyamova (2015), "Economic Assessment of Socio-economic Classes in Kazakhstan", Background paper to this report.

Ministry of Education and Science of the Republic of Kazakhstan (2015), Written contributions received in February 2015 and Official website, *www.edu.gov.kz/en*.

Ministry of Education and Science of the Republic of Kazakhstan (2014a), "National report on the status and development of education of the Republic of Kazakhstan", 2014.

Ministry of Education and Science of the Republic of Kazakhstan (2014b), "Key indicators of preschool and secondary education system, academic year 2012-2013", Astana -2012, in OECD Review of Policies to Improve the Effectiveness of Resource Use in Schools, Astana.

Ministry of Healthcare and Social Development of the Republic of Kazakhstan (2014), *Strategic plan for 2014–2018 of Ministry of Healthcare and Social Development of the Republic of Kazakhstan*, Ministry of Healthcare and Social Development of the Republic of Kazakhstan, Astana, *www.mzsr.gov.kz/en/taxonomy/term/217*.

Ministry of Healthcare and Social Development of the Republic of Kazakhstan, Official website (n.d.), *www.mzsr.gov.kz/*.

Ministry of National Economy of the Republic of Kazakhstan, Committee on Statistics, (n.d.), Official website, *www.stat.gov.kz/*.

Ministry of National Economy of the Republic of Kazakhstan (2015), Committee on Statistics, Kazakhstan, Written Contributions received in 2015.

Mun D. et al. (2015), "Social spending, taxes and income redistribution in Kazakhstan", Background paper for this report.

Murussov, A. and G. R. Arabsheibani (2013), "Informal self-employment in Kazakhstan", *Asian Institute of Management Working Paper* 14 – 006, AIM, Makati City, Philippines.

OECD (2015a), *Securing Livelihoods for All: Foresight for Action*, Development Centre Studies, OECD Publishing, Paris, *http://dx.doi.org/10.1787/9789264231894-en*

OECD (2015b), *In It Together: Why Less Inequality Benefits All*, OECD Publishing, Paris, *http://dx.doi.org/10.1787/9789264235120-en*.

OECD (2015c) *OECD Income Distribution Database (IDD)* (database), accessed July 2015, *www.oecd.org/social/income-distribution-database.htm*

OECD (2015d) *OECD Employment and Labour Market Statistics* (database), accessed July 2015, *http://dx.doi.org/10.1787/lfs-data-en*.

OECD (2014a), *PISA 2012 Results: What Students Know and Can Do – Student Performance in Mathematics, Reading and Science (Volume I, Revised edition, February 2014)*, OECD Publishing, Paris, *http://dx.doi.org/10.1787/9789264208780-en*.

OECD *(2014b)*, The *Social Institutions and Gender Index* (SIGI), *http://genderindex.org/* (accessed on 10 June 2015).

OECD (2014c), *OECD Territorial Reviews: Colombia 2014*, OECD Publishing, Paris, *http://dx.doi.org/10.1787/9789264224551-en*.

OECD (2014d), *Reviews of National Policies for Education: Secondary Education in Kazakhstan*, OECD Publishing, Paris, *http://dx.doi.org/10.1787/9789264205208-en*.

OECD (2014e), "Suicide", in *Society at a Glance 2014: OECD Social Indicators*, OECD Publishing, Paris, *http:dx.doi.org/10.1787/soc_glance-2014-24-en*

OECD (2014f), *Kazakhstan: Review of the Central Administration*, OECD Public Governance Reviews, OECD Publishing, Paris, *http://dx.doi.org/10.1787/9789264224605-en*.

OECD (2013a), *How's Life? 2013: Measuring Well-being*, OECD Publishing, Paris, *http://dx.doi.org/10.1787/9789264201392-en*.

OECD (2013b), *Multi-dimensional Review of Myanmar: Volume 1. Initial Assessment*, OECD Development Pathways, OECD Publishing, Paris, *http://dx.doi.org/10.1787/9789264202085-en*.

OECD (2012), "Green growth and environmental governance in Eastern Europe, Caucasus and Central Asia", *OECD Green Growth Papers*, No. 2012-02, OECD Publishing, Paris, *http://dx.doi.org/10.1787/5k97gk42q86g-en*.

OECD (2011a), *How's Life? 2011: Measuring Well-being*, OECD Publishing, Paris, *http://dx.doi.org/10.1787/9789264121164-en*

OECD (2011b), *Divided We Stand: Why Inequality Keeps Rising*, OECD Publishing, Paris, *http://dx.doi.org/10.1787/9789264119536-en*

OECD (2007), *Reviews of National Policies for Education: Higher Education in Kazakhstan 2007*, The World Bank, Washington, D.C./OECD Publishing, Paris, *http://dx.doi.org/10.1787/9789264033177-en*

OECD (2001), *The Well-being of Nations: The Role of Human and Social Capital*, OECD Publishing, Paris, *http://dx.doi.org/10.1787/9789264189515-en*.

OECD/ECLAC (2014), *Multi-dimensional Review of Uruguay: Volume 1. Initial Assessment*, OECD Development Pathways, OECD Publishing, Paris, *http://dx.doi.org/10.1787/9789264209459-en*

OECD/World Bank (2010), *Chile's International Scholarship Programme*, OECD Publishing, Paris, *http://dx.doi.org/10.1787/9789264086425-en*.

Pons, A. et al. (2015), *OECD Reviews of School Resources: Kazakhstan*, pre-publication version, OECD and the World Bank, *www.oecd.org/edu/school/OECD School Resources Review_Kazakhstan_FINAL_CRC_with cover.pdf*.

Presidency of the of the Republic of Kazakhstan (2010), Decree No.1118, dated December 7, 2010, in the "*State Program of Education Development of the Republic of Kazakhstan 2011 – 2020*".

Prosecutor General's Office (2014), prokuror.gov.kz, 11 March; Interfax-Kazakhstan, 14 March.

Rutkowski, J. (2011), "Promoting formal employment in Kazakhstan", Paper presented at the IZA/World Bank Workshop on Institutions and Informal Employment in Emerging and Transition Economies, Bonn, June, available at *www.iza.org/conference_files/InfoETE2011/rutkowski_j1928.pdf*.

Sapsford, R. and P. Abbott (2006), "Trust, confidence and social environment in post-communist societies", *Communist and Post-Communist Studies* No. 39, 59-71.

Sztompka, P. (1999), *Trust: A Sociological Theory*, Cambridge University Press, 1999.

Transparency International (2014), *Corruption Perception Index* (database).

UIS (2014), *UIS Data Centre* (database), UNESCO Institute for Statistics, *http://data.uis.unesco.org/*.

UNDP (2014), *International Human Development Indicators* (database), United Nations Development Programme, *http://hdr.undp.org/en/data*.

UNECE (2008), "Environmental Performance Reviews: Kazakhstan Second Review", Committee on Environmental Policy, United Nations, New York and Geneva.

UNESCO (2013), *UNESCO Country Programming Document (UCPD), Republic of Kazakhstan 2013-2014, http://unesdoc.unesco.org/images/0022/002239/223965E.pdf* (accessed on 10 April 2015).

UNODC (2014), *United Nations Office for Drugs and Crime* (database), *www.unodc.org/gsh/en/data.html*.

WHO (2014), *Kazakhstan: Health Profile*, World Health Organization, *http://who.int/countries/kaz/en/*.

World Bank (2015) *International Comparison Program Database*, the World Bank, Washington DC, *http://icp.worldbank.org/*.

World Bank (2014a), *World Development Indicators* (database), Washington DC, *http://data.worldbank.org*.

World Bank (2014b), PovcalNet: the on-line tool for poverty measurement developed by the Development Research Group of the World Bank, accessed 7 Nov 2014, *http://iresearch.worldbank.org/PovcalNet/*.

World Bank (2004), *Dimensions of Poverty in Kazakhstan*, Poverty Reduction and Economic Management Unit, Europe and Central Asia Region, World Bank, Washington DC.

World Bank and Ministry of Environment and Water Resources of the Republic of Kazakhstan (2013), *Towards Cleaner Industry and Improved Air Quality Monitoring in Kazakhstan*, Joint Economic Research Program (JERP), November 2013.

World Economic Forum (2014), *The Global Gender Gap Report 2014*, Geneva, *http://reports.weforum.org/global-gender-gap-report-2014/*.

World Life Expectancy, Official website: *http://worldlifeexpectancy.com*

World Values Survey (2014), *Wave 6* (online database), *http:/worldvaluessurvey.org/wvs.jsp*

Multi-dimensional Review of Kazakhstan
Volume 1. Initial Assessment

Chapter 3

Bolstering growth in Kazakhstan

Kazakhstan's economic performance has been impressive. The size of the economy has almost tripled since the turn of the century, and growth has been relatively inclusive. To further its economic development, Kazakhstan has set the ambitious target of belonging to the 30 most developed countries by 2050. Compared to its peers, Kazakhstan appears well placed to catch up with OECD income levels by then. However, bolstering growth is needed if the country's high ambitions are to be realised.

This chapter analyses past growth as well as the challenges and perspectives for future economic development. Growth remains very dependent on external conditions, most notably on oil prices and the economic conditions in some key trade partners. The challenges to economic stability posed by the oil-led growth are dealt with in a broadly adequate way, but financial sector weakness and exchange rate uncertainty have been weighing on private sector development. Prudent management of oil-related revenues has avoided large negative repercussions for non-oil economy activity. However, given the small size of the manufacturing sector, continuous efforts to diversify the economy are warranted, so as to strengthen growth perspectives and prepare for the eventual fading-out of the oil boom. Shifting labour to more productive sectors could considerably boost growth, but raising productivity is ultimately the key to sustaining higher growth. This would require raising investment from its current low levels. Future growth should make economic activity more sustainable to meet the country's own targets and to avoid a further aggravation of the current high toll on the environment if the economy expands at the envisioned high rate.

To realise Kazakhstan's high growth ambitions would require solid, broad-based and sustainable growth. Since the turn of the century, real gross domestic product (GDP) growth has amounted to almost 8% per annum, which makes Kazakhstan one of the top performers worldwide. Growth was fuelled by the large oil and gas sector, as both production and prices were increasing. The dependency on oil prices, however, became clear in 2008, and more recently in 2014-15, when lower commodity prices caused a significant economic slowdown. Kazakhstan aims to belong to the 30 most developed countries by 2050, which would require a broader economic base and a reversal of the recent slowdown in labour productivity. Moreover, given the high environmental toll of current economic activity, future growth should be more sustainable than in the past.

This chapter analyses past growth as well as the challenges and perspectives for future economic development. The first section describes Kazakhstan's recent economic performance, including its banking crisis of 2008-09, and puts the growth target in perspective. The chapter continues by discussing the external conditions that shape Kazakhstan's growth perspectives. The third section analyses how the oil-based growth is affecting macroeconomic and financial sector stability. It also discusses the effects on the non-oil economic sectors. The next section analyses the scope to raise growth by increasing labour utilisation, shifting labour to more productive sectors and raising labour productivity. Finally, the last section focuses on the environmental impact of the recent rapid growth and the implications for future growth.

Growth has been impressive, but needs to be sustained to realise Kazakhstan's high ambitions

Kazakhstan's economic performance since the turn of the century is remarkable. During the 1990s, the country had gone through a period of economic instability as it started its transition from a centrally planned to a market-based economy and suffered from the fallout of the Russian crisis in 1998. However, a large devaluation and rising oil prices helped the economy of Kazakhstan to reap the benefits of past reforms, resulting in an average annual growth rate of almost 8% since 2000 (Figure 3.1).

During this long period of high growth, the country was transformed in fundamental ways. Income per capita increased rapidly, as did many dimensions of well-being (see Chapter 2). Moreover, falling income inequality and the sharp reduction in poverty indicate that growth has been relatively inclusive. Partly because of the changed economic situation, the years of massive emigration came to an end in 2003 and the country became a net receiver of migrants. The birth rate picked up around the same time, and the population, which at the time had shrunk by 10% compared to 1990, has been expanding by 1.3% per annum since then. Just a few years after requiring financial aid from the International Monetary Fund (IMF) in the wake of the 1998 Russian crisis, the country established a sovereign wealth fund as oil-related revenues were increasing rapidly. As its economic weight was increasing, relations with other countries, both neighbouring and more distant, were strengthened, and co-operation with international organisations intensified.

Figure 3.1. **Recent growth of the economy of Kazakhstan is impressive**

Real GDP growth in %, average 2000-14

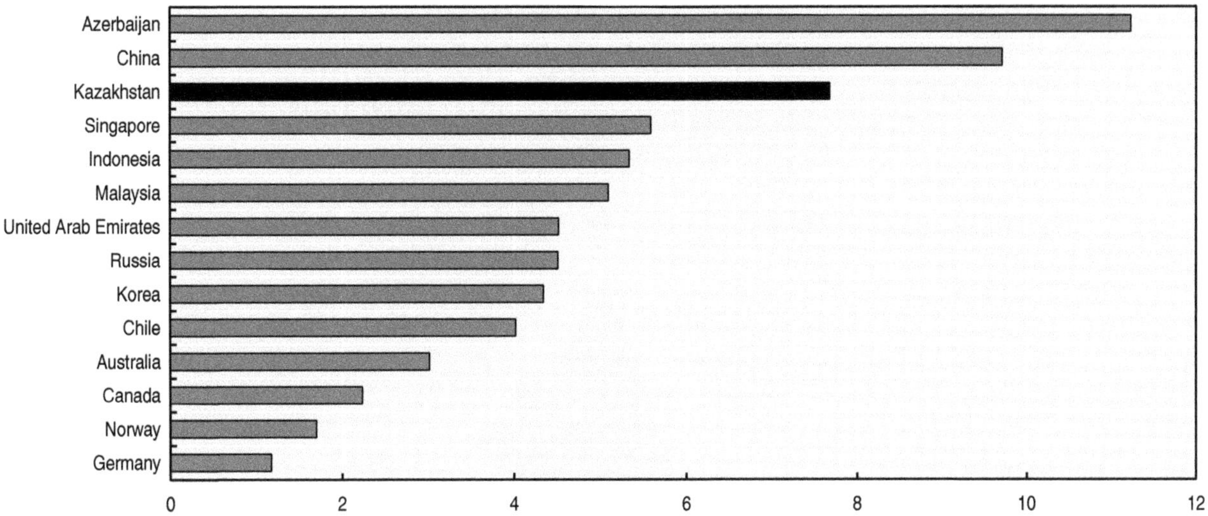

Source: World Bank (2014), *World Development Indicators* (database), *http://data.worldbank.org.*

StatLink http://dx.doi.org/10.1787/888933289307

Meanwhile massive capital inflows fuelled a real estate bubble in the major cities, ultimately leading to a banking crisis. Lending to the non-financial sector increased rapidly, since banks had easy access to foreign funding. As the finance and construction sectors became the major drivers of economic growth, the economy overheated (World Bank, 2013b). The bubble burst in 2008, when falling commodity prices turned the current account surplus into a deficit and pressures on the Kazakhstani tenge (KZT) increased. Foreign credit dried up, putting the banking sector under financial strains. Non-performing loans soared as real estate prices collapsed and the devaluation of the tenge put loans in foreign currency – around half of the loan portfolio – under pressure. Economic growth almost stalled and only resumed after a large anti-crisis support programme was put in place. Growth recovered in 2010 and has been around 6% on average since.

The country also had to deal with the effects of lower commodity prices during the banking crisis. After Russia, Kazakhstan has the largest oil reserves and oil production of the former Soviet republics. Because of Kazakhstan's dependence on the oil and gas sector, the fall in commodity prices had large repercussions on the current account, budget revenues and growth. Kazakhstan has a relatively narrow economic base, as extractive industries generate a large share of value added (Figure 3.2) and related activities also account for a substantial share of manufacturing, transport, trade and services. By some estimates, the oil and gas sector generates around 30% of gross domestic product (GDP), almost a third of budget revenues and close to two-thirds of exports.

Kazakhstan has ambitious growth targets, and, to judge by its recent performance, is in a good position to attain them. In his 2012 address to the nation, President Nursultan Nazarbayev introduced the Kazakhstan 2050 Strategy, which set multiple objectives under the overarching objective of being among the 30 most developed economies by 2050. The reform programme "100 Concrete Steps" followed up with a list of measures to support institutional reform and economic reform. Success will be judged not only on the basis of GDP per capita, but also on the basis of citizens' well-being and the transformation of the economy and society. Currently, a qualitative assessment of Kazakhstan's progress can only be done on the basis of GDP per capita, as indicators for the other dimensions are

Figure 3.2. **Even without accounting for related activities, extractive industries generate a large share of value added**

Share of GDP in %, average 2012-14

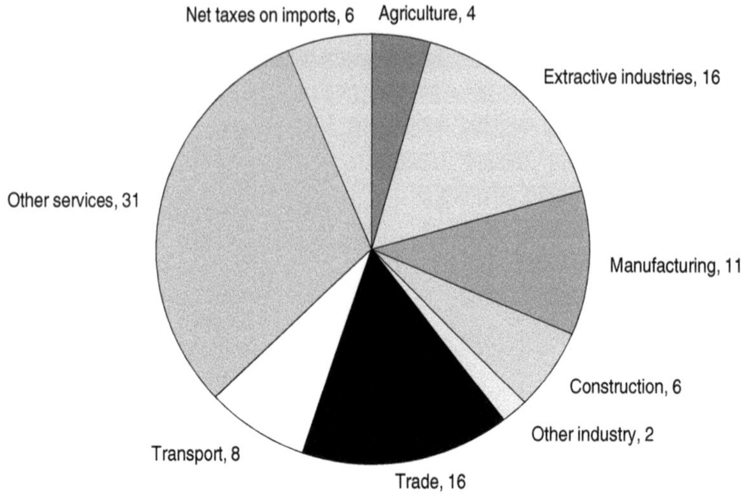

Source: Committee on Statistics, *www.stat.gov.kz.*

StatLink http://dx.doi.org/10.1787/888933289319

still being developed. The average annual growth rate required to reach average OECD GDP per capita by 2050 compares well with Kazakhstan's recent performance (Figure 3.3). The country seems better placed to converge than several other resource-rich middle-income economies, including Brazil, Mexico and South Africa, which would need higher growth in the next 35 years than in the most recent period. By contrast, for some countries identified as benchmarks for Kazakhstan, i.e. Azerbaijan, the People's Republic of China, Malaysia

Figure 3.3. **Based on recent performance, Kazakhstan appears well placed to catch up with OECD income levels**

Average real GDP growth 2000-12 and average growth needed to reach average OECD per capita income in 2050

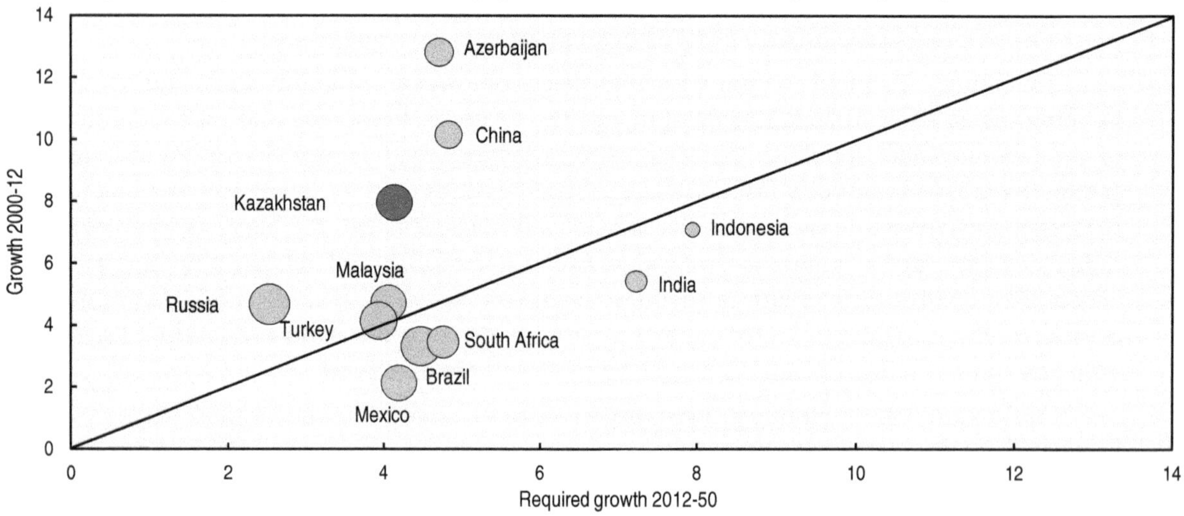

Note: The OECD per capita income level is a simple average of the 34 member countries, with Israel included for 2000-11. The statistical data for Israel are supplied by and under the responsibility of the relevant Israeli authorities. The use of such data by the OECD is without prejudice to the status of the Golan Heights, East Jerusalem and Israeli settlements in the West Bank under the terms of international law.

Source: OECD (2014), *Perspectives on Global Development 2014: Boosting Productivity to Meet the Middle-Income Challenge*, based on data from the World Bank (2014), *World Development Indicators* (database).

StatLink http://dx.doi.org/10.1787/888933289323

and Russia, maintaining past trend growth would also be sufficient for convergence with average OECD incomes by 2050.

Despite the encouraging point of departure, bolstering growth is necessary to realise the high ambitions. Growth has already decelerated in recent years and is expected to fall further in 2015 as a result of lower oil prices, the sharp economic slowdown of Russia and slower growth in China. In the longer run, growth should become less reliant on the oil and gas sector, which requires economic diversification and raising productivity of the non-oil economy. Improving the education and healthcare systems is also widely considered essential for generating higher growth, as is ensuring environmental sustainability.

External conditions largely shape Kazakhstan's current growth perspectives

Growth in Kazakhstan is dependent on the commodity markets and demand from several key trading partners. External conditions have been largely beneficial in the past as oil prices were high and the main neighbouring countries grew rapidly. The dependency on the outside environment, however, also makes the country vulnerable to external shocks, and lower commodity prices and the Russian crisis are already weighing on the economic outlook.

The current low oil prices highlight the economy's dependence on the oil and gas sector

The oil and gas sector has been an important driver of growth, especially during the beginning of the century when both production and prices increased (Figure 3.4). The share of GDP generated by the oil sector increased from some 25% during the early 2000s to almost 35% during 2005-08 before falling back to just below 30% in recent years. The large oil and gas sector has been beneficial to economic development in various ways. First of all, it is an important source of budget revenues. Taxes on oil production and exports are an important source of income, as are profits of state-owned enterprises involved in various oil-related activities. The large revenues provide fiscal space for maintaining the relatively low taxation of other economic activities. The oil and gas sector also provides employment, although most activities are not very labour-intensive, and is a source for technology and skill transfers from abroad. Importantly, wages in oil-related companies are considerably higher than for comparable work in other sectors (see Chapter 4). Finally, the oil and gas sector stimulates the local economy by creating demand for a wide range of supporting businesses, ranging from catering companies to highly specialised goods and service providers, and by bringing about infrastructure improvements. The advantages have a downside, though, as maintaining macroeconomic and financial stability becomes more complicated, while real exchange rate appreciation can mitigate government efforts to support economic diversification (see next section). In addition, the extraction and distribution of oil give rise to environmental concerns.

The current low oil prices affect economic prospects, but the link between developments in the oil and gas sector and growth of the overall economy is complex. It takes about a year for the effect of lower oil prices on growth to be felt, but over a longer time span the effect tends to disappear (Korhonen and Mehrotra, 2009). The slowdown in oil-sector growth from 2000 onwards has not been mirrored by the overall economy, which instead went through a boom-bust cycle (Figure 3.4). The main reason for this weak link is that only a few economic sectors benefit directly from oil activity, which to a large extent cushions the direct impact of developments in the oil and gas sector on non-oil growth (IMF, 2011). In addition, the differences in growth paths can also be attributed to the prudent management of oil-related revenues: by insulating the government budget from oil price movements, the sensitivity of the overall economy to developments in the oil and gas sector is reduced. Nevertheless, the impact of current low oil prices is already apparent.

Figure 3.4. **Economic growth appears less reliant on the oil and gas sector than a decade ago**

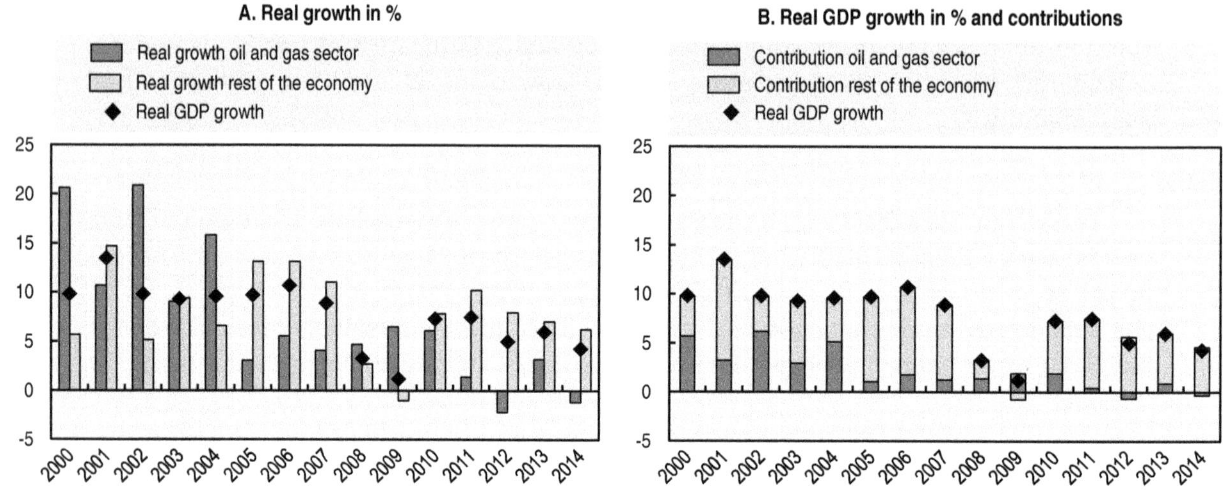

Source: International Monetary Fund *World Economic Outlook* database, *https://www.imf.org/external/pubs/ft/weo/2015/01/weodata/index.aspx.*

StatLink http://dx.doi.org/10.1787/888933289335

Oil production is expanding much more slowly than only a few years ago, and it will take several years before it will pick up again. Volume growth in recent years could not match the exuberant expansion of 1998-2007 as production at many established fields has peaked (Figure 3.5). The exploration of the huge Kashagan oil field could significantly boost production, but repeated delays have postponed the start of commercial production to 2017. The continuing expansion of several smaller oil fields will start to pay off at around the same time or even later.

Figure 3.5. **Oil production is slowing**

Annual actual production and short-term trends in millions of tonnes

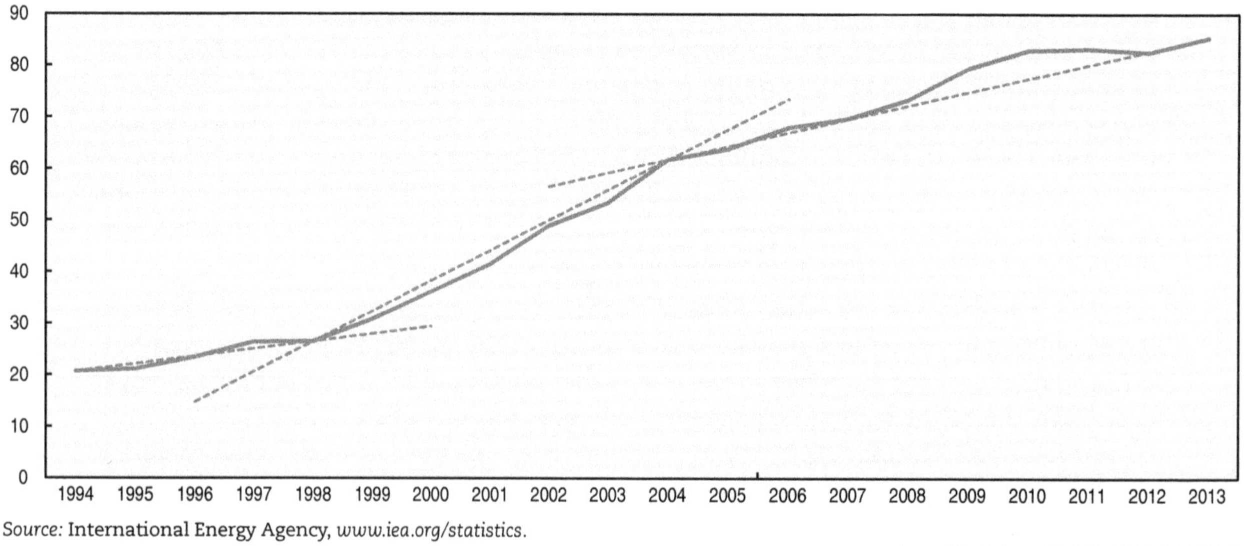

Source: International Energy Agency, *www.iea.org/statistics.*

StatLink http://dx.doi.org/10.1787/888933289349

Foreign direct investment (FDI) in Kazakhstan is failing to keep up with economic growth (Figure 3.6) as important oil-related projects reach completion and the risk appetite of foreign investors remains subdued in the aftermath of the financial crisis. Although in nominal terms net investment is close to its 2007 level, net inflows relative to the size of the economy are now about half their pre-crisis level. More than 70% of FDI inflows are related to the extraction of natural resources, and this high concentration indicates the substantial time and effort required to diversify the economy (OECD, 2012).

Figure 3.6. **Investment from abroad has failed to keep up with real GDP growth since 2010**

Foreign direct investment in Kazakhstan (net inflows)

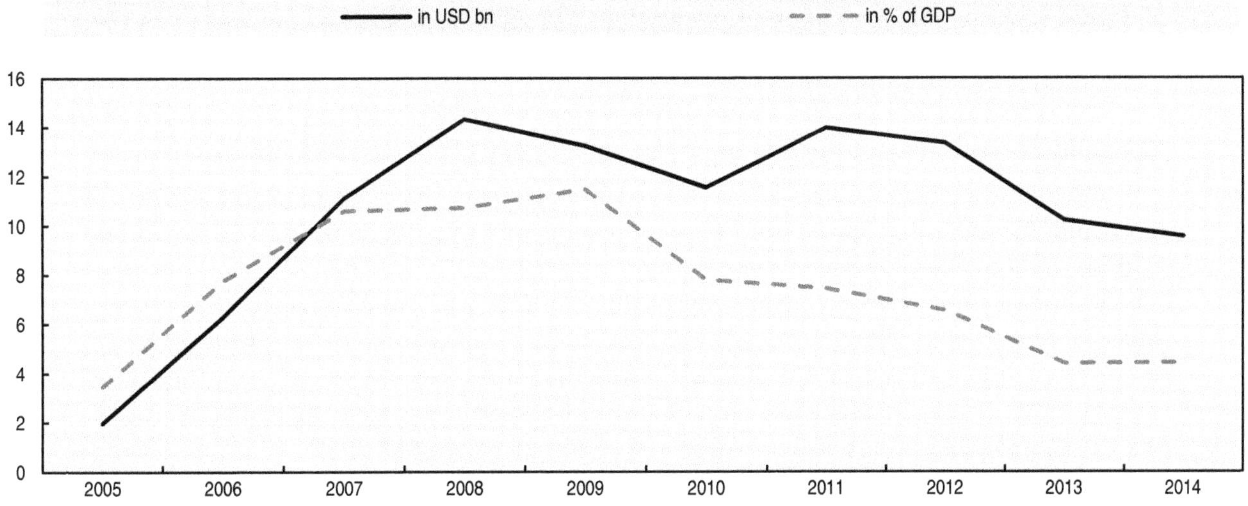

Source: Committee on Statistics and National Bank of Kazakhstan.

StatLink http://dx.doi.org/10.1787/888933289359

Not surprisingly, the composition of exports reflects the abundance of natural resources (Figure 3.7), but non-oil exports are slowly increasing. Non-oil exports have a low diversification as the number of exported products is low by international comparison

Figure 3.7. **Exports are dominated by commodities and distant destinations**

Breakdown of exports by product and by destination for 2012-14

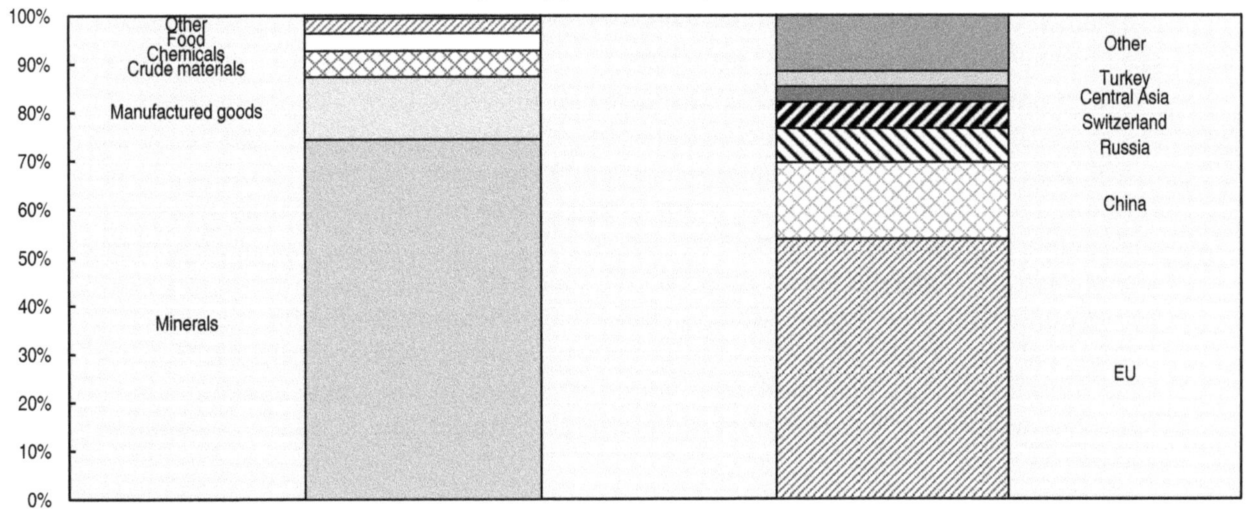

Source: *UN Comtrade* (database), *http://comtrade.un.org*.

StatLink http://dx.doi.org/10.1787/888933289366

(World Bank, 2013a). The value of non-oil exports is slowly increasing, though, and the product mix is gradually expanding as well. In recent years, Kazakhstan has gained market share in several of its major trade partners (Varela, 2013). Most importantly, non-oil exports to its largest trade partner, China, expanded by around 20% per year, which is two percentage points higher than world exports to China. However, the overall number of products exported declined between 2006-07 and 2010-11 (Varela, 2013). Raising non-oil exports, both existing and new products, is complicated by the often long distances involved and the many transport modes. The accession to the World Trade Organisation in the second half of 2015 will have a positive impact on exports, but many benefits have already been reaped during the two decades when negotiations were held and many of the required economic reforms were implemented. Moreover, especially in the short run the positive effect on the domestic economy and labour market will be dampened as not all sectors are ready to face the increased competition.

Geopolitical tensions and the economic situation of key trade partners hamper exports

Geopolitical tensions related to events in Ukraine pose a challenge to export growth, in particular for non-oil goods. Around 50% of Kazakhstan's exports are sold to EU countries (Figure 3.7), and a large share of these exports pass through Russian territory on their way. The trade sanctions imposed against Russia do not affect goods originating in Kazakhstan, but checks at the EU-Russia borders have been stepped up, leading to long waiting times and other complications for Kazakhstani goods that cross Russian territory on their way to Europe. With the ongoing expansion of the port of Aktau, transporting goods to Europe via the Caspian Sea, and thus bypassing Russia, will increasingly become an economically attractive alternative.

The precarious economic situation of Russia also has direct repercussions for Kazakhstan. With the Russian economy contracting and the ruble (RUB) depreciating against the tenge, exports to Russia have been hit hard. At the same time, cheaper imports put companies in Kazakhstan under strain, especially producers of motor vehicles and a wide range of food products. Economic linkages with Russia are mainly through these trade channels, as (recorded) remittances are small (Figure 3.8). The IMF estimates that a 1 percentage point lower growth in Russia reduces Kazakhstan's growth by 0.1-0.2 percentage points through lower trade and FDI (IMF, 2014a). The economy could be further harmed if Russian banks, which account for about 9% of bank assets in Kazakhstan, have to reduce their activities as a result of further sanctions.

Economic ties between Kazakhstan and Russia intensified as the Eurasian Economic Union (EEU) came into force on 1 January 2015. The creation of a common economic space, which also includes Armenia, Belarus and Kyrgyzstan, has the potential to boost regional trade, but the depreciation of the Russian ruble has diminished the benefits in the short term. Membership of the EEU makes mitigating contagion from Russia more complicated for Kazakhstan, as internal trade barriers are supposed to be removed. For example, the ruble depreciation has caused significant problems for the domestic non-oil industry, especially before the tenge was allowed to float freely, but imports from Russia were not restricted on a wide scale. Despite the single economic area, Kazakhstan has not followed Russia in imposing an import ban on a range of western goods.

Figure 3.8. **Strong economic linkages with Russia through large trade flows**

Larger bubbles indicate higher importance, average 2012-14

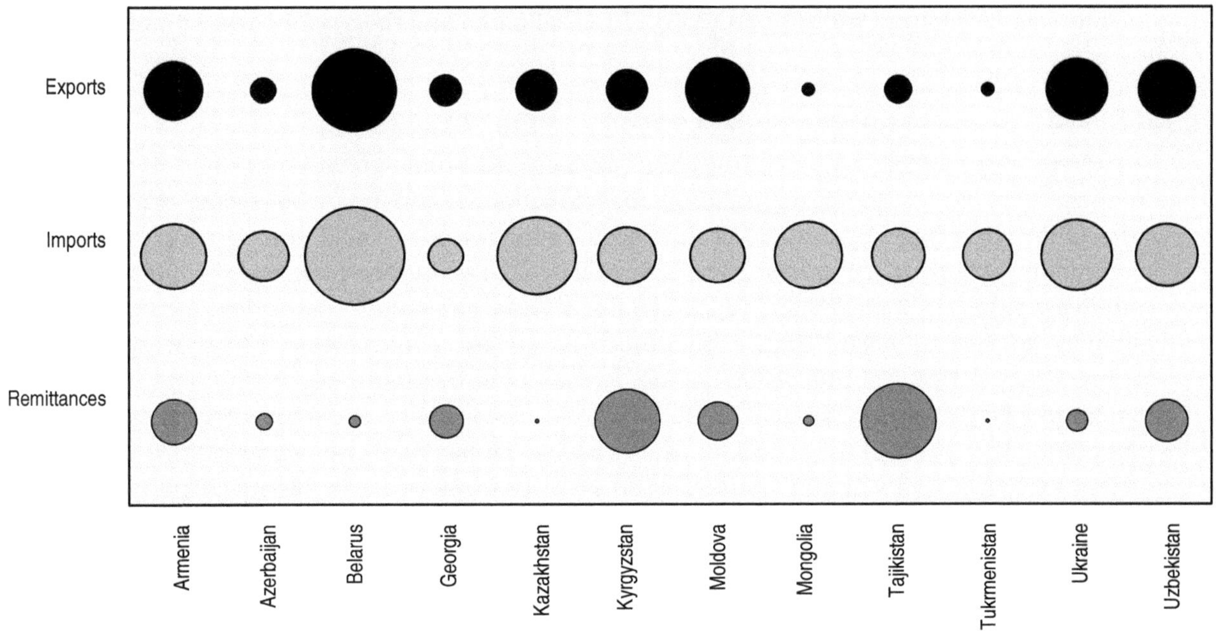

Note: Exports to Russia as share of a country's total exports; imports from Russia as share of a country's total imports; remittances from Russia as share of GDP; no 2012 data available for trade between Russia and Kazakhstan and remittances to Uzbekistan, average 2013-14 used.

Source: International Monetary Fund *Direction of Trade Statistics* database and World Bank *Migration and Remittances* database.

StatLink http://dx.doi.org/10.1787/888933289372

Meanwhile, trade with China has been flourishing although export growth is set to decline. Trade with China has been supported by the Shanghai Cooperation Organisation and the Central Asia Regional Economic Cooperation Program. Kazakhstan has been exporting large volumes of raw materials, while non-oil exports and imports expanded rapidly in most recent years. China has become a major investor in Kazakhstan, financing several projects related to oil extraction and distribution. As part of the Silk Road Economic Belt, Chinese investments also support upgrades of infrastructure networks to connect East Asia with Europe. A Special Economic Zone has been set up in Khorgos at the Chinese border, and the national railways operator is developing a major commercial and transport hub nearby. The dry port is connected by rail to Aktau, and goods can reach Europe within 15 days, which is much quicker than via sea routes. Construction is still in progress, but once finished, Khorgos will also serve as a distribution centre connecting the fast-growing east of China with Central Asia. However, the slowdown in China's growth is reducing prices and demand for metals and other resources from Kazakhstan, with lower export growth as a result.

Kazakhstan is the most prosperous country in Central Asia. GDP per capita based on purchasing power parity (PPP) is about 70% higher than in Turkmenistan and at least four times higher than in the other Central Asian countries, making Kazakhstan an attractive destination for labour migrants. Intra-regional trade is relatively limited, accounting for some 4% of total exports, although its share is significantly higher for the agriculture and food processing sectors and for several manufacturing industries. A substantial part of intra-regional trade is informal, in particular imports of light industry products made in China and re-exported through Kyrgyzstan (Mogilevskii, 2012). As the largest economy in

Central Asia, Kazakhstan is also home to the region's main financial centre, Almaty. Its continuing expansion in terms of size and services provided, including its growing role as a hub for Islamic finance, will support growth in Kazakhstan and the neighbouring countries.

Oil-based growth poses challenges for macroeconomic and financial sector stability and the development of the non-oil economy

Natural resources can be an important driver of economic growth, but their efficient management is crucial in maintaining macroeconomic and financial sector stability. The main challenge for natural resource-rich countries is to avoid that shocks to the commodity exporting sector have to be absorbed by the rest of the economy, which is often relatively small. In Kazakhstan, shocks to the oil and gas sector could affect economic stability in several ways. First, high oil-driven growth could create financial sector vulnerabilities if capital inflows sustained by the boom in the domestic economy make banks too dependent on foreign funding. Second, fiscal policy could transfer oil sector shocks to other parts of the economy when lower revenues necessitate expenditure cuts. Third, exchange rate volatility caused by oil price changes could invite speculation and harm foreign investment. It can also contribute to the large dollarisation of the economy, which in turn limits the effectiveness of monetary policy. Fourth, high revenues related to natural resources can trigger a reallocation of labour and capital, which weighs on the development of the industrial sector. Finally, large profits from the extractive industries can create incentives for corruption and rent-seeking, thus limiting the opportunities for institutional development and private sector growth (see Chapter 5).

The financial sector is dealing with the last effects of the 2008-09 crisis

The rapid oil-based growth of the economy triggered major inflows into the banking system. Increasing dependence on foreign borrowing, currency mismatches, lax credit standards and a real estate bubble created major financial vulnerabilities before 2008. In contrast to widely held beliefs at the time, the authorities did not use the accumulated oil wealth to prevent failures of large and systemically important banks. When banks got into trouble, creditors incurred heavy losses and the authorities injected close to USD 10 billion to avoid a further escalation. However, cleaning up the banking system has proven complicated, as non-performing loans still accounted for 26% of the total loan portfolio in December 2014, before falling to 10% at the end of June 2015. The problems of the banking sector reflect the erosion of financial discipline of firms by a weak enforcement of bankruptcy legislation and by the limited corporate governance exercised through domestic financial institutions and markets (EBRD, 2014).

In response to the crisis, banking supervision and regulation have been considerably strengthened. The capacity and effectiveness of banking supervision, particularly for larger banks, have been increased and prudential regulation stepped up. The National Bank of Kazakhstan (NBK) also introduced macroprudential measures to slow down the rapid growth in consumer lending, including a 30% ceiling on annual lending growth at the individual bank level. A resolution mechanism for large problem banks has been approved and the legal framework for bank restructuring has been updated. In spite of the overall progress in strengthening financial sector oversight and the resolution framework, important weaknesses remain (IMF, 2014b).

The quality of banks' balance sheets has improved markedly in recent years. Banks substituted deposits for wholesale funding denominated in foreign currency, which improved the loan-to-deposit ratio. The share of foreign currency lending has fallen to 30%, about 20 percentage points lower than during 2009 (Figure 3.9), partly in response to new lending rules for banks. In addition, several bank mergers involving troubled banks further strengthened the overall health of the banking sector. With the banking sector in a better condition, the devaluation of 2014 had a much smaller effect than the one of 2009. However, the considerable weakening of the tenge in August 2015 could still result in sizeable losses for banks as the credit quality of the loan portfolio is vulnerable to exchange rate movements given the still extensive dollarisation. The effect could be aggravated by the high concentration of exposures. An additional weakness is the high level of non-performing loans, which is mostly concentrated in some of the large banks. In December 2014, the capital of the fund for problem loans was raised and, as part of a merger involving one of the worst-hit banks, the fund subsequently took over a large share of bad loans. The NBK has stepped up efforts to deal with this crisis legacy and stipulated that all banks have to reduce the share of non-performing loans in their portfolio to 10% by the end of 2015. Sanctions for missing the target include the loss of eligibility for government funding, removal of management and, ultimately, revocation of the banking licence.

Figure 3.9. **Dollarisation has stabilised for loans, but continues to increase for deposits**

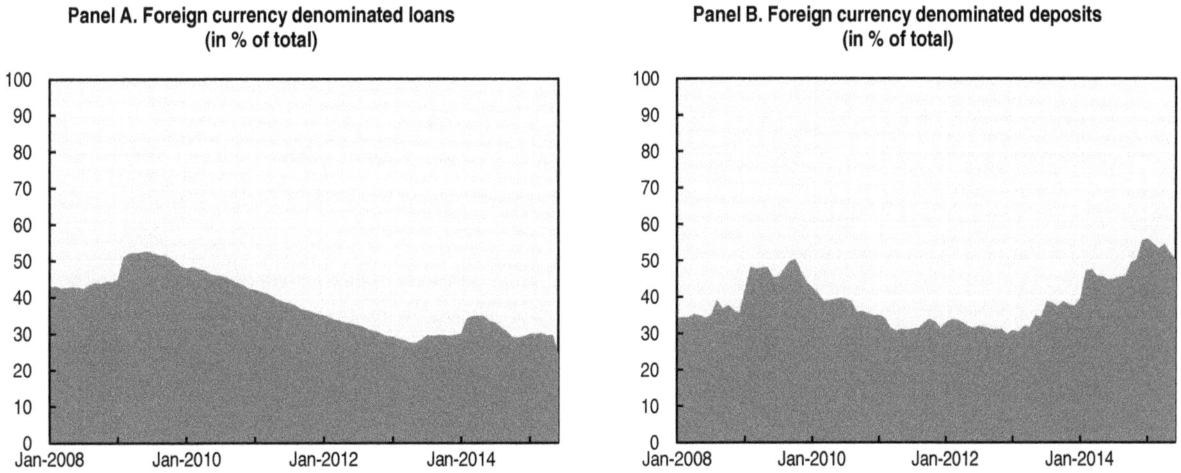

Source: National Bank of Kazakhstan.

StatLink http://dx.doi.org/10.1787/888933289385

The number of banks is declining because of mergers and the exit of several foreign banks. Medium-sized banks seized the opportunity to step up their activities, but a further consolidation of the banking industry is likely. The system's aggregate capital adequacy ratio stabilised at a comfortable 17% at the end of 2014, although several banks have a considerably weaker position. Despite banks' adequate capitalisation under current conditions, major deficiencies could arise under stress (IMF, 2014b). Banks' ability to increase capital is limited as the still sizeable stock of non-performing loans depresses profitability.

The prudent fiscal management of oil-related revenues dampens the effect of oil shocks

Fiscal management of natural resources has been responsible, striking an adequate balance between supporting economic development and accumulating savings. Over a third of the added value generated by the oil and gas sector flows to the public sector in the form of taxes and duties (Figure 3.10, Panel A). The bulk of these oil-related revenues are directly transferred to the National Fund (NF), managed by the NBK. This fund was established in 2000 with a goal of reducing the government's dependence on resource revenues, to shield the economy from unfavourable external shocks and to accumulate savings for future generations (OECD, 2015). Assets of the NF have increased rapidly thanks to high transfers and investment returns (Figure 3.10, Panel B). The vast majority of assets are denominated in foreign currencies, and the portfolio is managed by foreign companies.

Figure 3.10. **Oil revenues fuel the National Fund and the government budget**

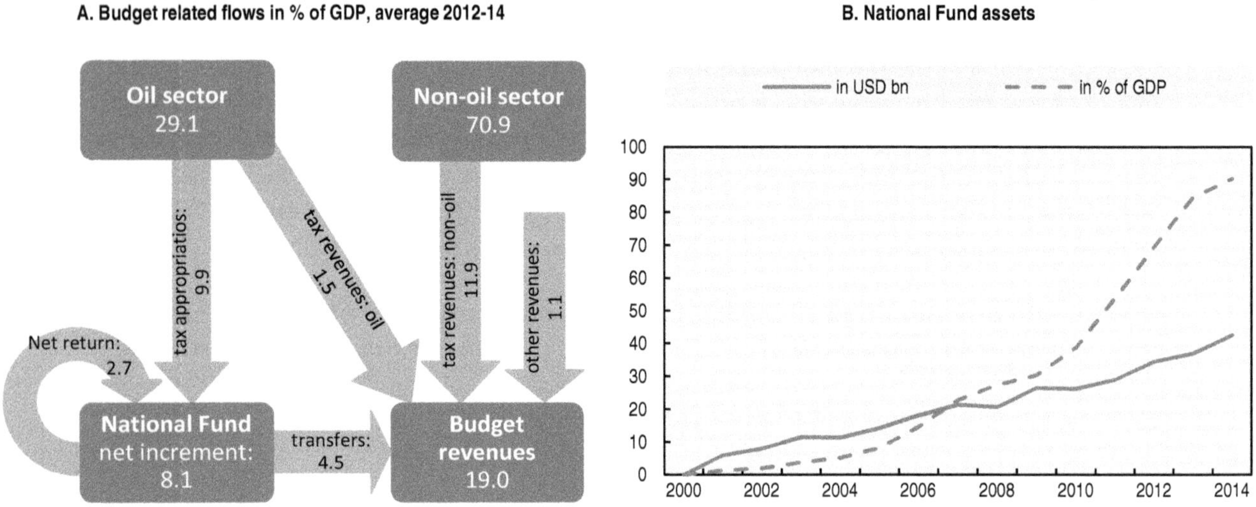

Note: Assets of the National Fund as share of GDP increased by 4.5 percentage points per annum during 2012-14, reflecting annual increments of 8.1% of GDP and the mathematical impact of GDP growth on the stock of assets.

Source: Ministry of National Economy and International Monetary Fund.

StatLink http://dx.doi.org/10.1787/888933289392

Annual guaranteed transfers from the NF to the budget of the central government amount to USD 8 billion plus or minus 15% depending on the phase of the economic cycle. In addition, targeted transfers can be made by presidential decree for socially significant projects if alternative funding sources are insufficient. For example, during 2014-15, targeted transfers of USD 5.4 billion were made mainly to support the recovery of the banking sector, to provide bank lending to small and medium-sized enterprises (SMEs) and to finance infrastructure projects. For the period 2015-17, annual transfers of USD 3 billion will support sustainable economic growth and employment within the new State Programme of Infrastructure Development (*Nurly Zhol*). Transfers from the NF are possible as long as its assets remain above 30% of GDP at the end of each financial year and annual expenditures on public debt service do not exceed 4.5% of assets managed. The overall framework ensures steady budget support, while providing sufficient flexibility to deal with transitory shocks to the economy, and the USD 8 billion rule governing transfers from the oil fund to the budget is consistent with the permanent income approach (World Bank, 2013b).

Of all oil-related revenues, only the proceeds of the oil export customs duty go directly to the state budget, accounting for some 8% of total budget revenues during 2012-14. Directing most oil-related revenues to the NF shields the government budget from developments in the oil and gas sector. As a result, the fiscal balance has been very stable during the last years, hovering between 2% and 3% of GDP (Figure 3.11). The stability also reflects prudent growth assumptions at the planning stage and the possibility of extra-budgetary public spending.

Figure 3.11. **The decline of the non-oil deficit has stalled**

In % of GDP

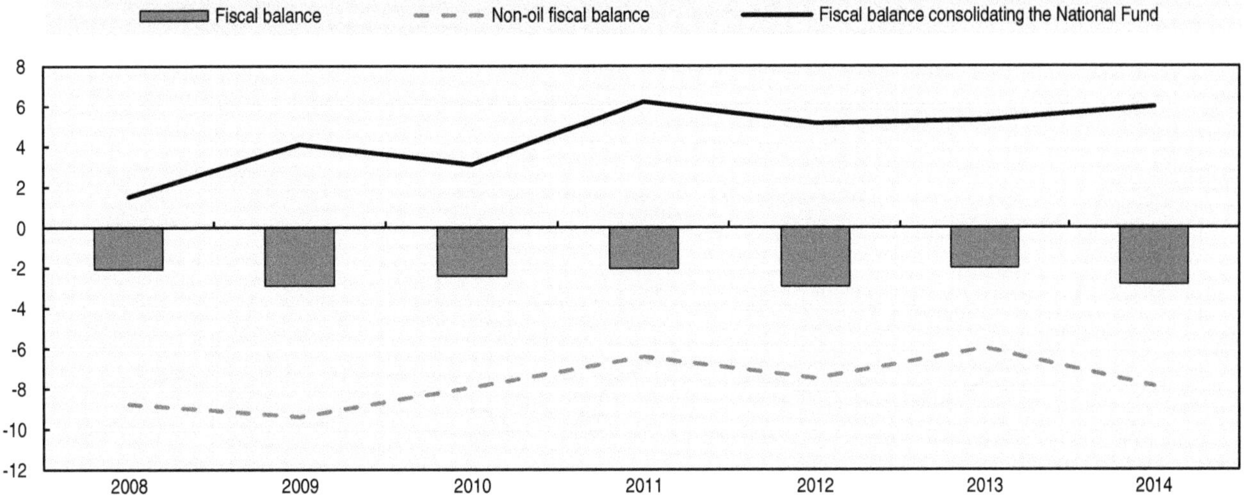

Note: The non-oil fiscal balance includes oil tax revenues, but not transfers from the National Fund; the fiscal balance consolidating the National Fund include tax appropriations received by the National Fund and its net return.

Source: Ministry of National Economy.

StatLink http://dx.doi.org/10.1787/888933289402

The non-oil fiscal balance is shrinking slowly. The fiscal performance and its long-term sustainability can be assessed by looking at the non-oil fiscal balance. This measure has improved since the crisis of 2008-09, when large additional stimulus measures were implemented, but has been stable or even declining during recent years. The government aims to decrease the non-oil deficit from its current level of around 8% of GDP to 2.8% of GDP by 2020, which is well below the 6% of GDP that is considered sustainable in the long-term (IMF 2014a). The authorities are improving fiscal coverage of the official statistics to account for the State Social Insurance Fund and operations of the quasi-fiscal sector, which could add 1 to 3 percentage points to the non-oil deficit (IMF, 2014a).

The transition to a free-floating exchange rate could support monetary policy and the business climate

The switch from a managed exchange rate regime to a freely floating tenge allows the NBK to strengthen its inflation targeting framework. Already before the transition, the primary objective of monetary policy was to maintain price stability. Since 2009, average inflation has been close to the midpoint of the target band of 6% to 8%, with occasional over- or undershooting (Figure 3.12). Until August 2015, the benchmark interest rate played little role in maintaining price stability as the NBK managed tenge liquidity through foreign-currency swap and repo operations. The NBK had already announced a new policy interest rate instrument to be implemented in the medium term, as the tenge was planned to float freely in three to five years. Effectively anchoring money market interest rates around a policy rate will be essential for conducting successful monetary policy.

The free-floating exchange rate will help the economy to absorb external shocks. Until August 2015, monetary policy focused primarily on the tight management of the exchange rate. The tenge was devalued by 18% against the US dollar in February 2009 and it remained

Figure 3.12. **Until August 2015, price stability was maintained through tight management of the exchange rate**

Increase of consumer price index during preceding 12 months in % and end-of-month exchange rate

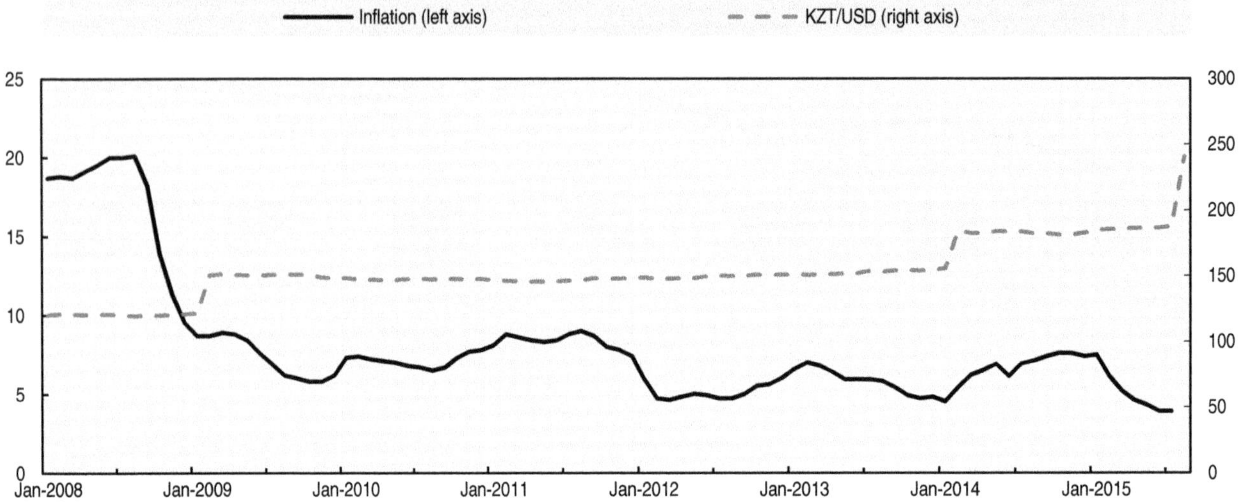

Source: Datastream and Committee on Statistics.

StatLink http://dx.doi.org/10.1787/888933289410

close to a level of 150 KZT/USD during the succeeding years. In February 2014, the NBK devalued the tenge by 19% to 185 KZT/USD because of deterioration in the current account balance, concerns about price competitiveness arising from the depreciation of the Russian ruble and a fall in central bank international reserves (IMF, 2014a). In August 2015, pressures on the tenge increased again following economic turbulence in Kazakhstan's key trading partners China and Russia and the lasting low oil prices. Instead of another devaluation, authorities decided to speed up the scheduled transition towards a free-floating exchange rate, which caused the tenge to lose about a quarter of its value immediately before recovering moderately.

The increasing dollarisation of the Kazakh economy had already indicated that the exchange rate regime did not provide enough security for many people and companies. Over 50% of deposits were denominated in foreign currency (Figure 3.9), while foreign currency lending had been fluctuating around 30% in recent years. With a high share of both assets and liabilities denominated in foreign currency, the financial system is vulnerable to exchange rate adjustments, and it will become clear over time how well it has coped with the recent transition.

After the economy will have adjusted fully to the new exchange rate regime, the increased flexibility is likely to be beneficial for the business climate. When monetary policy becomes more focused on maintaining price stability, greater exchange rate flexibility would reduce vulnerabilities to oil-price fluctuations and would better account for the different economic developments of key trading partners. In the past, limiting exchange rate volatility in the short run occasionally led to large devaluations when it became too costly to defend the peg. This weighted heavily on the business climate, and at times even devaluation expectations contributed considerably to the overall risks of doing business in Kazakhstan.

A "Dutch disease" has been largely avoided, but diversification of the economy remains a priority

The tenge had become uncompetitive, and the transition to a free-floating exchange rate is expected to bring the real exchange rate closer to its five-year average (Figure 3.13). When the NBK devalued the tenge in February 2014 in response to exchange rate pressures and outflows of official reserves, the exchange rate appeared moderately overvalued (IMF, 2014a). The devaluation provided a cushion for the steady appreciation in the second half of the year, which mainly reflected the fall of the Russian ruble. However, soon the real effective exchange rate started to rise again, and the effect on business activity was widely felt, as Kazakh companies reported losses in market share to Russian counterparts, both in Russia and Kazakhstan.

Figure 3.13. **The real exchange rate has been volatile**

Index 2000=100 and average for January 2010-May 2015

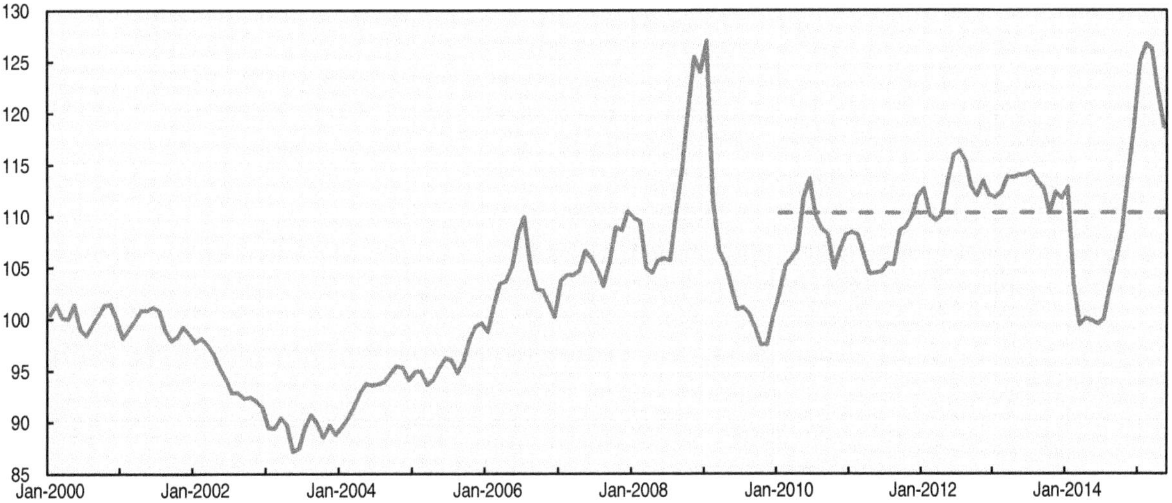

Source: National Bank of Kazakhstan.

StatLink http://dx.doi.org/10.1787/888933289428

Nevertheless, real exchange rate appreciation since 2000 has been modest, as prudent management of oil-related revenues limited pressures on the exchange rate. The national oil fund invests oil-related revenues in foreign assets, which sterilised a large part of oil-related capital inflows (World Bank, 2013b). As a result, the steady real exchange rate appreciation sometimes observed for commodity exporting countries, a phenomenon associated with the "Dutch disease", has been largely avoided (Box 3.1). The small appreciation of the real exchange rate since the beginning of the century might be attributable to the resource boom, but even so does not necessarily harm overall growth as it is in principle an equilibrium phenomenon that reflects a change in underlying fundamentals (Magud and Sosa, 2010).

Price developments exhibit some symptoms of a Dutch disease, but wages less so. Prices of non-tradeables have been growing consistently faster than prices of tradeables (IMF, 2013). Productivity performances in both sectors have been broadly similar though, so that the faster price increase of non-tradeables cannot be explained by a combination of high wage growth based on productivity in the tradeable sector, and lagging productivity

Box 3.1. **Characteristics of the "Dutch disease"**

The term Dutch disease refers to the decline of the manufacturing sector in the Netherlands after a large natural gas field was discovered in the 1950s. The windfall in revenues from natural resources caused a rise in the (real) exchange rate, which lowered the price competitiveness of tradeable goods. Assessing whether a country suffers from the Dutch disease is not straightforward as it is often impossible to disentangle the various factors that affect the real exchange rate and growth of the manufacturing sector. For example, a rising real exchange rate can also be due to a Balassa-Samuelson effect when productivity catches up with that in trading partners and the improvement for the tradeable sector is larger than for the non-tradeable sector. In this case, wage rises in the tradeables sector – justified by productivity growth and prices that are determined abroad – will cause wage rises in the non-tradeables sector that outpace productivity developments, which in turn triggers real price increases and a relative increase in the overall price level *vis-à-vis* partner countries.

The Dutch disease can operate through two channels (IMF, 2013). First, labour and capital might shift from non-resource sectors to the booming resource sector, which is referred to as "direct de-industrialisation". Prices of tradeables will not be affected as they are determined abroad, but prices of non-tradeables will increase with an appreciation of the real exchange rate as a result. However, as resource sectors are typically not very labour-intensive, this effect is often small. Second, when the resource revenues are spent, the increased demand for domestic non-tradeables increases prices and leads to real exchange rate appreciation. If in reaction to the increased demand, the non-tradeable sector attracts labour and capital from the tradeable sector, this results in "indirect de-industrialisation."

Occurrence of the Dutch disease could be inferred from various symptoms. A first sign would be a consistently higher price growth of non-tradeables compared to tradeables. A second effect would be direct or indirect de-industrialisation, with tradeables losing share in GDP and employment. Finally, rapid wage growth outpacing productivity developments would indicate pressures on the price competitiveness of the tradeable sector.

Source: IMF (2013), "Leveraging Oil Wealth for Development in Kazakhstan: Opportunities and Challenges", *Country Reports*, No. 13/291, International Monetary Fund.

growth in the non-tradeable sector. Increased domestic spending due to high oil-related revenues has thus fuelled growth of the non-tradeable sector. Wages, however, appear not to have risen excessively fast as they have been growing at the same pace as GDP since 2000 (Figure 3.14). Although wage growth outpaced productivity in the tradeable sector, this was also the case for the non-tradeable sector. Moreover, wage levels are still in line with productivity (see Chapter 4).

Nevertheless, the rapid oil-based growth has contributed to the changing economic structure. The GDP share of the manufacturing sector dropped by 5.6 percentage points between 2000 and 2009 before stabilising, while the share of services fluctuated but overall expanded by a similar quantity (Figure 3.15). Part of the opposing developments is explained by slower price increases in manufacturing than in services. However, even when correcting for this price effect, manufacturing was shrinking relative to the rest of the economy during 2000-09, while services were expanding. In real terms, manufacturing recorded positive growth rates, except for the crisis years, but it grew more slowly than services during almost all years. Since the crisis, the GDP share of manufacturing has kept up relatively well, in part due to the adoption of government programmes such as the

"30 Corporate Leaders of Kazakhstan" and the "Forced Industrial-Innovative Development for 2010-2014". Together with the vanishing price effect on the GDP share of services, this might indicate that oil-based revenues have a smaller effect on the development of the real economy than before 2009.

Figure 3.14. **Wages increased in line with GDP, but rose rapidly in dollar terms**

Index 2000 = 100

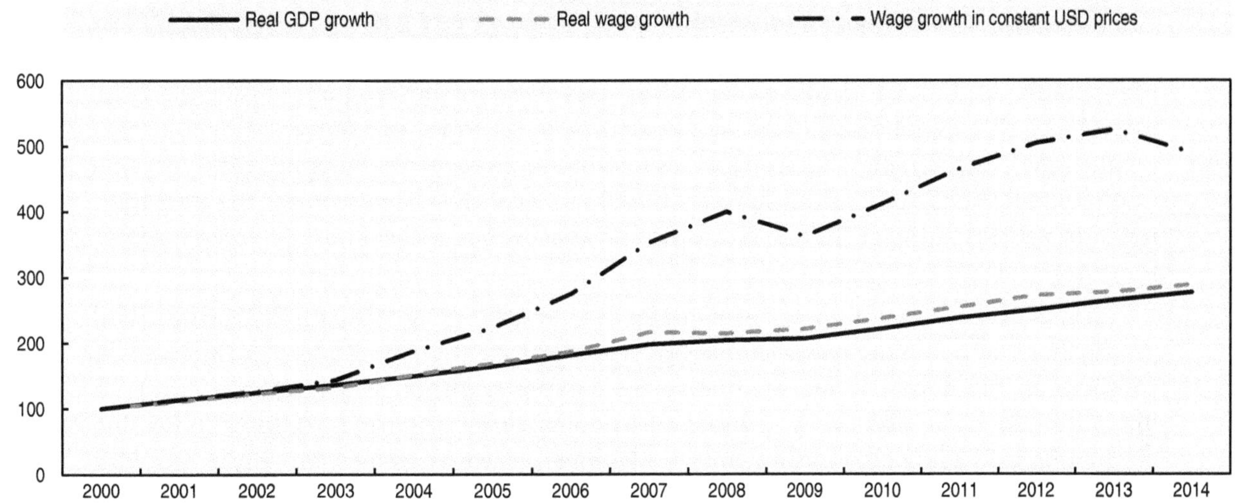

Source: Authors' calculations based on data from the Ministry of National Economy and the OECD Main Economic Indicators database.

StatLink http://dx.doi.org/10.1787/888933289437

Figure 3.15. **The GDP share of services has increased at the expense of the manufacturing share**

Evolution of the GDP share in %

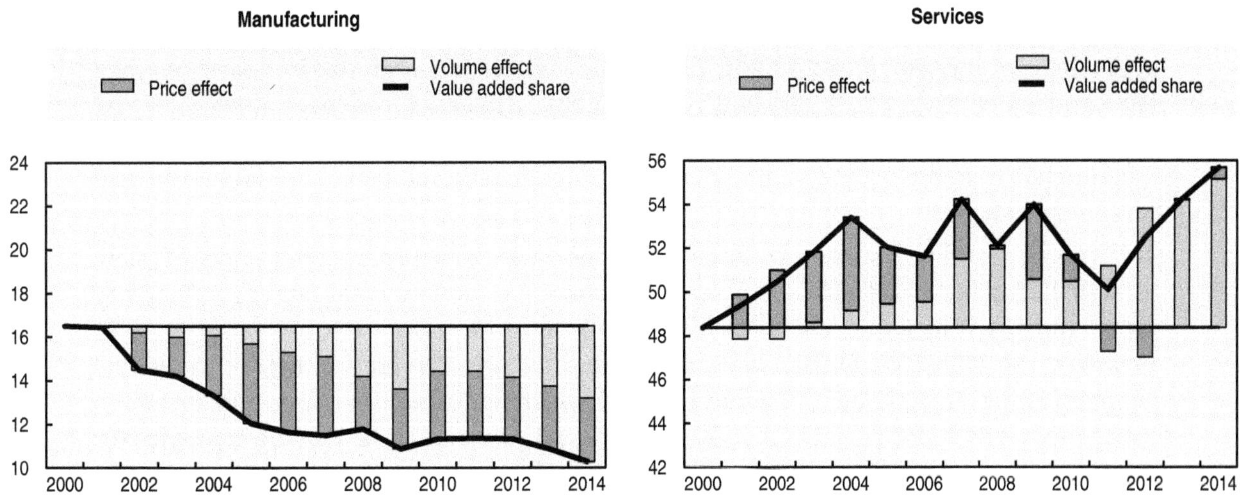

Note: The volume effect measures the change in GDP share since 2000 based on constant prices; the price effect is the difference between the changes in GDP share based on current prices and the change in GDP share based on constant prices.

Source: Authors' calculations based on data from the Committee on Statistics.

StatLink http://dx.doi.org/10.1787/888933289445

Bolstering domestic industry would support growth in the long run when the effect of the resource boom is fading. The government is actively promoting diversification of the economy to make the country less oil-dependent and to prepare it for the next development stage (see Chapter 4). For example, the need to diversify the economy figures prominently in the Kazakhstan 2050 Strategy. Support for developing the industrial base is given through, inter alia, tax incentives, regulatory advantages, public investments and policies to improve the overall business climate.

However, the past high volatility of the real exchange rate could have worked against diversification. High volatility could constrain private sector development in two ways (Hausmann, 2011). First, it makes investing, especially in the production of tradeables, more risky, thereby reducing funding opportunities for more innovative firms and new technologies. Second, high volatility will overwhelm microeconomic policy interventions to promote diversification, such as finely tuned tax incentives or subsidies. The transition towards a free-floating exchange rate is not a panacea, but will eventually make it easier for firms to plan for the future.

Diversification could also be hampered if wages grow structurally faster than productivity. Maintaining price competitiveness is essential for Kazakh businesses to compete on the domestic market and to raise exports. Although wages have grown in line with GDP since 2000, they quintupled in dollar terms (Figure 3.14), thereby making production in Kazakhstan more expensive. Moreover, as wages are now broadly in line with productivity (see Chapter 4), maintaining price competitiveness requires that future wage growth is sustained by increases in labour productivity.

Raising labour productivity is essential to achieving long-term growth

Labour productivity has increased steadily, thereby supporting income growth, but remains low in international comparisons. A decomposition of per capita incomes in Kazakhstan shows that growth over the last two decades has been due to improvements in labour productivity as well as increases in employment (Figure 3.16). The productivity spurt before the global economic crisis allowed Kazakhstan to increase average labour productivity by 50% between 2003 and 2013. However, the level of productivity is still low compared to more advanced countries. Closing the gap would require Kazakhstan to move up the value chain with higher technological sophistication and productivity levels.

The productivity slowdown highlights the risk of a prolonged period of slow growth. Economic growth has been mainly driven by growth in total factor productivity (TFP), and the contribution was comparable to that in Russia and China (Figure 3.17). However, the high contribution was mainly due to high TFP growth before the global economic crisis in 2008-09. TFP growth turned negative during the crisis, and, although it has recovered since, remains low. A growth slowdown in middle-income countries (or a "middle-income trap") is often associated with a significant slowdown in growth of productivity (Box 3.2).

Kazakhstan has various options to increase productivity, which should be exploited simultaneously. Many middle-income countries enter a period of lower economic and productivity growth when labour supply, labour composition and capital run out of steam as drivers. However, some of these factors can still be further exploited in Kazakhstan. In addition, the country needs to move up the value chain to further boost productivity and growth.

Figure 3.16. **Higher labour utilisation and productivity both raised incomes**

GDP per capita based on purchasing power parity, 2013

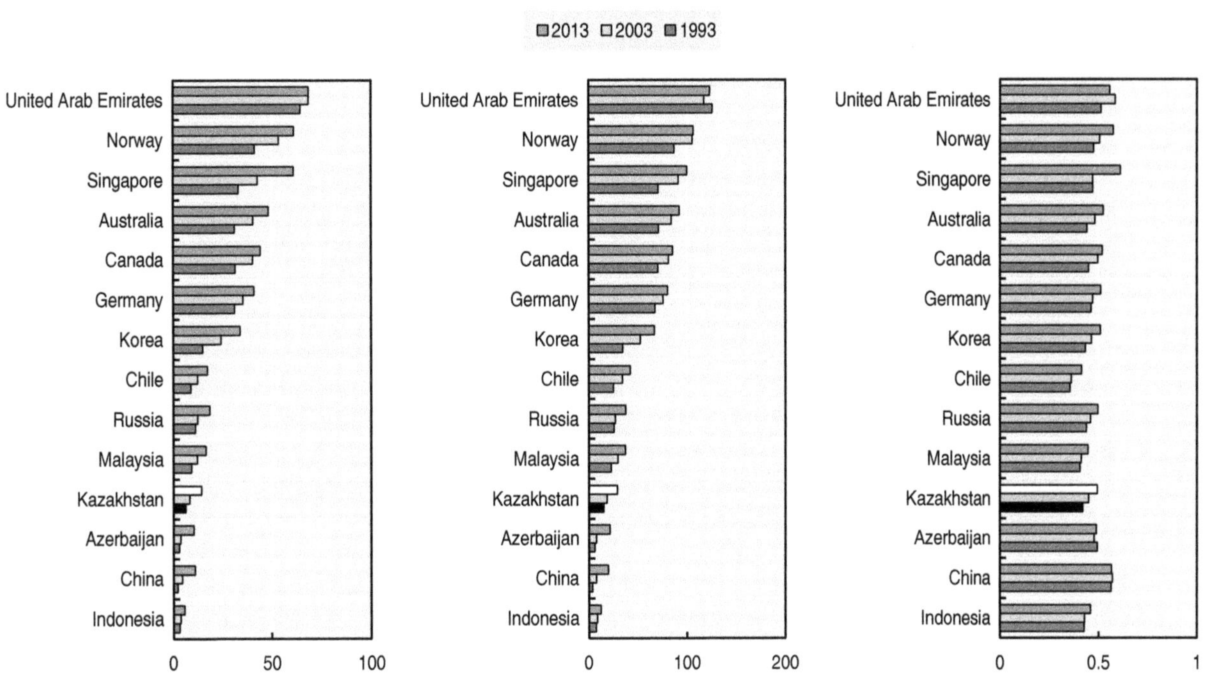

Note: For methodological details, see: *https://www.conference-board.org/data/economydatabase/*.

Source: Authors' calculations based on data from The Conference Board Total Economy database.

StatLink http://dx.doi.org/10.1787/888933289452

Figure 3.17. **Total factor productivity has been driving GDP growth in Kazakhstan, but is slowing**

Real growth in %

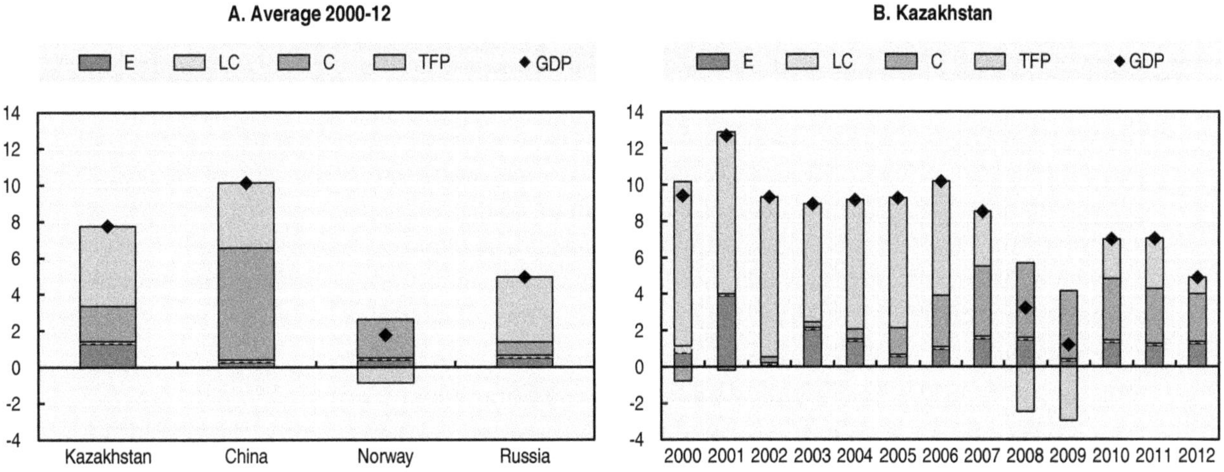

Note: E = Employment, LC = Labour Composition, C = Capital and TFP = Total Factor Productivity.

Source: Authors' calculations based on data from The Conference Board Total Economy database.

StatLink http://dx.doi.org/10.1787/888933289463

Box 3.2. **Growth slowdowns in middle-income countries are often associated with productivity slowdowns**

Middle-income countries often face sustained periods of lower growth. The theoretical foundation for a middle-income trap continues to be debated and there are no common criteria defining what makes a country become trapped in the middle-income bracket. Despite the absence of a common framework to identify the trap, there is broad agreement of its occurrence (see for example, Eeckhout and Jovanovic, 2007; Gill et al., 2007; or World Bank and DRC, 2012). Moreover, such growth slowdowns are often associated with significant slowdowns in growth of productivity (Aiyar et al., 2013; Eichengreen et al. 2011 and 2013), and on average 85% of the slowdown in the rate of growth of output is explained by the slowdown in total factor productivity growth (Eichengreen et al. 2011).

Productivity slowdowns can be associated with difficulties in moving up the value chain, away from a growth path driven by factor accumulation to one driven by knowledge and innovation. Many previously low-income countries have risen to middle-income status by exploiting labour cost advantages (OECD, 2014). These advantages vanish once the pool of surplus labour is exhausted and thus wages start to accelerate. Higher wages very often cannot be afforded as the economic, regulatory and governance environment is not sufficiently conducive to the innovations needed to sustain growth or to the development of the more sophisticated labour skills required for the production of higher value-added products. Moreover, in many middle-income countries, the availability and quality of infrastructure is not comparable with that in high-income countries. Infrastructure investment is in particularly beneficial to growth at later stages thanks to its productivity-enhancing impacts through network effects, density and scale economies and other externalities besides its direct additions to the capital stock.

Sources: Aiyar et al. (2013); Eeckhout and Jovanovic (2012); Eichengreen, Park and Shin (2011 and 2013); Gill and Kharas (2007); OECD (2014); World Bank and Development Research Centre of the State Council (DRC) (2012).

Labour utilisation can be improved only slightly

The rise to middle-income status is often accelerated by a demographic transition in which the working-age population increases faster than the population as a whole. When mortality rates decline faster than birth rates, the dependency ratio, which is the number of persons younger than 15 or older than 64 per 100 persons of working age, will start to decline after a while. This "demographic dividend" has been an important factor in explaining the rise of many Asian countries. For example, in India, much of the growth acceleration since the 1980s is said to be attributable to the demographic transition (Aiyar and Mody, 2011). When people of working age make up a larger share of the population, growth is primarily supported through a higher labour supply. In addition, as working people are likely to save more than those without jobs, it increases the household saving rate, which boosts resources available for productive investments and lowers the cost of capital.

Kazakhstan has reaped most of its demographic dividend, but population ageing will not arrive in the near future. The fall in population between the mid-1990s and the mid-2000s causes a peak in the dependency ratio around 2020 as the smaller generation born around 2000 enters the labour market (Figure 3.18). This will be followed by another fall in the dependency ratio until the effects of ageing finally start to be felt. The relatively long period of stability in the dependency ratio sets Kazakhstan apart from most other countries, including China, Russia and the more advanced countries. Kazakhstan might thus be able to benefit from a relative form of the demographic dividend as public expenditure does not have to be diverted from growth-enhancing spending to social security.

Figure 3.18. **Kazakhstan's dependency ratio will only rise marginally until 2050**

Persons aged 0-14 and 65+ per 100 persons aged 15-64

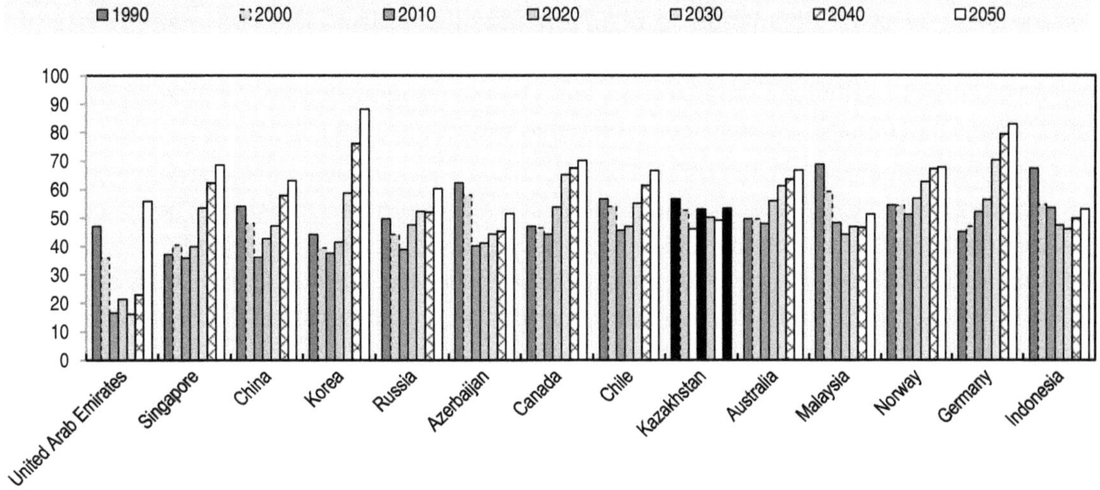

Note: Projections start in 2020 and correspond to United Nations' medium fertility estimates.

Source: United Nations World Population Prospects.

StatLink http://dx.doi.org/10.1787/888933289474

There is little room further to raise labour force participation. As the country created employment opportunities at a fast pace during the last decades, the labour force participation rate increased to almost 80% in 2013, up from 77% in 2000, while the unemployment rate fell from around 10% to just 4% during the same period (Figure 3.19). Kazakhstan's labour force participation rate is now comparable to that of more advanced countries including Germany, Australia and Norway.

Figure 3.19. **The high labour force participation leaves little room to further increase labour utilisation**

Labour force participation rate in % of total population (ages 15-64), 2013

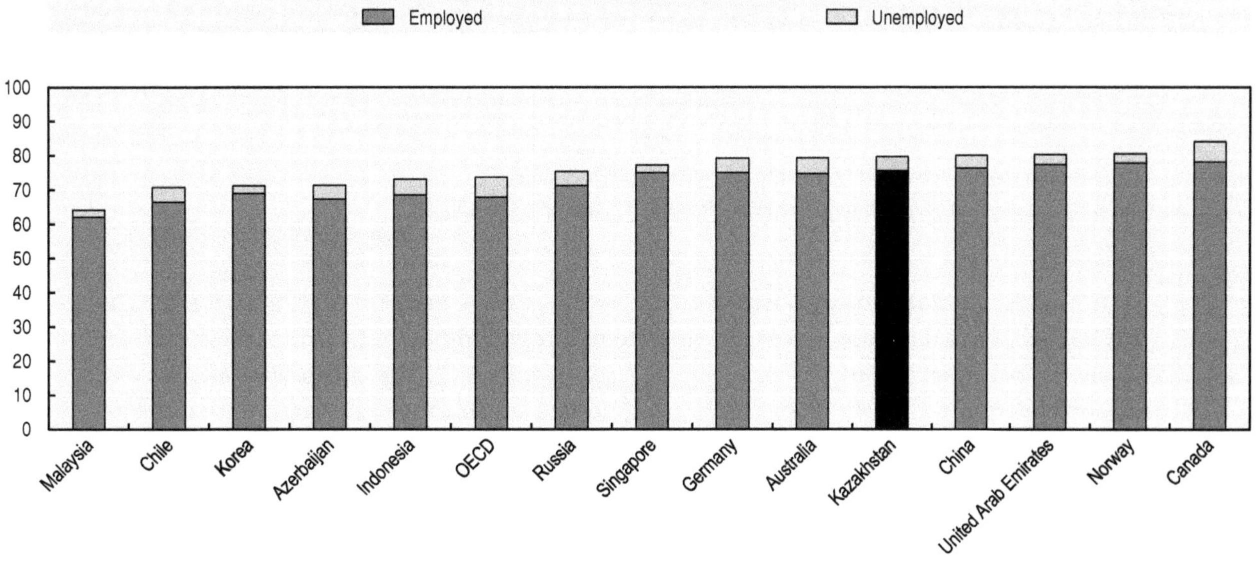

Note: The statistical data for Israel are supplied by and under the responsibility of the relevant Israeli authorities. The use of such data by the OECD is without prejudice to the status of the Golan Heights, East Jerusalem and Israeli settlements in the West Bank under the terms of international law.

Source: International Labour Organization and World Bank (2014), *World Development Indicators* (database).

StatLink http://dx.doi.org/10.1787/888933289489

Shifting labour to more productive sectors would raise productivity significantly

Countries reaching middle-income status have often succeeded by directing the fast-growing working population to relatively productive uses. The two main drivers of this change in employment composition are the migration of surplus workers from rural areas to cities in search of employment and the movement of labour inside agriculture, manufacturing and services to more productive subsectors (see Chapter 4).

Employment in Kazakhstan is concentrated in the least productive sectors; hence changes in the employment composition could result in significant productivity gains. The agricultural sector is both the least productive sector and the largest employer, accounting for around 24% of employment in 2013 (Figure 3.20; see Chapter 4 for a detailed productivity analysis at the sectoral level). At the same time, the level of urbanisation is low at around 50% and has been broadly stable during the last two decades. The level of urbanisation is around 80% in advanced countries such as Australia and Germany, but also in, for example, Russia, while urbanisation in China is lower but rising steadily. Supporting labour flows from rural areas to (intermediate) urban economic centres would allow the country to expand relatively productive, but low-cost and low-tech, manufacturing and services and thus to raise overall productivity.

Figure 3.20. **Employment is concentrated in the least productive economic activities**

Productivity in KZT and employment by economic activity, 2013

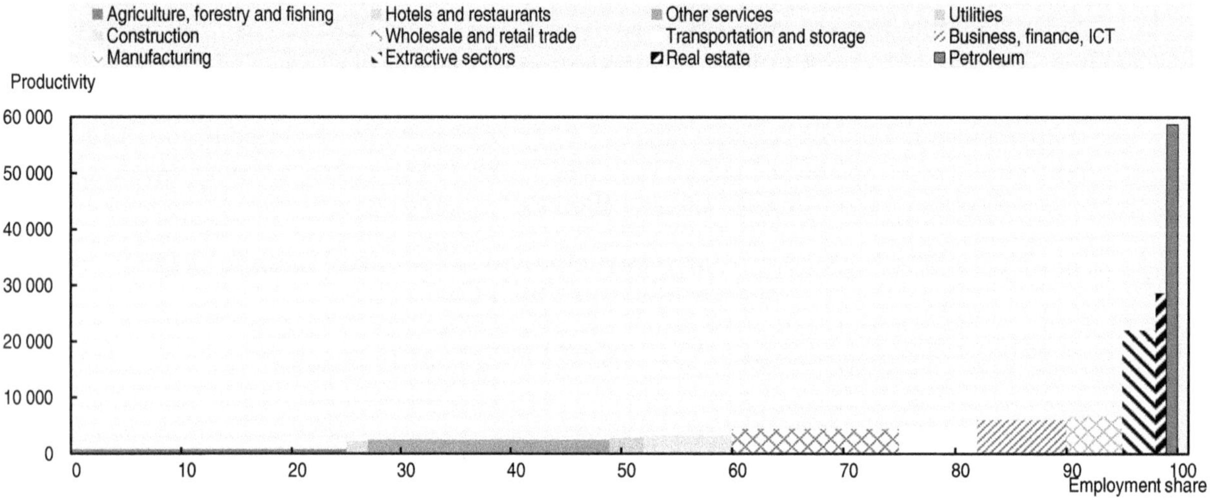

Note: Productivity for the public sector based on wages and other input measures.

Source: Authors' own calculations based on data from the Ministry of National Economy.

StatLink http://dx.doi.org/10.1787/888933289490

A broader manufacturing base would align the relative sectoral contributions to GDP with Kazakhstan's development stage. In spite of a high employment share in agriculture, the sector contributes only around 4% to GDP (Figure 3.2). The extractive sectors are responsible for a relatively large share, even compared to other resource-rich countries such as Australia, Canada and Russia. On the other hand, the GDP share of manufacturing is 11%, which is relatively low compared to other emerging economies as well as advanced, resource-rich countries. There is thus potential to broaden the industrial base, although reaching a GDP share of manufacturing comparable to China (33%) or even Indonesia (22%) will be challenging given Kazakhstan's smaller population and lower population density.

Shifting employment to more productive sectors would close about a fifth of the GDP per capita gap with OECD countries. Shifting labour from agriculture to manufacturing and services will take time, as present workers might not have the required skills and new entrants only make up a small part of the workforce each year. Training programmes would, however, support such a shift. If the labour distribution over economic activities in Kazakhstan were to reach the average labour distribution of OECD countries, GDP per capita would increase by 30% (Figure 3.21). However, GDP per capita would still need to increase by 111% to catch up with the OECD average, which highlights the need to increase labour productivity at the sectoral level.

Figure 3.21. **Even with large labour shifts to more productive sectors, GDP per capita would remain considerably below the OECD average**

GDP per capita in 1000 USD, 2013

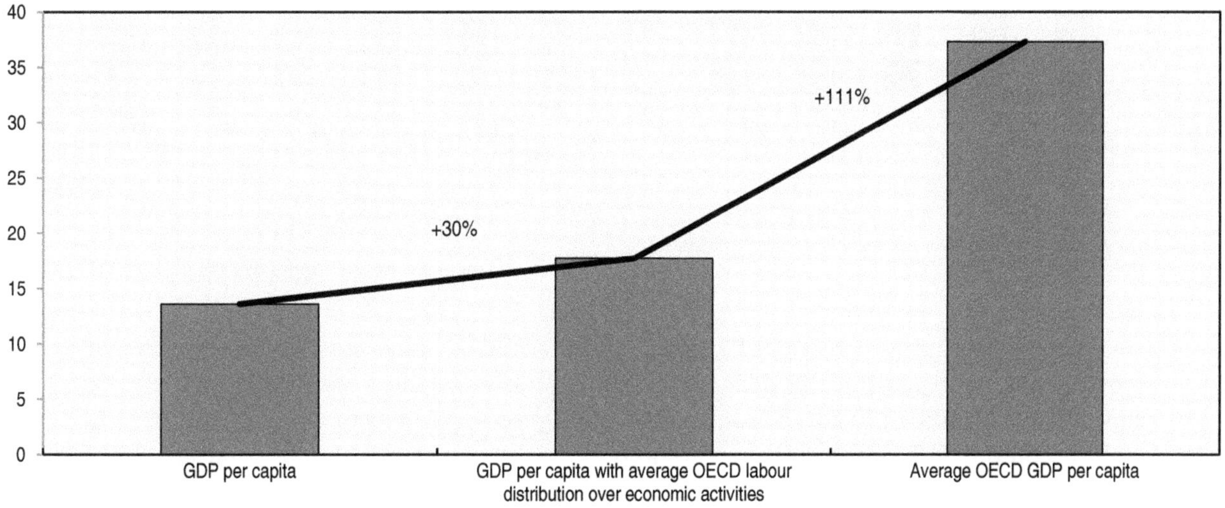

Note: Calculations for the labour distribution based on 24 OECD countries and six sectors of economic activities, namely agriculture, extractive industries, manufacturing, utilities, construction and services, keeping the share of employment in the extractive industries constant. The statistical data for Israel are supplied by and under the responsibility of the relevant Israeli authorities. The use of such data by the OECD is without prejudice to the status of the Golan Heights, East Jerusalem and Israeli settlements in the West Bank under the terms of international law.

Source: Authors' calculations based on data from the Ministry of National Economy and the OECD Annual Labour Force Statistics database.

StatLink http://dx.doi.org/10.1787/888933289508

Raising investment from its current low level is needed to increase productivity

A boost in efficient capital investment in Kazakhstan is needed as the stocks of capital available per worker are still very low. To a large extent, labour productivity is determined by the available capital stock, including infrastructure, real estate and business capital, per worker. The estimated aggregate capital intensity in Kazakhstan is broadly in line with its development stage, as it is slightly higher than the level in China, and slightly lower than that in Russia (estimates based on Berlemann and Wesselhoft, 2013). However, the gap with advanced countries is large: the capital stock per worker in Norway, for example, is around 15 times higher.

Nevertheless, annual investments are not impressive. Kazakhstan's investment share in fixed assets amounted to some 24% of GDP during 2011-13, which is on the low side – especially when compared to several Asian countries (Figure 3.22). But Norway, too, with its much higher capital stock recorded larger investment flows. The government has taken major steps to develop necessary, large-scale infrastructure projects during recent years (see Chapter 4). Unfortunately, the implementation of these projects and appropriate allocation of funds often remain challenging.

Figure 3.22. **Investment as a share of GDP is low given Kazakhstan's ambitious development objectives**

Share of gross capital formation in % of GDP, average 2011-13

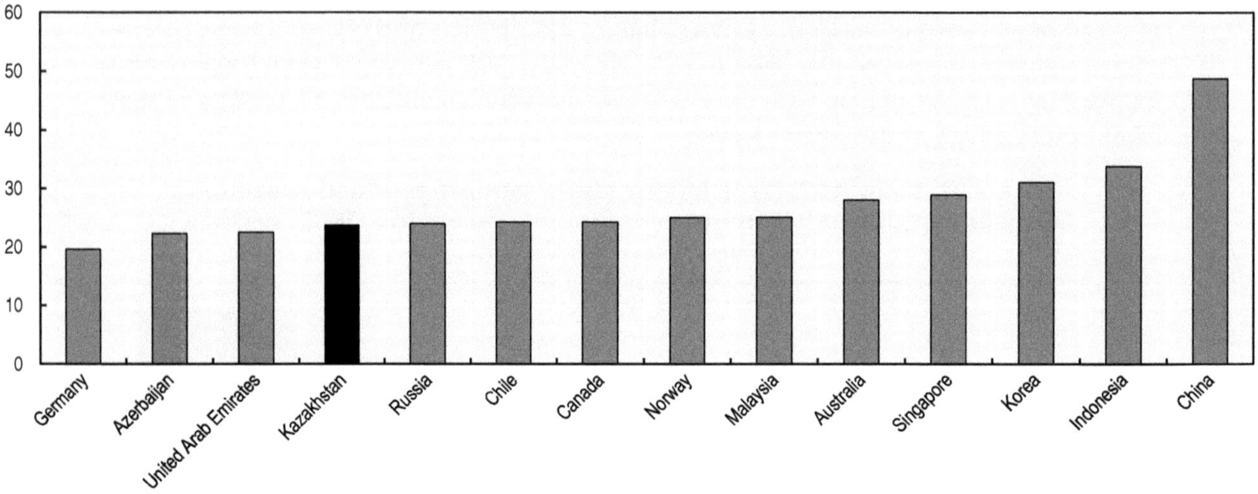

Source: World Bank (2014), *World Development Indicators* (database).

StatLink http://dx.doi.org/10.1787/888933289519

Increasing capital investment has a high potential to translate effectively into GDP growth. A growth accounting decomposition reveals that the accumulation of capital contributed significantly to economic growth (Figure 3.17). It was the most important growth component during recent years and contributed around 25% of total economic growth since 2000. In China, particularly high capital investment translated yet more successfully into growth; it contributed almost two-thirds in total growth. Future growth led by capital accumulation could still be effective for one or more decades in Kazakhstan, but unlocking investment as a growth driver would require addressing the various bottlenecks that hold it back.

Given the already high toll on the environment, future growth should make economic activity more sustainable

The high growth in Kazakhstan has come at a considerable cost to the environment. The energy intensity of the economy is high and the country is very much reliant on fossil fuels, which weigh on the environment, but also on price competiveness. Kazakhstan has a fragile ecology, in part as a result of its semi-desert geography, and is therefore vulnerable to climate change. The country is affected by water shortages and considerable pollution, which negatively affect public health. The economy can be made more sustainable by raising energy efficiency, developing renewable energy sources and improving the management of natural resources such as water, land and air.

The Kazakh economy has high greenhouse gas emissions, which reflect its high energy intensity

Greenhouse gas (GHG) emissions have been on an upward trend since 1999 and are high relative to production. GHG emissions shrank during the 1990s when the economy was contracting, but have almost doubled since 1999 (Figure 3.23). CO_2 accounted for almost 80% of Kazakhstan's GHG emissions in 2012. CO_2 emissions relative to GDP have been fairly stable in recent years, which indicates that the production process has not become more environmentally friendly despite ongoing technological progress. Moreover, a comparison with benchmark countries shows that emissions are very high given the level of production: relative to the size of the economy, CO_2 emissions are almost four times the Norwegian level and even about 15% above that of China.

Kazakhstan has demonstrated a commitment to tackling climate change through its participation in international agreements. The country ratified the United Nations Framework Convention on Climate Change in 1995 and signed the Kyoto Protocol in 1999. For the second commitment period of the Kyoto Protocol (2013-2020), Kazakhstan aims to keep the average annual GHG emissions below 95% of their 1990 level. Kazakhstan's (non-binding) targets under the Copenhagen Accord of 2009 are to reduce emissions by 15% in 2020, compared to 1990 levels, and by 25% in 2050, compared to 1990 levels. Projections based on current implemented policies predict that emissions in 2020 will be comparable to the 1990 level, while by 2030 a 24-37% increase on the 1990 level is forecast. Meeting

Figure 3.23. **High economic growth came with an increase in greenhouse gas (GHG) emissions**

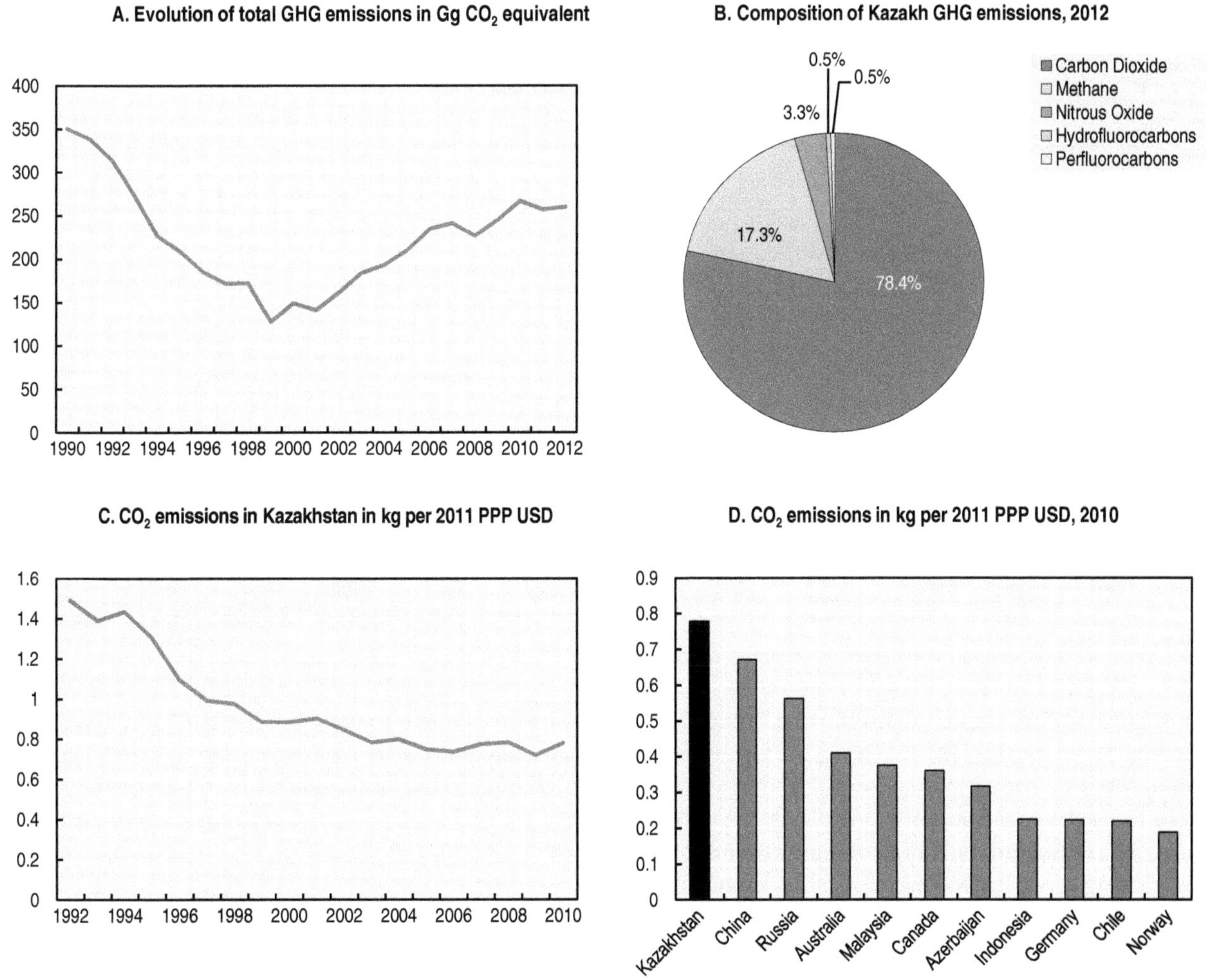

Note: Panel A: Including Land Use, Land-Use Change and Forestry (LULUCF) activities.

Source: Authors' calculations based on data from the World Bank *Sustainable Energy for All* database.

StatLink http://dx.doi.org/10.1787/888933289521

the targets thus requires the implementation of new policies, such as the Law on Energy Saving and Increasing Energy Efficiency of January 2012 and the comprehensive energy saving plan of the Ministry of Investment and Development, as well as the development of renewable energy sources (Box 3.3).

Box 3.3. **Kazakhstan has a large potential for developing renewable energy**

Renewable energy sources contribute a small share of Kazakhstan's electricity output and could be developed further. Kazakhstan is a vast country with a low population density, which makes it very suitable for various renewable energy sources. However, only 11% of electricity production in 2012 came from renewables (Figure 3.24) and almost exclusively from five hydropower plants on the Irtysh River built during Soviet times. Around 50% of Kazakhstan's territory, mostly the central and southern regions of the country and the Caspian Sea area, has a wind speed of 4-5 metres per second (m/s). The potential of wind energy is around 18 000 gigawatts hours (GWh) a year, which is over 25% of current energy consumption (Wind Energy and Electric Vehicle Review, 2014). Photovoltaic power also has considerable potential. The economically feasible production of hydropower was estimated at 35 000 GWh per year in 1997 (FAO, 2013).

Figure 3.24. **Renewables in Kazakhstan only account for a small share of total electricity production**

Renewable electricity production in % of total electricity production, 2012

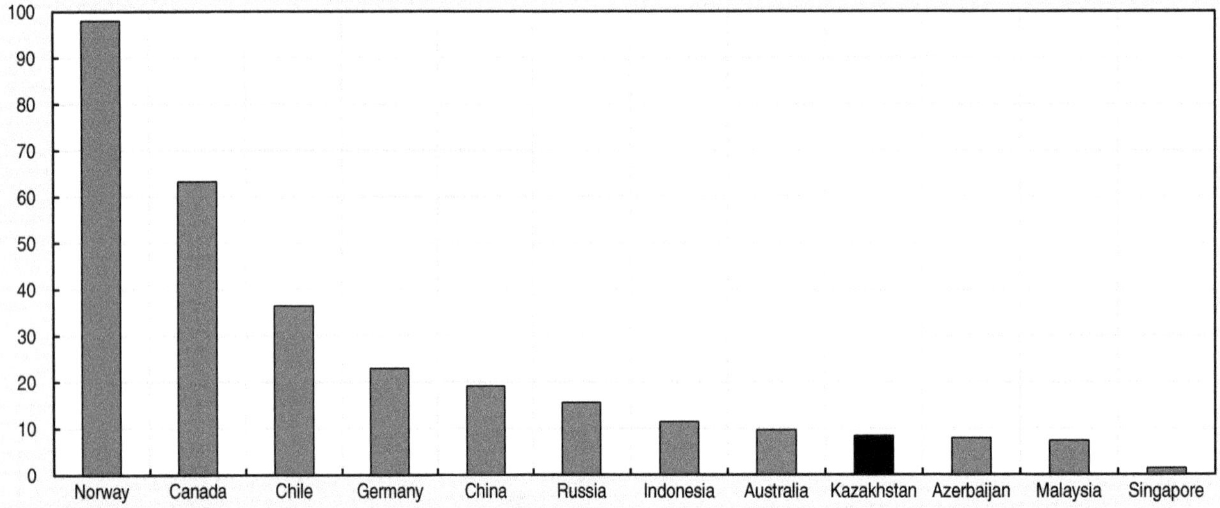

Source: World Bank (2014a), *World Development Indicators* (database).

StatLink http://dx.doi.org/10.1787/888933289536

Kazakhstan is stepping up efforts to increase the production of clean energy. Investment in renewable energy is increasing. For example, the country's first large-scale wind power project is being constructed, supported by the European Bank for Reconstruction and Development. In June 2013, a renewable energy law was introduced and in August 2013, Kazakhstan accepted a new feed-in tariff law to support renewable energy production. This type of legislation and its successful practical implementation are imperative for attracting private investment into the renewable sector.

Sources: FAO (2013), "Irrigation in Central Asia in figures, AQUASTAT Survey – 2012", *Water Reports*, No. 39, Food and Agriculture Organization of the United Nations, Rome; Wind Energy and Electric Vehicle Review (2014), *www.evwind.es/2014/11/28/ebrd-to-support-yereymentau-wind-farm-in-kazakhstan/49118*.

During recent years, Kazakhstan's energy consumption has grown in line with economic activity. A country's energy consumption is determined by the size of its economy, but also its energy efficiency, economic structure, behavioural factors and external causes such as the weather. Decompositions of energy end-use trends typically distinguish three main components: i) aggregate activity, to capture changes in the level of activity; ii) sectoral structure, to account for changes in the composition of economic activities, particularly shifts between sectors with different energy intensities; and iii) energy intensity, reflecting changes at the sector level (International Energy Agency and the World Bank, 2014). For Kazakhstan, growing activity explains more than the actual rise in energy consumption (Figure 3.25). As the economic structure has been very stable, the difference is explained by a lower energy intensity. However, after significant improvements in the beginning of the century, the energy intensity has been relatively constant in recent years.

Figure 3.25. **Energy consumption increased only marginally more slowly than economic activity**

Index 2000 = 100

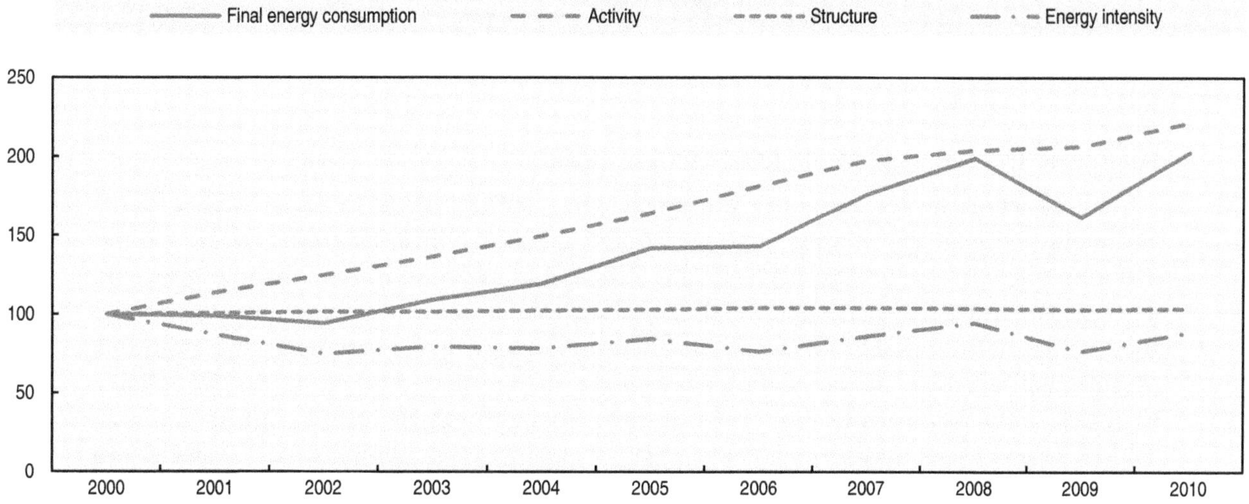

Source: Authors' calculations based on data from the World Bank *Sustainable Energy for All* database.

StatLink http://dx.doi.org/10.1787/888933289545

The energy intensity of the Kazakh economy remains at a very high level. Similar to GHG emissions, energy use relative to production is the highest in the benchmarking group. Although this partly reflects Kazakhstan's economic structure, disaggregating energy intensity by sector shows that the industrial sector in particular has a considerably higher energy intensity than in the benchmarking countries, including oil-exporting countries such as Russia (Figure 3.26). This would suggest that there is considerable scope to bring down energy consumption in the industrial sector. The potential for energy reduction in other sectors, including agriculture, is lower, albeit still sizable, as their energy intensity is average.

Energy efficiency in Kazakhstan remains low but has improved over time. Kazakhstan loses around 40% of energy in the transformation and distribution of raw fuels into energy available to end-users, which is high in international comparison. This raises the required amount of total crude energy consumption relative to GDP, which is indeed higher than in all benchmarking countries except for Russia. Energy efficiency at the industry level has seen some positive developments, however, with falling energy use relative to value added for several manufacturing industries.

Figure 3.26. **The high energy intensity of the Kazakh economy is driven by the industrial sector**

Energy intensity in MJ per 2005 PPP USD, 2010

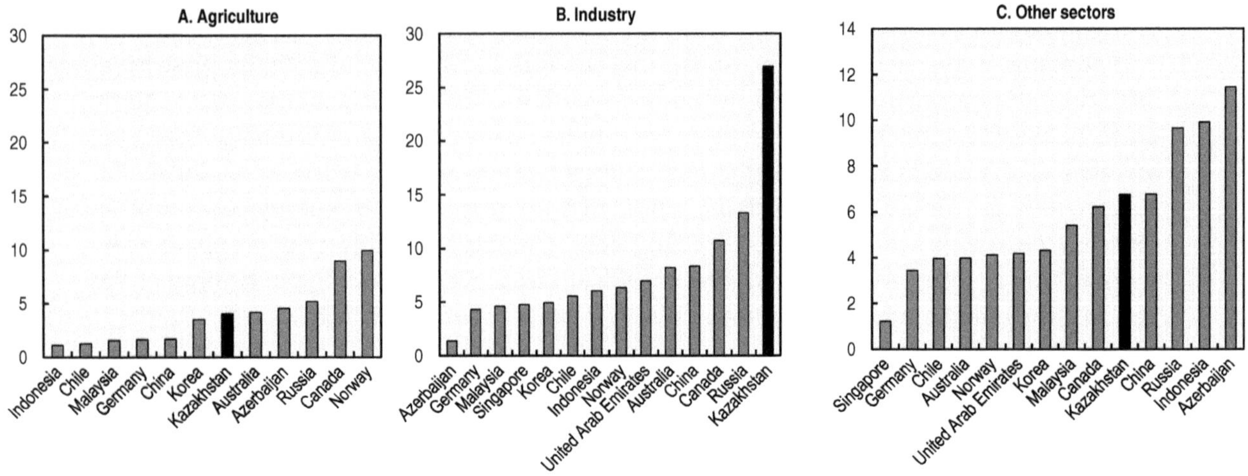

Source: World Bank *Sustainable Energy for All* database.

StatLink http://dx.doi.org/10.1787/888933289552

Past growth weighs on water, land and air quality

Kazakhstan's water resources are small. The country tends to experience hot dry summers and cold dry winters. Average annual precipitation is estimated to be around 250 mm with high evaporation levels and considerable variation in rainfall among regions (FAO, 2013). Surface water accounts for almost 90% of total water withdrawal, but Kazakhstan's total volume of renewable surface water is low compared to its benchmarking countries (Figure 3.27). Moreover, surface water resources are not distributed evenly across the country with 75% of the resources in river basins in the east and northeast of the country and only 3% located in central Kazakhstan. The dangers of exhausting the limited water supplies are well-known as large-scale irrigation has led to environmental disasters in the past (Box 3.4).

Improving management of the water supply is essential. Around 11% of the gross volume supplied by the water industry was lost during transport in 2013. Importantly, Kazakhstan was the first country in Central Asia to implement water fees in 1994, which are used to fund maintenance of hydraulic structures and water facilities. A Water Code has been in place for more than 20 years and has been recently updated twice. Nevertheless, given the vastness of the country and the fact that surface water resources are concentrated in certain areas of the country, improving the efficiency of water transportation is imperative (FAO, 2013).

The large agriculture sector accounts for the largest share of water usage in Kazakhstan and contributes to several other environmental problems. Not surprisingly, given its economic and social importance, agriculture accounts for over 75% of land use. It also consumes about two-thirds of water, as agriculture in the semi-arid regions is typically very water-intensive. A number of other environmental problems relate to Kazakhstan's large agriculture sector, including soil degradation and erosion, pastureland degradation from overgrazing, and consumption of pesticides. Given the large share of land used for agriculture, environmental degradation related to agriculture has the potential to be extensive.

Figure 3.27. **Kazakhstan's level of renewable surface water is low, especially given the country's size**

Total renewable surface water in billion cubic metres per year, 2014

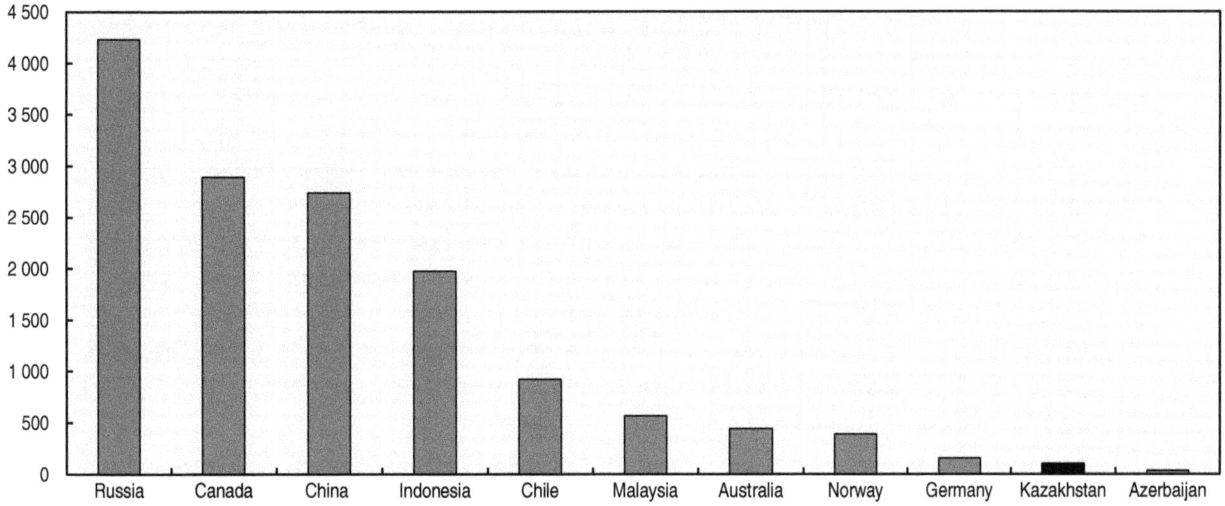

Source: Food and Agriculture Organization AQUASTAT database.

StatLink http://dx.doi.org/10.1787/888933289565

Box 3.4. **The Aral Sea disaster and partial revival**

The Aral Sea lies in Central Asia, covering southern Kazakhstan and the northern part of Uzbekistan. In the 1950s, it was the fourth largest saline lake in the world. However, the Soviet government implemented a programme designed to irrigate the desert region surrounding the sea in order to boost agriculture, particularly cotton. The two rivers that fed into the lake were diverted, cutting the lake off from its major sources of water supply with a dramatic decrease in its water level as a result. Moreover, as a result of considerable water wastage, between 25% and 75% of the diverted water was soaked up by the desert. By 1990, the Aral Sea had split into the North Aral Sea in Kazakhstan and the larger South Aral Sea on the Kazakh-Uzbek border.

As the water level fell, the inflow of salt exceeded the salt discharged and salinity levels rose. The rise in salinity made it impossible for many species of fish to survive and by 1980 commercial fishing, which in 1960 had yielded over 43 000 tonnes of fish per year, had stopped. Detrimental consequences of the Aral sea desiccation also included significant desertification as surrounding land and natural resources deteriorated to the point where they became no longer usable. The desertification process was intensified by the increased salinisation of the lands and led to soil erosion, which has been cited as one of the major reasons for widespread fertiliser use. Dust and salt storms have also become more common and significant wind strengths have meant that even soil far away from the Aral Sea has been negatively affected.

Since the 1990s there have been continuing efforts to save the sea. Between 2005 and 2007, Kazakhstan and the World Bank funded extensive restoration projects in the North Aral Sea, including the 13km long Kokaral Dike to help conserve waters from the Syr Darya River and hydraulic facilities channel more water to the sea basin. These measures have resulted in a rising water level in the North Aral Sea, an increase in its size and a visible recovery in the biodiversity of the whole area. This partial recovery is impressive but the seas, particularly the southern one, remain in a very delicate state and require continued attention.

Sources: Columbia University (2015), "The Aral sea crisis", available at: *www.columbia.edu/~tmt2120/introduction.htm*, consulted on 10th March 2015; World Future Society (2015), "Reviving the Aral Sea", available at: *www.wfs.org/node/1163*, consulted on 3rd April 2015.

Efforts to address the growing amount of industrial waste need to be stepped up. In the past, achieving high growth was often considered more important than minimising or appropriately disposing of waste (Suleimen, 2014). Industrial waste, sometimes toxic, is frequently dumped or buried and this harms natural resources by degrading land quality and polluting water supplies. It can also pose a serious threat to public health. Kazakhstan lacks appropriate facilities for processing recyclable materials, which is inefficient as materials that could be re-used are discarded. Existing regulations on waste management in Kazakhstan are inadequate as they operate at the regional level and are not sufficiently binding or uniform to change the behaviour of industries (Suleimen, 2015). National regulations and more effective monitoring are essential to compel industries to invest in suitable waste management. The national sovereign wealth fund, Samruk-Kazyna, is taking steps to improve waste management by investing in research on resource management and waste minimisation. This is a considerable challenge given the large amount of existing hazardous waste that must be disposed of and the need to develop and promote techniques that generate less waste.

Despite the high levels of CO_2 emissions, the air quality in Kazakhstan is average, which to a large extent reflects the large size of the country and the low level of urbanisation. Air pollution, as measured by the mean annual exposure to particulate matter (PM) 2.5 pollution, is average compared to the benchmark countries (Figure 3.28). However, air quality varies considerably across the country as the two main polluters, industry and traffic, are concentrated in and around cities. For example, Almaty has a particularly high level of air pollution as a result of the city's geographical position: it is surrounded on one side by mountains and on the other side by factories. Based on a ranking using air quality and other indicators related to health and environment, Almaty has been assessed as the ninth most polluted city in the world (Mercer Human Resource Consulting, 2008). Reducing emissions from transport and industry is imperative as the high levels of pollution have adverse health effects on the population of Kazakhstan's largest city.

Figure 3.28. **Air pollution in Kazakhstan is mid-range**

Particulate matter (PM) 2.5 pollution, mean annual exposure in micrograms per cubic metre, 2010

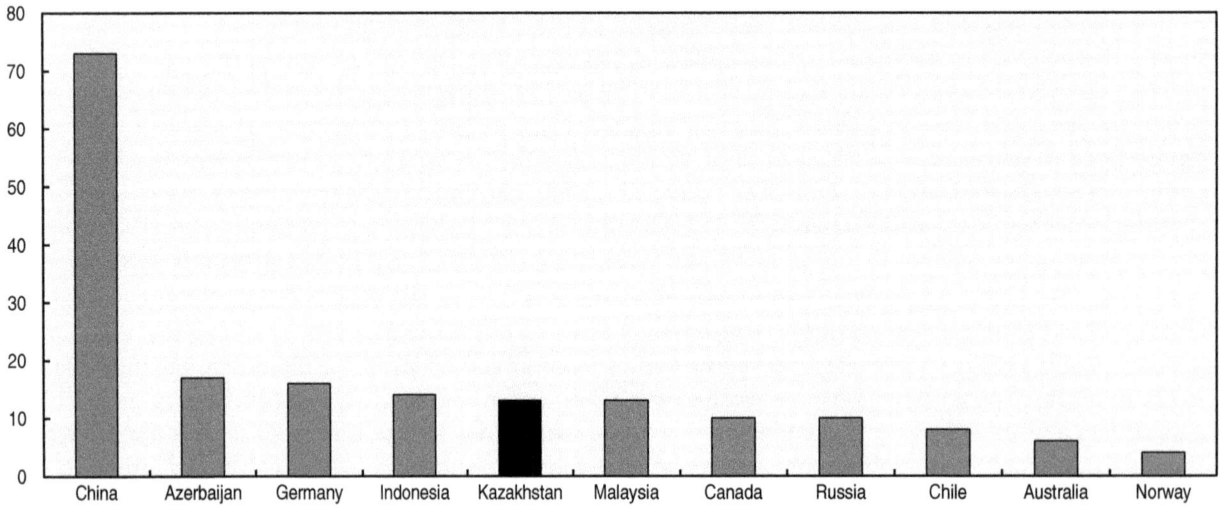

Source: World Bank (2014), *World Development Indicators* (database).

StatLink http://dx.doi.org/10.1787/888933289573

References

Aiyar, S. and A. Mody (2011), "The demographic dividend: Evidence from the Indian states?", *IMF Working Paper* No. 11/38.

Aiyar, S., R. Duval, D. Puy, Y. Wu and L. Zhang (2013), "Growth slowdowns and the middle-income trap", *IMF Working Paper* No. 13/71.

Berlemann, M. and J-E. Wesselhoft (2013), "Estimating aggregate capital stocks using the perpetual inventory method – New empirical evidence for 103 countries", *www.hsu-hh.de/berlemann/index_VQxdoUqt6VmSoYt6.html.*

Columbia University (2015), "The Aral sea crisis", available at: *www.columbia.edu/~tmt2120/introduction.htm*, consulted on 10 March 2015.

EBRD (2014), "Transition report 2014. Innovation in transition", European Bank for Reconstruction and Development, London.

Eeckhout, J. and B. Jovanovic (2012), "Occupational choice and development", *Journal of Economic Theory* Vol. 147(2), pp. 657-683.

Eichengreen, B., D. Park and K. Shin (2013), "Growth slowdowns redux: New evidence on the middle-income trap", *NBER Working Papers* No. 18673, Cambridge, MA.

Eichengreen, B., D. Park and K. Shin (2011), "When fast economies slow down: International evidence and implications for China", *NBER Working Papers* No. 16919, Cambridge, MA.

FAO (2013), "Irrigation in Central Asia in figures, AQUASTAT Survey – 2012", *Water Reports*, No. 39, Food and Agriculture Organization of the United Nations, Rome.

Gill, I. and H. Kharas (2007), *An East Asian Renaissance: Ideas for Economic Growth*, World Bank, Washington, DC.

Hausmann, R. (2011), "Ensuring a competitive and stable real exchange rate: A macroeconomic policy strategy", in *Growth and Competitiveness in Kazakhstan: Issues and Priorities in the Areas of Macroeconomic, Industrial, Trade and Institutional Development Policies*, R. Hausmann et al. (eds.)

IMF (2014a), "Article IV consultation – Staff report", *Country Reports*, No. 14/242, International Monetary Fund, Washington DC.

IMF (2014b), "Financial system stability assessment", *Country Reports*, No. 14/258, International Monetary Fund, Washington DC.

IMF (2013), "Leveraging oil wealth for development in Kazakhstan: Opportunities and challenges", *Country Reports*, No. 13/291, International Monetary Fund, Washington DC.

IMF (2011), "Selected Issues III. Oil wealth and development: What does this mean for Kazakhstan?", *Country Reports*, No. 11/151, International Monetary Fund, Washington DC.

International Energy Agency and the World Bank (2014), *Sustainable Energy for All 2013-2014: Global Tracking Framework Report*, Washington DC.

Korhonen, I. and A. Mehrotra (2009), "Real exchange rate, output and oil: Case of four large energy producers", *Bank of Finland Institute for Economics in Transition Discussion Papers*, No. 6/2009.

Magud N. and S. Sosa (2010), "When and why worry about real exchange rate appreciation? The missing link between Dutch disease and growth", *IMF Working Paper*, 10/271, Washington DC.

Mercer Human Resource Consulting (2008), *Health and Sanitation Rankings 2007*.

Mogilevskii, R. (2012), "Trends and patterns in foreign trade of Central Asian countries", *University of Central Asia Working Paper*, No. 1, 2012.

OECD (2015), "Comparative analysis on the performance of stabilisation funds and investment options", forthcoming, OECD, Paris.

OECD (2014), *Perspectives on Global Development 2014: Boosting Productivity to Meet the Middle-Income Challenge*, OECD Publishing, Paris, *http://dx.doi.org/10.1787/persp_glob_dev-2014-en.*

OECD (2012), *OECD Investment Policy Reviews: Kazakhstan 2012*, OECD Publishing, Paris, *http://dx.doi.org/10.1787/9789264121812-en.*

Suleimen, U. (2015), "Growth but not at any cost", *Astana Times*, *www.astanatimes.com/2015/01/growth-cost/*

Suleimen, U. (2014), "A green future for Kazakhstan", *CIWM Journal Online*. *www.ciwm-journal.co.uk/archives/11131.*

Varela, G. (2013), "How do ECA countries do in diversifying export destinations?", *World Bank Policy Research Paper*, No, 6472, Washington DC.

Wind Energy and Electric Vehicle Review (2014), *www.evwind.es/2014/11/28/ebrd-to-support-yereymentau-wind-farm-in-kazakhstan/49118.*

World Bank (2014), *World Development Indicators* (database), *http://data.worldbank.org.*

World Bank (2013a), *Beyond Oil. Kazakhstan's path to Greater Prosperity through Diversifying*, Washington DC.

World Bank (2013b), *Oil rules. Kazakhstan's Policy Options in a Downturn*, Joint Economic Research Program, Washington DC.

World Bank and Development Research Centre of the State Council (DRC) (2012), *China 2030 – Building a Modern, Harmonious and Creative High-Income Society*, World Bank, Washington, DC.

World Future Society (2015), "Reviving the Aral Sea", available at: *www.wfs.org/node/1163*, consulted on 3rd April 2015.

Multi-dimensional Review of Kazakhstan
Volume 1. Initial Assessment

Chapter 4

Enhancing sectoral competitiveness in Kazakhstan

Following the global economic crisis, Kazakhstan initiated extensive industrial development and innovation programmes with the aim of enhancing overall productivity and decreasing dependence on growth in extractive sectors. Since their initiation in 2010, the country has made some progress in terms of productivity improvements within non-resource sectors and boosting employment in manufacturing and some knowledge- and information-intensive services.

This chapter studies trends in Kazakhstan's competitive stance in different sectors and identifies enabling and constraining factors for competitiveness in the future. Based on past trends, it highlights the risk in Kazakhstan of a slower diversification process if resource sectors were to experience another boom. While recent economic reform efforts have been fruitful for Kazakhstan's competitive stance and diversification, implementation, co-ordination between policies, and regulatory burdens remain challenges. Moreover, facilitating access to external financing will support investment and private sector development. The government has put in place a strategy and the related institutions to develop a highly qualified workforce with adaptable and more practical skills. The actual implementation of this strategy, and reaching sufficient scope for the various programmes, will be essential. Finally, enhancing innovation capabilities, particularly through augmented leveraging of information and communications technologies (ICTs) and related services, is a fundamental requirement for Kazakhstan's competitiveness and greening of the economy in the future.

Competitiveness is the ability of a country (or firms within a country) to offer products and services that meet the quality standards of the local and world markets at international market prices and provide adequate returns on the resources employed or consumed in producing them. Low productivity levels and specialisation in low value added sectors may be aligned with the competitive stance of a country. For example, low labour costs and low productivity would reveal a competitive advantage in sectors and segments of sectors at the lower end of the value chain.

Sustained competitiveness requires that countries move up the value chain and diversify their economic structure. Sectoral competitiveness and comparative advantage change with economic development; for example, labour cost advantages may fade when the pool of surplus labour is exhausted and thus wages start to accelerate. To remain competitive continuously, countries need to move up the value chain both by shifting labour to more productive sectors and increasingly by shifting to activities with higher added value within sectors. The previous chapter revealed that Kazakhstan can still significantly boost growth and productivity by sectoral reallocation of labour. Moreover, sustaining competitiveness means developing a sufficiently diversified economic structure – both in terms of sectors and trading partners – so as to be less vulnerable to economic shocks and to be more embedded in diverse value chains. This is particularly relevant for resource-dependent economies such as Kazakhstan (Box 4.1). As shown in Chapter 3, Kazakhstan's economy is highly concentrated in resource sectors and exports to only a few key trading partners. The country is thus extremely vulnerable to external shocks. The falling commodity prices since mid-2014 and the economic crisis in its key partner country, the Russian Federation, have already lowered growth prospects for the coming years. Moreover, the economic slowdown in the People's Republic of China, which has been the driver of the commodity boom during the last decade, will further put a burden on growth prospects in Kazakhstan. Thus, if the country is going to become a competitive economy in the long run, it needs to make enormous efforts to become less dependent on the extractive sectors and diversify geographically.

This chapter studies trends in Kazakhstan's competitive stance and identifies enabling and constraining factors for competitiveness in the future. The first section benchmarks Kazakhstan's current competitive stance and studies whether the country is moving up the value chain and diversifying in order to sustain competitiveness and become less dependent on resources. Following the global economic crisis, Kazakhstan initiated extensive industrial development and innovation programmes. The section studies progress made since the initiation of these programmes in 2010. The second section reviews patterns of export diversification in Kazakhstan during the recent resource price boom, which has been a blessing for growth but produced challenges for diversification. The following sections discuss factors and policy areas determining competitiveness and compares Kazakhstan to its peers, including in the areas of governance and regulation, finance, investment, skills, and innovation.

Box 4.1. **Where natural resources meet a favourable environment, initial dependence can quickly be overcome, even as the natural resource sectors keep growing**

The historical paths of resource-rich countries suggest that, at low levels of development, resource commodities are the main income earners and account for large proportions of exports and gross domestic product (GDP). In other words, the economy's dependence on resources is high. This is expected as resources are comparatively easy to produce and export. In a small or underdeveloped economy the resource sector will therefore account for most exports and a significant share of GDP. As investments pour in, production expands quickly and often further reserves are proven. Both abundance and dependence increase (see Figure 4.1 in this box for cross-sectional evidence of this pattern).

As the resource sector expands it creates opportunities for the rest of the economy: resource production requires a large range of supplies, from food for its workers to higher technology activities such as software design, chemical analysis and customisation of machinery. At the same time resource exports generate important revenues for the state that can be invested in human capital (education and health) and public capital (infrastructure and public services) thereby creating opportunities for economic activities that are relatively intensive in these types of capital. The original comparative advantage in natural resources can thus be used to push the production possibility frontier outwards and create new comparative advantages through diversification.

If the country manages to use its resource endowment to develop opportunities for other sectors, over time resources will become less important as the rest of the economy becomes larger. During this process resource production and the amount of proven assets are even likely to continue growing, as new technology and an improving regulatory framework lead to new discoveries, but resources lose importance relative to the rest of the economy. In the case of mineral and energy resources abundance will finally decrease as the existing reserves are depleted or become unviable for economic (relative price of labour and capital), social (harm done to neighbouring communities) or environmental (environmental damage of extraction, climate change) reasons (see Figure 4.1 in this box showing that resource-rich high-income countries are still on the upward sloping section of the abundance curve). This need not be the case for soft resources which do not face depletion as long as they are not exploited beyond their rate of regeneration.

Figure 4.1. **While resource abundance increases with economic development, countries' dependence on extractive sectors decreases**

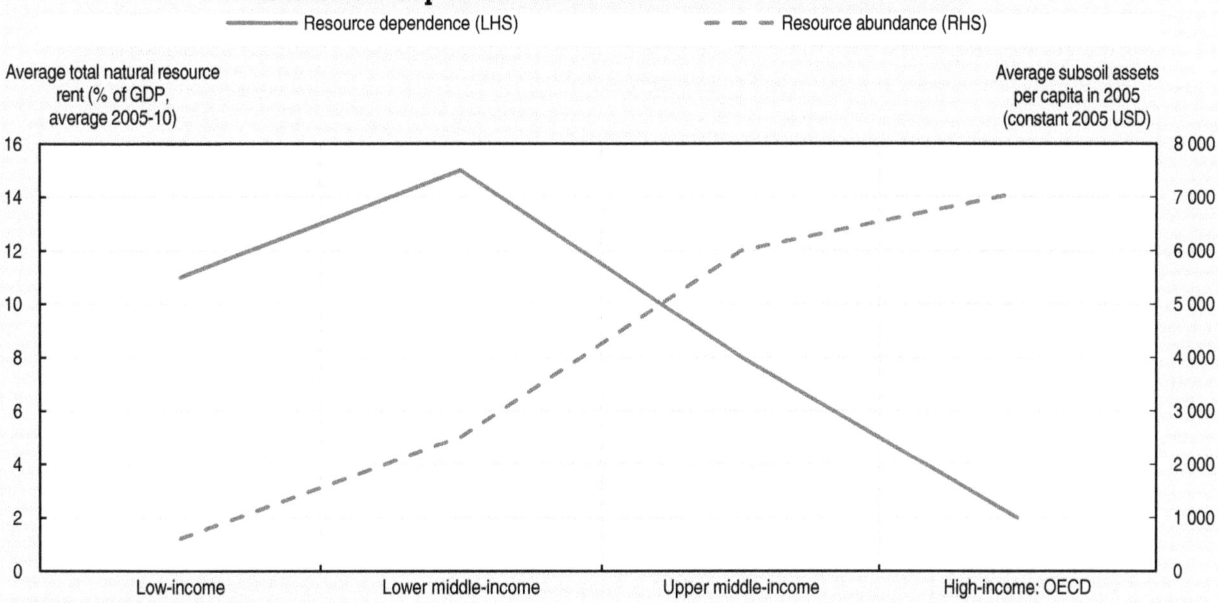

Note: The sample only includes countries that are extracting resources of any type.

Source: OECD (2013a), *African Economic Outlook 2013: Structural Transformation and Natural Resources*, *http://dx.doi.org/10.1787/aeo-2013-en.*

StatLink http://dx.doi.org/10.1787/888933289580

Kazakhstan is making some improvements in its competitive stance in non-resource sectors

Kazakhstan is still almost exclusively internationally competitive in products based on natural resources. Between 2010 and 2014, the country had on average a revealed comparative advantage (RCA) in exporting goods in 55 (out of approximately 1 000) products (see next section for an international comparison). Around 30% were raw material or agricultural products and two-thirds corresponded to processed natural resources including a few chemical products. Fewer than 5% of the RCA products were products not based on resources, including, for example, rail locomotives, tugs and vessels. In services, Kazakhstan's RCA is in transport services, which is also a resource-dependent sector shipping overseas products based on natural resources.

The average labour productivity level in Kazakhstan, defined by value added per person employed, is lagging significantly behind the level in benchmarking countries. For example, labour productivity is around three times higher in Germany or Canada compared to Kazakhstan (see Figure 3.16 in Chapter 3). The gap in productivity is yet higher with countries such as Singapore, Norway and the United Arab Emirates. Average labour productivity is slightly above the levels in Azerbaijan, China and Indonesia.

Average productivity growth across all sectors has been impressive during the last two decades. Economy-wide average productivity doubled between 1993 and 2013 (see Figure 3.16 in Chapter 3). Productivity received a particular boost during the last decade, mostly driven by the commodity price boom benefiting all countries worldwide that are rich in natural resources. These countries have enjoyed rising terms of trade, increasing exports, and improving current account balances (OECD, 2014a). While this has been a windfall economic gain and also made it possible to boost per capita incomes, productivity growth driven by increased demand for resources can lead to wrong conclusions. Most resource-rich countries have seen their competitiveness challenged in the manufacturing and other sectors. The commodity price boom, mainly prompted by the rise of China, reduced the level of export diversification in these countries because (depending on the country) of price effects or possible Dutch disease effects (see section on export diversification further below illustrating this challenge for Kazakhstan).

Recent growth was supported by strong labour productivity growth in services, agriculture and manufacturing

Kazakhstan's productivity gap in the largest economic sectors remains considerable. In a classification of 25 economic sectors, the six largest sectors (in terms of share of GDP) in Kazakhstan are the wholesale and retail trade, extractive sectors, real estate, transportation and storage, construction and agriculture sectors (see Annex Table 4.A1.1). Together they were responsible for more than 50% of GDP in 2013. Productivity in the largest sectors is lagging considerably behind levels in more advanced countries such as Australia and Canada (see Annex Figure 4.A1.1). This gap is most dramatic in agriculture and related sectors. Australia is more than 25 times as productive as Kazakhstan in agriculture; this factor is around 15 and 6 compared to Canada and Germany, respectively.[1] The reason is that the self-employment rate in agriculture is, at around 50%, extremely high. Self-employed agricultural workers engage in low productivity activities, mostly for subsistence.[2]

But overall economic growth during the most recent years was supported by significant productivity improvement in four of the largest sectors, which are all non-resource sectors. Compound annual growth of productivity over 2010-13 was 20% or above in wholesale and retail trade; real estate; professional, scientific and technical services; and agriculture (Figure 4.2). Of course, given the very low level of productivity in agriculture in Kazakhstan even high growth rates mean a long process to catch up with productivity levels in other countries. Productivity growth in the extractive sector was stagnant over 2010-13.[3]

Figure 4.2. **Labour productivity in the transport equipment as well as chemical and pharmaceutical sectors experienced a boost over 2010-13**

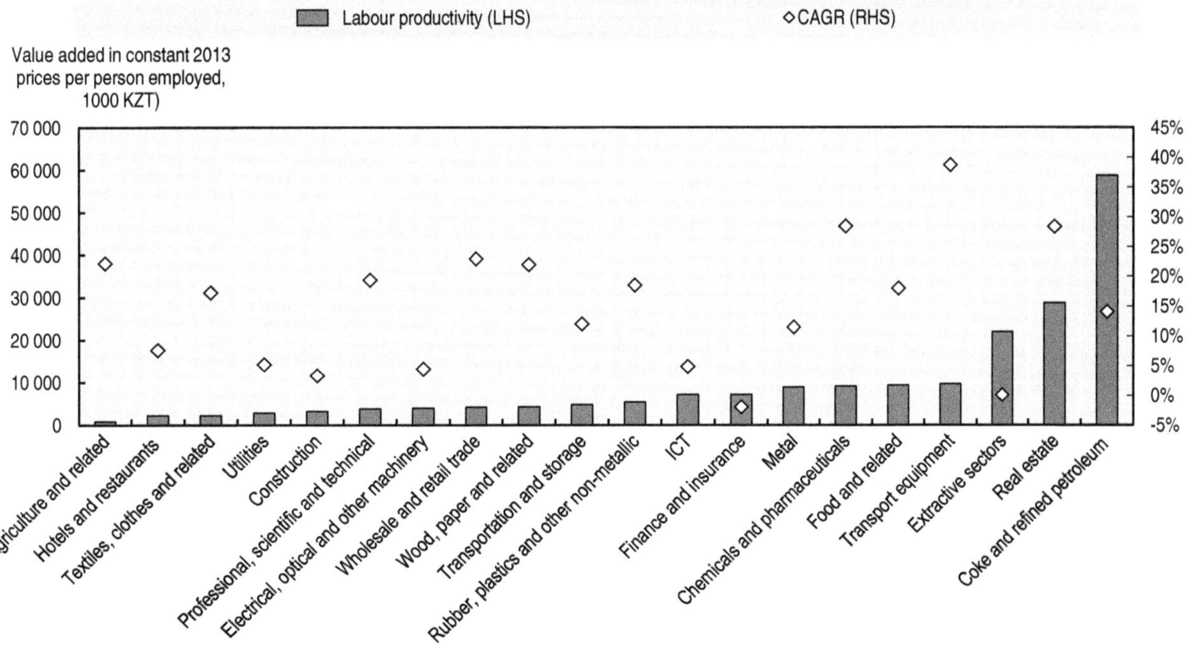

Notes: CAGR stands for compound annual growth rate. Sectors are ordered from the least productive (left) to the most productive sectors. The labour productivity levels and growth in labour productivity of (mostly non-commercial) public and social services are not included in the figure. Raw data for 2014 were not available. However, productivity growth figures for 2014 for some sectors were provided by the Ministry of National Economy: food and related (-13%), transport equipment (-35%), basic pharmaceuticals (-32%), coke and refined petroleum (-21%), chemicals (+13%), textiles, clothes and related (+15%), electrical equipment (+12%), iron and steel (+19%).

Source: Authors' calculations based on data received from the Ministry of National Economy.

StatLink http://dx.doi.org/10.1787/888933289590

Labour productivity in the fastest growing manufacturing sectors is higher in Kazakhstan compared to peer developing countries. Kazakhstan's fastest growing manufacturing sectors include the transport equipment, chemicals and pharmaceuticals, rubber, coke and refined petroleum, and food sectors. Except for coke and refined petroleum, advanced economies such as Australia and Canada still have considerably higher productivity levels in these sectors compared to Kazakhstan (Figure 4.3). The difference varies by a factor of 1.5 and 4 for these two countries. But in these manufacturing sectors the productivity level in Kazakhstan is generally higher than in China, Indonesia and the Russian Federation.

Moreover, productivity is improving in these manufacturing sectors, particularly in the transport equipment and chemical-pharmaceutical sectors. Individual manufacturing sectors remain relatively small in economic terms in Kazakhstan. Together they were responsible for approximately 11% of GDP over the last four years. Growth was particularly high in the production of transport equipment. Since 2010, annual growth was around 60% in this sector; largely driven by productivity improvements at an annual rate of 40% over 2010-13. However, in 2014, productivity decreased by 35% in this sector (not reported in Figure 4.3). The sector remains very small at 0.5% of total GDP in 2013. The government has identified the transport equipment sector as one of the focus sectors to boost growth through government incentives in its industrial policy programme 2010-14, introduced as a reaction to the economic slowdown in Kazakhstan following the global financial and economic crisis.[4] The chemical and pharmaceutical sector has also experienced very fast growth in productivity at 30% annually over 2010-13. In 2014, productivity continued to increase by 13% in the chemical sector, but decreased in the pharmaceutical sector (not reported in Figure 4.3).

Figure 4.3. **In the fastest growing manufacturing activities, labour productivity levels in Kazakhstan are above the levels in peer developing countries**

Labour productivity as a factor of the level in Kazakhstan in 2013

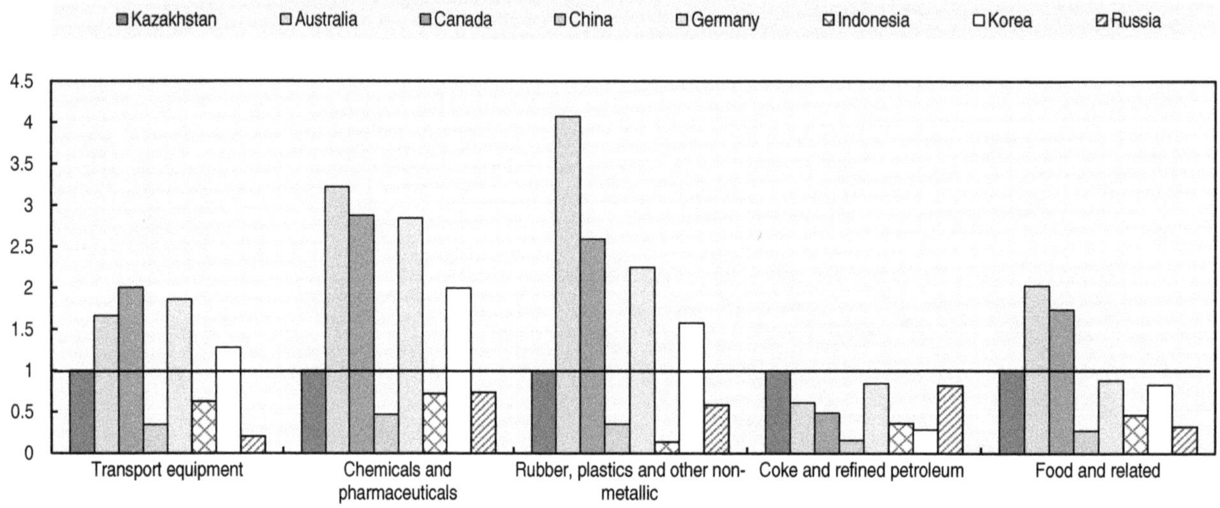

Notes: The sectors illustrated in the figure correspond to the five fastest growing manufacturing sectors in Kazakhstan over 2010-13. In fact, wholesale and retail trade was, with a growth rate at 28%, also among the fastest growing. However, the productivity differential could not be conducted for this sector as comparable statistics for benchmarking countries were not available. Productivity figures correspond to 2013 figures for Kazakhstan and 2011 for all other countries.

Source: Authors' calculations based on data received from the Ministry of National Economy.

StatLink *http://dx.doi.org/10.1787/888933289601*

Employment shifts towards manufacturing and knowledge-intensive services also enhanced recent growth and productivity

Manufacturing and knowledge-intensive services have relatively low employment shares in Kazakhstan. About 24% of total employment in Kazakhstan is in the agricultural sector (Figure 4.4). Despite agriculture's big employment share the sector only contributes 5% to total GDP, illustrating its relatively low productivity (see Figure 4.2). Another quarter of all workers are employed in wholesale and retail trade as well as in the construction sector. The extractive sector employs only around 3% of all workers. This low share is due to the capital-intensive characteristic of this sector and boosting employment could thus not be a policy strategy. The employment share of manufacturing at around 5% was still very low in 2013. Similarly, knowledge-intensive services such as information and communications technology (ICT), finance and insurance and professional, scientific and technical services have very low employment shares in Kazakhstan; together they employ around 8% of all workers. In more advanced service economies such as Australia, Canada or Germany, employment shares in these sectors are at around 20%. An expansion of these services has significant employment potential, given their labour-intensive characteristics.

Figure 4.4. **Job creation was fastest in the transport equipment, finance and insurance as well as hospitality sectors**

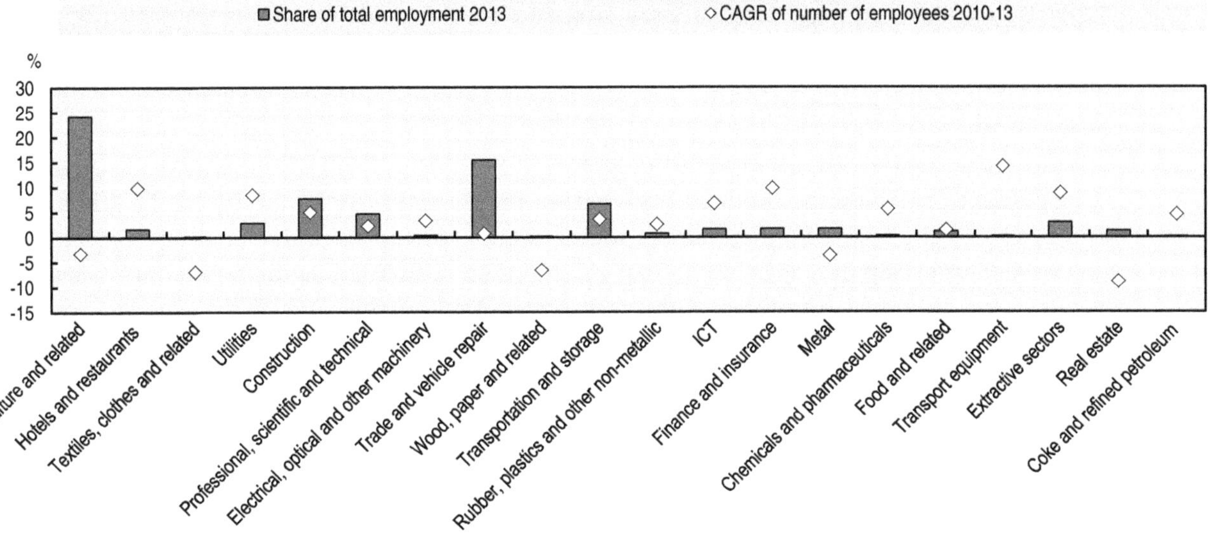

Notes: CAGR stands for compound annual growth rate. Sectors are ordered from the least productive (left) to the most productive sectors (see Figure 4.2). Employment shares and growth in employment of (mostly non-commercial) public and social services are not included in the figure.

Source: Authors' calculations based on data received from the Ministry of National Economy.

StatLink http://dx.doi.org/10.1787/888933289611

But from 2010 to 2013, employment expanded considerably in manufacturing and some knowledge-intensive service sectors. Job creation has been relatively high over recent years in Kazakhstan. Growth in employment has been around 2% each year since 2010, a satisfactory growth figure given Kazakhstan's relatively high labour force participation and low unemployment rate. Job creation was particularly high in manufacturing and some knowledge-intensive services (Figure 4.4). For example, annual growth in employment stood at around 15% in the transport equipment manufacturing sector and at around 10% in the financial and insurance sectors. Continuously boosting employment in manufacturing and knowledge-intensive services would increase aggregate productivity and growth. As also illustrated in Chapter 3, Kazakhstan still has significant potential to shift labour to more productive sectors. It is interesting to note that in agriculture, the least productive sector in Kazakhstan, employment decreased over 2010-13. Thus, the recent employment shifts are in the right direction.

Kazakhstan has competitive wage levels in the manufacturing sector

An important indicator of whether a country is in line with its comparative advantage is the comparison of productivity growth in the various economic sectors with real wage growth. If wages are increasing faster than productivity, the competitiveness of a country in a given sector may suffer. Higher wages may not be affordable as the economic, regulatory and governance environment is not sufficiently conducive to the innovations needed to sustain growth or to the development of the more sophisticated labour skills required for the production of higher value-added products.

Because of the booming commodity sector over the last decade wages have increased rapidly (see also Chapter 3). Even during the most recent years, when the commodity boom started to fade, compound annual growth of wages was at least 5% over 2010-13, in most sectors closer to 10% or more (see Annex Figure 4.A1.2). The only commercial sectors which experienced negative wage growth were the construction and hospitality sectors. High wage growth may offer a challenge to the development of low-cost and low value added manufacturing sectors, which would be needed to develop a strong manufacturing base in Kazakhstan.

However, in selected manufacturing sectors, the wage levels in Kazakhstan still seem to be competitive given the productivity levels in these sectors. Productivity can be taken as a proxy for the level of technological sophistication within the value chain of a given sector. A comparison of wages and labour productivity with Kazakhstan's peer countries in the food, chemical-pharmaceutical and automotive sectors shows that wages are still lower than those in comparator countries with lower or similar productivity levels than in Kazakhstan (Figure 4.5). For example, Kazakhstan may operate with a higher technological sophistication (or higher up the value chain) than Indonesia, the Russian Federation and China in the transport equipment industry but still has lower wage levels in that sector.

Kazakhstan's diversification process would be challenged by a future resource boom

Kazakhstan experienced a period of relative specialisation into the resource sector during the pre-crisis commodity price boom. While recent economic growth in Kazakhstan was mostly reliant on robust growth in non-resource sectors (see previous section), extractive sectors were driving overall growth during the early 2000s (see Chapter 3). A key challenge faced by the country may thus be to continue a process of relatively faster growth in non-resource as compared to resource sectors, to sustain the diversification process, even if the commodity markets become more favourable again.

Economic diversification, associated with sophistication of production, is fundamental to ensuring sustainable competitiveness. It makes countries less vulnerable to shocks. It may also make countries' economic structures more adaptable to longer-term evolutions in comparative advantages in the world markets. Indeed, diversification – if it comes with sophistication of production – may go along with a more diversified skills supply, as well as with a range of productive firms among different sectors. Therefore the economy may be more capable of grasping rapidly new opportunities and facing challenges implied by changes in competitive edges (OECD, 2014a; UNIDO, 2009). Conversely, over-specialisation may lead to rents, economic inefficiencies, and a low incentive to invest in other sectors. Excessive specialisation in some economies also leads to issues of limited labour absorption capacity, with only a few productive sectors to take on high numbers of workers. Countries which specialise in natural resources, such as Kazakhstan, have a particular challenge to diversify and thus difficulties in absorbing labour in productive sectors.

Exports of non-resource goods and services lost ground during the commodity price boom

Kazakhstan is exporting considerably fewer non raw-material goods than an average country of similar economic weight would; and even fewer than a decade ago. The ratio of Kazakhstan's share in world's total non raw-material exports and its share in global GDP – a simple measure of export competitiveness relative to economic size – was 0.5 in 2013,

Figure 4.5. **Wages in selected manufacturing sectors are competitive in Kazakhstan**

2013

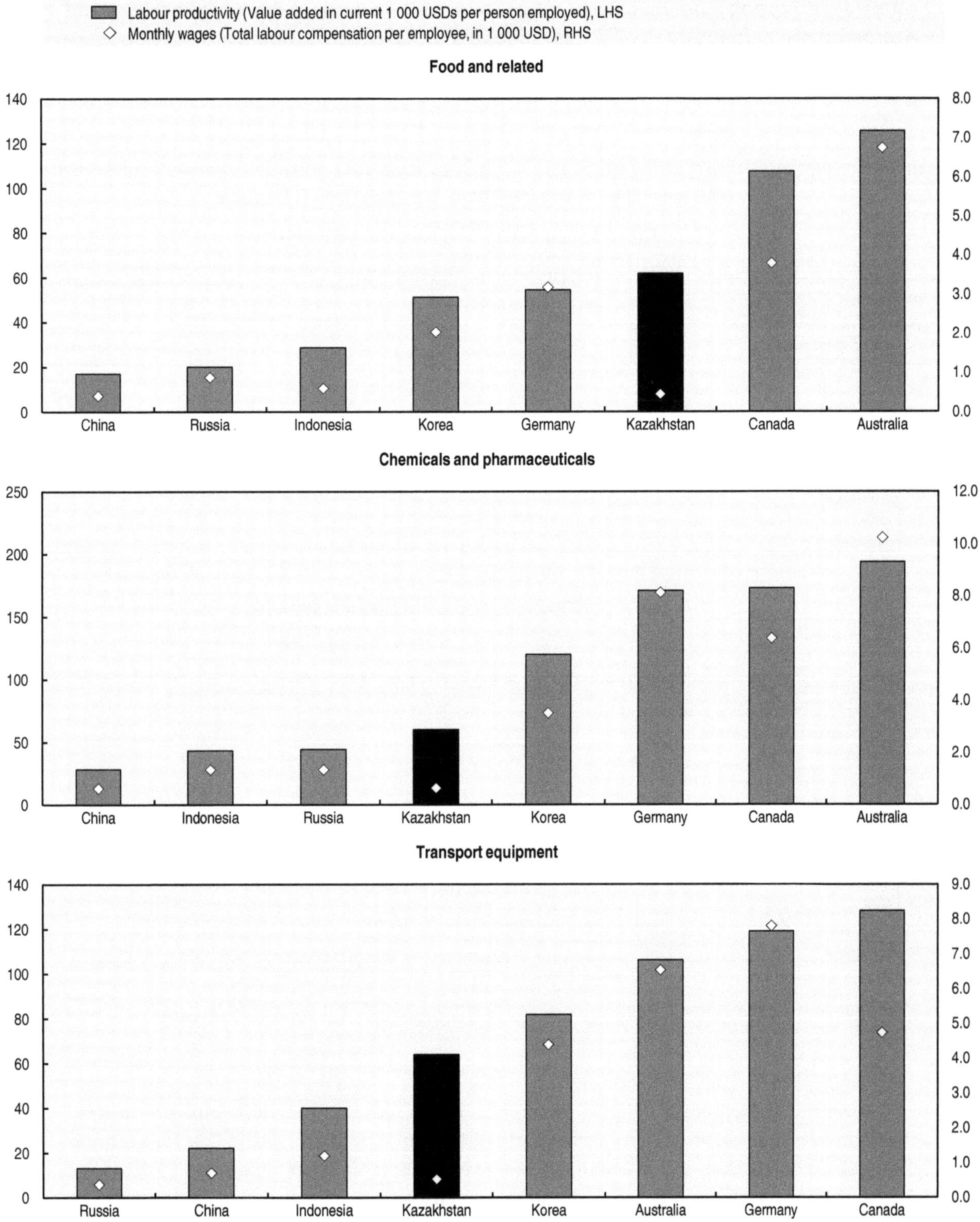

Source: Authors' calculations based on data received from the Ministry of National Economy.

StatLink http://dx.doi.org/10.1787/888933289622

down from 0.8 in 2004 (Figure 4.6, Panel A). A value of 1 of this ratio means that the country's competitive stance is in line with its economic size. A value higher than 1 means that the country is exporting more than expected given its GDP. Australia, a developed country, and Azerbaijan are performing even worse compared to Kazakhstan. China also saw its score in this ratio fall over the last decade, driven by the rising domestic market, but it is still in line with its economic size. Singapore, Malaysia and Korea have all very high scores at 2 and above.

Figure 4.6. **Lagging export competitiveness both in non-raw material goods and services**

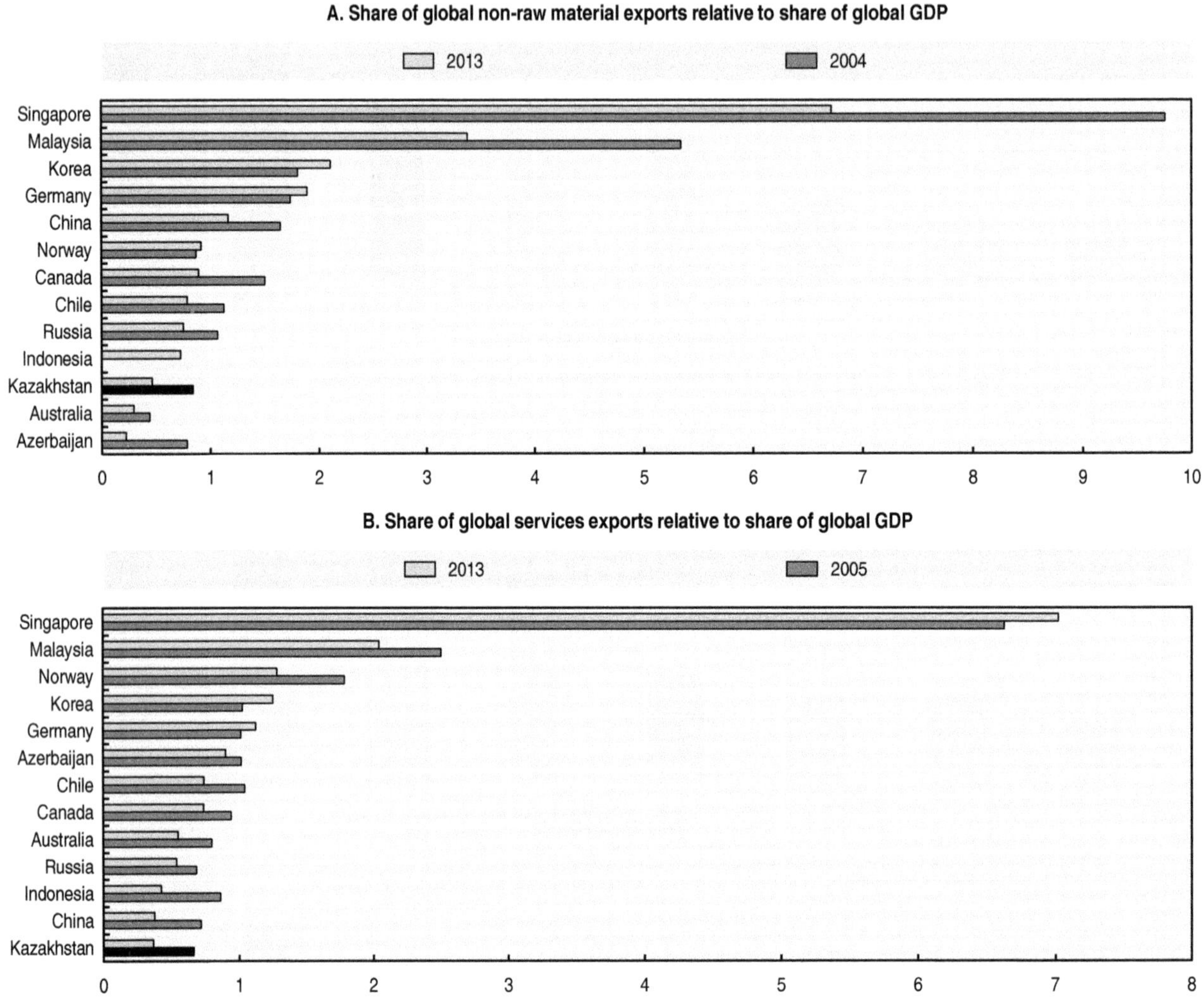

Source: A: World Bank (2015a), *World Integrated Trade Solution* (database), *http://wits.worldbank.org/*. B: World Bank (2015b), *World Development Indicators* (database) *http://data.worldbank.org/data-catalog/world-development-indicators*.

StatLink http://dx.doi.org/10.1787/888933289632

Similarly, the potential of services exports is not reaped in Kazakhstan. The ratio of the country's share in global services exports relative to its share in world GDP was around 0.4 in 2013; down from 0.7 in 2005 (Figure 4.6, Panel B). This score is similar to those for China, Indonesia or the Russian Federation, which could all boost growth by developing their services sector and thus services exports (OECD, 2014a). Services exports are largely concentrated in transport and travel services in Kazakhstan. Together, exports in those sectors are responsible for more than 80% of all service exports. Kazakhstan has still relatively underdeveloped knowledge-intensive services (see section above and further below). Developing these services could boost overall growth and exports in Kazakhstan.

Kazakhstan's exports are highly concentrated in raw materials and even more so than two decades ago

Exports of Kazakhstan are concentrated in just a few resource-based products; and increasingly so over time. The top five products exported by Kazakhstan were together responsible for around 80% of total merchandise exports in 2014 (Figure 4.7). With the commodity boom over the last two decades concentration of exports has even increased. In 1996, the top five export products were responsible for only around 50% of total merchandise exports. Azerbaijan experienced a similar trend with a share of the top five products in total exports of around 15% in the mid-1990s and above 90% in 2014. The increase in export concentration is less dominant in the Russian Federation; the share of the top five products in total exports increased from around 55% to 72% between 1995 and 2011. Well-diversified economies such as Germany and China kept the concentration of top five export products at below 30%, relatively constant over the last 20 years.

Figure 4.7. **Kazakhstan's exports are highly concentrated**

Share of top five exported products, in % of total exports

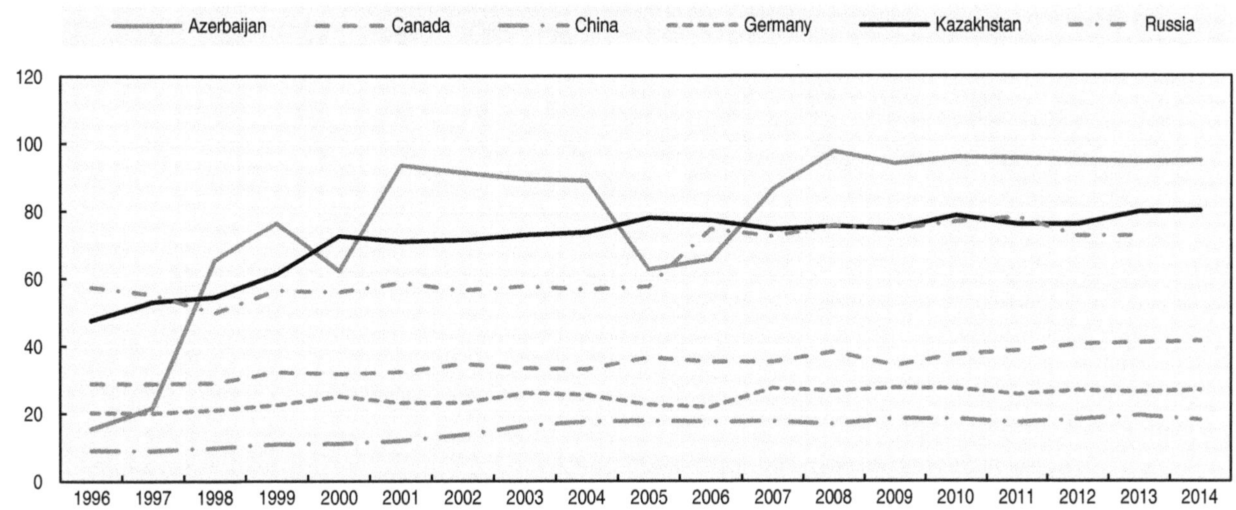

Notes: Product classification used is SITC. Rev3, 4-digits. For example in 2014, top five products for Kazakhstan included: crude oil (3330), commodities not classified elsewhere (9310), copper (5251), radio-isotopes (3432), and natural gas (6821).

Sources: Authors' calculations based on Word Bank (2015c), *World Integrated Trade Solution* (database), *http://wits.worldbank.org/*

StatLink *http://dx.doi.org/10.1787/888933289648*

Similarly, the number of products with a revealed comparative advantage (RCA) is relatively low in Kazakhstan compared to its peers. RCA is a measure to indicate the relative advantage or disadvantage of a certain country in a certain class of goods as evidenced by trade flows. In a classification including around 1 000 product categories, Kazakhstan had a revealed comparative advantage in around 60 products between 2010 and 14, down from an average number of around 90 products from 1996 to 2000 (Figure 4.8).[5] It should be noted those products that have no longer an RCA in the 2010s were responsible for only very small shares of total exports in Kazakhstan. The reduction does however indicate that some product categories are at the margin to be globally competitive and have lost ground recently. Among the 13 benchmarking countries, only Azerbaijan and the United Arab Emirates had a lower level of export diversification than Kazakhstan measured by RCA over the same period. Singapore and Malaysia, for example, had around 140 and 200 products over 2010-2014. The respective numbers were above 400 in China and Germany over the same period. Countries rich in natural resources, including Kazakhstan, experienced a period of specialisation, showing their difficulty in remaining competitive in. and moving into, non-resource sectors particularly during a period of high commodity demand and prices.[6] As pointed out in the previous section, in terms of RCA, only around 5% of RCA products in Kazakhstan are not based on natural resources. These products include railway locomotives, tugs and special purpose vessels.

Figure 4.8. **Kazakhstan has fewer products with a revealed comparative advantage than two decades ago**

Average number of products with a revealed comparative advantage for indicated time period

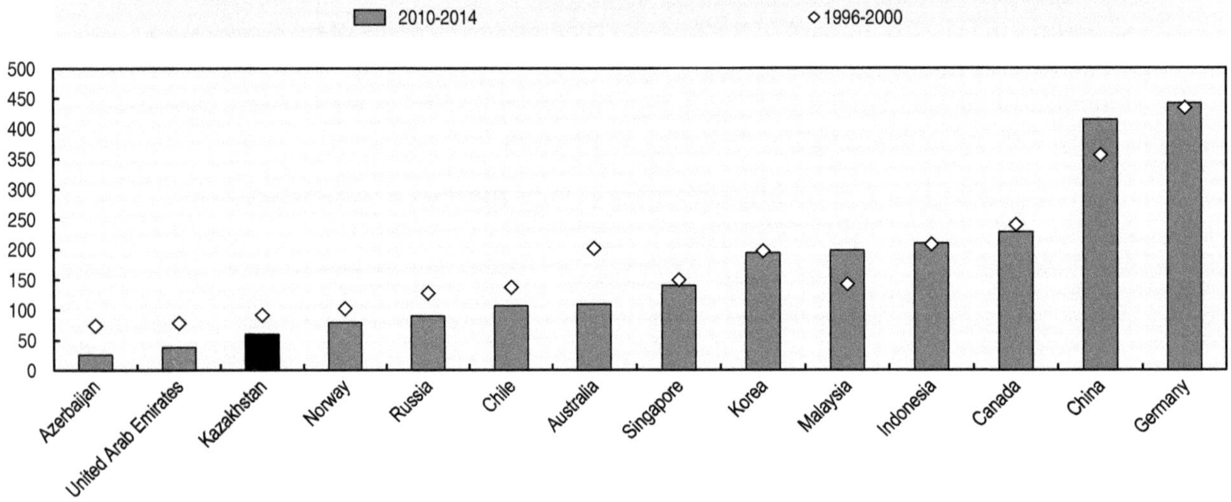

Notes: Product classification used is SITC. Rev3, 4-digits. RCA is a measure to indicate the relative advantage or disadvantage of a certain country in a certain class of goods as evidenced by trade flows.

Sources: Authors' calculations based on World Bank (2015a), *World Integrated Trade Solution* (database). World Bank, Washington, DC, *http://wits.worldbank.org/*

StatLink http://dx.doi.org/10.1787/888933289652

Concentrating exports in raw materials does not only make the country vulnerable to shocks, it also corresponds to a missed opportunity to move up the value chain. In fact, exporting unprocessed goods which are further exported by importing countries plays an increasingly important role in Kazakhstan. This so-called forward integration was responsible for around 30% of Kazakhstan's total exports in 2011, considerably higher than in advanced resource-rich countries such as Australia, Canada or United Arab Emirates.

Access to external financing is important for private sector development

The financial sector has developed rapidly since the turn of the century, but its role in supporting private businesses could be expanded. Kazakhstan ranks lower in a large range of financial indicators when compared to other middle-income countries: credit to the private sector is comparatively low, the stock market and local capital markets are still small. Bank lending is the most important source of external financing for firms, but since the banking crisis lending growth has been subdued. To achieve balanced economic growth, it is essential that the financial sector, and in particular the banking sector, fulfil their economic role of channelling savings to productive investments. Further analysis of the sector in the next phase of this MDRC, including on concessional financing conditions and take-up, will shed light on whether the relative weakness of lending to the private sector is primarily a supply-side or demand-side issue.

Bank lending to the private sector is relatively low

Although Kazakhstani firms rely on banks for external financing, domestic credit to the private sector is low. As in most middle-income economies, Kazakhstani firms mostly rely on internal funding when financing investments. Bank lending is the most important external funding source, and accounts for more than half of all external financing (World Bank, 2015c). Bank penetration is high, with over 90% of firms having a checking or savings account. Nevertheless, only 19% of firms have a bank loan or credit line. Domestic credit to the private sector stands at around 40% of GDP, which is relatively low (Figure 4.9).

Figure 4.9. **Domestic credit to the private sector is low**

Domestic credit to private sector in % of GDP, average 2010-13

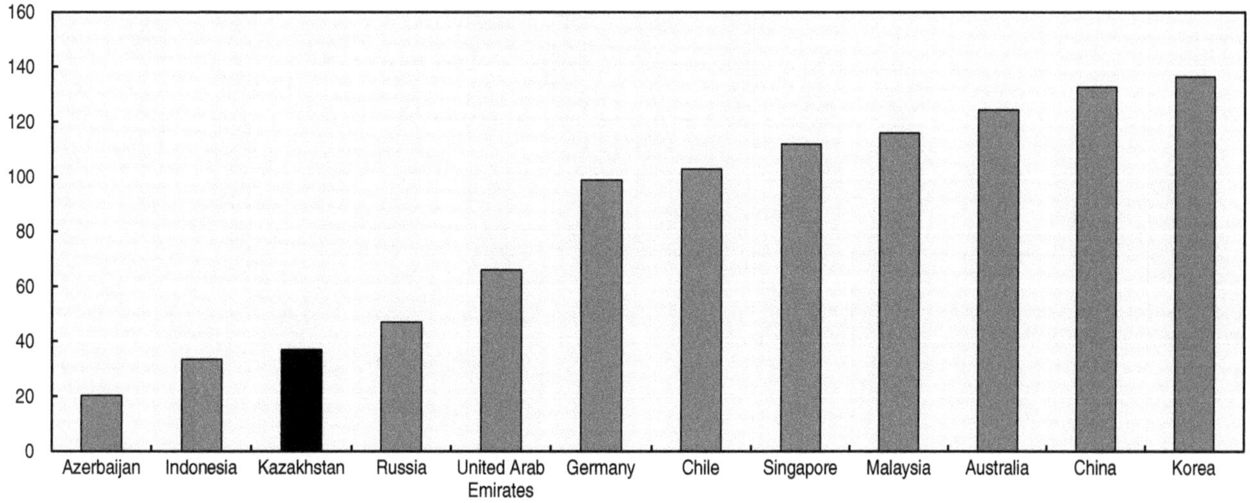

Notes: The average for United Arab Emirates is based on 2010-12.

Source: Authors' calculations based on World Bank (2015b), *World Development Indicators* (database), *http://databank.worldbank.org/data/.*

StatLink *http://dx.doi.org/10.1787/888933289661*

Bank lending has stalled as an engine of growth. After the crisis, the banking sector underwent a marked deleveraging (Figure 4.10). The effect on the economy, however, was limited, as it coincided with a necessary downsizing of the construction sector (IMF, 2014). During recent years, bank lending increased in nominal terms, but just enough to grow in line with economic activity. The still high stock of non-performing loans limits banks' ability to extend credit. It also depresses profitability and thereby slows down the strengthening of banks' capital positions. As minimum capital requirements are rising as a result of the gradual phasing-in of Basel III, while the current comfortable solvency situation could quickly deteriorate in case of stress, capital could become an important constraint on future credit growth.

During recent years, growth in corporate lending has been especially weak. Retail lending grew faster than corporate lending for almost three years in a row (Figure 4.11). Since 2012, the portfolio of corporate loans has increased by just 6% in real terms, compared to 42% for retail loans. Lending to households has been relatively profitable because of the high interest margins (Figure 4.12).[7] To avoid excess lending to consumers, the central bank has capped interest rates for unsecured consumer loans at 56% since 2013, which in particular limited lending growth by microfinance institutions. In addition, growth of the consumer loan portfolio was limited to 30% at the individual bank level in 2014. Although retail lending has slowed down, there has been no pick-up in corporate lending.

Figure 4.10. **During recent years, the expansion of bank lending was just in line with economic growth**

Outstanding loans to the economy at year end, in % of GDP

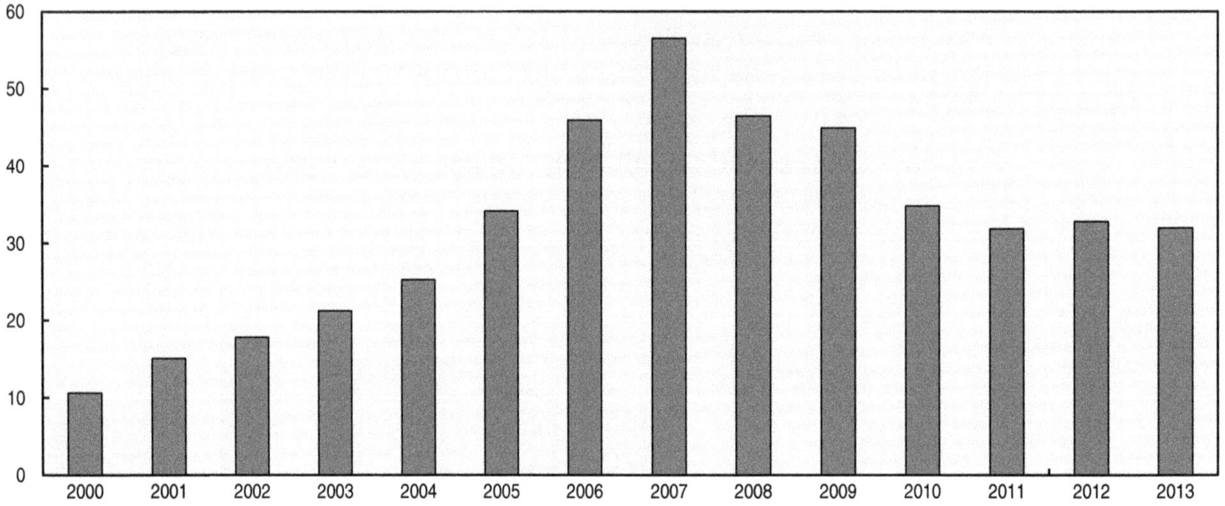

Source: Authors' calculations based on National Bank of Kazakhstan (2015), *Official Internet Resource of the National Bank of Kazakhstan* (database), *www.nationalbank.kz/?docid=127&switch=english*.

StatLink http://dx.doi.org/10.1787/888933289672

Figure 4.11. **Retail lending has grown faster than corporate lending since mid-2012**

Annualised growth of outstanding loans, in %

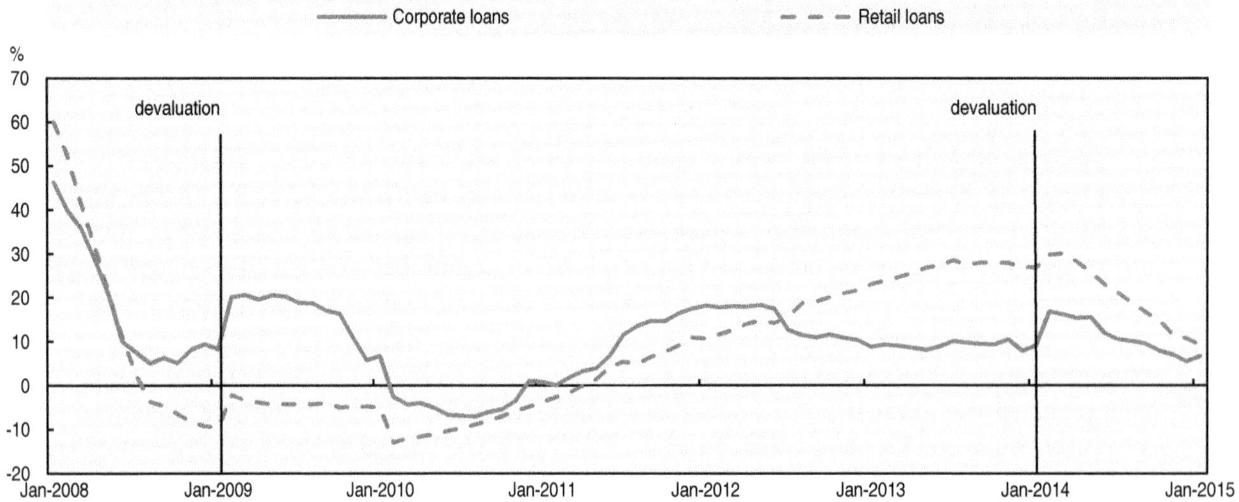

Source: Authors' calculations based on National Bank of Kazakhstan (2015), *Official Internet Resource of the National Bank of Kazakhstan* (database), *www.nationalbank.kz/?docid=127&switch=english*.

StatLink http://dx.doi.org/10.1787/888933289682

Figure 4.12. **Comparatively high interest rates on retail loans make lending to businesses less attractive**

Interest rates on loans in domestic currency, in %

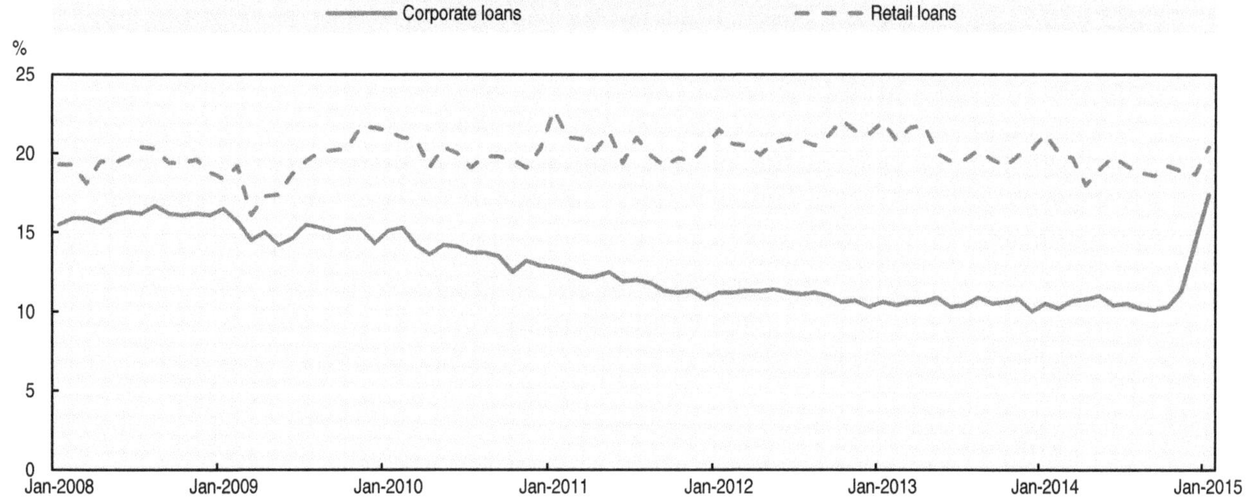

Source: Authors' calculations based on National Bank of Kazakhstan (2015), *Official Internet Resource of the National Bank of Kazakhstan* (database), *www.nationalbank.kz/?docid=127&switch=english.*

StatLink http://dx.doi.org/10.1787/888933289695

Defying the overall developments in corporate lending, loans to small businesses have started to recover. Outstanding loans had been decreasing continuously in real terms during 2009-13, but recorded 30% growth in 2014 (Figure 4.13). Although this growth was partly due to the devaluation of the tenge, loans to small businesses also increased as a share of the total lending portfolio. The improvement was entirely due to higher small and medium-sized enterprises (SMEs) lending, as loans to individual entrepreneurs declined slightly.

Figure 4.13. **Lending to small businesses was hit by the banking crisis, but has started to recover**

Outstanding portfolio in real terms, index 2002=100, and in % of the total lending volume

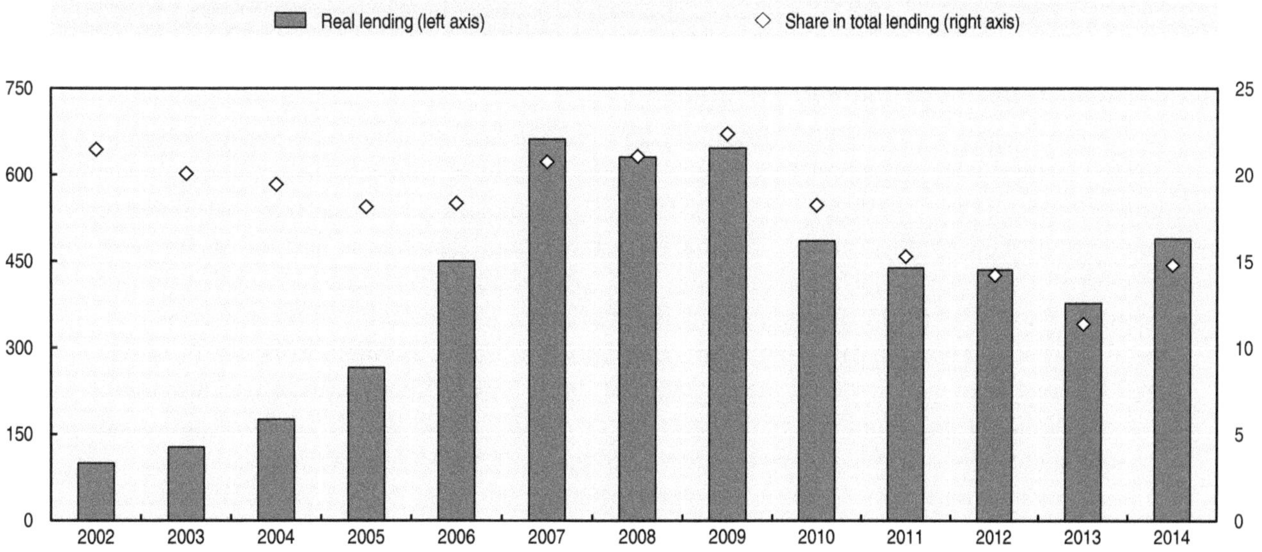

Notes: Nominal loans to small businesses deflated by the private consumption deflator.

Source: Authors' calculations based on National Bank of Kazakhstan (2015), *Official Internet Resource of the National Bank of Kazakhstan* (database), *www.nationalbank.kz/?docid=127&switch=english.*

StatLink http://dx.doi.org/10.1787/888933289700

Despite the recent improvements for SMEs, the scarce availability of bank credit limits firms' access to finance. Many in Kazakhstan consider access to finance as a key constraint on their development (see Annex Figure 4.A1.4), which is in line with the low credit to the domestic sector, the 30% rejection rate on loan applications (World Bank, 2015c) and the relatively high collateral requirements (Figure 4.14). Aware that access to finance for SMEs is a bottleneck for private sector development, the government has a wide range of supporting programmes in place. As mentioned in the previous section, insufficient co-ordination and implementation of such programmes are bottlenecks in Kazakhstan, but steps to improve have been put in place. In addition, the central bank has stepped up activities to increase financial literacy.

Figure 4.14. **Collateral requirements are high**

In %, 2013 or most recent

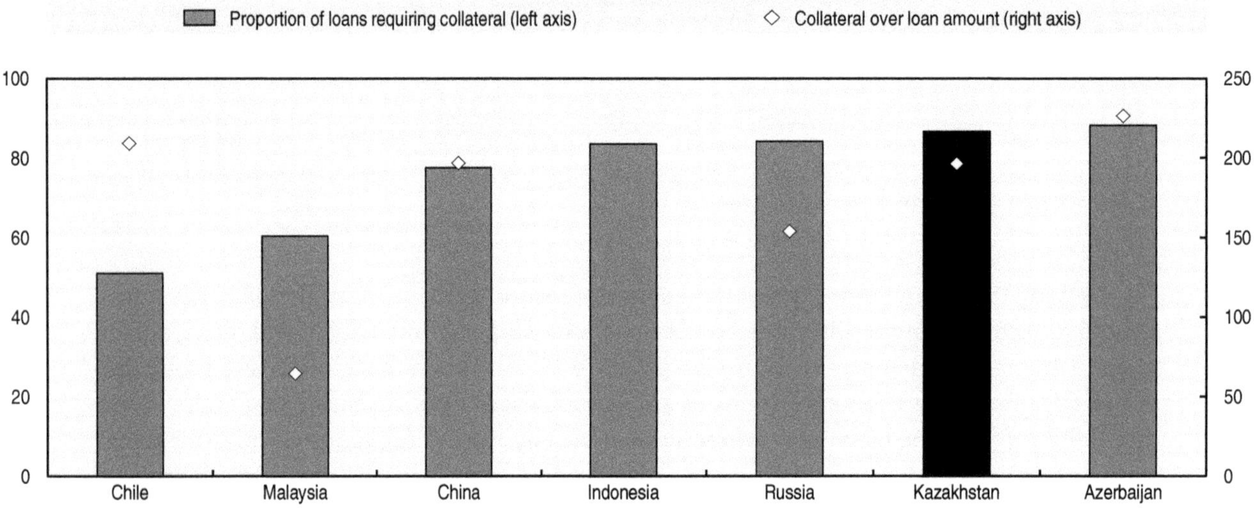

Notes: No comparable data on collateral values available for Indonesia. Latest data for Chile (2012), China (2012), Indonesia (2009) and Malaysia (2007).

Source: Authors' calculations based on World Bank (2015c), *Enterprise Surveys* (database), *www.enterprisesurveys.org*

StatLink *http://dx.doi.org/10.1787/888933289719*

Local stock and bond markets are undeveloped

Beyond bank loans, external financing sources are limited. The stock market is small with a market capitalisation of listed companies of around 25% of GDP on average over 2010-12; and 27% in 2015 (Figure 4.15). Market capitalisation corresponds to the share price multiplied by the number of shares outstanding. Despite its limited size, there are currently some 130 listed companies. The local bond market has a capitalisation of around 16% of GDP (in 2015) when government bonds are excluded. The bond market was negatively affected when the country's pension funds were consolidated into a single entity in 2013, as the merger lowered market liquidity and reduced competition for new bond issues (OECD, 2013b). Bond financing could become more important for the non-financial private sector when corporate governance improves and the credit rating and evaluation framework is enhanced (IMF, 2010). The authorities aim to develop the local capital market further, making it an attractive alternative for bank loans and foreign funding, through the establishment of the planned Astana Financial Centre, which will be built on the site of the Expo2017.

Figure 4.15. **The stock market is underdeveloped**

In % of GDP, average 2010-12

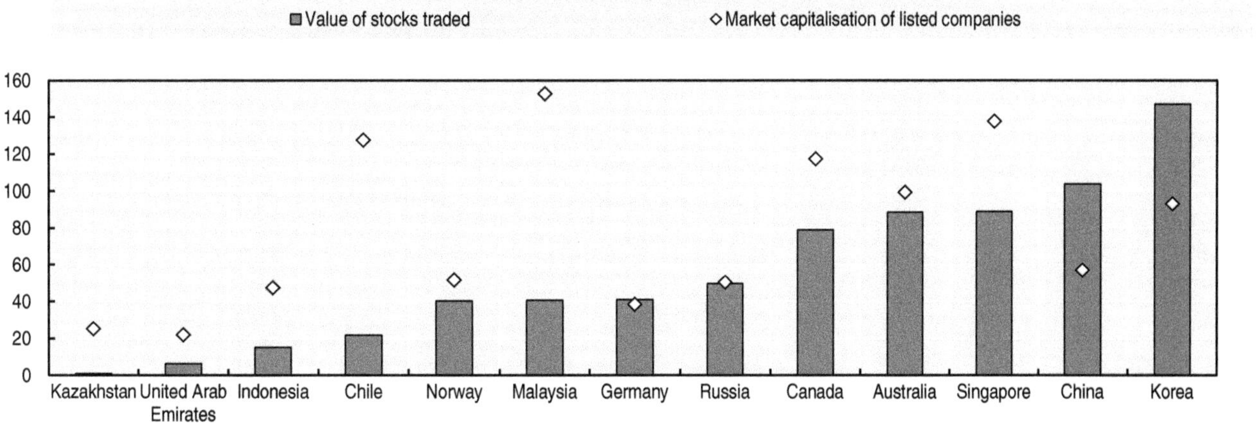

Notes: Market capitalisation (also known as market value) is the share price times the number of shares outstanding. Listed domestic companies are the domestically incorporated companies listed on the country's stock exchanges at the end of the year. Listed companies do not include investment companies, mutual funds, or other collective investment vehicles.

Source: Authors' calculations based on World Bank (2015b), *World Development Indicators* (database), *http://databank.worldbank.org/data/*

StatLink http://dx.doi.org/10.1787/888933289721

Sustained competitiveness requires a boost in private, public and foreign investment

Investment growth in Kazakhstan is lower than growth in GDP and the share of private investment is shrinking. Kazakhstan's share of gross fixed capital formation was around 39% of GDP in 1990, decreased to 17% in 2000 was at levels between 20% and 30% during recent years (Table 4.1). The investment share of GDP is at a similar level in the Russian Federation. These investment shares are relatively low compared to those in China, at 40% in the 1990s and almost 50% during recent years, as well as many more advanced countries. Moreover, constraints on obtaining external financing of the private sector have led to a shrinking share of private investment in total gross capital formation in Kazakhstan. Nonetheless, private investment at almost 70% of total investment remains relatively high in Kazakhstan.

Kazakhstan could boost investment to move sustainably up the value chain. As shown in Chapter 3, the capital stock available per worker in Kazakhstan is only 5-10% of the levels in advanced countries and thus investment will continue to translate effectively into growth and productivity improvements. Moreover, foreign investment makes it possible to absorb global knowledge and to develop domestic capabilities (see section below).[8] The government has taken major steps to develop big and needed infrastructure projects as well as to accelerate domestic and foreign private sector investment. However, as highlighted in previous sections, implementation of these projects, transparent allocation of funds, over-regulation and access to external funds remain major obstacles. Also, accelerating both domestic and foreign investment is challenged by a deteriorating external environment, including lower commodity prices and thus lower expected returns on investment (Magud and Sosa, 2010).

Table 4.1. **Unlike in most benchmarking countries, Kazakhstan's investment intensity is shrinking as is the share of private investment**

	1991-2000		2001-2010		2011-13	
	Total investment (% of GDP)	Private investment (% of total)	Total investment (% of GDP)	Private investment (% of total)	Total investment (% of GDP)	Private investment (% of total)
China	39.0	..	42.6	..	48.7	..
Indonesia	26.7	..	26.0	..	33.8	..
Korea, Rep.	32.5	..	31.8	..	31.0	..
Singapore	34.6	..	24.7	..	28.9	..
Australia	24.8	..	26.9	..	28.1	..
Malaysia	35.8	65.0	22.6	48.6	25.1	58.1
Norway	21.8	..	21.7	..	25.0	..
Canada	19.9	..	22.2	..	24.3	..
Chile	25.0	..	22.0	..	24.2	..
Russian Federation	24.3	64.4	21.6	79.3	24.0	78.6
Kazakhstan	**21.4**	**92.5**	**28.9**	**75.5**	**23.7**	**68.0**
United Arab Emirates	..	..	22.6	59.9	22.5	64.8
Azerbaijan	20.7	120.4	31.5	101.5	22.3	..
Germany	23.8	..	19.9	..	19.6	..

Source: Authors' calculations based on World Bank (2015b), *World Development Indicators* (database).*http://databank.worldbank.org/data/*.

Kazakhstan attracts most foreign direct investment in the region, but relative to growth in GDP, inward FDI flows have slowed

Inward FDI flows have increased considerably over the last decade and Kazakhstan attracts a significant share of the world's total foreign direct investment (FDI). With a volume of gross FDI inflows of USD 22.5 billion in 2012, up from USD 5 billion in 2003, Kazakhstan emerged as one of the top FDI -receiving countries worldwide (also see Figure 3.6. in Chapter 3 for net FDI flows over time). Within the region, Kazakhstan is clearly the largest receiving country. Among Central Asian countries it received 85% of all investment in 2012; among the Commonwealth of Independent States the share was 42% (International Trade Center, 2015).

But inflows of FDI have recently slowed relative to GDP. Inflows relative to the size of the economy are now much lower compared to the 2006-09 period according to statistics of the National Bank of Kazakhstan (Figure 4.16, Panel A). While inward foreign investment as a percentage of GDP was around 10% in the years before the crisis, this share has decreased since 2009 to around 4% in 2014. Throughout the last two decades or so, inward FDI flows relative to GDP have been higher than in the Russian Federation, China and Korea. This also holds for inward FDI stocks, which have been increasing from around 50% of GDP in 2005 to 60% in 2013 (Figure 4.16, Panel B).

Non-resource sectors attract most domestic investment but still not much foreign investment

A snapshot of the investment patterns indicates relatively high domestic investment in non-resource sectors. In 2012, the manufacturing sector received one-third of domestic gross capital formation in Kazakhstan (Figure 4.17). This relatively high share is consistent with fast growth in value added and productivity in this sector (see first section of

Figure 4.16. **Inward FDI flows and stocks in Kazakhstan are high compared to peer countries**

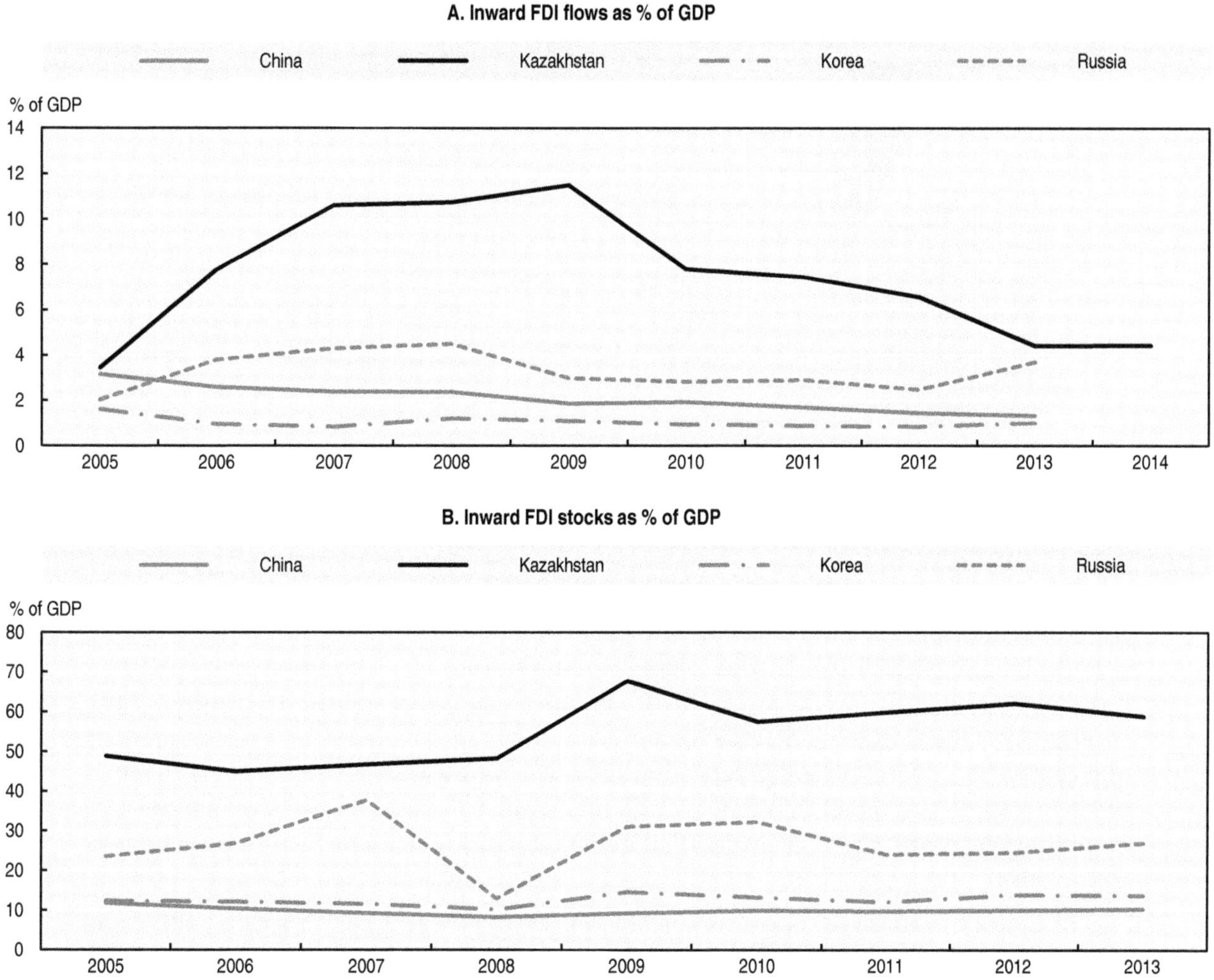

Notes: Panel A shows net investment from abroad as a percentage of GDP. For Kazakhstan, FDI data used is from the National Bank of Kazakhstan and GDP data was received from the Ministry of National Economy. The rest of the data is from UNCTAD. Data used in Panel B is from UNCTAD, including for Kazakhstan.

Source: Authors' calculations based on National Bank of Kazakhstan (2015), *Official Internet Resource of the National Bank of Kazakhstan* (database), *www.nationalbank.kz/?docid=127&switch=english*, data received from the Ministry of National Economy and UNCTAD (2015), *UnctadStat* (database), *http://unctadstat.unctad.org/ReportFolders/reportFolders.aspx*

StatLink http://dx.doi.org/10.1787/888933289730

this chapter). Another 10% went to knowledge- and information-intensive services such as business, financial and ICT. In the future, the development of, and strong investment in, these strategic services are crucial for Kazakhstan's development and competitiveness more broadly (see section below). Despite the banking crisis in 2008, initiated by the bursting of a real estate bubble (see Chapter 3), the construction sector still received more than 40% of total investment in 2012. This is also consistent with a high share of lending to households. Finally, the resource-related sectors accounted for less than 5% of total investment in 2012.

Figure 4.17. **Recent investment is concentrated in manufacturing and construction**

Domestic gross fixed capital formation, by aggregate sectors, 2012

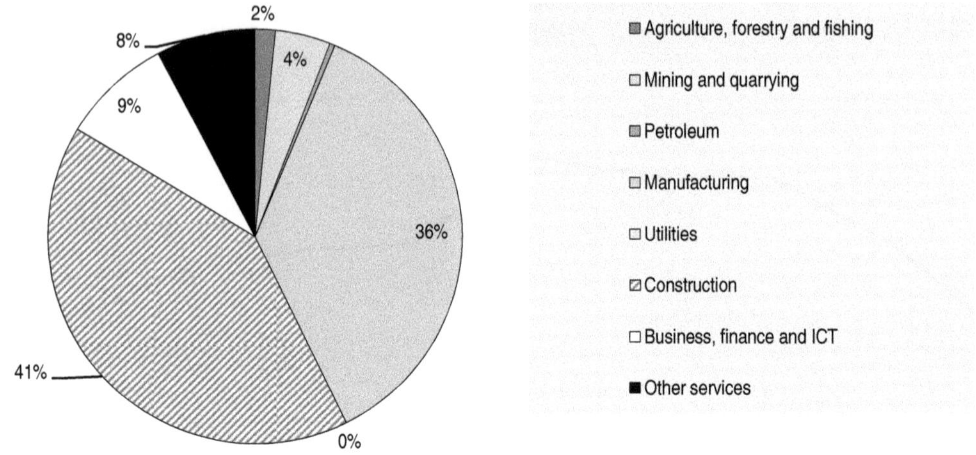

Source: Authors' calculations based on data received from Ministry of National Economy.

StatLink http://dx.doi.org/10.1787/888933289741

More than half of inward foreign investment goes into the extractive sectors. The share of inflows of FDI into activities related to natural resources stood at around 50-60% in Kazakhstan over 2010-14, down from 70-80% before the global economic downturn in 2008. Foreign investment in the extractive sector is split into equal shares for mining activities and geological exploration and prospecting activities (Figure 4.18 and OECD, 2012). In terms of FDI stocks, 55% of total FDI is in exploration and prospecting activities and another 15% in mining. The share of foreign investment in manufacturing remained at around a modest 15% in 2014.

In addition to the high concentration of FDI in extractive sectors, FDI inflows also come from just a few countries of origin. FDI in Kazakhstan is dominated by big investors from only a few countries, particularly the Netherlands and the United States with shares in FDI stocks at 40% and almost 20% (OECD, 2012). Just as with international trade, concentration of inward FDI in terms of countries of origin makes Kazakhstan very vulnerable to economic shocks in these countries, which could lead to the pulling out of investment from Kazakhstan.

Successful implementation of domestic and international investment projects to enhance logistical performance is fundamental

High transaction costs and poor logistics limit the competiveness of Kazakhstan. The country underperforms in the World Bank's Logistical Performance Index (LPI) relative to all the benchmarking countries except Azerbaijan and Russia. The index ranges from 1 (worst) to 5 (best) and measures perceptions of countries' logistics based on six elements. In 2014, Kazakhstan had an overall LPI of 2.7, placing it in 88th place out of 160 countries. Higher LPI is correlated with higher labour productivity implying that Kazakhstan's relatively low logistics performance could be damaging labour productivity (see Annex Figure 4.A1.5). Kazakhstan performs particularly poorly in terms of efficiency of customs procedures

Figure 4.18. **Extractive sectors still attract most foreign investment**

Share of inward FDI flows, by sector aggregates, 2005-14

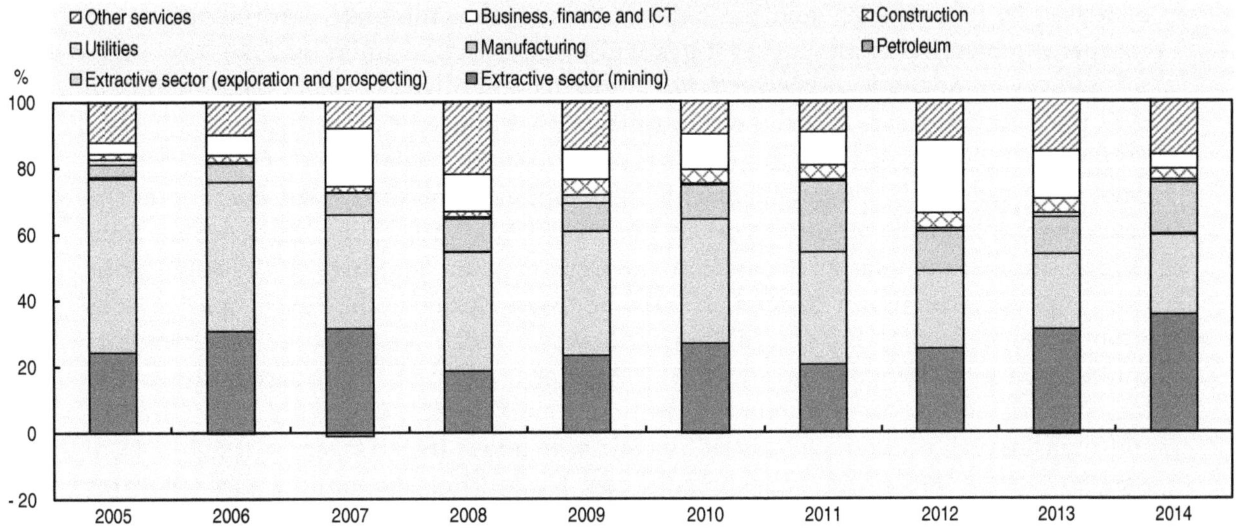

Source: Author's calculations based on International Trade Center (2015), *FDI database*, *www.intracen.org/itc/market-info-tools/statistics-inward-country-industry/*.

StatLink http://dx.doi.org/10.1787/888933289752

and the quality of trade and transport-related infrastructure. In the LPI, the scores of both of these sub-components deteriorated between 2010 and 2014 in Kazakhstan. An Asian Development Bank (ADB, 2013) study estimated that improvements in the transport infrastructure had the potential to reduce road travel time between provincial capitals by 35%; increase rail line-haul by 71%; and decrease the cost of intermodal rail and road container shipment by 24% in Kazakhstan. In other areas of logistics performance, such as the quality of logistic service, tracking and tracing, and ease of arranging competitively priced shipments Kazakhstan also performs relatively badly compared to peers. Part of the relatively bad logistics performance is also a legacy problem of infrastructure links designed for a previous economic structure and the challenge of modernisation in the large territory of Kazakhstan.

The logistic performance of the region is poor and this impacts negatively on Kazakhstan. As Kazakhstan is a landlocked country, its LPI score takes into consideration markets in neighbouring countries that connect them to the world market.[9] Trade links within the CIS countries (except with the Russian Federation) are very weak and markets are not well integrated. Resolving this is a priority and most international organisations active in Kazakhstan such as the *Economic and Social Commission for Asia and the Pacific* (ESCAP), the Eurasian Development Bank, the World Bank and the ADB have implemented various initiatives to expand regional trade opportunities by developing better transport infrastructure and trade facilitation activities.

Despite the challenges that Kazakhstan continues to face in terms of logistics, there are areas where considerable progress is being made. China's New Silk Road will bring many opportunities to Kazakhstan. For manufacturers in inland China, transportation time by sea can take up to 60 days and Kazakhstan offers an alternate route. Following the opening of a railway border crossing at Khorgos on the Eastern border with China in 2012, the volume of 40 foot containers passing from China to Europe through Kazakhstan increased by 80% to 6 600 and the head of Kazlogistics, the state run transportation company, projects that annual revenues will reach USD 3.5 billion by 2020. The state-run railway company Kazakhstan Temir Zholy has promised to spend USD 44 billion over the next five years to reduce the transit time between Chongqing in south-west China and Duisburg in Germany via Kazakhstan, Russia, Belarus and Poland from 14 days to 10. Growth in cargo transport is also supported by the recent opening of the Lianyungang logistics terminal port in the Yellow Sea, providing a direct route from Europe through the Russian Federation and Central Asian countries to the Asia-Pacific region. A customs union formed in 2011 between Kazakhstan, Russia and Belarus supports facilitated traffic across Eurasia: however recent geopolitical developments could jeopardise this (Mkrtchyan, 2013).[10] Further integration of Kazakhstan into the international transport and communication routes is planned with the "Eurasian transcontinental transport corridor", which will allow free transit of freights from Asia to Europe. Moreover, Kazakhstan's new Nurly Zhol economic policy allocates considerable funding to well-targeted infrastructure projects (see more details in section below).

Governance and regulation are fundamental for Kazakhstan's economic reform process

Boosting productivity and diversification as proposed in the country's 2050 Strategy requires effective industrial policies and a competitive business environment. Diversification and productivity will help to overcome the potential threat of a middle-income trap and support the country's goal to become one of the 30 most developed nations by 2050. More broadly, the 2050 Strategy involves ambitious objectives in many areas such as developing economic policies based on the principles of profitability, return on investment, and competitiveness; providing support to entrepreneurship, particularly SMEs and public-private partnerships (PPPs); re-launching the privatisation process; designing new social policies that balance social guarantees and personal responsibility; and advancing the development of a knowledge-based, sustainable economy.

Effective implementation and co-ordination of industrial policy programmes can support competitiveness and diversification

In co-ordination with the 2050 Strategy, the government has launched various medium-term industrial policy programmes. The industrial policy programmes are implemented by the Ministry of Energy, the Ministry of Investment and Development, and the Ministry of Agriculture. The financing of the various projects is primarily channelled through the Development Bank of Kazakhstan (for big infrastructure projects, loans are at least KZT 30 million or USD 165 000), Baiterek National Holding and particularly the DAMU Entrepreneurship Development Fund (for financial support of SMEs) and KazAgro (for financial support to rural and agricultural areas). Before the 2050 Strategy and associated programmes Kazakhstan already had an active industrial policy to foster diversification, with limited success (Box 4.2).

The State Programme on Accelerated Industrial and Innovative Development (SPAIID, 2010-2014) was initiated in 2010, four years before the announcement of the 2050 strategy (see Table 4.1). Singapore and Malaysia, among other countries, were taken as peers to develop the programme. In fact, Singapore, today a leading service economy, also went through profound industrialisation with a strategic and well-implemented industrial policy (Box 4.3).

Box 4.2. **Kazakhstan has been repeatedly hit by external economic crises and its past policy efforts were not sufficient to make the country more resilient through a more diversified economic structure**

The industrial strategy of the government of Kazakhstan has evolved in the period since independence. Between 1991 and 1995 real GDP decreased by 31% as the economy suffered in the aftermath of the breakup of the USSR. There was significant migration of ethnic Russians, Germans and Slavs; Soviet trade links collapsed; production networks were disrupted; and from 1992-1994, the country experienced hyperinflation in excess of 1 000% per year. The government responded by trying to liberalise the economy and pursued reforms including deregulating prices; abolishing public bodies responsible for planning and distribution; removing import substitution barriers; and developing banking and customs systems.

By 1996-1997, the Kazakhstani economy was relatively stable. But the Russian currency crisis of 1998 forced the country to devalue the tenge in order to maintain macroeconomic stability and to boost exports. In 1997 President Nursultan Nazarbayev outlined the Kazakhstan 2030 Strategy which was inspired by the experiences of countries such as Canada, the Republic of Korea, Malaysia and Norway. The goal of the strategy was to transform Kazakhstan into a modern industrial and service-based economy by 2030. Long term priorities included economic growth founded on an open market economy; domestic political stability; and improving the health, education and well-being of citizens. Public policy focused on specific sectors with the goal of meeting the basic needs of the population; taking advantage of the country's natural resources and geography; and reducing the share of imported products particularly in sectors such as agriculture where they accounted for 60% and pharmaceuticals where they made up 94%.

Between 2000 and 2007, the average growth rate was 10%, driven by high commodity prices, the effects of the continuing structural reforms and practical policies designed to promote diversification. The government approved a strategy of industrial innovation development for 2003-2015 as part of the long term strategy of Kazakhstan 2030. Recognising that a successful modern industrial economy should not be overly reliant on oil, the plan aimed to triple the 2000 level of labour productivity by 2015, promote an average annual growth rate of 8% to 8.4% in the processing industries, increase research and development (R&D) expenditure as a share of GDP and to halve the 2000 level of energy intensity. Public institutions such as the Development Bank of Kazakhstan and the National Innovation Fund were also established by the government to help implement the Kazakhstan 2030 strategy.

The global economic crisis and the domestic banking crisis of 2008-09 adversely affected Kazakhstan's industrial policies. As a result of low domestic deposits and underdeveloped local financial markets, banks had borrowed excessively in international capital markets to fuel credit expansion. The Kazakhstani banks were overly dependent on cheap money based on the expectation of the country's future resource revenues. As a result of the crisis, economic growth in Kazakhstan has been constrained by insufficient credit as bank assets have deteriorated and non-performing loans are high. The number of products exported with comparative advantage fell considerably between 2005 and 2010. A favourable oil price contributed to the reduction in diversification implying that the various diversification programmes had failed substantively to promote sustained diversification.

Source: ADB (2013) and Ministry of Industry and New Technologies of the Republic of Kazakhstan (2014).

There were a number of possible objections to the design of SPAIID 2010-14. The plan highlighted seven priority sectors (agriculture, construction and construction material, oil and gas products and infrastructure, metallurgy and metal products, chemicals and pharmaceuticals, energy, and transport and telecommunications infrastructure). In itself, the selection of these broad sectors was reasonable given that Kazakhstan has a RCA in some specific products in all these sectors and thus further diversification into related sectors could be targeted (see previous section). But the design was imprecise with respect to the way in which the various sectors were to be supported and what part of the value chain was supposed to be developed. Also, the vast number of different available support measures and initiatives made a co-ordinated development of these industries

Box 4.3. **Singapore, a leading service economy, went through profound industrialisation with a strategic and well implemented industrial policy**

Singapore is a small economy with an estimated population of 5.4 million (2013) and an area that makes the city-state one of the smallest countries in the world. Nevertheless it has been a conspicuous example of economic growth since its independence from Malaysia in 1965. Even then, its geographic situation had made its port a major hub for trade. At independence, however, it had a small domestic market and much of the population lived in poverty (IDE-JETRO and WTO, 2011).

Ever since the government established the Economic Development Board, it has pursued a strategy of export-led growth in combination with well-targeted, successful industrial and technology policies. On independence, Singapore implemented a strategy of openness and sought to attract foreign direct investment (FDI). It invested heavily in education to build a skilled workforce and in physical infrastructure to facilitate logistics. In the 50 years to 2010, the share of manufacturing in GDP increased from 11% in the 1960s to almost 30% in the 1990s. By 2010 it had slipped to 23%, while the share of services had risen.

FDI helped not only to boost the economy directly; it also facilitated the transfer of technology and innovation, which provided leverage for further innovations. Continuous investment in infrastructure, logistics, the development of services, and education attracted FDI and enticed multinational corporations to stay (Lee and Tan, 2006).

When other Asian countries emerged as competitive manufacturers, the development of products related to ones already existing helped facilitate Singapore's gradual diversification into new, higher-technology products. The government reacted early and quickly to adjust to changing conditions, promoting structural change that incorporated technology upgrades and the development of services. Over the last decade, the focus of services has shifted from basic commercial activities to business and financial services, which today make up 27% of GDP (IMF, 2005 and Jankowska et al., 2012).

Nevertheless, challenges lie ahead. Other cities, especially in China, are exerting increasing economic pull and Singapore's ageing population will be an obstacle to any kind of growth strategy. The government is seeking to address those challenges through targeted migration strategies and priority investment in skills and education, especially adult learning (OECD, 2013c). The aim is to support innovation and new sources of growth and enable Singaporean firms to seize emerging opportunities. Singapore is also supporting SMEs and their R&D capacities as part of a multi-agency assistance strategy to help local enterprises enhance their productivity.

Given the particular characteristics of Singapore, not all its strategies are transferable to any developing country. Nevertheless, it is a major showcase for skills and education being a continuous advantage at all stages of development. Development policies are designed with clear vision and quantitative targets, while dedicated agencies ensure implementation and monitor results. High and continuously improving standards of education have helped to attract and maintain high levels of FDI, move the manufacturing sector up the product ladder, and sustain the recent shift towards more modern service activities. With the emergence of ICT-based services, the importance of the services sector for development has become even more pronounced. Nevertheless, the country's strong manufacturing base has been its growth base and its interaction with the service sector has delivered multiplier effects on economic growth.

difficult (Table 4.2). State support to these sectors included the state-funded development of physical infrastructure (information and communications, energy, and transport) and development of human capital, lower administrative barriers particularly in special economic zones (SEZs), guidelines on technical regulations and the creation of a more business-friendly environment to attract FDI. Support allocated directly to firms was only available for Kazakhstan firms. Moreover, various central government bodies and institutes were responsible for the co-ordination of the programme, making a co-ordinated and well-structured implementation difficult. At the same time, involvement in the implementation of the programme of regional governments and businesses themselves was limited. Financing came exclusively from the state budget.

Table 4.2. **The design of the new industrial policy programme (2015-19) is built on the experience of the previous 2010-14 programme**

	SPAIID 2010-14	New SPAIID 2015-19
Goal	• Economy diversification, increase in manufacturing industry share and reduction of oil dependence	• Smart diversification – accelerated development of manufacturing industry
Support receivers	• Imprecise industry focus, many industrial programmes • Support of Kazakhstan companies only	• Focus on narrow set of industrial activities and national clusters • Flexible approach to industrial priorities through ranking • Competitive selection of companies in regional clusters for receiving state support • Support possible for foreign companies
Support measures	• Wide instruments spectrum for all industries • Many instruments were not used	• Limited set of instruments • Different set of instruments for three sector groups (primary, market-oriented, innovation sectors) • Centralisation of project selection procedures to increase effectiveness and transparency
Action plan	• Many industrial programmes • Some actions are undeveloped	• Cancellation of unused industrial programmes • One unified action plan • Attention to the elaboration and details of individual events
Realisation	• Several departments take responsibility for Programme's realisation • Some development institutes are also responsible for Programme's realisation	• Creation on the basis of several development institutes by a unified National Institute of Industrial Development • Introduction of performance contracts
Roles of business and regions	• Minimisation of business and regions involvement in the Programme development • Business and regions are executors of the Programme	• Active business participation in Programme's development and realisation. Effective collaboration with National Chamber of Entrepreneurs • Active participation of regions in Programme. Realisation of regional industrial development strategies, new role of social entrepreneur corporations
Financing model	• Programme is mainly antirecessionary • Full-scale financial state support of business	• Balanced financing model • Active attraction of private funds for Programme realisation

Source: Foreign Investors' Council (2013), *Industrialization Concept 2015-2019*.

Despite these possible flaws in the programme design, the process of diversification of the economy was successfully launched through SPAIID 2010-14. The development of the manufacturing industry, for example in the area of transport equipment and chemical products, has been accelerated since its initiation (see first section of this chapter). Nonetheless, non-resource industries remain very small in Kazakhstan and only a few of these sectors are internationally competitive (also see previous sections in this chapter).

The succeeding programme "Industrial and innovative development programme 2015-19" was announced by the president in 2014 with the aim of drastically accelerating industrial development.[11] The programme is a logical continuation of SPAIID 2010-14 and takes into account the experience of its implementation (Table 4.2). While the new programme still prioritises many different sectors (including the iron and steel industry; non-ferrous metallurgy; refining; oil and gas chemistry; food; agricultural chemistry; chemicals for industry; transport equipment, accessories and engines; electrical machinery and apparatus; agricultural machinery; railway equipment; machinery and equipment for the extractive sectors; machinery and equipment for oil refining and oil extracting industry; construction materials), it focuses primarily on the development of processing activities within these sectors. Kazakhstan already has an RCA in selected products in all priority sectors and thus fostering the development in related sector is appropriate. The over-arching objectives of the programme are: accelerating the development of the manufacturing industry, improving the efficiency and increasing the added value in the priority sectors, increasing exports of non-resource products, keeping productive employment, creating innovation clusters, and promoting entrepreneurship and development of SMEs in manufacturing. Target indicators to measure success of the programme in the priority sectors include real output growth, productivity growth, employment growth, reduction of energy intensity.

The new programme has clearly defined instruments for support that are targeted at specific recipients (companies, regional bodies, industries as a whole). They include: i) access to financing (debt financing, interest rate subsidies, government guarantees and financial incentives for large investment projects) targeted mostly at companies; ii) infrastructure development and modernisation (including for SEZs and industrial parks) targeted primarily at regional bodies but also directly at companies; iii) specialised services (special grants for example for innovation projects or export support, and education programmes) for companies and regions; iv) effective regulation (roadmap for administrative barriers reduction, technical regulation, tariff regulation) applied most directly to specific industries; and finally government procurement (Ministry of Industry and New Technologies of the Republic of Kazakhstan, 2014, and Foreign Investors' Council, 2013).

In addition, the recently announced countercyclical economic policy "Nurly Zhol" (The Path to the Future) (2015-19) is being implemented to accelerate structural reforms. During the last decades the country has diverted funds from exports of raw materials to the National Fund (see Chapter 3). The president announced Nurly Zhol is to use some of these funds during the current economic slowdown for the acceleration of structural transformation, in particular the development of transport, energy, industrial and social infrastructure and SMEs.[12]

Enhancing government effectiveness in the area of industrial policy is crucial (see also Chapter 5). In the end, implementation of the newly launched programmes will depend on the success of attracting FDI. For example, the share of government budget funds in the total amount of funding required for SPAIID 2015-19 amounts to only 20%. Similarly, the share of state funds required for the implementation of Nurly Zhol corresponds to 15% (Nazarbayev, 2014). To attract the required funds and successfully realise the objectives, Kazakhstan's industrial policy programmes require better co-ordination across ministries and key stakeholders including the private sector (Ministry of Industry and New Technologies of the Republic of Kazakhstan, 2014). A well-structured overview of all programmes and co-ordinated objectives, implementation and evaluation is missing. In the future, with the creation of the Industrial Development Commission and the National Institute of Industrial Development, the various industrial development initiatives could become more co-ordinated and implementation facilitated. Moreover, contracts will be increasingly performance-based. The experience of the SPAIID 2010-14 showed the importance of improvement in this area: many programmes were delayed and faced difficulties in being implemented; many of the programmes that were implemented failed to meet their objectives: the practical implementation of around 30% of the projects was unsuccessful. For example, it was planned for a project in the textile sector to be supported by public funds, but the relevant government agency was not yet prepared for cotton production (e.g. customs and legislations to export cotton had yet to be established).

Further privatisation and private sector development require an enabling environment for enhanced competition and private investment

State companies and conglomerates dominate the business landscape. Public ownership has fallen compared to the Soviet era, but state entities still account for some 30% to 40% of GDP. The first wave of privatisation created powerful businessmen, who have built up conglomerates stretching across various sectors from resource exploitation and the manufacture of high-value goods in state or private firms to banking (Rahmetov, 2011) (Figure 4.19). They have strong incentives to oppose market reforms that threaten their respective monopolies or oligopolies. Beyond extensive financial assets, powerful business groupings have influential allies in state structures, their own banks and media outlets, as well as direct or mediated access to the president. The president has carefully managed a complex system of these competing groups and skilfully ensured a balance of power between these major business groupings (Kjærnet et al., 2008).

Figure 4.19. **Wealthiest individuals have a relatively high net worth**

Combined net worth of the five wealthiest individuals in % of GDP, 2013

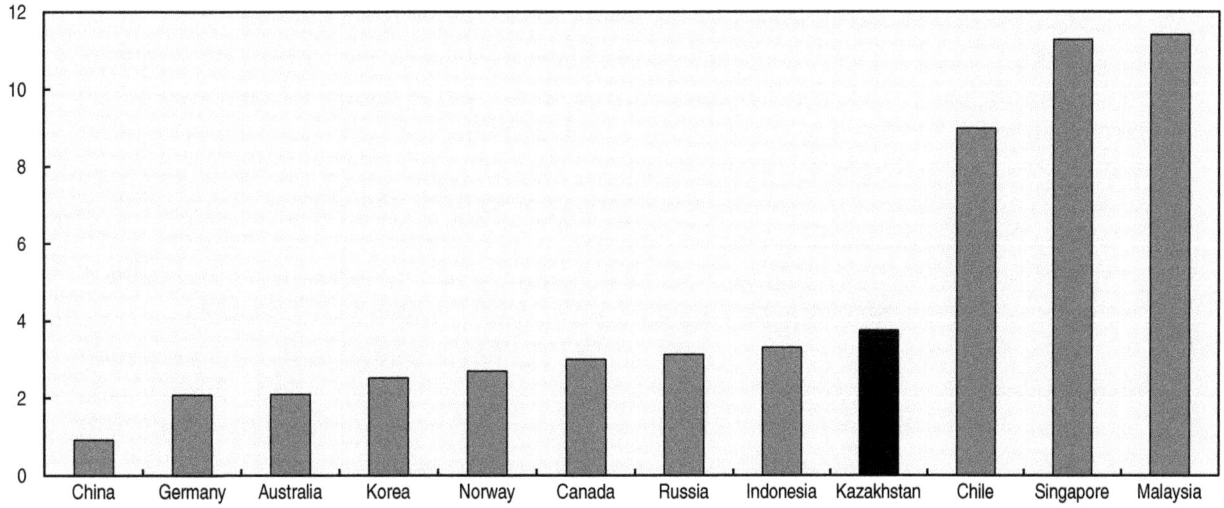

Notes: No individuals in Azerbaijan with recorded net worth over USD 1 billion; only four in the United Arab Emirates.

Source: Authors' calculations based on Forbes (2015), *Forbes The World's Billionaires*, *www.forbes.com/billionaires/list/#version:static* and World Bank (2015b), *World Development Indicators* (database), *http://databank.worldbank.org/data/.*

StatLink *http://dx.doi.org/10.1787/888933289760*

The sovereign wealth fund Samruk-Kazyna was established to enhance the competitiveness and sustainability of the national economy, and to limit the effects of negative external shocks on domestic economic growth. At the end of 2013, its assets amounted to USD 92 billion, roughly half the country's GDP. The fund manages all non-financial public companies, including the oil and gas company KazMunayGas and the national railway company Kazakhstan Temir Zholy. Most of these companies have been owned by the state since the Soviet era. It also owns the banks rescued during the recent banking crisis, although they are gradually being sold. The fund is run on a commercial basis and aims to increase the long-term value of its assets. It is managed separately from the state budget, but most of its profits are paid to the budget as dividends, while sometimes loans or transfers are received to make targeted investments.

Baiterek assists sustainable economic development of the non-oil economy by providing financial and investment support to priority sectors. With this core mission, the holding also aims to foster the diversification process, attract more investment, develop innovation clusters and improve the corporate governance system in its subsidiaries. Its subsidiaries include the Kazakhstan Development Bank, the Investment Fund of Kazakhstan, the Housing Construction Savings Bank of Kazakhstan, the Kazakhstan Mortgage Company, the KazExportGarant, the Damu Entrepreneurship Development Fund, the National Agency for Technological Development, the Kazakhstan Mortgage Guarantee Fund, the Kazyna Capital Management, and the Stress Assets Fund. At the end of 2013, the holding owned assets of USD 12 billion. Its strategy is closely linked to the state programmes, in particular "Business roadmap – 2020", and "Sustainable housing – 2020".

Kazakhstan has announced a new wave of privatisations. A review of all state-owned companies was carried out in 2014 as part of a comprehensive privatisation plan. Of the 782 assets to be transferred to the private sector, around 100 belong to Samruk-Kazyna and 34 are organisations owned by the central government. The remaining assets are currently controlled by municipalities, or socio-entrepreneurial corporations (developed by regional institutions, mainly to support agriculture). Assets in both the atomic energy and oil and gas sectors will also be sold, along with stakes in electricity distribution networks. The privatisation would allow Samruk-Kazyna to focus on its core business and develop industries that are deemed profitable in the long run and in the national interest, e.g. green energy. An additional 380 state entities will be reorganised or liquidated. Moreover, in April 2015, amendments to the competition law limit and reduce state involvement in business activities (through the so-called "Rules of the yellow pages"). The amendments prohibit the establishment of SMEs by legal entities with more than 50% government participation and hinder the creation of subsidiaries by such state entities, if private companies are already doing business in a given sector. Informed by the competition authority, the government will annually publish a list of state entities to be privatised.

While privatisation processes are transparent, the implementation of the privatisation plan is subject to challenges. Managing the privatisation process in a transparent way is complicated given the underdeveloped local capital market (see also next section) and the potential to further strengthen the already powerful conglomerates. The first of the "people's initial public offerings", which exclusively target Kazakhstan's citizens, raised considerable interest. By July 2015, 189 assets had already been privatised, generating KZT 69 billion. The bidding process is made transparent using electronic tools, which lower the possibility of influencing the results. Moreover, the results are published in printed newspapers as well as specialised websites.[13] To reach prospective buyers in remote areas, the national post service acts as an agent for brokers.

Smooth privatisation and development of a competitive private sector are also complicated by a non-transparent regulatory environment. Interest by local and foreign investors in purchasing privatised assets or in competing in markets dominated by large state or private firms may be reduced because of (sometimes non-transparent) regulatory burdens and price controls, including, for example, in the energy distribution networks and in telecommunications. For instance, a monopoly on fourth-generation (4G) licences in Kazakhstan is acting as a barrier to competition in the telecommunications sector, where one small, state-owned company enjoys the exclusive right to operate 4G services. The telecoms regulator argues that no additional frequencies are available, has defended the monopoly on national security grounds, and has indicated that new 4G licences will not be issued until 2018 (EIU, 2014). Such a policy is likely to have a negative impact on local and foreign investment and may affect investment appetite in other sectors.

More generally, Kazakhstan has ample room to lower regulatory burdens and improve the business climate. Kazakhstan ranks 77th out of 189 countries based on the ease of doing business (World Bank, 2015b). Although it has narrowed the gap with the best performers, ample room remains for improvement, in particular in the fields of arranging construction permits, trading across borders and getting electricity. On the other hand, registering property and paying taxes are found to be very straightforward. Also, according to OECD's FDI restrictiveness index 2013, Kazakhstan has relatively low restrictions compared to, for example, China, Indonesia and Malaysia (see Annex Figure 4.A1.3). The relative ease of starting a business has led to a high share of inactive firms, over 50% in 2015, as many starting entrepreneurs are presumably caught off guard by administrative procedures and encounter difficulties in closing their business (World Bank, 2014). Moreover, Kazakhstani firms most frequently mention corruption as the key constraint in doing business (World Bank, 2015c). Despite a small improvement in recent years, corruption is perceived to be widespread (Figure 4.20; see also Chapter 5). In particular, more than half of the respondents in the latest Transparency International survey felt that police, judiciary, education systems, medical services and civil servants were corrupt (Transparency International, 2014), reflecting that public power is often used for private gain (Satpayev, 2014). The recent anti-corruption strategy for 2015-2025 aims to eradicate conditions that foster corruption, fight corruption in the public, quasi-public and private sectors and intensify public control.

Figure 4.20. **Corruption is perceived to be widespread**

Index from 0 (highly corrupt) to 100 (very clean), 2014

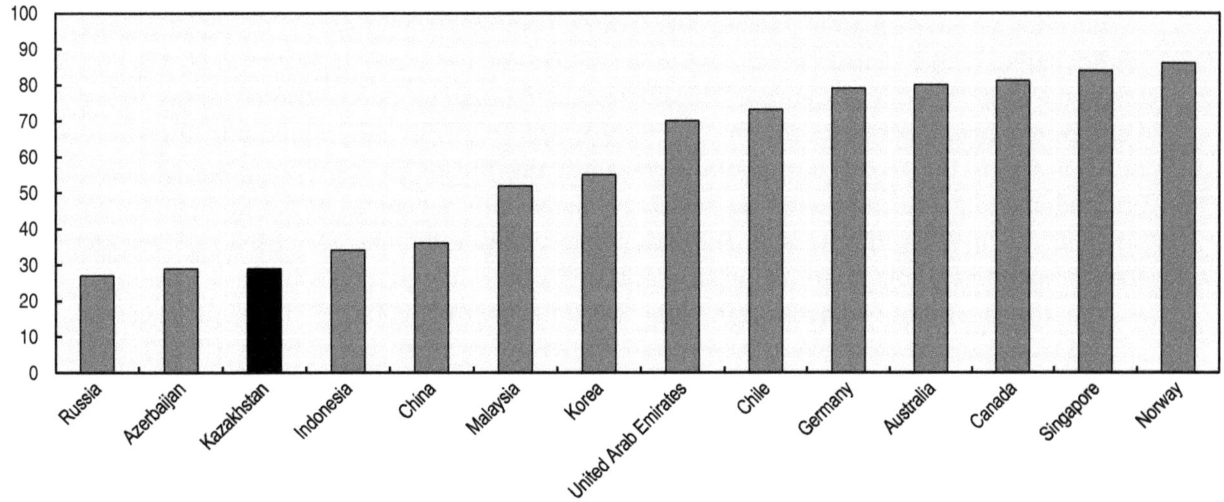

Source: Authors' calculations based on Transparency International (2014), *Corruption Perceptions Index* (database); *www.transparency.org/cpi2014*

StatLink http://dx.doi.org/10.1787/888933289777

These constraints make the development of a prosperous SME sector difficult. The share of SMEs in Kazakhstan's GDP remains low, hovering between 17% and 20% depending on oil prices (Jappar and Jandosova, 2013). The state programme "Business Roadmap – 2020" aims to increase the SME share in GDP to 50% by 2020. Small and medium-sized business entities are already increasingly important for job creation, accounting for some 30% of total employment compared to 26% a decade ago. Effective implementation of the privatisation plan could provide an important impetus to the expansion of the SME sector.

Developing high-quality and flexible skills is essential

Tight coherence between education policies and technological absorption mechanisms contributes to an upgraded, more diversified economy. In many middle-income countries, recent improvements in educational attainment and deeper integration into value chains have often not been sufficient to ensure the competitiveness of the labour force and continuously increasing market shares. This suggests that education policies need to make it possible continuously to adapt the supply of skills to the changing needs in the economy.

Educational attainment is improving, but the quality of education remains low and skills may be better adapted to needs

Educational attainment has progressed continuously, but the quality of education is still an issue in Kazakhstan. In 2010, the average number of years of total schooling stood at above 11 in Kazakhstan; almost as high as in OECD countries (see Annex Figure 4.A1.6). The strikingly higher attainments of secondary and tertiary education could yield a larger crop of skilled labour at competitive labour costs and increase the share of young people in good jobs. However, the quality of education is still lower in Kazakhstan than in many of its peers. According to the latest results of the Programme for International Student Assessment (PISA), out of 65 entities (countries or cities), Kazakhstan students at the age of 15 years ranked 49th in mathematics, 63rd in reading and 52nd in science (see Chapter 2 for a more detailed discussion and Box 4.2. below on recent policies to address the problem of quality).

Compared with some middle-income countries, the share of firms considering an inadequately educated workforce as a constraint is low. Compared to the 13% of firms mentioning an inadequately educated workforce as a key constraint in the 2013 survey for Kazakhstan, this share is much higher in Chile (41%), the Russian Federation (25%) and Malaysia (20%). The lower figure in Kazakhstan could also be due to the economy being still less sophisticated compared to the comparator countries mentioned and the share of firms facing that constraint could increase in the future. In contrast to Kazakhstan, an inadequately educated workforce is more likely to be a constraint for SMEs than for larger firms in Chile, the Russian Federation, Germany and China (Figure 4.21). Despite the comparatively low share of firms mentioning an inadequately educated workforce as a major constraint in Kazakhstan, only two other factors (corruption and practices of the informal sector) were mentioned more often. Among all surveyed firms in 2013, 63% expected that total annual sales would increase if an inadequately educated workforce was no longer an obstacle.

There may still be a skills mismatch in Kazakhstan's manufacturing sector. As many as 80% of the workers in manufacturing received some training or education, before or after joining the firm, and can thus be considered as skilled (Annex Figure 4.A1.7). This share is high compared to most other benchmarking countries, which contrast with an inadequately educated workforce being mentioned among the most important constraints in Kazakhstan. Indeed, employers in Kazakhstan do not seem particularly satisfied with the support they receive from government to develop workforce skills (Álvarez-Galván, 2014). Thus, manufacturing workers' skills and competencies may not be adapted to the current or the future needs of firms; trained workers may not have a pivotal position within manufacturing firms; or the quality of training/professional skills could be low and efforts spent in training are not reflected in the firm's business operations.

Figure 4.21. **An inadequately educated workforce is more likely to be a key constraint among larger firms in Kazakhstan**

Percentage of firms, by size

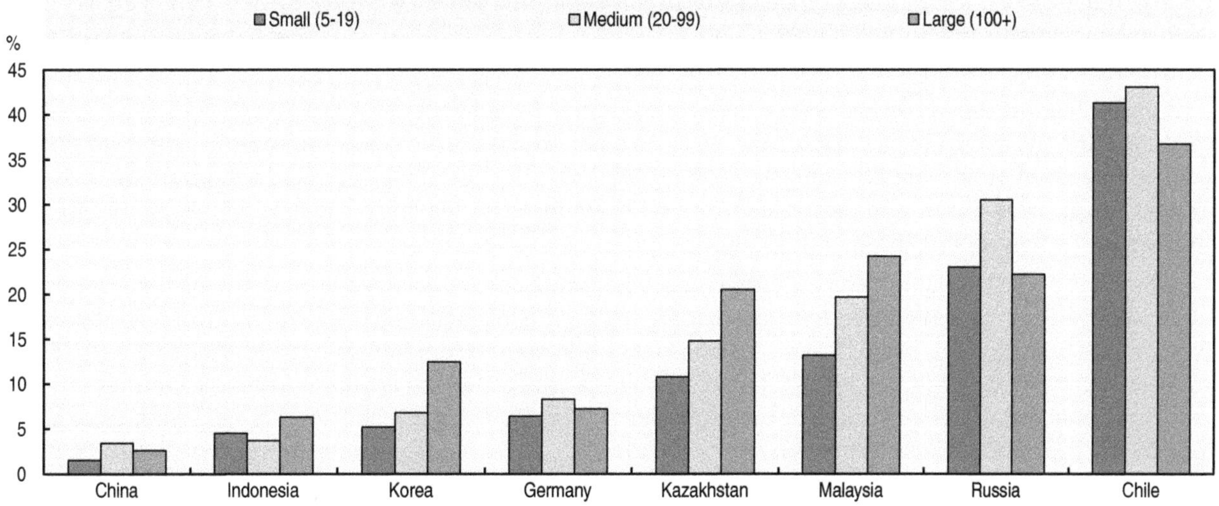

Notes: Year of survey in parentheses: Kazakhstan (2013), Azerbaijan (2013), Russia (2013), Chile (2012), China (2012), Indonesia (2009), Malaysia (2007), Germany (2005), Korea (2005). Six hundred firms were surveyed in Kazakhstan.

Source: Authors' calculations based on World Bank (2015c), *Enterprise Surveys* (database), *www.enterprisesurveys.org*.

StatLink *http://dx.doi.org/10.1787/888933289789*

Kazakhstan has a new strategy to enhance the quality of education and better to supply the changing skills needed

Education and skills policies should address the issue of coherence between investment in skills and technological needs in the economy (OECD, 2013a). Indeed, converging economies often follow imitation-based development strategies. They do not, therefore, require the same type or amount of investment in advanced education as countries close to the technological frontier (Aghion et al., 2005). This even applies to within-country investments. As an example, a study of the long-term growth effects of educational spending in the 50 states of the United States showed that returns to education spending are higher when states distant from the technological frontier invest in technical education and when states at the technological frontier invest in research-type education (Acemoglu et al., 2006).

Kazakhstan invests to enhance the quality of skills and to better co-ordinate their development with the demand from industry. Education systems need to be flexible to respond to the demand of their economies. To that end, countries can assess the skills needs of their economies with surveys, including those directed towards firms, and then allocate public funding accordingly, especially in tertiary education and vocational training. Kazakhstan invests to improve skills in the economy, for example, through the training programmes of the Damu Entrepreneurship Development Fund or the Roadmap of employment 2020 adopted in 2007. More recently, Kazakhstan has recently increased efforts to improve the quality of education, particularly of vocational training, better to supply the changing skills needed (Box 4.4). The strategy involves the development of "points of growth" – selected new, world-class educational institutions in the area

Box 4.4. Kazakhstan's recent efforts to upgrade the educational system

School enrolment is compulsory between the ages of 6-7 and 17 and compulsory schooling is provided free of charge. A distinction exists between public schools, the 97 special schools, and the 16 "Nazarbayev intellectual schools" which select and educate 10 655 pupils and are used to test curricula and pedagogical reforms. In addition, the country has 99 private schools. At the tertiary level, Kazakhstan has 126 universities with the Nazarbayev University being the most selective and prestigious.

A big problem of the education system is the low quality of teachers and this relates to the poor incentive pay structure. Teachers are paid badly; they work on an hourly basis for 18 hours a week (but their workload can be increased to at most 27 hours) and the profession is not socially esteemed in the country. In 2012, a new system was put in place to create three different levels of teachers under which teachers can get higher pay by progressing through the levels.

In September 2011, Holding Kasipkor, under the Ministry of Education was created with the goal of developing a network of leading vocational educational institutions capable of educating the workforce to a high standard and in line with the needs of employers. The aim is that the expertise developed in the leading colleges will be transferred to 278 state colleges by 2020. Kazakhstan has a total of 467 state colleges. Technical and vocational education and training (TVET) can play an important role in improving the skill level of the labour force as it can fill the gap between basic education and occupation-specific training provided by employers. TVET is also valuable in allowing workers to upgrade their skills or move into more relevant industries.

The current system of TVET in Kazakhstan is not appropriately aligned with the needs of employers, teachers lack appropriate experience and the resources of the colleges are out of date. The TVET system is not considered prestigious and this motivates teenagers to aim for higher education as opposed to vocational training. One of Holding Kasipkor's initiatives has been to implement a mandatory independent qualification certificate which aims to separate the education process from the assessment of education quality. The goal is to develop teachers who are practice- orientated and to ensure they receive training and up-skilling at least once every five years.

The new TVET system aims to create two world-class colleges between 2015 and 2017 that will train 3 060 students in tourism and hospitality; construction and utility services; computing; the energy industry; engineering and design. In conjunction, four new inter-regional centres with a capacity of 2 800 students will be opened. The idea of these colleges is to combine classroom and applied learning. They aim to engage employers at every stage of the creation and operation of the colleges to ensure that syllabuses are designed with the needs of the labour market in mind.

In the area of tertiary education, Kazakhstan has co-developed with the World Bank and a series of leading education institutes (Duke, Carnegie, and Kennedy School of Government) an agenda to better integrate education, science and industry. Accordingly, early in 2011, Kazakhstan's Majilis passed a new law, "On the status of Nazarbayev University, Nazarbayev Intellectual Schools and Nazarbayev Fund." The enactment granted the Nazarbayev University and the "Intellectual Schools" a range of "special status" exemptions from education ministry regulations and mandates. The law granted NU administrators the authority to set academic and governance practices in line with "Western educational standards." It also called for the "integration of education, science and industry – the inseparability of educational process from scientific and practical activities in [the] university and [the] provision of strategic partnerships with science and business organisations."

Source: Kasipkor (2014), Republic of Kazakhstan (2007), Ruff and Horn (2012).

of secondary education, vocational training and tertiary education –, which after full implementation can spill over to the entire educational system. With respect to vocational training, the curricula of students (including practical, workplace training – "dual system") are increasingly conducted in co-ordination with firms in the respective industries – a good practice from the perspective of the OECD and well implemented in Germany and Switzerland, for example (OECD, 2014a). Effective implementation of these plans is essential for Kazakhstan's long-term competitiveness.

Beyond improving the educational system as such, Kazakhstan can support firms by encouraging life-long training, in-house or external to the firm. In fact, the government has a key role to play, as firms may have little incentive to finance training for their employees, if they are then hired by competitors. Recent research into Chinese and Indonesian manufacturing firms shows that companies that invest in training their workers enjoy higher productivity levels than firms which do not (OECD, 2014a). Training helps workers use equipment more effectively and can be used to standardise production processes. The effects of workforce training, however, vary from company to company and facility to facility, shaped by a host of other factors, including employees' educational qualifications and skills levels. Put briefly, the development of human capital tends to involve many mutually complementing factors. The returns to investment in job training may be higher among the educated or experienced who are more productive, regardless of the additional training they receive at work. Firms also benefit most when training costs are distributed over a longer period of time, increasing the relative returns of training younger and longer term employees (Carneiro and Heckman, 2003).

Figure 4.22. **Firms in Kazakhstan are less likely to offer formal training compared to most peers**

Percentage of firms

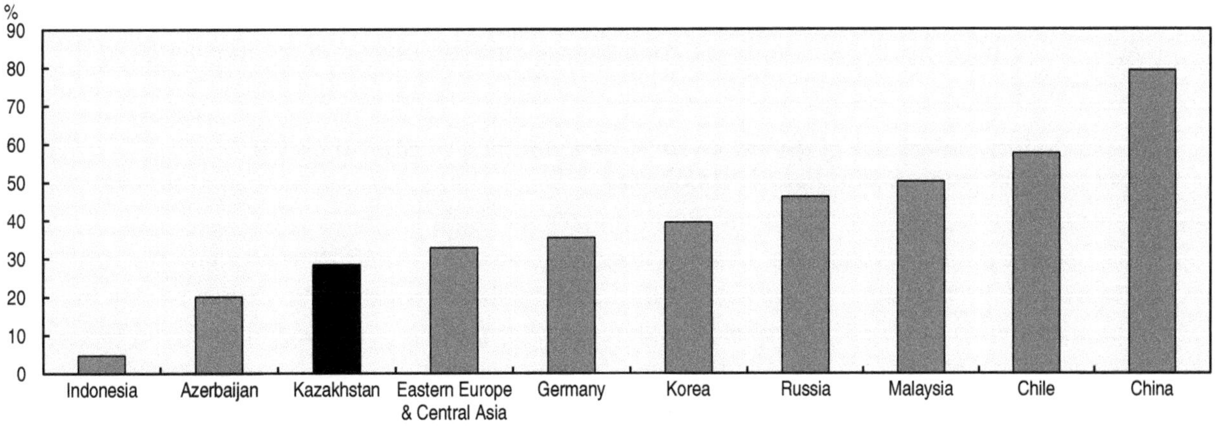

Notes: Year of survey in parentheses: Kazakhstan (2013), Azerbaijan (2013), Russia (2013), Chile (2012), China (2012), Indonesia (2009), Malaysia (2007), Germany (2005), Korea (2005). 600 firms have been surveyed in Kazakhstan.

Source: Authors' calculations based on World Bank (2015c), *Enterprise Surveys* (database), *www.enterprisesurveys.org*.

StatLink http://dx.doi.org/10.1787/888933289791

The share of firms in Kazakhstan offering formal training to their employees is relatively low compared to its peers. In 2013, around 30% of the firms surveyed by the World Bank offered formal training to their employees (Figure 4.22); the share is higher for manufacturing firms. Large and medium enterprises provide more training than small firms, in line with their higher perception of having an inadequately educated workforce. In the three countries that consider an inadequately educated workforce as one of three major constraints (Chile, the Russian Federation, and Malaysia), the proportion of firms offering formal training is higher than in Kazakhstan (between 40% and 60%). In the future, increasing incentives for firms – including SMEs – to develop training programmes in Kazakhstan would be necessary. In fact, through its various support programmes to SMEs, Kazakhstan has introduced training programmes for employees. Studying their scale, scope and effectiveness would be useful in enhancing the development of appropriate skills for sustained competitiveness.

Enhancing innovation capabilities is a requirement for Kazakhstan's competitiveness in the future

Kazakhstan can seize the opportunities to move up the value chain afforded by adopting global knowledge and developing domestic innovation capabilities, among others through knowledge- and information-intensive services. Innovation, i.e. the capacity to create new and better products and services, as well as new business models, is increasingly needed in Kazakhstan to sustain productivity growth and to compete effectively in global markets. In this context, in addition to the accumulation of physical and human capital, Kazakhstan can continue to take advantage of technology and knowledge that already exists elsewhere in the world and potentially revisit its strategy in doing so. This involves, among other things, making effective use of imports of technology embodied in capital goods and components; FDI; technology licensing; getting technology, designs, production and management assistance from foreign buyers; consulting firms, and technical experts; foreign education and training; trade fairs, technical conferences, databases; copying and reverse-engineering products and services. Future competitiveness and innovation capability in all sectors are also determined by domestic research and development (R&D) and increasingly by the existence of competitive services intensive in knowledge and information.

Kazakhstan makes use of global knowledge embodied in capital goods and benefits from sending students abroad

Over the last decade, Kazakhstan has imported capital goods on a massive scale. At the beginning of the 2000s, the share of capital goods imports in GDP was around 10% (Figure 4.23). It was lower in the second half of the 2000s at around 7%. This is largely in line with trends in China, which used capital goods imports as a strategic tool to develop innovation capability over the last decades. The share of capital goods imports in GDP has been clearly lower in the Russian Federation, at between 3% and 6% over the last decade. Some benchmarking countries use the adoption of foreign technologies through imports as a much more prominent tool to move the economy up the value chain than Kazakhstan. Singapore and Malaysia had shares of capital goods imports at above 30% and 50% during the same period (not shown in figure).

Making effective use of global knowledge can also be fostered by sending students abroad – a strategy successfully implemented in Kazakhstan. China has tapped global knowledge through a policy of sending students abroad for tertiary education (OECD, 2014a). It has the largest number of students in the world at the tertiary level studying outside their home country, 567 000 (15% of the world total). In relative terms, Kazakhstan sends yet more students abroad than China: among all tertiary students, the share of those studying abroad is, at almost 7%, highest in Kazakhstan compared to comparator countries; with the exception of Singapore's share at almost 9% (see Table 4.3 below). China has in fact a considerably smaller share at around 2%. Kazakhstan's success in using global knowledge through foreign education is boosted by the so-called Bolashak International Scholarship, which is awarded to high-performing students from Kazakhstan to study overseas and pays for all students' expenses, provided that they return to Kazakhstan to work for at least five years after graduation (see Chapter 5 for more details on this programme).

Figure 4.23. **Kazakhstan adopts foreign technologies through capital goods imports**

Share of capital goods imports in GDP

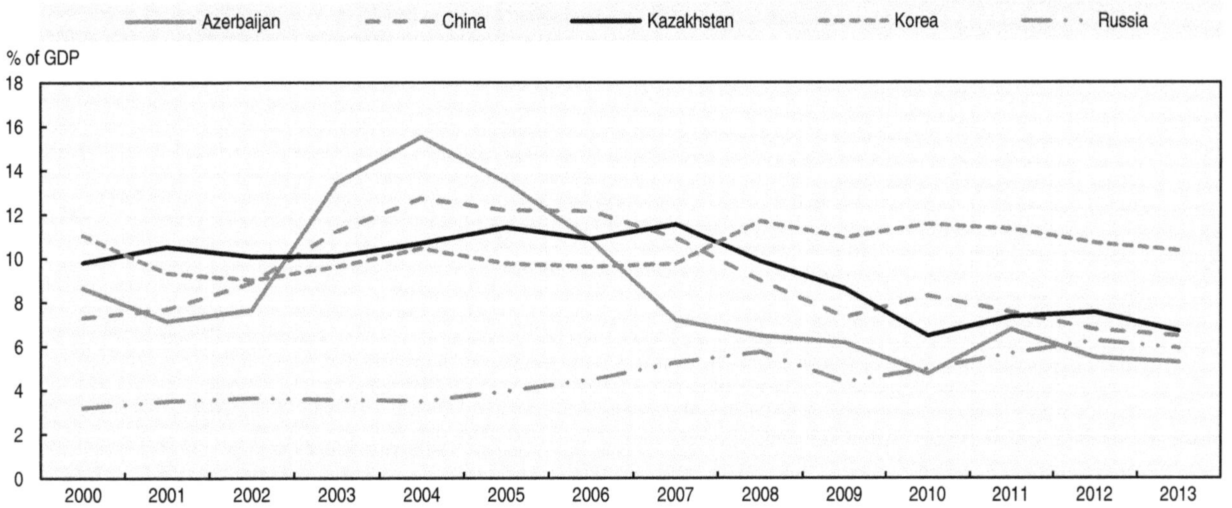

Notes: All figures are in nominal terms. Two benchmarking countries, Singapore and Malaysia had shares of capital goods imports at above 30% and 50% over the same period.

Source: Authors' calculations based on World Bank (2015b), *World Development Indicators* (database), *http://databank.worldbank.org/data/*.

StatLink http://dx.doi.org/10.1787/888933289806

The development of domestic innovation capabilities through R&D remains marginal in Kazakhstan

During the last decade, Kazakhstan's R&D expenditures amounted to 0.2% of GDP, which is low compared to its peers. Emerging countries such as Malaysia and the Russian Federation had shares above 1% in 2011 and China reached almost 2% (Table 4.3). Although relative R&D spending is still lower than in OECD countries, they have made great progress in the last decades: China was the second largest spender on R&D in the world in 2011, and the Russian Federation has spent about as much as Italy or Spain (OECD, 2014a). Moreover, most of the efforts are driven by public research institutions or state-owned enterprises (SOEs), compared to Germany or Korea, for example, where business R&D accounts for more than 70% of total R&D spending (Veugelers, 2013). Similarly, the number of researchers in R&D relative to its population is lowest in Kazakhstan compared to some comparator countries (China, Malaysia, Russian Federation, Korea, Singapore, and Germany).[14] Kazakhstan has set an ambitious target to increase funding for science up to the level of 3% of GDP while focusing on building global solutions in mobile and multimedia, nano- and space-technologies, robotics technology, gene engineering, search and discovery of energy.

Table 4.3. **Kazakhstan is less active in R&D than the benchmarking countries**

	Kazakhstan	China	Malaysia	Russian Federation	Korea	Singapore	Germany
Tertiary students studying abroad as percentage of total number of tertiary students							
2001	5.2	1.8	7.1	0.4	2.4	.	.
2006	3.6	1.7	6.0	0.5	3.3	.	.
2012	6.6	2.1	5.2	0.6	3.7	8.9	4.0
Research and development expenditure (% of GDP)							
2001	0.2	1.0	.	1.2	2.5	2.1	2.5
2006	0.2	1.4	0.6	1.1	3.0	2.2	2.5
2011	0.2	1.8	1.1	1.1	4.0	2.2	2.9
Researchers in R&D (per million people)							
2001	.	577	.	3 460	2 951	4 161	3 163
2006	.	923	368	3 231	4 229	5 425	3 342
2011	652	963	1643	3 120	5 928	6 494	4 085
Patent applications, residents, per 1 million people							
2001	108	24	11	170	1 557	126	607
2006	94	93	20	196	2 594	142	583
2011	85	309	37	185	2 773	204	574
Patent applications, non-residents, per 1 million people							
2001	7	26	237	64	652	1 965	127
2006	8	67	162	69	842	1 940	153
2011	19	82	187	104	821	1 686	152
Scientific and technical journal articles							
2001	114	21 134	472	15 658	11 008	2 434	42 678
2006	86	49 575	724	13 562	17 910	3 838	44 550
2011	87	89 894	2 092	14 151	25 593	4 543	46 259

Notes: Resident patent applications are those for which the first-named applicant or assignee is a resident of the state or region concerned.
Source: Authors' calculations based on World Bank (2015b), *World Development Indicators* (database), *http://databank.worldbank.org/data/*.

The outputs of Kazakhstan's R&D and other innovation efforts are not yet commensurate with the inputs. Kazakhstan ranked 69th among 142 countries in an Innovation Input Sub-Index including aspects of institutions, human capital and research, and infrastructure as well as market and business sophistication (Table 4.4). It ranks 101st, significantly lower, in the Innovation Output Sub-Index including knowledge and technology outputs as well as creative outputs. As in other emerging economies such as China, Chile and the Russian Federation, which have upgraded their capabilities, there is still room for progress.

Table 4.4. **Innovation indices partially reflect recent production upgrades**

Rankings out of 142 economies, selected benchmarking countries in the WIPO Innovation Indices

	Global Innovation Index	Innovation Output Sub-Index	Innovation Input Sub-Index
Korea	16	15	16
Malaysia	33	35	30
China	29	16	45
Chile	46	54	37
Russian Federation	49	45	56
Kazakhstan	79	101	69
Indonesia	87	60	117

Note: The Global Innovation Index is a compilation of existing indicators. It includes two sub-components: the Innovation Input Sub-Index and the Innovation Output Sub-Index. The Innovation Input Sub-Index includes aspects of institutions, human capital and research, infrastructure, market sophistication, and business sophistication. The Innovation Output Sub-Index includes aspects of knowledge and technology outputs as well as aspects of creative outputs.

Source: Cornell University, INSEAD and WIPO (2014), *The Global Innovation Index 2014: The Human Factor in Innovation*, *www.globalinnovationindex.org*.

Two measures of the output side are scientific and technical journal articles and patents. Scientific and technical journal articles can be taken as a proxy for the generation of knowledge. Patents generally can be taken as a proxy for knowledge that has some commercial value. Researchers based in Kazakhstan had clearly the lowest output in terms of scientific and technical journal articles among selected benchmarking countries over the last decade (Table 4.3). The number of articles was actually considerably lower in 2011 compared to ten years earlier. The smaller number is, of course, also due to the smaller population compared to other benchmarking economies. Nonetheless, in the small country of Singapore, the number of articles was more than 50 times higher than in Kazakhstan in 2011. In terms of patents, the number filed by residents of Kazakhstan also decreased over the last decade. The number filed by residents per million people was among the lowest compared to benchmarking countries; only Malaysia had a lower ratio (Table 4.3). All selected benchmarking countries have a considerably higher number of non-resident patent applications per million people than Kazakhstan.

But Kazakhstan is scaling up its innovation efforts

Spurring innovation at the firm level and stimulating the interactions for innovation (e.g. knowledge triangles and clusters) are priorities for Kazakhstan. Attracting anchor innovators (e.g. in the Silicon Valley, Lockheed and Fairchild served as the anchors, in Cambridge UK, it was Acorn, Cambridge Consultants and later Advanced RSIC) is a pressing challenge and has been recognised by the president, who has recently set the objective for the Investment Promotion Agency, Kaznex Invest, to attract ten multinational enterprises (MNEs) in the next two years. Moreover, Kazakhstan has launched various initiatives to foster diversification and innovation such as the Accelerated Industrial and Innovative Development programme or SPAIID 2010-2014 (see section above), the National Innovation Fund, or the launch of the Council on Technology Policy chaired by the prime minister and operated by the Ministry of Investment and Development. Despite these efforts, innovation may be hampered as a result of, for example, difficulties in hiring foreign experts who would be needed to engineer the results of R&D into commercial products or the not fully developed intellectual property rights (IPR) protection framework. Developing competitive knowledge- and information-intensive services would have transformative effects for the economy.

The importance of services as a new driver of growth at the middle-income level has been recognised widely. Beyond economic benefits, an efficient and high-quality service sector helps countries to ensure social inclusiveness and environmental sustainability. Services are essential for industrial upgrading, and in particular for the reduction of energy consumption and emissions, through their provision of wide-ranging productive factors, including knowledge, information, improved processes and a high-quality labour force. A well-developed service sector can help to capture increased gains from trade, deepen the position in global value chains, and reshape the competitive advantage of an economy in the international market. In addition, demand for modern consumer services is rising with per capita incomes and thus the provision of them becomes crucial in meeting people's expectations (OECD, 2014a).

Kazakhstan has underdeveloped knowledge- and information-intensive services. While Kazakhstan is on a par with more developed benchmarking countries such as Germany with regard to the development of traditional services, the share of knowledge- and information-intensive services is considerably lower. In 2013, the share of business services in GDP stood at around 5% in Kazakhstan compared to around 14% in Germany.

An important aspect enabling higher value-added production in developed and developing economies is that they make growing use of business-related services and that they outsource these services to independent firms. Examples of these services are labour recruitment, information technology (IT), marketing, customer contacts, market analysis, and R&D. Outsourcing of these services in developed countries is an "Adam Smithian" process driven by the gains from specialisation and scale economies. Such gains are not automatic – they may be achieved only if the right conditions – modern ICT infrastructure, stable contract enforcement, intellectual property rights – are in place.

Kazakhstan does not make use of services and particularly of business services to the extent many benchmarking countries do. Services inputs as share of total intermediate inputs in agriculture, manufacturing and extractive sectors are low compared to respective shares of most of its more developed peers, such as Germany, Australia and Canada (Figure 4.24). The share of business services as an input into production is particularly low in Kazakhstan; in manufacturing it is almost 0% in Kazakhstan compared to more than 10% in Germany.

Figure 4.24. **The share of services inputs in agriculture, extractive sectors and manufacturing is lower in Kazakhstan compared to developed countries**

Service inputs as share of total intermediate inputs, by aggregate sectors

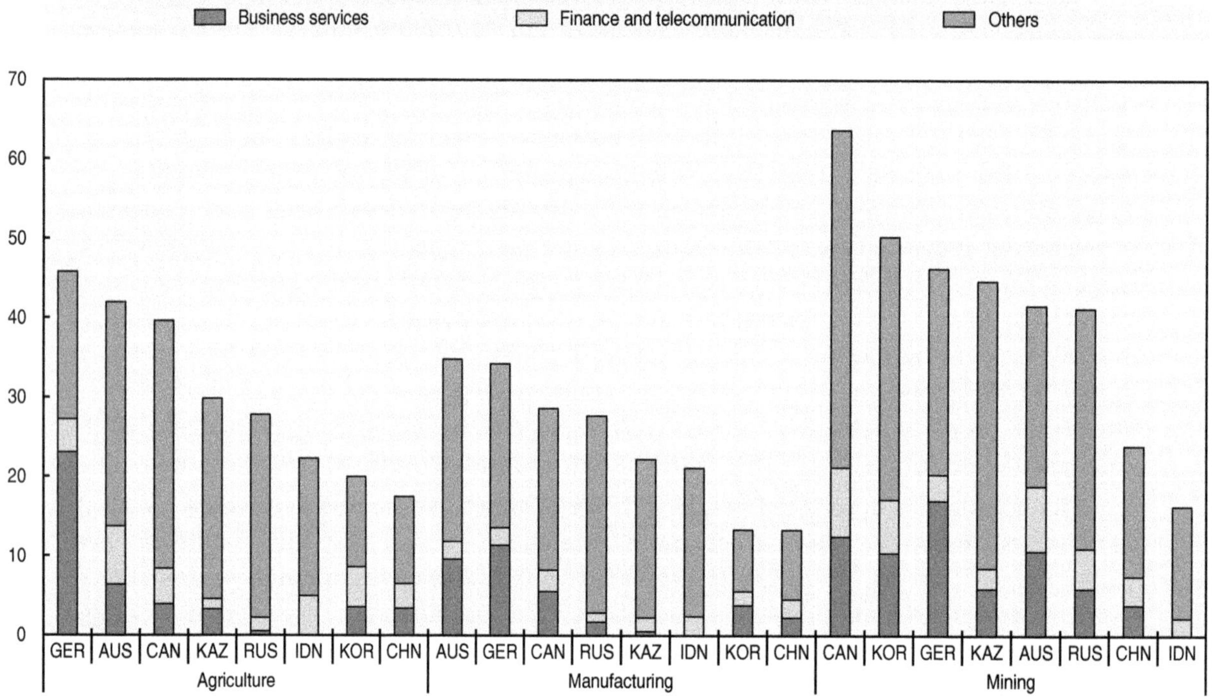

Sources: Authors' calculations based on Timmer, M.P. (ed) (2012), "The World Input-Output Database (WIOD): Contents, Sources and Methods", *WIOD Working Paper*, Number 10, *www.wiod.org/publications/papers/wiod10.pdf* and data received from the Ministry of National Economy.

StatLink *http://dx.doi.org/10.1787/888933289818*

Analysis highlights significant differences between developed and emerging economies in manufacturing structures. Developing countries' efforts to improve their production capacity may in fact grind to a halt because of their below-benchmark use of outsourced business services (Evangelista et al., 2013). Computerisation and R&D, for example, become increasingly critical to competitive, innovative manufacturing as countries grow richer and have to compete on productivity rather than costs. Furthermore, countries that are productive manufacturers are also productive providers of business services and use them intensively in manufacturing (Annex Figure 4.A1.8). Boosting productivity in Kazakhstan's business services, from the current low levels would most likely support productivity growth in manufacturing as well, if links are well managed. This comparison does not, however, allow any conclusions to be drawn about causal links between manufacturing and business services. More intensive use of business services in manufacturing may have a learning-by-doing effect, which boosts productivity in those services. In contrast, business services may be used more intensively because their productivity has reached a high enough level to improve competitiveness in manufacturing, too.

Rapid progress in ICT – and particularly the Internet – has allowed economies of scale in the production of most services and positive spillover effects to be realised. In future, these knowledge and information-intensive services, including applications based on big data analytics and cloud computing, will increasingly become a strategic asset for a country to be internationally competitive in the long run (McKinsey Global Institute, 2014; and OECD, forthcoming; Box 4.5 for the case of China). For industrial upgrading, exploiting the potential of the "Internet of Things" will become a crucial competitive asset.

Box 4.5. **How knowledge and information-intensive sectors can drive competitiveness: The case of China**

China's digital transformation has largely been driven by consumers and the country boasts a dynamic technology sector, hugely successful social networks and the largest e-tailing (on-line selling) market in the world. Through the internet, millions of transactions and communications happen every day and this contributes significantly to GDP. By 2013, China's Internet economy as a share of GDP had surpassed that of the United States, France and Germany.

China is now on the brink of a second wave of digital transformation as enterprises increasingly look towards web technologies to improve the efficiency of their operations. This will increase productivity, and in addition, by creating new markets for digital goods and services it will also generate growth that is based on productivity, innovation and consumption. This new source of growth will be crucial to sustaining high growth as the capital investment and labour force expansion that supported China's development over the last two decades decline.

The Internet and ICT improvements in general have allowed China to create economies of scale in the production of most services, and these knowledge- and information-intensive sectors will play an important role in ensuring the country's future competiveness. Fostering services as a source of inclusive growth is an important part of China's 12th five-year Plan for National Economic and Social Development (2011-2015). Through targeting improvements in a variety of services including services for SME's, e-commerce, energy saving services and next generation ICTs China has increased the service sector's share of GDP by almost four percentage points.

Exploiting the potential of new technological developments such as big data analytics and cloud computing will be important in ensuring that China's service sector continues to develop and that the country moves towards an inclusive and sustainable development path. Being at the forefront of new technological developments such as the "Internet of Things" will be a crucial competitive advantage and one that the Chinese authorities intend to target through the country's forthcoming 13th five year plan (2016-2020) (OECD, forthcoming).

Source: SAS (2012), "Intelligence Quarterly: Journal of Advanced Analytics 4Q 2012", SAS Institute Inc.; OECD (forthcoming), Strategies for China's knowledge- and information-intensive services".

Kazakhstan has a lot of room to enhance the use of ICTs. The World Economic Forum's Networked Readiness Index measures the environment for ICTs, the readiness of a society to use ICTs, the actual usage of all main stakeholders and finally the impacts that ICTs generate in the economy and society. Kazakhstan ranked 38th out of 148 countries in the overall Networked Readiness Index in 2014 (Figure 4.25, Panel A). It has improved the leveraging of ICTs considerably over the last decade; back in 2006/07 it ranked 73rd in the same index. Benchmarking countries like Singapore, Korea and Germany already make much better use of ICTs, ranking among the best 12 countries worldwide. China only ranked 62nd in 2014, losing ground since 2009 when it was still ahead of Kazakhstan. Compared to Germany, the regulatory and business environment for ICT development in Kazakhstan lags (Figure 4.25, Panel B). The same holds for its readiness to use ICTs in terms of infrastructure and digital content and skills, with the exception of the affordability of ICT services. In terms of actual usage, only the government in Kazakhstan uses ICTs to a similar extent as the German government. Businesses and individuals make less use of ICTs in Kazakhstan compared to Germany. As a result, leveraging ICTs also affects the economy to a smaller extent in Kazakhstan compared to Germany.

Figure 4.25. **Kazakhstan has improved the leveraging of ICTs over time**

A. Networked Readiness Index Rankings

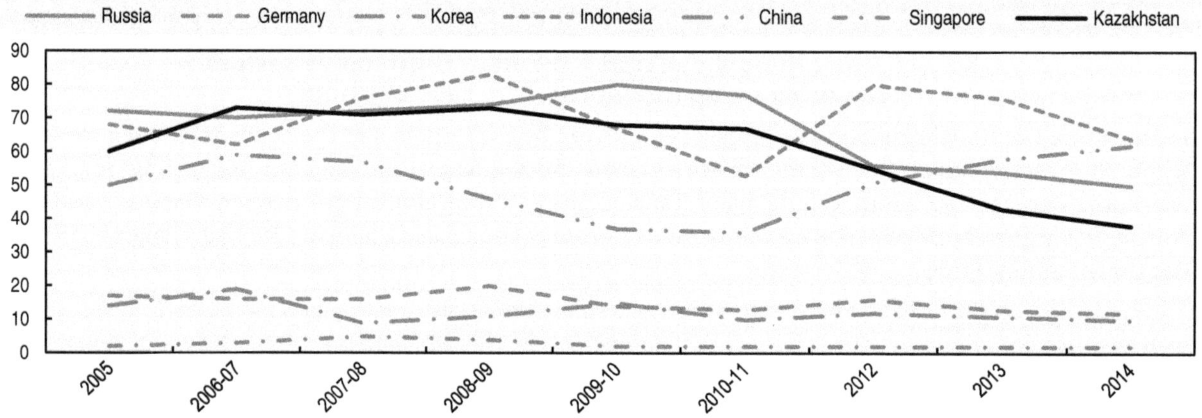

B. Decomposition of the Networked Readiness Index

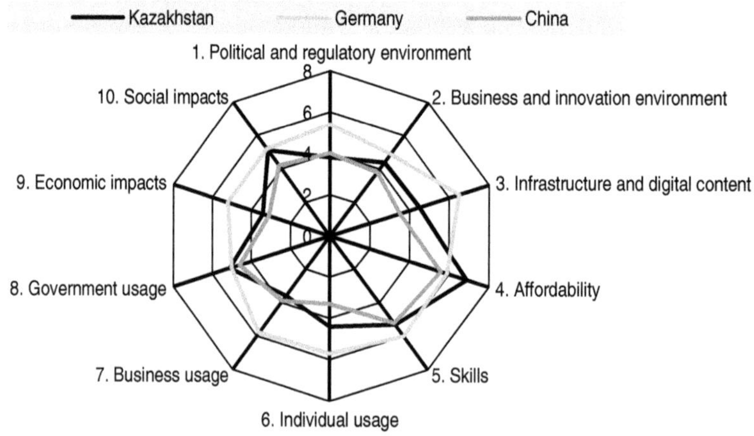

Source: Authors' calculations based on WEF (2013), *The Global Information Technology Report 2014*, *www.weforum.org/reports/global-information-technology-report-2014*.

StatLink http://dx.doi.org/10.1787/888933289827

Notes

1. Significant productivity differences across countries can have various causes, some of them are not related to the relative competitiveness of countries, and have to be regarded with some scepticism. For example, in the extractive sectors an important reason for differences can simply be a different composition of commodities, which all have considerably different prices, yielding substantially different productivity levels. In that sector, productivity is relatively high in all countries, pointing to the fact that it is a very capital-intensive sector. Productivity statistics for services, particularly non-tradeable services such as real estate and construction, are associated very much with purchasing power parities of countries (OECD, 2014a; Triplett and Bosworth, 2008; and Schreyer, 2001). Thus, productivity tends to be higher in countries where prices and the cost of living are higher. The analysis in this chapter does not correct for purchasing power parity (PPP) in the different economies. Making use of a PPP rescaling might reduce the productivity gap between emerging and advanced economies. The non-availability of sectoral PPP figures in the countries under consideration excludes this correction..

2. Important structural reforms have been made in the agricultural sector since independence, leading to the introduction of private ownership of land and the privatisation and restructuring of collective farms. The reforms to land ownership and the farm structure resulted in a substantial reallocation of production from large-scale agricultural enterprises to small-scale producers (OECD, 2013d). The ambitious agricultural development programme (2013-2020) aims to overcome low investment in the sector, outdated technological level of the industry's equipment, low-intensity agriculture, low genetic potential and low productivity of farm animals (OECD, 2014b). Moreover, for selected agricultural products, the government has set the target to export up to half of the produced goods to CIS countries within three years and increasingly to substitute imports. These development programmes will be based on the experiences of New Zealand's Fronterra and Denmark's Arla.

3. Growth of value added in the extractive sector over 2010-13 was on a par with employment expansion, leading to stagnant labour productivity growth over the same period.

4. Kazakhstan manufactures cars, trucks, buses, agricultural vehicles as well as locomotives, tugs and vessels. Cars are manufactured by two large enterprises – Joint Stock Companies AgromashHolding (Kostanay) and "AZIA AVTO" (Ust-Kamenogorsk). The total output of cars amounted to approximately 95% of all vehicles produced in Kazakhstan in 2013. The government has adopted a range of programmes to foster domestic and foreign investment in the sector, including financial support and a zero tax regime in special economic zones. The government is also planning a special scheme for the development of the car component sectors, which will include financial support for technology purchases and infrastructure development among others. Car sales in Kazakhstan are supported by privileged credit schemes. Credits for local car purchases benefit from a 50% subsidy on interests. See for example: *www.abiz.ru/en/170/297/554/?nid=843&a=entry.show*; *www.just-auto.com/regions/kazakhstan_cid109*; *http://investkz.com/en/journals/84/713.html*; *http://en.trend.az/casia/kazakhstan/2323583.html*.

5. The average number of RCA products in Kazakhstan has slightly increased since the global economic crisis to an average of 58 products over 2012-14, up from around 50 over 2007-11.

6. Around one-third of all products where Kazakhstan has an RCA are raw material products. Two-third of the RCA products are categorised as semi-finished products. Kazakhstan has an RCA in only a few finished products. Compared to its benchmarks, Kazakhstan ranks low in terms of export diversification in all three categories. The number of RCA raw material products is naturally higher in Kazakhstan compared to non resource-rich countries, but Kazakhstan still ranks below other resource-rich countries such as the Russian Federation, Chile or Australia. Interestingly, Kazakhstan has fewer products with an RCA in all three categories, even in raw materials, than two decades ago.

7. The recent hike in interest rates of corporate loans can be explained by the expected devaluation causing a higher demand for tenge loans.

8. Foreign direct investment (FDI) is not only supportive to economic growth but can also be a tool to develop domestic capabilities through jobs. Over 2003-13, FDI inflows created around 5 000 jobs per year, with two positive outliers in 2008 and 2011 thanks to higher FDI inflows in those years. While FDI inflows are much lower than before the crisis, the average number of jobs created by USD million invested has doubled from 1.5 jobs over 2003-08 to 3 jobs since 2010 (fDi Intelligence, 2015). The creation of jobs relative to investment volumes is also relatively high in Azerbaijan, but much lower in Norway and Chile for example.

9. Data for the World Bank LPI comes from surveys where logistic experts are asked to evaluate eight markets on the six core dimensions discussed. These markets include a combination of the most important export and import markets of the country of interest, randomly selected markets, and for landlocked countries like Kazakhstan, markets from neighbouring countries that link them to the world market. Therefore the poor performance of the region is reflected in Kazakhstan's score.
10. In October 2014, Russia threatened to impose countersanctions by preventing Western food products from passing through to Kazakhstan (The Economist, 2014).
11. The Decree of the President of the Republic of Kazakhstan No. 874 "On approval of the state program of industrial-innovative development of Kazakhstan for 2015-2019" was signed on 1 August 2014.
12. Through Nurly Zhol funds are allocated in various areas. For example, KZT 81 billion are reserved in 2015 for the "dry port" complex infrastructure project at Khorgos and the National Industrial Petrochemical Technological Park in Atyrau and Taraz. The policy sets also aside KZT 29 billion in 2015 to expand Astana airport with the aim of increasing capacity from 3.5 million passengers to 7.1 million by 2017 (Nazarbayev, 2014). Important regions (Centre-South, Centre-East, and Centre-West) will be better connected with Astana through roads, railways and airlines. Around KZT 300 billion will be allocated for the reconstruction of highways in 2015 and 2016.
13. See *https://www.gosreestr.kz/* for further details on privatisation plan and bidding mechanisms.
14. The group of comparator countries has been selected at random.

References

Acemoglu, D., P. Aghion and F. Zilibotti (2006), "Distance to frontier, selection, and economic growth", *Journal of the European Economic Association*, MIT Press, Vol. 4, No.1, pp. 37-74.

ADB (2013), *Report to the Government of Kazakhstan: Policies for industrial and service diversification in Asia in the 21st Century*, Asian Development Bank.

Aghion, P. et al. (2005), *Exploiting States' Mistakes to Identify the Causal Impact of Higher Education on Growth*, mimeo.

Álvarez-Galván, J. (2014), *A Skills beyond School Review of Kazakhstan*, OECD Reviews of Vocational Education and Training, OECD Publishing, Paris, *http://dx.doi.org/10.1787/9789264221826-en*

Carneiro, P. and J. Heckman (2003), "Human capital policy", *NBER Working Paper* No. 9495, Cambridge, *www.ucl.ac.uk/~uctppca/HCP.pdf.*

Cornell University, INSEAD and WIPO (2014), *The Global Innovation Index 2014: The Human Factor in Innovation*, Geneva, Ithaca and Fontainebleau, *www.globalinnovationindex.org/*

DAMU (2013), *Report on the Status of Development of Small and Medium Enterprises in Kazakhstan and its Regions*, edition 5, JSC Damu Entrepreneurship Development Fund and Ministry of Regional Development of the Republic of Kazakhstan.

Economist (2014), "Hardly an oasis", *http://economist.com/news/asia/21632595-kazakhstan-turns-geography-advantage-china-builds-new-silk-road-hardly-oasis*

EIU (2014), "Monopoly on 4G hampers telecoms development", *Economist Intelligence Unit*, October 16.

Evangelista, R., M. Lucchese and V. Meliciani (2013), "Business services, innovation and sectoral growth", *Structural Change and Economic Dynamics*, Vol. 25, pp. 119-132.

fDi Intelligence (2015), *fDi Intelligence* (database), *http://fdiintelligence.com/*

Forbes (2015), *Forbes The World's Billionaires*, *http://forbes.com/billionaires/list/#version:static*

Foreign Investors' Council (2013), *Industrialization Concept 2015-2019*, *fic.kz/uploads/files/Presentation_Eng.pdf*

IDE-JETRO and WTO (2011), "Trade Patterns and Global Value Chains in East Asia: From Trade in Goods to Trade in Tasks", World Trade Organization, Geneva.

IMF (2014), "Financial system stability assessment", *Country Reports*, No. 14/258, International Monetary Fund, Washington DC.

IMF (2010), "Selected Issues III. Financial market development in Kazakhstan?", *Country Reports*, No. 10/237, International Monetary Fund, Washington DC.

IMF (2005), "Singapore: Selected issues", *IMF Country Report* No. 05/140, International Monetary Fund, Washington, DC.

International Trade Center (2015), FDI database, *www.intracen.org/itc/market-info-tools/statistics-inward-country-industry/*

Jankowska, A., A. Nagengast, and J. R. Perea (2012), "The product space and the middle-income trap: Comparing Asian and Latin American experiences", *OECD Development Centre Working Paper* No. 311, April, OECD Publishing, Paris, *http://dx.doi.org/10.1787/5k9909j2587g-en.*

Jappar, A. and J. Jandosova (2013), "Kazakhstan: Improving capacity to support SME development", *Asian Development Bank Technical Assistance Consultant's Report.*

Kasipkor (2014), "New TVET system in Kazakhstan", Kasipkor.

Kjærnet, H., Satpaev, D. and Torjesen, S. (2008), *Big Business and High-level Politics in Kazakhstan: An Everlasting Symbiosis?*, *www.isn.ethz.ch/Digital-Library/Publications/Detail/?lang=en&id=55285.*

Lee, H. H. and H. B. Tan, (2006), "Technology transfer, FDI and economic growth in the ASEAN Region", *Journal of the Asia Pacific Economy*, Vol. 11, No. 4.

McKinsey Global Institute (2014), *China's Digital Transformation: The Internet's Impact on Productivity and Growth*, *www.mckinsey.com/insights/high_tech_telecoms_internet/chinas_digital_transformation*

Ministry of Industry and New Technologies of the Republic of Kazakhstan (2014), *www.fic.kz/uploads/files/programme_eng.docx*

Ministry of National Economy (2014), Data received from Kazakhstan in December

Magud N. and S. Sosa (2010), "When and why worry about real exchange rate appreciation? The missing link between Dutch disease and growth", *IMF Working Paper 10/271.*

Mkrtchyan, A. (2013), *The Customs Union Between Russia, Belarus and Kazakhstan: Some Evidence from the New Tariff Rates and Trade Flows*, Forum for Research on Eastern Europe and Emerging Economies, *http://freepolicybriefs.org/2013/10/07/the-customs-union-between-russia-belarus-and-kazakhstan-some-evidence-from-the-new-tariff-rates-and-trade-flows/.*

National Bank of Kazakhstan (2015), Official Internet Resource of the National Bank of Kazakhstan (database), *www.nationalbank.kz/?docid=127&switch=english.*

OECD (forthcoming), "Strategies for China's knowledge- and information-intensive services".

OECD (2015), *FDI Restrictiveness Index* (database), *www.oecd.org/investment/fdiindex.htm.*

OECD (2014a), *Perspectives on Global Development 2014: Boosting Productivity to Meet the Middle-Income Challenge*, OECD Publishing, Paris, *http://dx.doi.org/10.1787/persp_glob_dev-2014-en*

OECD (2014b), *Kazakhstan: Review of the Central Administration*, OECD Public Governance Reviews, OECD Publishing, Paris, *http://dx.doi.org/10.1787/9789264224605-en*

OECD (2013a), *African Economic Outlook 2013: Structural Transformation and Natural Resources*, African Development Bank, OECD, UNDP and UNECA, Paris, *http://dx.doi.org/10.1787/aeo-2013-en.*

OECD (2013b), *Capital Markets in Eurasia: Two Decades of Reform, Corporate Governance*, OECD Publishing, Paris, *http://dx.doi.org/10.1787/9789264203976-en.*

OECD (2013c), *Perspectives on Global Development 2013: Industrial Policies in a Changing World*, OECD Publishing, Paris, *http://dx.doi.org/10.1787/persp_glob_dev-2013-en.*

OECD (2013d), *OECD Review of Agricultural Policies: Kazakhstan 2013*, OECD Publishing, Paris, *http://dx.doi.org/10.1787/9789264191761-en*

OECD (2013e), *Southeast Asian Economic Outlook 2013: With Perspectives on China and India*, OECD Publishing, Paris, *http://dx.doi.org/10.1787/saeo-2013-en.*

OECD (2012), *OECD Investment Policy Reviews: Kazakhstan 2012*, OECD Publishing, Paris, *http://dx.doi.org/10.1787/9789264121812-en.*

Rahmetov, A. (2011), *Kazakhstan's Presidential Elections 2011: Nazarbayev Postpones Succession*, *www.ispionline.it/it/documents/Analysis_51_2011.pdf*

Republic of Kazakhstan (2007), *Law on Education of the Republic of Kazakhstan*, dated July 27, 2007, No.319-III

Ruff A. and Horn S. (2012), *The World Bank and Higher Education in Kazakhstan*, counterpunch, *www.counterpunch.org/2012/12/14/the-world-bank-and-higher-education-in-kazakhstan/.*

SAS (2012), *Intelligence Quarterly: Journal of Advanced Analytics 4Q 2012*, *https://www.sas.com/news/intelligence_quarterly/q412.pdf*

Satpayev, D. (2014), "Corruption in Kazakhstan and the Quality of Governance", *IDE discussion paper*, No. 475, Institute of Developing Economies.

Schreyer, P. (2001), "The OECD Productivity manual: A guide to measurement of industry-level and aggregate productivity", *International Productivity Monitor*, No.2, pp. 37-51.

Timmer, M.P. (ed) (2012), "The World Input-Output Database (WIOD): Contents, Sources and Methods", *WIOD Working Paper* Number 10, *www.wiod.org/publications/papers/wiod10.pdf*.

Transparency International (2014), *Corruption Perceptions Index* (database), *www.transparency.org/cpi2014*.

Triplett, J. and L. Bosworth (2008), "The state of data for services productivity measurement in the United States", *International Productivity Monitor*, No. 16, pp. 53-70.

UNCTAD (2015), *UnctadStat* (database), *http://unctadstat.unctad.org/ReportFolders/reportFolders.aspx*.

UNIDO (2009), *Industrial Development Report*, United Nations Industrial Development Organisation, Vienna.

Veugelers. R. (2013), "The world innovation landscape: Asia rising?" *Bruegel Policy Contribution*, Issue 2013/02, *www.bruegel.org/publications/publication-detail/publication/766-the-world-innovation-landscape-asia-rising/*

WEF (2014), *Global Competitiveness Report* 2014-2015, World Economic Forum, *http://www3.weforum.org/docs/WEF_GlobalCompetitivenessReport_2014-15.pdf*

WEF (2013), *The Global Information Technology Report* 2014, World Economic Forum, *www.weforum.org/reports/global-information-technology-report-2014*

Word Bank (2015a), *World Integrated Trade Solution* (database). World Bank, Washington, DC, *http://wits.worldbank.org/*.

World Bank (2015b), *World Development Indicators* (database). World Bank, Washington, DC, *http://databank.worldbank.org/data/*

World Bank (2015c), *Enterprise Surveys* (database), *www.enterprisesurveys.org*.

World Bank (2014), "Kazakhstan: Growth slows as external pressures rise", World Bank Group Macroeconomics Fiscal Management.

ANNEX 4.A1

Table 4.A1.1. **Trade and extractive sectors were the two largest economic sectors in 2013**

	Share of total value added 2013 (%)	CAGR of value added 2010-13 (%)
Wholesale and retail trade	16.9	28
Extractive sectors	16.7	3
Real estate	9.2	21
Transportation and storage	8.3	16
Construction	6.5	15
Agriculture and related	4.9	4
Professional, scientific and technical	4.7	21
Metal	3.8	5
Education	3.1	20
Finance and insurance	3.0	3
Other service activities	3.0	33
ICT	2.9	35
Food and related	2.7	12
Public administration and defence	2.2	20
Utilities	2.1	15
Administrative and support	1.9	24
Coke and refined petroleum	1.9	15
Health	1.8	20
Rubber, plastics and other non-metallic	1.0	19
Hotels and restaurants	1.0	22
Other social	0.7	31
Chemicals and pharmaceuticals	0.7	31
Transport equipment	0.4	58
Electrical, optical and other machinery	0.4	7
Wood, paper and related	0.2	9
Textiles, clothes and related	0.1	3
Other manufacturing	0.0	17
Total	100	24

Notes: Sectors are ordered from the biggest to the smallest sector in terms of value added.

Source: Authors' calculations based on data received from the Ministry of National Economy.

Figure 4.A1.1. **The labour productivity gap is significant in Kazakhstan's largest economic sectors**

Labour productivity as a factor of the level in Kazakhstan in 2013

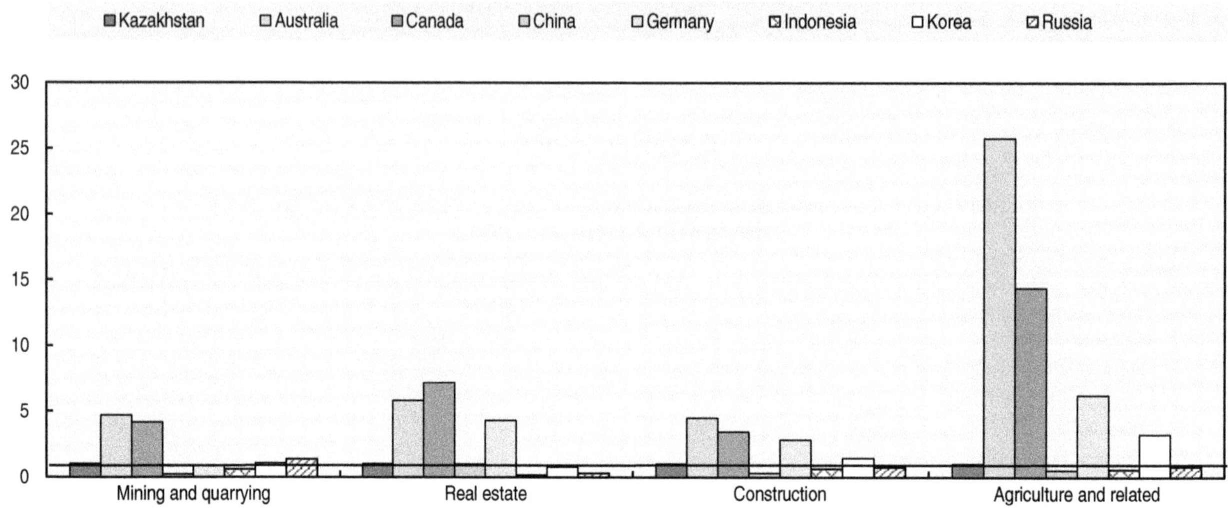

Notes: The sectors illustrated in the figure correspond to four of the six largest economic sectors in Kazakhstan in 2013. For wholesale and retail trade as well as transportation and storage the productivity differential could not be conducted as comparable statistics for benchmarking countries were not available. Productivity figures correspond to 2013 figures for Kazakhstan and 2011 for all other countries.

Source: Authors' calculations based on data received from the Ministry of National Economy.

StatLink http://dx.doi.org/10.1787/888933289838

Figure 4.A1.2. **Monthly wages increased fast in most sectors over 2010-13**

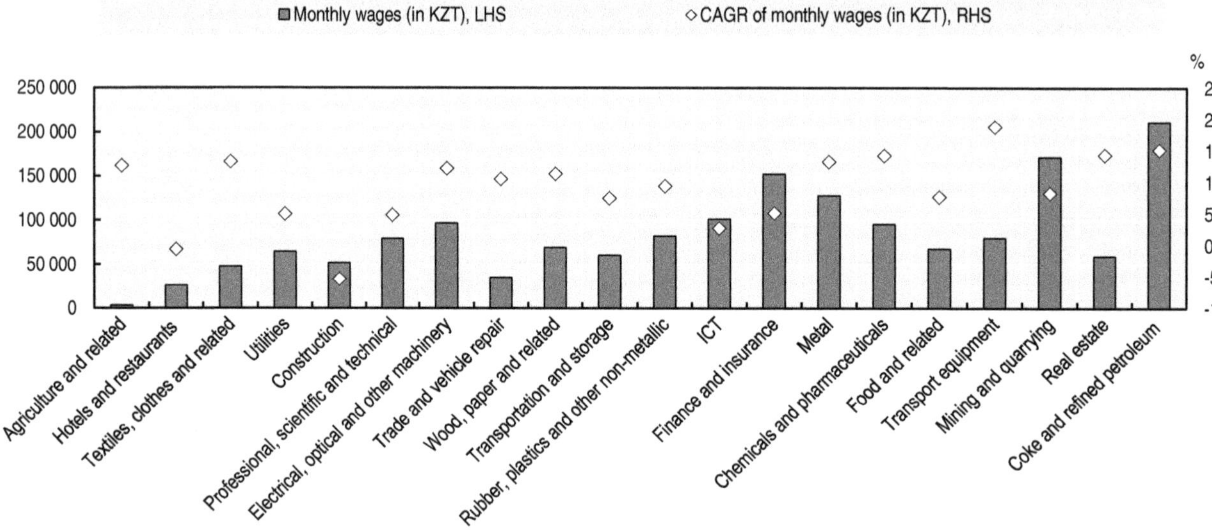

Notes: Sectors are ordered from the most productive (top) to the least productive sectors. The monthly wages and growth in wages of (mostly non-commercial) public and social services are not included in the figure.

Source: Authors' calculations based on data received from the Ministry of National Economy.

StatLink http://dx.doi.org/10.1787/888933289841

Figure 4.A1.3. **Kazakhstan has relatively low FDI restrictions**

Index between 0 and 1 (a higher figure stands for higher restrictions), 2013

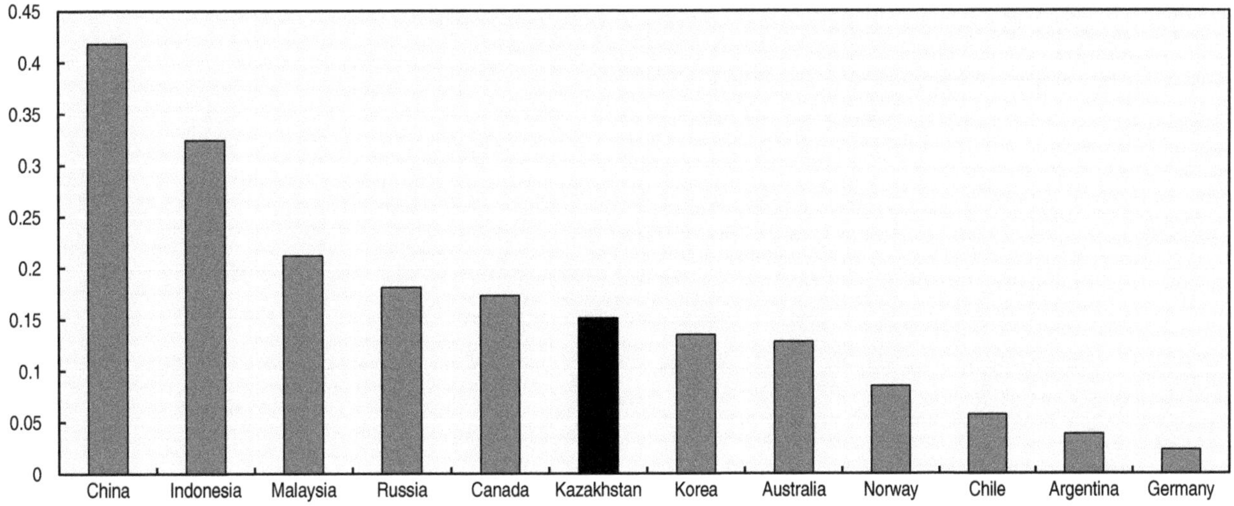

Source: OECD (2015), *FDI Restrictiveness Index* (database), *www.oecd.org/investment/fdiindex.htm.*

StatLink http://dx.doi.org/10.1787/888933289852

Figure 4.A1.4. **Access to finance is a key constraint for doing business**

Relative importance of access to finance as a key constraint, with the relative importance of 16 possible key constraints, in percent, 2014

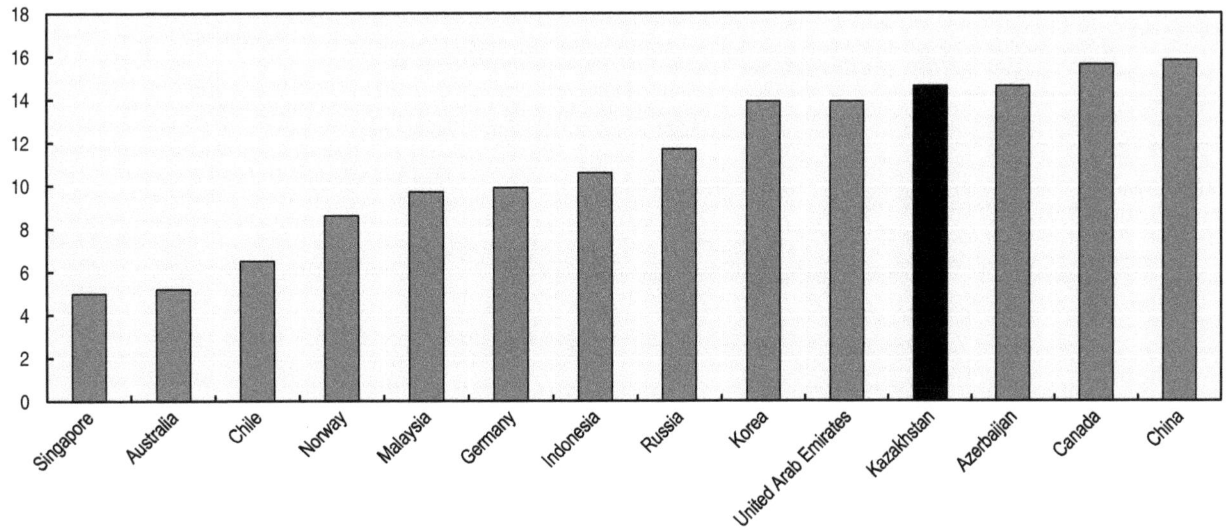

Source: WEF (2014), *Global Competitiveness Report 2014-2015, www3.weforum.org/docs/WEF_GlobalCompetitivenessReport_2014-15.pdf.*

StatLink http://dx.doi.org/10.1787/888933289862

Figure 4.A1.5. **Better logistics are associated with higher productivity**

Logistics performance index versus labour productivity

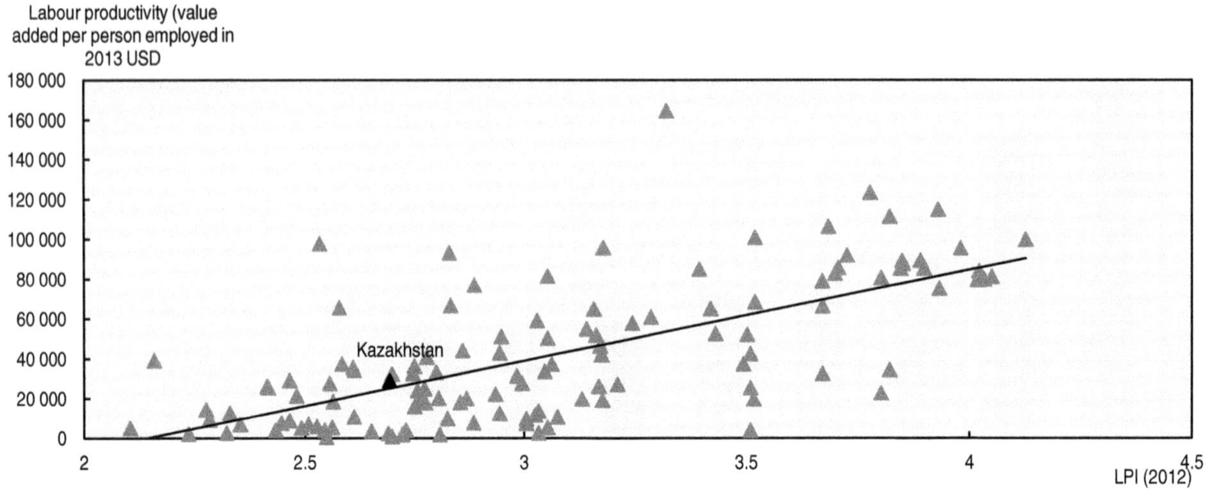

Source: Authors' calculations based on data received from the Ministry of National Economy and World Bank (2015b), *World Development Indicators* (database), *http://databank.worldbank.org/data/*.

StatLink http://dx.doi.org/10.1787/888933289879

Figure 4.A1.6. **Educational attainment in Kazakhstan is nearing OECD levels**

Average years of total schooling, age 15+, total, 1990 and 2010

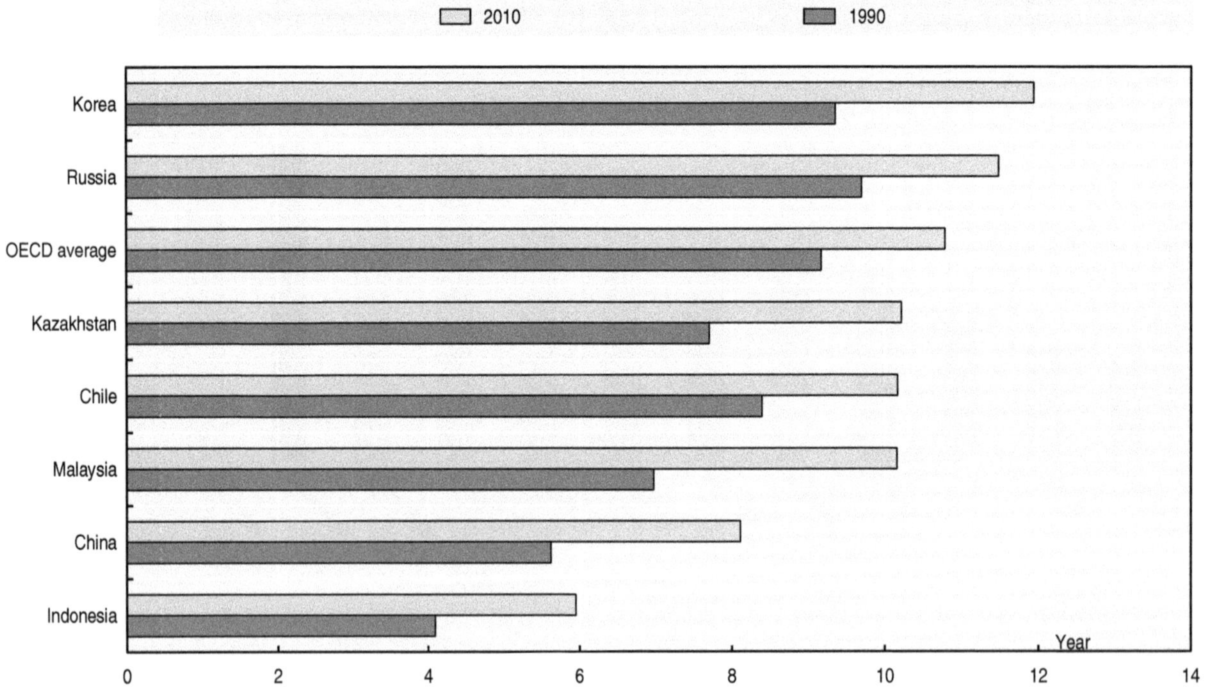

Source: Authors' calculations based on World Bank (2015b), *World Development Indicators* (database), *http://databank.worldbank.org/data/*.

StatLink http://dx.doi.org/10.1787/888933289886

Figure 4.A1.7. **Proportion of unskilled workers in manufacturing activities is relatively low in Kazakhstan**

Percentage of unskilled workers among all production workers

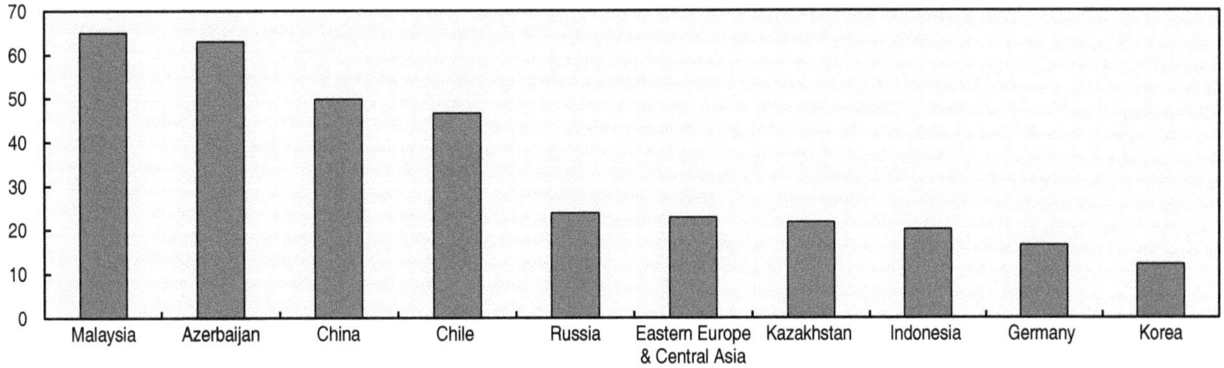

Notes: Year of survey in parentheses: Kazakhstan (2013), Azerbaijan (2013), Russia (2013), Chile (2012), China (2012), Indonesia (2009), Malaysia (2007), Germany (2005), Korea (2005). Six hundred firms were surveyed in Kazakhstan.

Source: Authors' calculations based on World Bank (2015c), *Enterprise Surveys* (database), *www.enterprisesurveys.org*.

StatLink http://dx.doi.org/10.1787/888933289892

Figure 4.A1.8. **Business service productivity and intensity of use are positively associated with manufacturing productivity**

Labour productivity in business series versus labour productivity in manufacturing

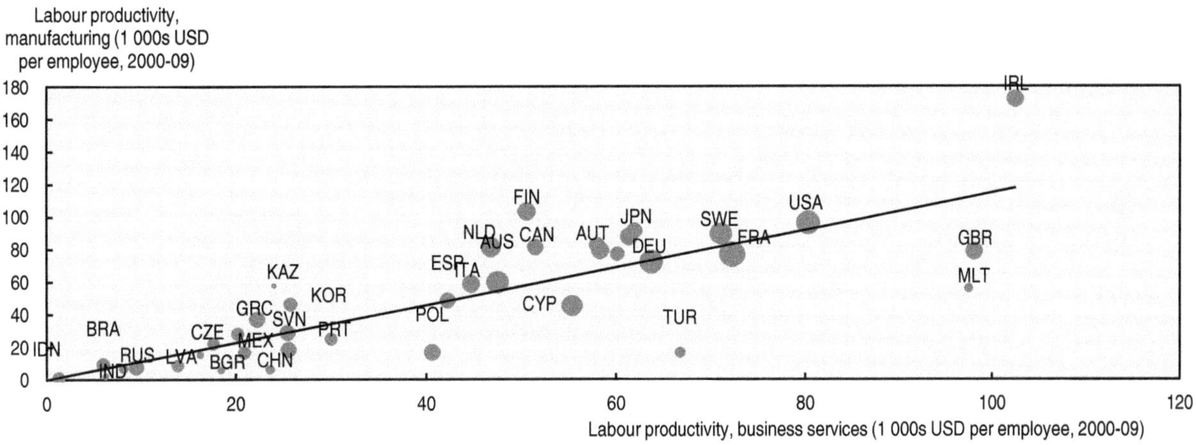

Notes: The bubble size denotes the share of business services inputs in the total inputs used in manufacturing. The shares of business service inputs in total inputs used in manufacturing range from 0.01% in Indonesia to 11% in Germany. The share in Kazakhstan is at 0.5%. The sectors are classified according to the International Standard Industrial Classification Revision 3 (ISIC Rev. 3). Business services are defined by ISIC sectors 71-74. Country names are abbreviated by 3-digit ISO codes.

Sources: Authors' calculations based on Timmer, M.P. (ed) (2012), "The World Input-Output Database (WIOD): Contents, Sources and Methods", *WIOD Working Paper*, Number 10, *www.wiod.org/publications/papers/wiod10.pdf* and data received from the Ministry of National Economy.

StatLink http://dx.doi.org/10.1787/888933289908

Multi-dimensional Review of Kazakhstan
Volume 1. Initial Assessment

Chapter 5

Enhancing governance and institutions for sustaining inclusive growth and well-being

This chapter uses the framework of the OECD series "Government at a Glance" (OECD, 2013, 2015a), incorporating interaction with institutions, to assess the key governance constraints which shape policy effectiveness in delivering the desired public service outcomes to sustain inclusive growth and well-being.

Kazakhstan has adopted a culture of continuous improvement to enhance its governance and institutions. Reforms are continuing to professionalise and modernise public service administration. It has strengthened the transparency and accountability of the national budget and of revenues from extractive industries. At the same time, it has stepped up its anti-corruption drive and rolled out open-government initiatives to improve policy transparency and accountability.

Control of corruption remains a key cross-cutting governance challenge, transcending the scope of action of anti-corruption authorities. Corruption can hold back private sector development and economic diversification as well as the delivery of public services. Public procurement, which forms a sizeable share of government expenditure, is viewed as particularly corrupt. The delivery capacity of public administration remains low. This is exacerbated by weak government capacity and co-ordination across government agencies, which underscore the need to professionalise the civil service and instil a culture of meritocracy to harness talent and enhance integrity. In conjunction, institutional reforms must be pursued to enhance the rule of law, regulatory quality, and the openness and inclusivity of policy making.

Government is a major actor in modern economies and societies. Public policies play an essential role in shaping economic growth and individuals' well-being through fiscal policy, through spending on areas such as education, health, research and development or infrastructure, and through economic regulation. Hence, how well, how effectively and how efficiently government performs these tasks is critical, as citizens increasingly demand more from governments in terms of services that better meet their needs and the transparent and accountable use of resources. The ability of governments to operate effectively and efficiently depends in part on their management policies and practices, including budgeting practices that support fiscal sustainability, human resource management practices conducive to good performance, regulatory management capacity, principles of public sector values and ethics, and the effective use of e-government tools. The transparency and participatory nature of these practices are also critical.

Good governance and institutions are essential preconditions for government effectiveness to enable sustainable and inclusive development. Countries face different binding constraints at different stages of development, and good governance will more likely help support growth and development when it diminishes those constraints (Rodrik, 2008). Empirical literature suggests that for middle-income countries to transit to higher-income status, an improvement in governance quality such as citizen participation and government accountability is entailed, as well as development of world-class institutions. In addition, better governance improves well-being beyond any impacts it has on income or transaction costs. Good governance may improve life evaluations either directly, because people are happier living in a context of good government, or indirectly, because good governance permits people to achieve higher levels of satisfaction that is directly important to their well-being (Helliwell et al., 2014).

More importantly, enhancing institutions and governance will provide a basis for governmental effectiveness in the implementation of development plans and public service delivery. As countries progress, they require modernisation of the governance system. At the core of this transformation is the need to improve government capacity and guarantee more effective co-ordination across institutions, while meeting the needs of societies that are more demanding of the country's governance situation. At the same time, governance could be enhanced at the local level with decentralisation as well as encompassing greater participation from civil society in the delivery of public services. In other words, the development process also requires a path of governance and institutional change. The two processes do not always move at the same pace, and frequently, advances in economic and social areas are not accompanied by parallel progress in the governance framework, creating a problem that may affect the sustainability of the development process. This situation particularly affects middle-income countries, as they are the nations which undergo the most accelerated transformations.

This chapter assesses the key governance and institutional constraints which limit government effectiveness in Kazakhstan. While there is no consensus view of which specific governance features matter most for successful development, there are some notable initiatives which produce a useful conceptual framework for analysing and benchmarking the key elements of good governance performance (Oman and Arndt, 2010). One of these initiatives is the OECD's biennial publication "Government at a Glance" (OECD, 2013, 2015a). The publication compares countries' political and institutional government frameworks, their public revenues, expenditures and employment, and their government policies and practices in terms of regulatory management, budgeting, integrity and e-government. However, as institutions, both formal and informal, as well as participation by civil society are important in shaping the dynamic of public services delivery outcomes, these elements have been supplemented in the conceptual framework (Box 5.1).

Box 5.1. **OECD conceptual framework for diagnosing governance constraints**

Governance can be defined as the set of rules and institutions by which political, economic and administrative authority is excised as necessary to manage a nation's affairs (OECD, 2006). It can be described as a situation where the relationship between the government, private sector and civil society is well-functioning. The OECD (OECD, 2009a, 2011, 2013) has identified the following elements of good governance:

- **Accountability:** the government is able and willing to show the extent to which its actions and decisions are consistent with clearly defined and agreed-upon objectives.
- **Participatory:** fairness in dealings with citizens, including mechanisms for consultation and participation.
- **Transparency:** government actions, decisions and decision-making processes are open to an appropriate level of scrutiny by other parts of government, civil society and, in some instances, outside institutions.
- **Integrity:** the alignment of government and public institutions with broader principles and standards of conduct that contribute to safeguarding the public interest while preventing corruption.
- **Fairness:** in a procedural sense the consistent treatment of citizens (and businesses) in the policy-making and policy-implementation processes.
- **Rule of law:** the government enforces equally transparent laws, regulations and codes.
- **Efficiency and effectiveness:** the government strives to produce quality public outputs, including services delivered to citizens, at the best cost, and ensures that outputs meet the original intentions of policy makers.
- **Responsiveness:** the government has the capacity and flexibility to respond rapidly to societal changes, takes into account the expectations of civil society in identifying the general public interest and is willing critically to re-examine its role.
- **Forward-looking vision:** the government is able to anticipate future problems and issues based on current data and trends and to develop policies that take into account future costs and anticipated changes (e.g. demographic, economic, environmental changes).
- **Whole of government approach:** consistency and coherence in policy formation and implementation.

Box 5.1. OECD conceptual framework for diagnosing governance constraints *(cont.)*

Figure 5.1. Conceptual framework for diagnosing governance constraints

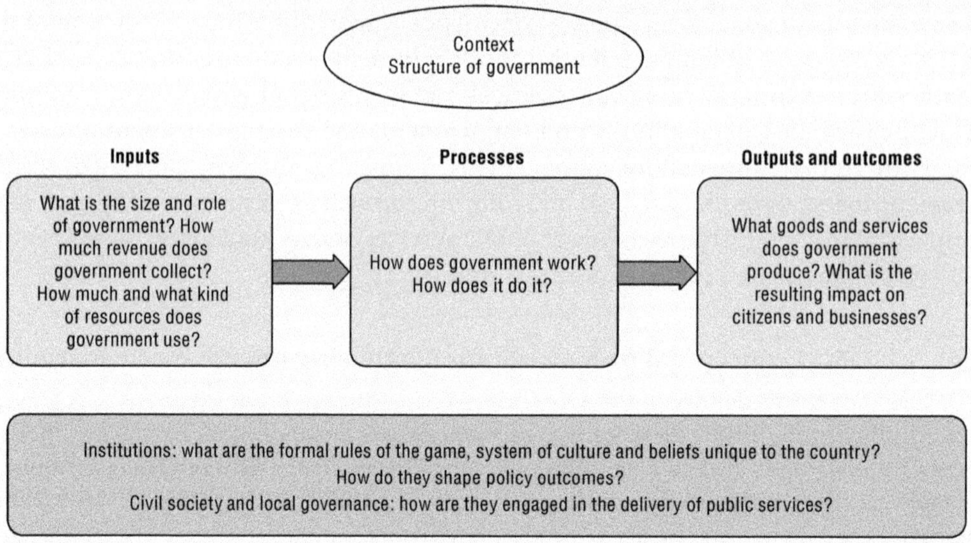

Sources: Hatry (1999) *Performance Measurement: Getting Results*; Pollitt and Bouckaert (2004), *Public Management Reform: A Comparative Analysis*; OECD (2013), *Government at a Glance 2013*; W.K. Kellogg Foundation (2004), *Logic Model Development Guide*.

Corruption and the institutional framework hold Kazakhstan back

Corruption remains a cross-cutting governance challenge

Government effectiveness in Kazakhstan has appeared limited hitherto, with corruption as a cross-cutting governance issue. As discussed in preceding chapters, government effectiveness appears limited in view of the mixed results of the implementation of certain strategic development plans and in the final public service delivery outcomes of state-dominated entities, such as health and education. While some of the constraints to government effectiveness are sector-specific, such as the legacy of underinvestment in primary health care or the difficulties in human resource management in the education sector, others largely reflect constraints in governance and institutions. Notably, corruption is perceived to be prevalent in the Corruption Perception Index produced by Transparency International (2014) and is one of the key constraints for doing business in Kazakhstan according to the 2013 World Bank Enterprise Survey[1] (World Bank, 2015).

Corruption can hold back private sector development and economic diversification. Findings from the World Bank's Enterprise Survey showed that "bribery depth", a measure of the prevalence of bribery, in Kazakhstan is on average much higher than in OECD countries as well as other comparators except Indonesia (Table 5.1). However, the value of the gifts expected in order to secure a government contract is relatively small in Kazakhstan, compared to Russia or Indonesia, and slightly higher than that in OECD countries. This suggests that petty corruption could be the underlying issue. If so, that would imply that corruption was a particular impediment to diversification and development of SMEs, given that such firms have fewer financial resources. While the evidence is not conclusive, this would be consistent with what other indicators show in respect of the strength of investor protection. In other words, Kazakhstan would need to do much more to create a more conducive business environment for entrepreneurship (OECD, 2014a). In particular, in these circumstances, corruption could pose a microeconomic risk, resulting in low appropriability[2] of firms and hence low investment in private sector and entrepreneurship (Hausmann, Rodrik and Velasco, 2005).

Table 5.1. **Corruption can hold back private sector development, particularly for SMEs**

	High income: OECD	Kazakhstan	Russia	Azerbaijan	Chile	China	Indonesia
Year of Survey		2013	2012	2013	2010	2012	2009
Bribery depth (percentage of public transactions where a gift or informal payment was requested)	1.2	22.0	9.7	13.2	0.8	9.9	23.0
Value of gift expected to secure a government contract (percentage of contract value)	0.5	0.8	2.5	0.0	0.0	0.2	1.8
Bribery incidence (percentage of firms experiencing at least one bribe payment request)	1.7	26.7	14.2	15.3	1.3	11.6	26.9
Percentage of firms expected to give gifts in meetings with tax officials	0.8	22.3	7.3	11.8	0.4	10.9	14.0
Percentage of firms expected to give gifts to secure government contract	10.7	19.1	30.9	49.9	1.0	42.2	53.0
Percentage of firms expected to give gifts to get an operating licence	2.8	15.8	12.6	38.8	1.2	7.8	25.9
Percentage of firms expected to give gifts to get an import licence	1.5	27.9	27.5	38.7	0.3	19.2	19.5
Percentage of firms expected to give gifts to get a construction permit	1.7	27.0	26.8	41.6	1.5	18.8	37.1
Percentage of firms expected to give gifts to get an electricity connection	0.5	34.4	25.8	6.1	0.6	3.0	23.3
Percentage of firms expected to give gifts to get a water connection	0.4	26.5	12.7	12.5	0.1	6.2	22.3
Percentage of firms expected to give gifts to public officials "to get things done"	8.4	20.4	20.5	6.8	0.7	10.7	14.9
Percentage of firms identifying corruption as a major constraint	10.8	19.6	33.1	4.7	17.5	0.9	14.1

Source: World Bank Enterprise Survey, various years. Firm-level survey of a representative sample of an economy's private sector, covering manufacturing firms only.

Corruption also undermines trust in government institutions and affects service delivery outcomes. Corruption can increase the cost to consumers if a bribe is demanded in addition to the official payment, something that reduces demand for services and therefore may worsen outcomes (Azfar and Gurgur, 2008). Similarly, if corruption takes the form of the official pocketing the payment intended for the government, this reduces government resources allocated to service delivery, which would also worsen outcomes. Indeed, survey data from the European Bank for Reconstruction and Development (EBRD) Life in Transition Survey II (2011) showed the reported prevalence of unofficial payments in developing countries in Central Asia (Figure 5.2). In particular, for Kazakhstan, the prevalence of unofficial payments is in key public services which have poor delivery outcomes such as health and education. Moreover, studies have shown that in countries which are rated as very corrupt or are rated to have a very ineffective bureaucracy, public spending on social services at the margin will be ineffective (Rajkumar and Swaroop, 2008).

Figure 5.2. **Reported prevalence of unofficial payments in Kazakhstan in key public services such as health and education where the delivery outcomes are poor**

Percentage of respondents that report unofficial payments are usually or always needed

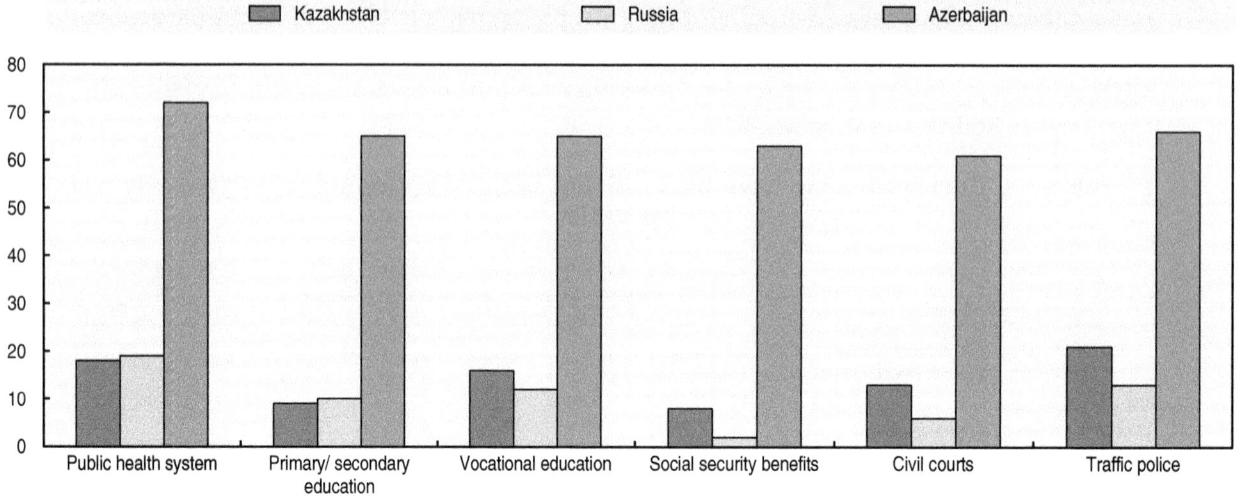

Source: EBRD (2011), *Life in Transition Survey II.*

StatLink http://dx.doi.org/10.1787/888933289911

The government has identified control of corruption as one of the key priorities in the strategy *Kazakhstan 2050* and has undertaken several anti-corruption measures to reduce its influence on the various spheres of society. The legislation stipulates that all state bodies and officials must strive against corruption within their area of competence. The Civil Service and Anti-Corruption Agency was established in August 2014 to co-ordinate the implementation of anti-corruption policy. A number of other agencies and institutions play an important role in tackling corruption, including the Ombudsman and the General Prosecutor's Office. In terms of anti-corruption measures and programmes, the state anti-corruption programme was implemented in 2011-2015. With the goal of improving efficiency in fighting corruption, this programme served as fundamental regulation in the anti-corruption policy that provides a set of systemic measures in the medium term. At the end of 2014, a new "Anti-Corruption Strategy of the Republic of Kazakhstan for 2015-2025" was developed and approved as part of the action plan to implement the presidential address setting out the Kazakhstan 2050 strategy. This new programme aims to improve anti-corruption activities and involve the participation of the non-governmental sector and the public in the fight against corruption. The measures included in the implementation of the strategy aim to minimise incentives for corruption, by, among other things, increasing the transparency of price-setting for regulated monopolies, reducing administrative barriers and strengthening the control of natural monopolies.

Nevertheless, control of corruption remains a key governance challenge. Progress on the implementation of anti-corruption measures has been mixed. In the third round monitoring of the Istanbul Anti-corruption Action Plan, it was noted that while Kazakhstan has taken some steps forward in the area of anti-corruption policy, there has, on the whole, been a lack of progress in the areas of criminalisation of corruption and prevention of corruption (OECD, 2015b). Moreover, a weak judicial system compromises Kazakhstan's extensive legal framework for dealing with corruption (Business Anti-Corruption, 2015).

Institutional reform in the rule of law is an area where Kazakhstan has achieved some progress, but key gaps remain

Kazakhstan has made some progress in institutional reform in the rule of law. According to the constitution, judicial power is exercised through civil, criminal and other forms of judicial procedure. The courts include the Supreme Court, local and other courts. The Supreme Court is the highest judicial body for civil, criminal and other cases that are under the jurisdiction of local and other courts; it supervises their activities and provides interpretation on issues of judicial practice. The president appoints judges to the Supreme Court and local courts, as well as members of the Supreme Judicial Council (OECD, 2014c). The development of better regulation policies in Kazakhstan has taken place in the context of the transition to an independent state with a market-based economy. In the aftermath of independence in 1991, the government carried out a broad set of reforms to transform the economy and integrate it into the international trading system, and to put in place institutions and a legal system based on the rule of law. Hundreds of new laws and decrees were adopted in key areas, including the institutional framework, justice, the banking and financial system, customs and taxes, environment, labour, health care.

However, key elements of the rule of law such as constraints on government powers need to be further improved and restrict private investment. Although Kazakhstan's constitution recognises the separation of powers and safeguards the independence of the judiciary, independent assessments often raise concerns about the independence of the judiciary, which seem to have increased following the 2007-08 constitutional amendments (see for example, Global Integrity, 2010). The World Justice Project (World Justice Project, 2014), measures the rule of law through nine composite indicators. They include an indicator of limits on government powers which measures whether authority is distributed, whether by formal rules or by convention, in a way that ensures that no single government organ has the ability to exercise unchecked power.[3] Another dimension is an indicator of fundamental rights that captures the protection of fundamental human rights and as a result, it is a normative measure. Compared to the benchmark countries, Kazakhstan's performance in these two dimensions of rule of law is similar. While Kazakhstan's scores for these two indicators are on a par with those of the People's Republic of China and Russia in 2014, they are lower than the rest of the comparators (Figure 5.3).

Figure 5.3. **Limits on government powers and the protection of fundamental rights are weak**

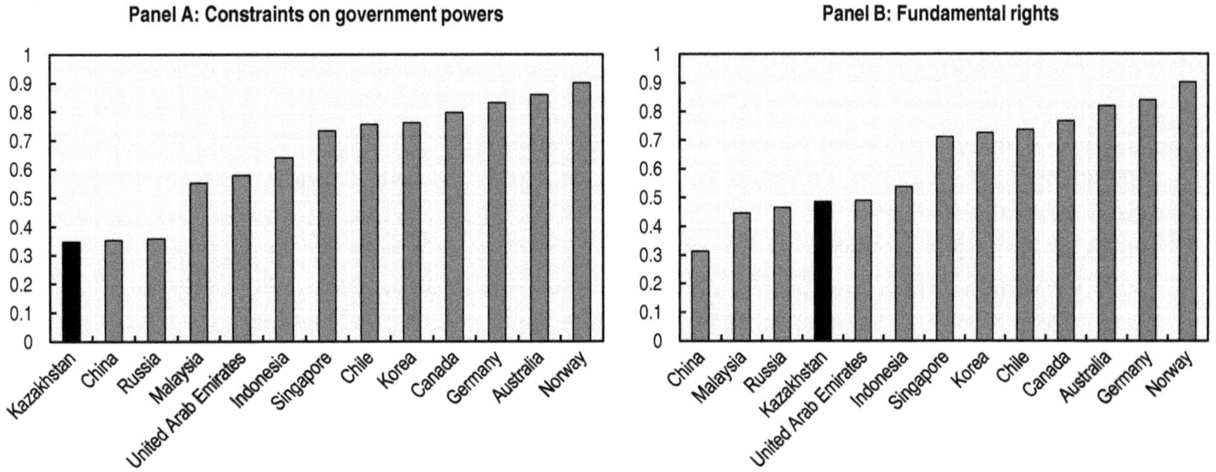

Source: World Justice Project (2014), *Rule of Law Index 2014*, *http://worldjusticeproject.org/sites/default/files/files/wjp_rule_of_law_index_2014_report.pdf.*

StatLink http://dx.doi.org/10.1787/888933289927

There are also gaps in regulatory enforcement and civil justice. The regulatory enforcement composite indicator measures the extent to which regulations are fairly and effectively enforced. It does not assess what and how government regulates, just how regulations are implemented and enforced. It considers areas of regulation that all countries regulate to some degree, such as public health, workplace safety, environmental protection and commercial activity. On the other hand, the civil justice composite measures whether ordinary people can resolve their grievances effectively through the civil justice system, which requires that the system be accessible, affordable, effective, impartial and culturally competent.[4] Similarly, while Kazakhstan's performance in these two elements is on a par with those of China and Russia in 2014, it is lower than the rest of the comparators (Figure 5.4).

Figure 5.4. **There are also gaps in regulatory enforcement and civil justice**

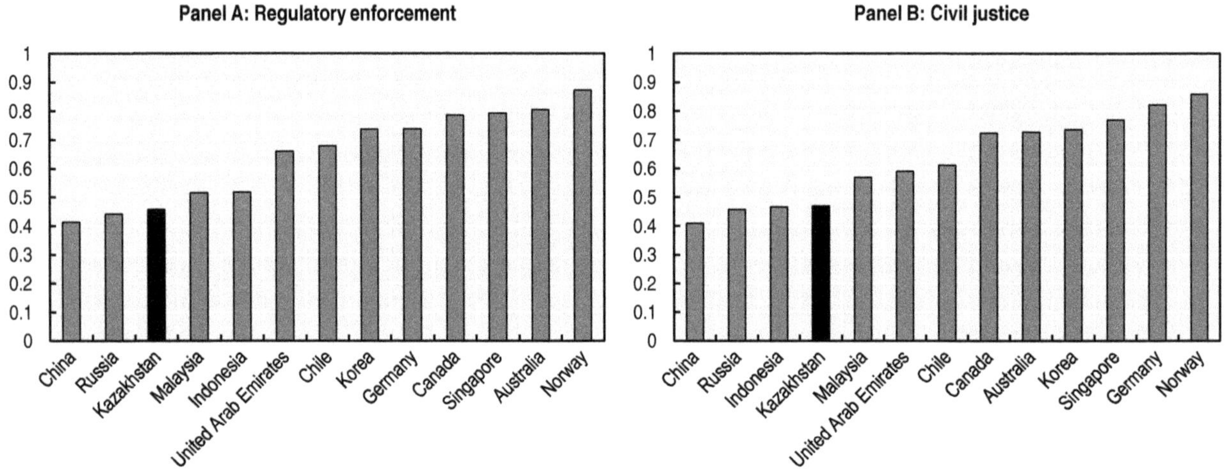

Source: World Justice Project (2014), *Rule of Law Index 2014*, *http://worldjusticeproject.org/sites/default/files/files/wjp_rule_of_law_index_2014_report.pdf.*

StatLink http://dx.doi.org/10.1787/888933289937

Similar conclusions are also drawn using governance indicators such as the World Bank Governance Indicators on rule of law or the Bertelsmann Stiftung Transformation Index (BTI). For example, BTI (2014) noted that there is still limited separation of powers as the head of the judiciary continues to be appointed by the president. Formal and informal methods continue to be used to disrupt checks and balances. While the constitution states that the judiciary is independent, practical implementation of that independence is not guaranteed. This is crucial for attracting foreign direct investment (FDI) in the underdeveloped non-extractive sectors for diversification of economic structure, particularly the manufacturing sector and high value services sectors, which typically require high-quality institutions and the rule of law. Moreover, the EBRD Judicial Decisions Assessment found the impartiality of courts in Kazakhstan to be questionable. In their judgments, courts are believed to show particular deference to the government and entities in which the state has a substantial interest (EBRD, 2014). Hence, much remains to be done to enhance the rule of law in Kazakhstan, and instil greater confidence in the judiciary system, which is crucial for attracting FDI and economic diversification.

Regulatory burdens have been reduced and transparency has improved, but key regulatory challenges remain

Over the years, Kazakhstan has increased the focus on improving transparency and regulatory quality, in order to create conditions for the development of a market economy. Following a large wave of regulatory reforms, increased attention has been given to improving the consistency of the regulatory framework and improving the legal quality of regulations, including through *ex ante* evaluation. In more recent years, efforts to diversify the economy away from natural resources have spurred initiatives to reduce administrative burdens with a view to building a more competitive economy and attracting foreign investment. These efforts have largely focused on the simplification for businesses of licences and permits. In particular, the "Concept of Further Reforming of the Licensing System of the Republic of Kazakhstan for 2012-2015" was introduced to improve the licensing system with the aim of reducing regulatory burdens and simplifying procedure to obtain licences. Currently, licences are issued in electronic format through the public database "E-licensing" and the time period for issuing licences has been reduced from 30 to 15 days. Reducing bureaucracy and red tape will also help to reduce both incentives and opportunities for bribery and corruption. The government's ambition to play an increasing role in international relations has also given prominence to the adoption of international best practices (OECD, 2014a). The progress in improving regulatory transparency and quality is reflected in the improvement of Kazakhstan's rating in indicators in the *World Competitiveness Report* (Figure 5.5).

Figure 5.5. **Transparency of government policy and regulatory burden have improved in Kazakhstan**

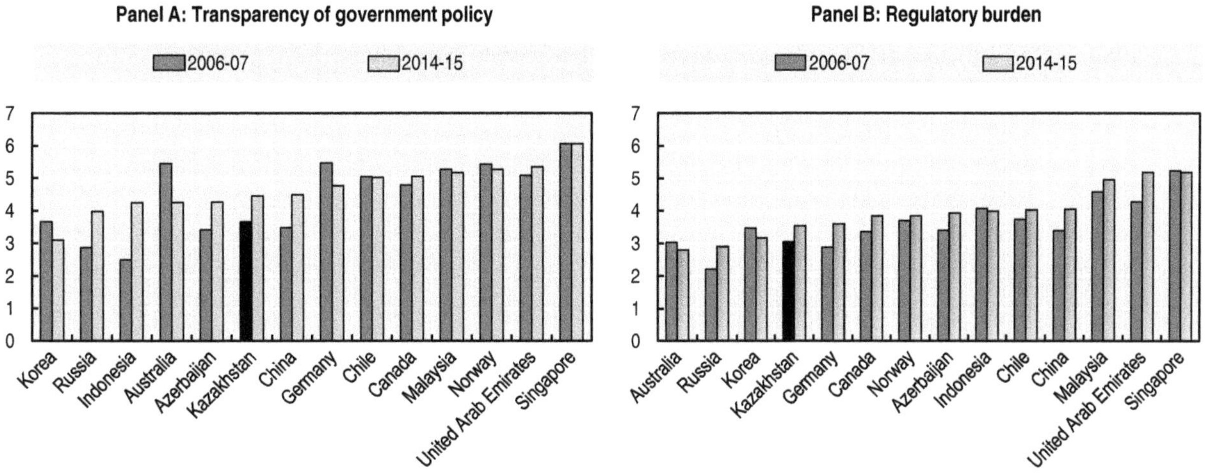

Note: Based on score of 1 (Worst) to 7 (Best).

Source: WEF, *Executive Opinion Survey of the Global Competitiveness Report*, *http://reports.weforum.org/global-competitiveness-report-2014-2015/* (various years).

StatLink http://dx.doi.org/10.1787/888933289942

However, several key regulatory challenges remain. First, regulatory reform efforts have not been framed into a comprehensive national policy or action policy, and the approach to regulatory policy has been largely patchy (OECD, 2014a). The new "Concept of State Regulation of Business Activities by 2020" shows a positive move towards a more comprehensive approach to regulatory policy. Second, strengthening regulatory policy requires adapting the institutional setting and promoting ownership of better regulation across the administration. The government so far does not have a body specifically charged with promoting and sustaining regulatory policies. Development of regulatory tools and processes is done within each ministry, in a "silo" way, and there is a general need for more practical co-operation across government bodies, and increased outreach to external stakeholders. Third, providing training, building capacities and raising awareness are essential to embedding better regulation in administrative culture and practice. The issue is particularly acute in Kazakhstan where a formal approach usually prevails. Fourth, discrepancies in implementation and interpretation of laws represent a significant issue, especially at the local level. Moreover, a lack of data on compliance with regulation hampers the monitoring of enforcement quality. Lastly, progress can be achieved by developing practical tools and training in support of the work of officials, such as defining common methodologies and guidelines for the preparation of regulations, public consultation, and inspections, *ex ante* impact assessment and *ex post* review of legislation. The current focus of ministries' performance efforts appears to be more on ensuring the legal implementation of strategic initiatives rather than on the effectiveness of the programmes themselves. There currently does not seem to be an incentive for ministries to undertake impact assessments of proposed regulations, as the main provisions for such regulations often stem from the planning process.

The flawed regulation of utilities creates significant negative externalities in the form of decaying infrastructure and environmental damage

Affordable district heating is an essential public service in Kazakhstan, but suffers from underinvestment. District heating is very common in Kazakhstan, with over 50% of the urban heating demand in the country covered by district heating. However, the sector is plagued by high levels of heat loss caused by aged infrastructure. Investment in infrastructure maintenance is low as a result of the indirect subsidy through the pricing mechanism. While blanket consumer subsidies have been eliminated, consumers are subsidised indirectly, by keeping end-user prices low and by providing support to producers. Tariff regulation and low end-user charges are a major obstacle to investment by network companies. Tariffs for regulated monopolies are set through the *cost plus* method, under which a standard mark-up is added to the cost of production of a good or service. Historically, this pricing regime has not provided sufficient incentives to promote investment (an insufficient rate of return on investment and inadequate allowance for the depreciation of assets), as well as suffering from a more general tendency not to cover key costs.

Compared with most Central and Eastern European countries, heating tariffs for district heating in Kazakhstan are low. The low tariffs in Kazakhstan are mostly the result of low-cost fuel used in heat generation and the exclusion of capital expenditure (CAPEX) from user tariffs. Through the cost-based calculation, the regulator approves not only the pricing but also the different cost items in operating costs. In particular, the exclusion of CAPEX from tariffs is one of the main barriers hindering the modernisation of the district heating sector in Kazakhstan. Depreciation accounts for 3% of total operating expenses (OPEX) while the profit margin is set at around 2.4% of OPEX. The expenses on repairs correspond to only 1% of OPEX. Currently, in most district heating utilities in Kazakhstan, the tariffs allow the (partial) coverage of OPEX but not CAPEX.

The low heating tariffs and the mode of calculation limit opportunities and incentives for investment. In many cases, regulated maintenance expenditure by the utilities is also very low, which results in further degradation of the existing infrastructure. Moreover, since the cost structure is approved by the regulator on a regular basis, incentives to reduce production costs, including through greater energy efficiency, are severely diminished. To keep the utilities running, the state needs to provide additional support. Direct subsidies to operations and maintenance (O&M) in the district heating sector are limited to several underdeveloped regions. Between 2008 and 2012, transfers for fuel purchases amounted to about KZT 8 billion (EUR 50 million). These subsidies are allocated from the respective local budgets. As a consequence, the renewal and modernisation of district heating infrastructure currently falls largely under the national and regional budgets rather than being carried out by regulated actors.

The cost-based price-setting mechanism seems to favour Astana and Almaty, the two richest cities in the country. The level of heating prices is heavily dependent on fuel costs, which make up about 70% of costs. Low fuel prices account partially for the low level of tariffs. Differences in the type of fuel used (gas in Southern Kazakhstan, in Taraz and Kyzylorda, coal in Northern Kazakhstan, in the cities of Astana, Karaganda and Pavlodar) and in distance to the sources of fuel lead to significant differences in cost and therefore in pricing. For example, the heat price in Almaty is the highest in Kazakhstan (KZT 101.16 per m^2). However, in terms of affordability (share of households' income spent on heating), it is Shymkent (South Kazakhstan), followed by Taraz and Kyzylorda, that pay most for heating. Heating prices in Astana are relatively more affordable, with households spending 2.2% of their income on heating (Table 5.2).

Table 5.2. **While Almaty has the highest heating price, heating is more affordable than in Shymkent, Kyzylorda and Taraz**

City	Heat price 2012 KZT/m^2	Household disposable income (KZT per capita 2012) KZT/person/month	Estimated monthly expenditures on heating KZT/month	Estimated affordability (% income spent on heating) %
Astana	69.74	41 645	4 561	2.2
Almaty	101.16	49 793	6 058	3.3
Aktau (Mangystau)	47.08	29 878	2 655	1.8
Atyrau	95.79	32 209	4 479	2.6
Aktobe	62.34	34 609	2 627	1.5
Karagandy	67.04	41 692	3 593	1.9
Kostanay	105.69	31 759	5 181	3.7
Kyzylorda	66.95	31 182	4 800	3.8
Kokshetau (Akmola)	77.81	33 257	4 046	2.3
Oral (West Kazakhstan)	85.49	29 530	4 360	3.2
Oskemen (East Kazakhstan)	48.38	35 756	2 196	1.5
Pavlodar	48.94	33 096	2 514	1.5
Petropavlovsk (North Kazakhstan)	81.27	33 809	4 037	2.5
Taraz (Zhambyl)	69.63	23 978	3 969	3.8
Taldykorgan (Almaty)	34.98	37 920	6 169	3.7
Shymkent (South Kazakhstan)	86.63	21 852	6 307	6.3

Source: Household disposable income is the measure of household income used for consumption provided by the Committee on Statistics of the Republic of Kazakhstan, other data from OECD (2014b).

Regulatory reform is needed to bring heating price tariffs closer to a level that would allow agents to invest in infrastructure maintenance and modernisation. Full cost recovery pricing is usually limited by two constraints: the affordability of heating and the need for households to be able to consume sufficient heating. According to international benchmarks (e.g. the World Bank) the maximum affordable expenditures for heating should not exceed

8% of disposable household income. Model-based estimates (OECD, 2014b) show that while prices in Kazakhstan are low, the scope to increase prices to the affordability threshold of 8% (which would imply rises from 27% to 433% in the price per m^2 across cities) is limited by the need to provide sufficient heating. Nevertheless, there is substantial scope for price increases, with the exception of Shymkent, where heating already commands 6.3% of household expenditures (Table 5.2). The removal of the hidden subsidy could help finance the upgrading of infrastructure and at the same time restrain excessive consumption. Upgrading of equipment would also help reduce air pollution. It is estimated that the

Box 5.2. Regulation of the district heating sector in Kazakhstan and impact on air pollution

There are 42 large district heating (DH) systems in the country connected to 38 large co-generation plants (CHPs) and 30 big central-heat only boilers (HOBs). The efficiency of the DH systems is generally low with heat losses reaching up to 50% of the primary energy used. The high level of heat losses is primarily the result of old, obsolete equipment (typically between 25 and 40 years old) and inadequate maintenance.

Most of the power generation is coal-fuelled. Kazakhstan has a developed infrastructure of heat supply. The installed capacity of heat power plants is more than 6 700 MWs (38% of the capacity of all power plants of the country). They cover about 40% of the heat consumption and about 46% of the electricity consumption in Kazakhstan. There is no natural gas supply infrastructure in the urban centres; as a result, district heating companies face no competitive pressure from natural gas suppliers. The lack of alternatives is an important factor in the low disconnection rate.

The district heating sector accounts for a significant share of Kazakhstan's greenhouse gas (GHG) emissions. According to national statistics, some 110 terawatt-hours (TWH) of heat (served through large district heating networks or through smaller local ones) are consumed each year, with additional heat generated in individually heated buildings. Of this, around 75 TWh are consumed by residential, public and commercial buildings; the remainder accounted for by industrial heat consumption. The associated emissions are close to 20% of the national total, at 47 MtCO2 (NERA Economic Consulting and BNEF, 2011).

Furthermore, a significant share of air pollution is attributable to electricity and heat production in thermal power plants. This is particularly related to emissions of sulphur oxides (SOx), nitrogen oxides (NOx), carbon monoxide (CO) and ash. According to UNECE (2008), much of this pollution is caused by the use of very low quality coal as well as the inefficient gas purification systems in thermal power plants, notably the lack of de-nitrification and de-sulphurisation units. Mean estimates of mortality risk attributable to air pollution are about 16 000 cases per year (Kenessariyev et al., 2013), which constitutes a significant contribution to the environmental burden of diseases. In relative terms, the impact of air pollution on premature mortality in Kazakhstan is notably higher than in Russia and the Ukraine

Modernising the obsolete infrastructure will help to reduce air pollution. By improving the energy efficiency of the existing DH systems and by further promoting cogeneration, the total conservative GHG emission reduction potential has been estimated at about 4.6 million tonnes of CO2 equivalent per year. The installed electrical capacity of the power plants in Kazakhstan is about 18 gigawatts (of which coal-fired power plants account for 87.5% and hydroelectric stations 12.4%).

Source: OECD (2014b) "Energy Subsidies and Climate Change in Kazakhstan", *Final Draft Report*, OECD Publishing, Paris.

difference between current prices and a higher level that would still guarantee households can consume sufficient heating would increase heating revenues by KZT 78 million and lead to substantial reduction in energy production and therefore greenhouse gas emissions (of 12% of the annual emissions of the sector). However, there is tendency to keep tariffs down rather than introduce full-cost recovery rates, because of the vital role of heating for social welfare in Kazakhstan's climate (OECD, 2014b. See Box 5.2).

The government of Kazakhstan is addressing the pricing problem by changing the tariff determination mechanism. The programme for tariff policy in the sphere of natural monopolies in the Republic of Kazakhstan, adopted in 2014, aims to shift the mode of regulation from the current system, where standard prices are determined for relatively short periods on the basis of the approval of the entire cost structure, to a model of *ceiling tariffs* by 2018. In this alternative model, caps on prices are approved for a longer period (one to five years and more) subject to the regulated agent carrying out an investment plan. Regulated agents are allowed to provide services below, but not above, the regulated cap. The extension of this system builds on its application to power generation since 2009. The predictability in pricing and larger allowance for non-specified costs, including capital expenditure costs, in the determination of prices is meant to provide greater incentives for regulated actors to invest, maintain and modernise the existing infrastructure.

Government and public administration suffer from a lack of capacity

Critically, the successful implementation of the vision of a strategic centre and delivering on ambitious national objectives require the development of necessary capacities at the centre, both at the individual and organisational levels. The OECD Review of Central Administration for Kazakhstan (2014c) identified three main areas of capacity gaps in the public administration:

- Ministerial capacity: while ministries are developing capacities to implement strategic documents, gaps remain elsewhere, including policy analysis, research and risk management capacities. The government of Kazakhstan is already taking steps to build capacities in the public sector (e.g. strengthening the Academy of Public Administration, developing competency frameworks), but major gaps still remain and there is a lack of a strategic approach to skill development in the public service.
- Role of policy-making and policy capacity: the role of the ministries in relation to the management of their human resources appears rather limited. The OECD review found evidence that many ministerial services, especially departments, are overburdened with their current tasks and unable to cover the complete range of their missions because of human resource constraints. In addition, departments seem to suffer from a chronic lack of specialised staff, a result of a non-targeted recruitment policy and high turnover among civil servants. The mobility of civil servants, which would be particularly beneficial if it took place within ministries to help them accumulate relevant experience, occurs in fact essentially between ministries and leads to a permanent loss of capital.
- Capacity of central agencies: the centre of government in Kazakhstan would need to develop strategic capacities to lead and steward a modern public administration, including the development of skills in new management areas, such as financial management and audit, effectiveness evaluation, policy analysis, procurement as an economic function, strategic human resources management. Moreover, having the sufficient capacities to deliver on the strategic role of the centre also calls for ensuring the appropriate level of staffing with the appropriate background and skills. Investment in information and

communications technology, research and building policy networks, inside and outside government, to develop seamless access to data and knowledge will also be critical.

Reflecting the capacity gaps, Kazakhstan's performance in governance surveys has been lagging behind more advanced economies. For example, the Institutional Policy Profiles of public governance published by the French *Centre d'Études Prospectives et d'Informations Internationales* (CEPII)[5] showed that Kazakhstan has a slightly above average performance in terms of capacity for sectoral reforms (score of 2.6 out of 4.0) and lags behind more advanced economies. However, a positive note is that Kazakhstan has a slightly better score for having long-term sectoral reforms, and its performance is better than those of Chile and Korea (Figure 5.6). This highlights that capacity gaps are the more fundamental issue in Kazakhstan.

Figure 5.6. **While Kazakhstan has a slightly above average performance in terms of capacity for sectoral reforms, it lags behind more advanced economies**

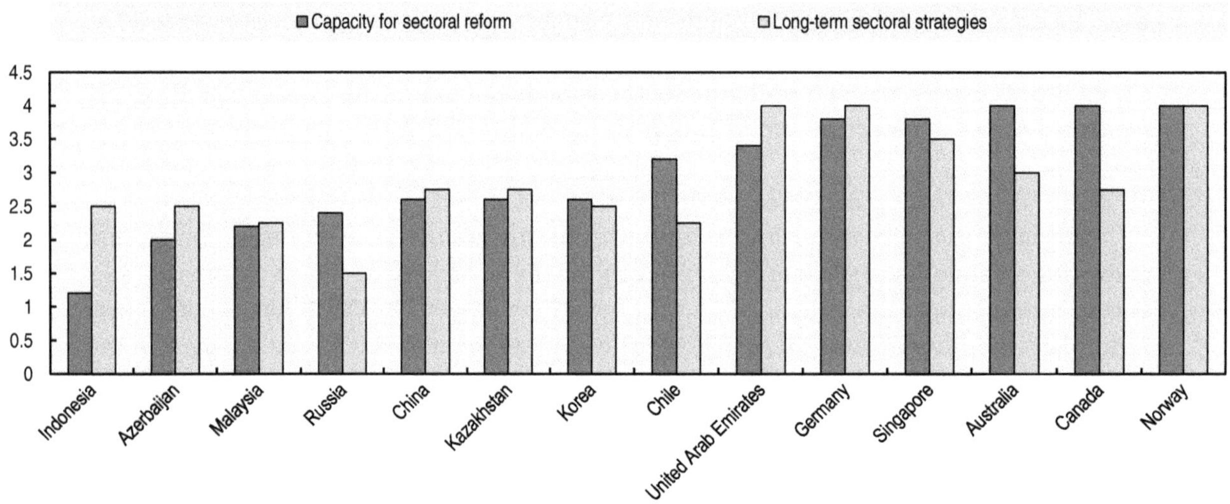

Notes: Capacity for sectoral reform measures "Authorities' ability to decide and actually implement" (scores range from 0 = very weak capacity; to 4= strong capacity). Long-term sectoral strategies measures whether "... the public authorities have a long-term strategic vision" (scores range from 0 =very weak strategic vision; to 4 = strong strategic vision).

Source: CEPII, *Institutional Profiles Database*, Centre d'Études Prospectives et d'Informations Internationales, Paris. *www.cepii.fr/institutions/EN/ipd.asp*.

StatLink http://dx.doi.org/10.1787/888933289951

The public administration needs merit-based and competitive recruitment and remuneration

The current cohort of civil servants is relatively young. As of April 2013, Kazakhstan's public sector employed 96 976 civil servants, including 403 political appointees and 96 573 administrative civil servants. The central state bodies included over 60% of civil servants, of which about 16% were in the central offices and the rest in the regional offices. The average age of political appointees is 48 and that of administrative officials 39. The civil service in Kazakhstan is relatively young, according to the data of the Civil Service and Anti-Corruption Agency: 24.6% of civil servants are under 30, 30% are 30 to 40 years old, 22.3% are 40 to 50 and 23.1% are over 50 (OECD, 2014c).

The capacity gaps highlight the importance of professionalising the civil service as well as skills and training development, to make the best use of talent. Importantly, having civil service remuneration competitive with private sector could help to retain and attract talent, and professionalise the public administration. This will also help to reduce incentives for corruption. In Kazakhstan, one of the main reasons for leaving the civil service is to find better paid jobs in state-owned enterprises and the private sector (OECD, 2014c). The average civil service experience is 10.4 years, with about three years in the same position. Over 88% of civil servants have a higher education degree, mostly in economic, legal, technical and educational areas. Many have graduated from the Academy of Public Administration under the President of the Republic of Kazakhstan and the presidential scholarship programme Bolashak. Undertaking steps to reduce the turnover of top civil servants in Kazakhstan, however, will be critical to ensuring effective and sustainable implementation of government strategies (OECD, 2014c). Having civil service salaries competitive with the private sector will also help to reduce incentives for corruption, particularly as decision-making is very centralised.

At a more fundamental level, the government could take the lead in instilling an informal institutional culture of meritocracy to strengthen equality of opportunity and enhance the integrity of the civil service. A system of corruption thrives on inequality or lack of fairness, as it provides a fertile breeding ground for corruption; and, in turn, it leads to further inequalities (Rothstein and Uslaner, 2005). Moreover, individuals may view the circumvention of rules and norms in a positive light, if they can be framed as redressing such underlying inequities, i.e. unlawful activity such as corruption might be viewed as redistribution by other means (Kline, Galeotti and Orsini, 2014). Hence, instilling a culture of meritocracy in the civil service is crucial to enhancing integrity. Meritocratic hiring underpins the notion of fairness and equality of opportunity; and meritocratic promotion serves as a pro-market incentive system to reward individuals' effort and hard work (Box 5.3).

Box 5.3. **Establishing a culture of meritocracy**

During Singapore's formative years, with its survival dependent on the ability of its people, it was critical that the incentive to achieve be maintained, and society had to reward, and be seen to reward, hard work and enterprise. A culture of leadership by example which transmits strong values and principles of good governance socially rather than formally throughout the public sector was created.

Singapore's late founding prime minister Lee Kuan Yew held strong beliefs about the need to build up an effective civil service – based on integrity, meritocracy and results – to facilitate economic growth and social development. He explained the need for a corruption-free Singapore: "The moment key leaders are less than incorruptible, less than stern in demanding high standards, from that moment the structure of administrative integrity will weaken, and eventually crumble. Singapore can survive only if ministers and senior officers are incorruptible and efficient ... Only when we uphold the integrity of the administration can the economy work in a way which enables Singaporeans to clearly see the nexus between hard work and high rewards." (Speech to Parliament, 1979)

Meritocracy is expressed through the selective recruitment of the "best and brightest" talent in the country without extraneous favour or prejudice. Over time these founding values have been internalised by the civil service, and have stood as guiding principles for its policies. Today, a merit-based incentive system permeates all levels of Singapore society and is the foundation of the integrity of the civil service. Indeed, Singapore has been consistently ranked at the top of the Corruption Perceptions Index and is perceived to be one of the least corrupt countries of all those surveyed.

Source: Authors' elaboration.

Countries with weak merit-based incentive systems are associated with higher perceptions of corruption (Di Tella, 2011). Survey findings from Gallup show across the benchmark countries that those which have lower belief in meritocracy tend to have poorer scores in the Corruption Perceptions Index (CPI): that is higher perception of corruption in their public sector. In particular Kazakhstan and regional peers Azerbaijan and Russia have relatively lower proportion of respondents who agree that working hard will bring success, corresponding to lower scores in the CPI (Figure 5.7). Similar findings are also shown in the Executive Opinion Survey conducted by the World Economic Forum. Again, lower scores in CPI for Kazakhstan, Azerbaijan and Russia are associated with hiring practices in the work place which are more likely to be perceived to be based on connections without regard for merit[6] (Figure 5.8).

Figure 5.7. **Weaker belief of meritocracy is associated with higher perception of corruption**

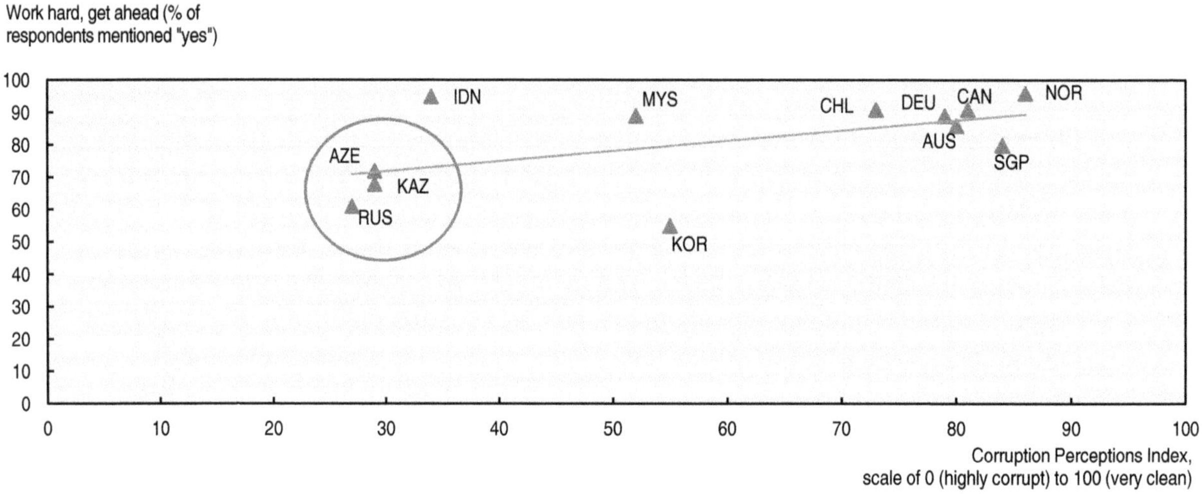

Sources: Gallup World Poll (2014), Question: "Can people in this country get ahead by working hard, or not?"; Transparency International (2014), *Corruption Perceptions Index.*

StatLink http://dx.doi.org/10.1787/888933289961

Figure 5.8. **Hiring practices in the work place perceived to be based on connections without regard for merit are associated with higher perception of corruption**

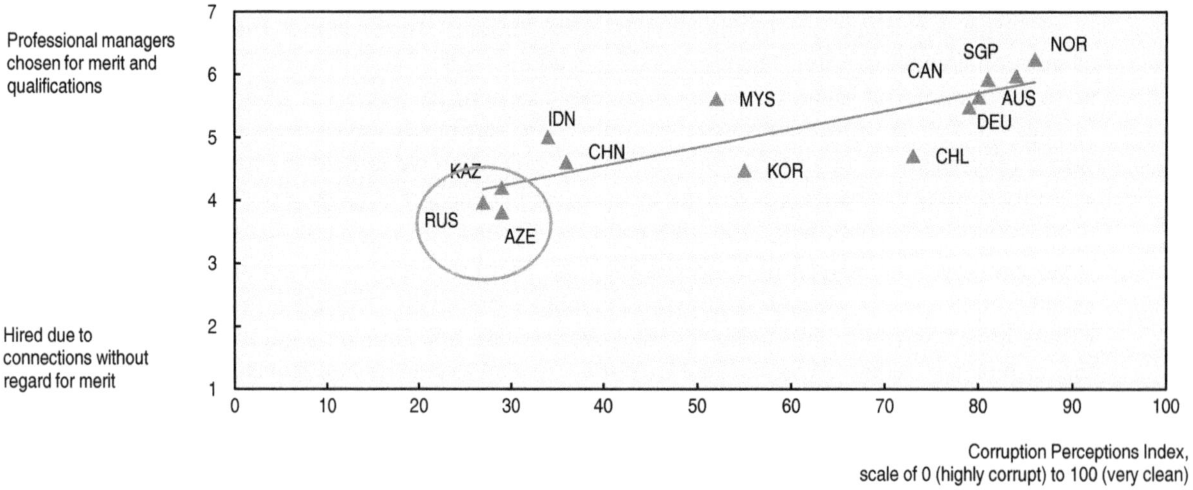

Sources: World Economic Forum (2014), *Executive Opinion Survey, Global Competitiveness Report 2014-2015*; Transparency International (2014) *Corruption Perceptions Index.*

StatLink http://dx.doi.org/10.1787/888933289977

Human resource management capacity needs to be improved and play a more strategic role in building talent in the civil service. While the Civil Service and Anti-Corruption Agency monitors qualifications, staff reserves, certain regulations and base pay, there is very limited oversight, including of the mechanisms ensuring the meritocracy of recruitment decisions and the allocation of individual bonuses. There is mandatory reporting on the staffing process, but the framework leaves room for major shortcomings in the recruitment. Weaknesses in guidance and oversight lead to opacity in the attribution of bonuses, allowances and housing (OECD, 2014c). Human resource management capacity should also include having an oversight of current and future skills gaps in the civil service and develop a skills and training and development roadmap to address this.

Following the Kazakhstan 2050 vision, the government has taken positive steps to invest heavily in the future of the public administration. It has rolled out reforms aimed at modernising and professionalising the civil service through the introduction of performance standards for public services in all central and local government bodies, as well as public organisations such as hospitals, the police and schools. The 2011 Concept of the New Model of Civil Service in Kazakhstan, with the subsequent Law on Civil Service aimed to modernise the civil service to become more centred on the profession and citizen by:

- strengthening meritocracy, for example by strengthening the requirements for admission to the civil service while centralising and standardising recruitment procedures into a three-step process evaluating knowledge and competencies prior to the interview process;
- creating a managerial corps (Corps A) and Corps B for professional public servants;
- strengthening integrity and reducing corruption by introducing a code of conduct, standards of ethics and other measures;
- improving the mechanisms of human resources (HR) management; and
- strengthening personnel management services, established with organisational independence.

Kazakhstan has created the National Personnel Policy Commission to regulate public sector recruitment, career development and performance. The introduction of Corps A aims to professionalise civil service management and includes executive secretaries and heads of administrations of regional authorities, chairmen of committees, governors of regions and towns. Kazakhstan is also reducing its number of political appointees by 80% from 3 271 to 400 to encourage transparent, merit-based selection and to reduce potential political influence-peddling in the civil service. Key legislation includes the Law on Civil Service and the Law on the Fight against Corruption. Written tests for civil service appointments have been computerised to minimise manipulation, interview processes and procedures have been tightened, and committees are used to ensure that the selection of candidates is objective. All of this has diminished the role of patronage, though it continues to exist. Civil servants with financial assets need to place them in trusts when taking office (OECD, 2014c).

The modernisation and professionalisation of the civil service is one of five key institutional reforms launched in April 2015 by President Nazarbayev. The action plan entitled "100 concrete steps" is a major initiative as part of the implementation of the Kazakhstan 2050 strategy. The action plan includes 15 specific reforms in the area of civil service development, including changes to recruitment processes, the introduction of performance pay, the introduction of regular on-the-job training, the strengthening of meritocracy in promotions as well as the development of ethics and anti-corruption institutions.

Insufficient co-ordination between government agencies hampers effectiveness

There are also co-ordination capacity gaps amongst government agencies. Although Kazakhstan has extensive co-ordination mechanisms at the high level both for central agencies and ministries, they appear too formal, and insufficient to deal with increasingly cross-cutting policy issues (OECD, 2014c). Hence, there is a need to strengthen interministerial and central agency co-ordination by encouraging working level contacts among ministries in the areas related to common objectives and among central agencies, including the chancellery and the presidency. Specifically, there are gaps in horizontal collaboration within the government. For example, while ministries are usually closely linked with their mandates, many issues cannot be compartmentalised and require cross-ministry co-operation. Currently, relations between ministries are confined within the framework of their respective strategic plans. Other modes of co-ordination are not common, and there is little exchange of information at the level of policy implementation and monitoring. Findings from CEPII showed co-ordination gaps are a constraint in Kazakhstan's public sphere compared to most of the benchmark countries (Figure 5.9).

Figure 5.9. **Co-ordination in Kazakhstan's public sphere is lower than most of the benchmark countries**

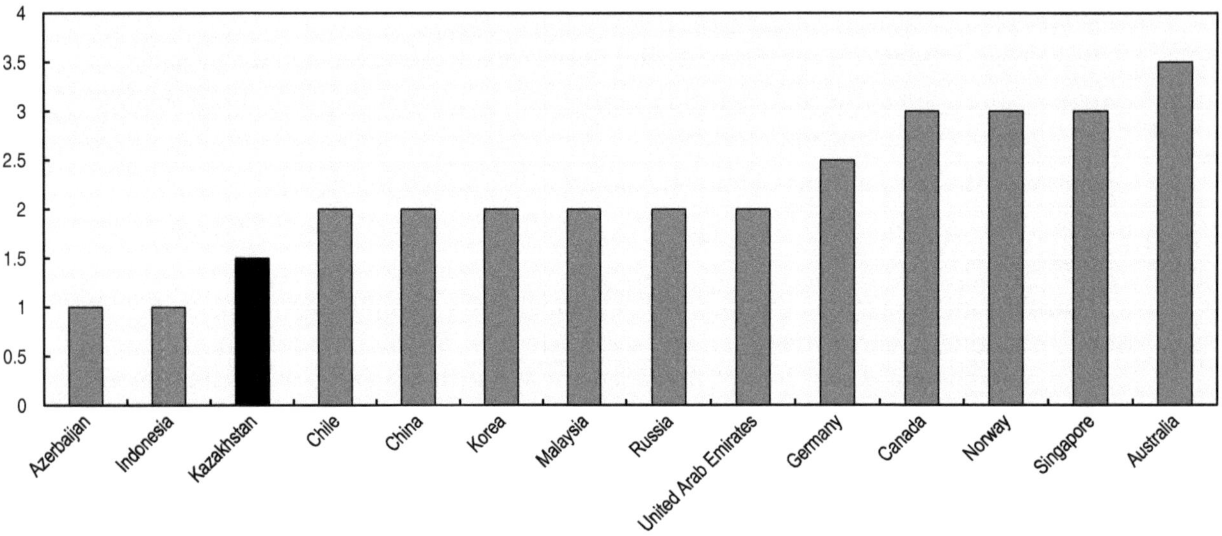

Note: The indicator measures the "degree of co-ordination/collaboration between ministries; Degree of coordination/collaboration between administrations" (scores range from 0 = very little co-ordination; to 4= strong co-ordination).

Source: CEPII (2012), *Institutional Profiles Database*.

StatLink http://dx.doi.org/10.1787/888933289987

Thus, the mechanism for horizontal collaboration needs to be solidified among ministries. This could be facilitated through the creation of ministerial posts for cross-cutting problems, strengthening accountability frameworks for horizontal activities, developing rotational programmes for government managers and policy communities, and improving the formal channels and informal networks of co-operation between ministries and agencies at decision-making, managerial and working levels (OECD, 2014c). In addition, co-ordination across ministries and government agencies could be strengthened with better alignment of strategic plans, budgeting and monitoring and evaluation of policy outcomes (Box 5.4).

Box 5.4. **Strengthening links between strategic plans and budgeting for better co-ordination**

While Kazakhstan is already taking steps towards results-based medium-term expenditure frameworks (MTEF) budgeting, there are gaps in implementing an effectively functioning and more integrated system. First, the links between planned results included in the strategic plans, budget programmes and resource allocations are not yet very clear. This could also be explained by the fact that the parliament does not receive ministerial strategic plans, which outline expected achievements. Yet it is ultimately the parliament that decides on the allocation of budget to ministries and across the government. Currently the process of resource allocation is based on the ministerial functions and competencies fixed in the legislation. Moreover, while strategic planning has a critical role in implementing a national vision and ensuring co-ordination across the government, its top-down and all-encompassing nature is detrimental to the sense of initiative and responsibility for a policy field in ministries.

More importantly, there should be a targeted focus towards outcome results indicators, rather than process and output indicators. Currently, Kazakhstan establishes key results indicators for agencies as part of the budget process, and these are used as an accountability mechanism between individual ministers and the prime minister. In this respect, the performance budgeting system can be enhanced through the use of programme reviews and programme effectiveness evaluations tied back into the resource allocation process. In addition since programmes may contribute to multiple objectives, cross-cutting sectoral programme reviews are an important tool to enhance the effectiveness and cost-effectiveness of Government programmes.

Source: OECD (2014c) *Kazakhstan: Review of the Central Administration, http://dx.doi.org/10.1787/9789264224605-en.*

Recent reforms have led to a reduction in the concentration of state functions in the centre of government. With the aim of increasing the efficiency of the administration, 5 000 jobs were transferred from central government agencies to local executive bodies in 2013. In August and September 2014, a significant reorganisation of ministerial portfolios took place, followed by amendments to constitutional law setting out the division of competencies between levels of government. As a result, a number of functions were transferred from the centre of government to cabinet ministers and to local authorities. Control and monitoring functions in the sphere of land relations, architecture, civil registration, veterinary services and crop production were transferred to local agencies, which were also strengthened with over 2 000 staff members.

Integrity is a key governance issue in public procurement

As a major part of the economy and public spending, public procurement is a major government activity. Reliable procurement systems are central to public service delivery. They can be harnessed as a policy lever to pursue economic, social and environmental goals while ensuring value for money and efficiency of spending. Many OECD countries have used innovative vehicles to achieve economies of scale, restructuring their purchasing functions, consolidating their purchases and adopting information and communication technologies (ICTs) in the procurement process. Moreover, public procurement policies are utilised by many OECD member countries not only to foster value for money but also to pursue other policy objectives. These policy objectives are designed to spur innovation, promote sustainable growth, support the development of SMEs and level the playing field for access to economic opportunities (OECD, 2013).

The procurement expenditure of the government is a major source of aggregate demand in Kazakhstan. According to statistics compiled by the United Nations Economic and Social Commission for Asia and the Pacific (ESCAP) (2014), for a sample of 19 countries, including Australia, China, India, Japan, Kazakhstan, New Zealand, the Russian Federation and Singapore, the total amounted to USD 582 billion in 2010. In particular, in Kazakhstan, the procurement expenses of the general government as a share of GDP reached 6.6% in 2010. This was higher than benchmark countries such as Singapore and Korea and comparable to Russia and Australia (Figure 5.10). Indeed, amongst the 19 countries, Kazakhstan had the largest procurement expenditure as a share of total governmental expenses at 43%.

Figure 5.10. **Government procurement expenditure forms an important part of GDP**

Procurement expenses of the general government, 2010, as % of GDP, 2010

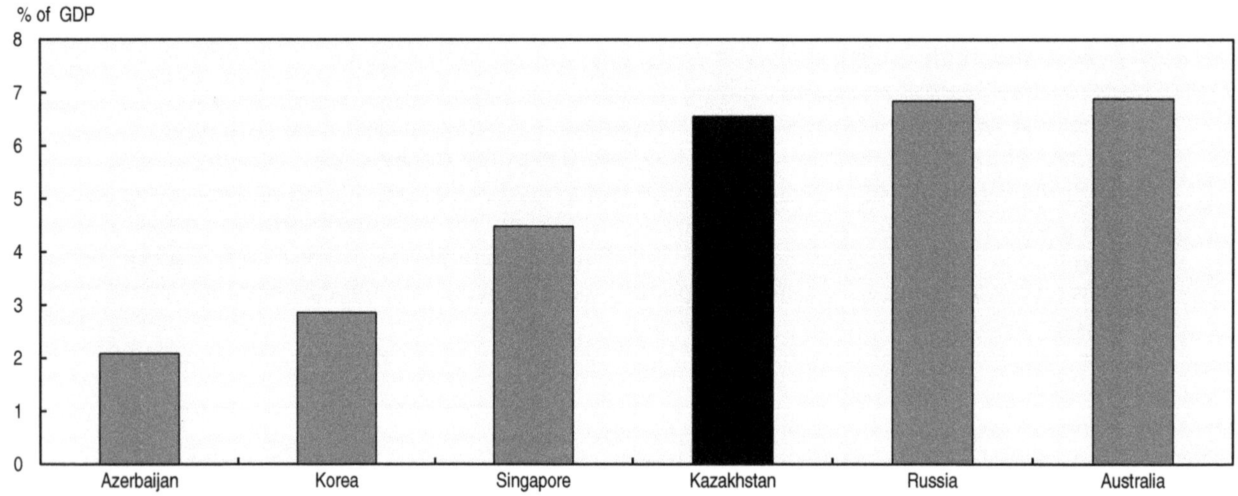

Source: UNESCAP (2014), "Governments can use sustainable public procurement to foster inclusive and sustainable development in Asia and the Pacific", *Working Paper*.

StatLink http://dx.doi.org/10.1787/888933289994

Ensuring efficiency and integrity in public procurement is essential for ensuring sound public service delivery and maintaining citizens' trust in government. This is particularly imperative as public procurement is a major risk area for mismanagement, fraud and corruption. The financial interests at stake, the volume of transactions on a global level, the close interaction between the public and private sectors, and the tensions created by introducing other policy goals (e.g. innovation and environmental) has made public procurement particularly vulnerable to corruption (OECD, 2009b). For example, according to the *Executive Opinion Survey* conducted by the World Economic Forum (WEF, 2014) for the *Global Competitiveness Report 2014-2015*, public procurement and the judiciary are the government activities with the highest perception of bribery risk in Kazakhstan (Figure 5.11). Kazakhstan's bribery risk in public procurement is ranked 64th globally in the GCR 2014-2015. While this placed Kazakhstan above regional countries such as

Figure 5.11. **Bribery risk in public procurement is high**

Frequency of irregular payments and bribes in Kazakhstan, 2014-15

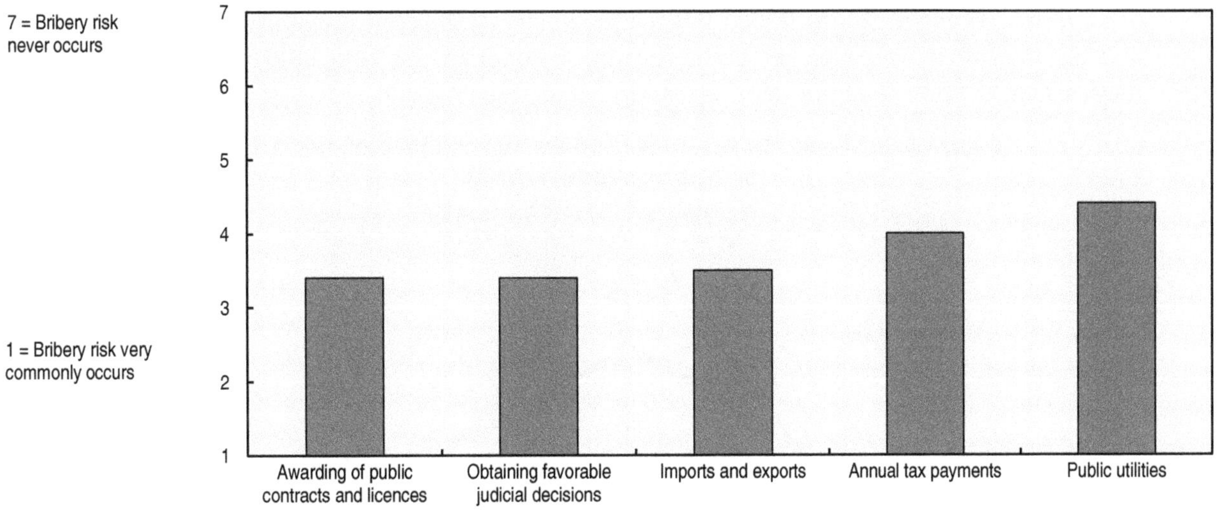

Note: The data reflect answers to the following question: In your country, how common is it for companies to make undocumented extra payments or bribes in connection with the following: awarding of public contracts and licences, obtaining favourable judicial decisions, imports and exports, annual tax payments and public utilities? [1 = very commonly occurs; 7 = never occurs].

Source: WEF (2014), Executive Opinion Survey, Global Competitiveness Report.

StatLink http://dx.doi.org/10.1787/888933290009

Azerbaijan and Russia, its performance is lower than the rest of the benchmark countries, with significant gaps compared to OECD countries as well as the United Arab Emirates and Singapore.

In terms of legislative framework, the first Law on State Procurement was adopted in Kazakhstan in 1997 and was based on the 1994 United Nations Commission on International Trade Law (UNCITRAL) Model Law. The public procurement legislation went through a number of revisions, with the current Public Procurement Law (the PPL) developed and enacted in 2007, and entering into effect on 1 January 2008. The public procurement system in Kazakhstan is regulated by a separate body of law; the PPL is the centrepiece of the country's public procurement legislation, setting out the basic principles and the general procedures of public procurement. The PPL covers both local and government procurement. Further, the civil legislation forms an integral part of the procurement framework in Kazakhstan, with the Civil Code regulating key contractual aspects of the procurement process. Furthermore, the Civil Code also contains provisions on guarantees, which apply to guarantees used by contracting entities in public procurement procedures (EBRD, 2014).

Kazakhstan has introduced e-procurement which has helped to improve its performance in key areas of public procurement governance

One of the major reforms in the public procurement system was the introduction of mandatory e-procurement procedures from 1 July 2012. The PPL provides for mandatory e-procurement procedures and requires that relevant information be published at every stage of the procurement. The e-procurement portal uses standard forms of procurement reports, which also ensure that procurement records are not manipulated and are easily accessible. In addition, the e-procurement platform maintains a blacklist of suppliers and contractors temporarily banned from participation in public procurement procedures.

However, regulatory gaps remain and there is scope for further development of the e-procurement platform to ensure well co-ordinated processes and real-time recording of all procurement decisions (EBRD, 2014). Indeed, accountability, transparency, efficiency and enforceability were the key areas of improvement in the 2012 EBRD Regional Self-Assessment of Public Procurement Legislation study (Figure 5.12).

Figure 5.12. **Kazakhstan has made progress in various areas of public procurement**

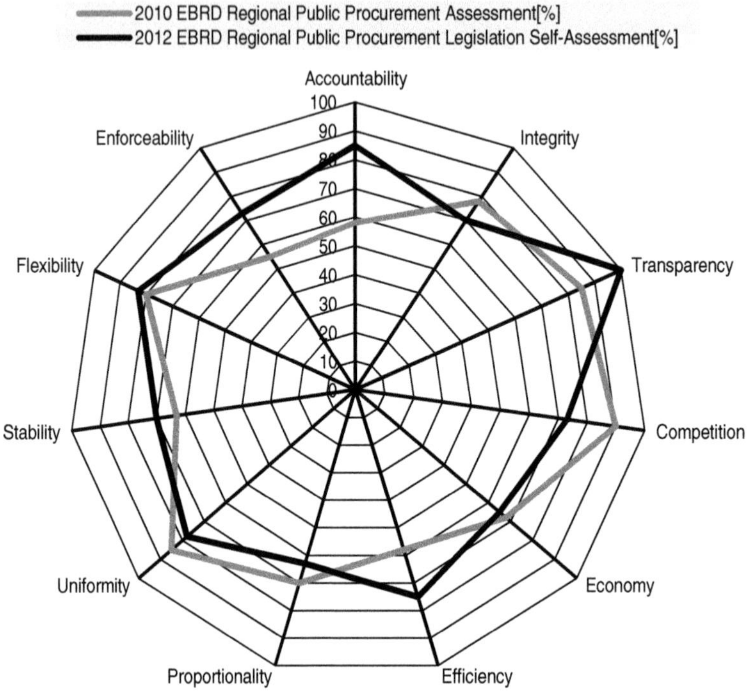

Note: The chart presents the scores for the quality of the legal framework in subsequent assessments of the national public procurement legislation completed between 2009 and 2013. The scores have been calculated on the basis of a legislation questionnaire based on the EBRD Core Principles for an Efficient Public Procurement Framework and answered by local legal advisors and/or national regulatory authorities. The scores are presented as a percentage with 100% representing the optimal score for each Core Principles benchmark indicator.

Source: EBRD (2010), "Regional Public Procurement Assessment"; EBRD (2012), "Regional Public Procurement Legislation Self-Assessment".

StatLink http://dx.doi.org/10.1787/888933290010

Key challenges are in areas such as integrity and competition of public procurement regulation

Nevertheless, there still several fundamental challenges in public procurement regulation. Specifically, as shown in Figure 5.12, Kazakhstan's performance worsened in the 2012 survey compared to 2010 in the integrity (-8 percentage points), competition (-17 percentage points), proportionality (-7 percentage points) and uniformity (-7 percentage points) aspects of public procurement regulation. Moreover, these are also the key areas in which Kazakhstan lags when compared to benchmark countries in the region, notably Russia, as well as Hungary (an OECD country with the best score in quality of public procurement laws covered in the EBRD study). In addition, there is also scope to improve efficiency of public procurement policies in Kazakhstan compared with Russia and Hungary (Figure 5.13).

Figure 5.13. **There are several key challenges, such as integrity and competition**

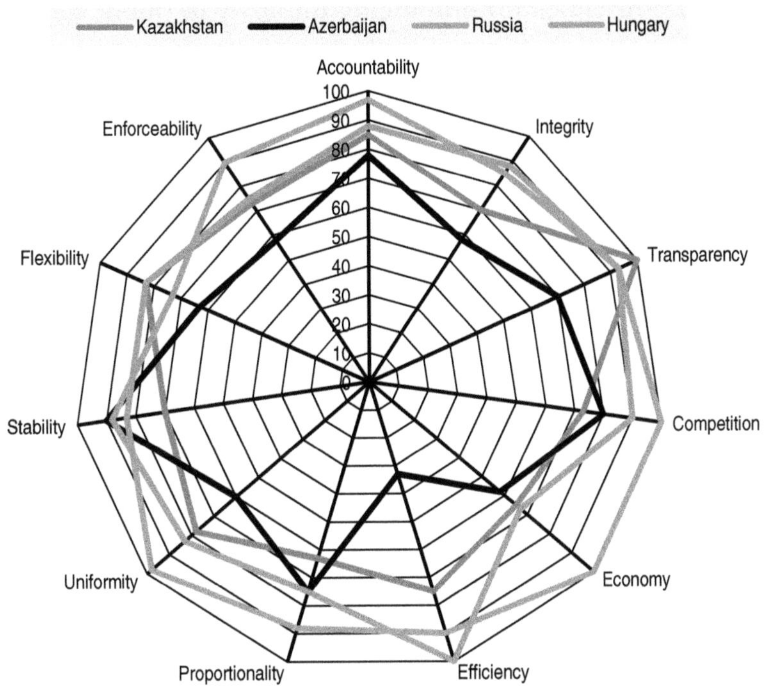

Source: EBRD (2012), "Regional Public Procurement Legislation Self-Assessment".

StatLink http://dx.doi.org/10.1787/888933290027

Among these key regulatory challenges, it is vital to enhance the integrity of public procurement as it is one of the key elements in anti-corruption and transparency safeguards (Box 5.5). In particular, transparency safeguards have always been a major element in procurement policy-making, and should still be considered of paramount importance as a regulatory factor, especially for countries where corruption is perceived to be a problem (EBRD, 2013). Second, Kazakhstan's current public procurement legal framework does not commit itself to the proper balance between attracting local and international participants to public tenders as appropriate. Ensuring a level playing field for potential suppliers to gain access to government contracts remains a major hurdle, especially at the international level (OECD, 2013). Third, Kazakhstan's public procurement legal framework allows heavy centralisation and does not promote the required level of uniform coverage of all public contracts, with excessive coverage exceptions and no clear differentiation between state and utilities procurement. Fourth, the public procurement legal framework does not provide for sufficient incentives for achieving best value for money from procurements or proper contract management of public contracts (EBRD, 2014).

Indeed, with such large expenditure on procurement, it is critical for Kazakhstan to enhance the integrity of public procurement to harness the potential of its strategic role. For example, public procurement can create synergies between innovation, development of SMEs and environmental protection. In particular, Kazakhstan can harness on the potential of sustainable public procurement to tap into green growth opportunities, which range from natural resource management (renewable and non-renewable, exhaustible and cultivated) to energy, urban and manufacturing systems (OECD, 2012).

Box 5.5. OECD Principles for enhancing integrity in public procurement

Developed and agreed upon by all OECD member countries, the OECD Principles for Enhancing Integrity in Public Procurement represent common standards for preventing waste, fraud and corruption in the entire procurement cycle, from the definition of needs to bidding, contract management and payment. These principles provide a blueprint for enhanced transparency, good management, prevention of misconduct, and control and accountability to map out and minimise the risk of corruption and provide a level playing field for businesses. The principles stress the importance of procedures to enhance transparency, good management, and prevention of misconduct as well as accountability and control in public procurement.

A. Transparency

1. Provide an adequate degree of transparency in the entire procurement cycle in order to promote fair and equitable treatment for potential suppliers.
2. Maximise transparency in competitive tendering and take precautionary measures to enhance integrity, in particular for exceptions to competitive tendering.

B. Good management

3. Ensure that public funds are used in procurement according to the purposes intended.
4. Ensure that procurement officials meet high professional standards of knowledge, skills and integrity.

C. Prevention of misconduct, compliance and monitoring

5. Put mechanisms in place to prevent risks to integrity in public procurement.
6. Encourage close co-operation between government and the private sector to maintain high standards of integrity, particularly in contract management.
7. Provide specific mechanisms to monitor public procurement as well as detect misconduct and apply sanctions accordingly.

D. Accountability and control

8. Establish a clear chain of responsibility together with effective control mechanisms.
9. Handle complaints from potential suppliers in a fair and timely manner.
10. Empower civil society organisations, media and the wider public to scrutinise public procurement.

Source: OECD (2009b), *OECD Principles for Integrity in Public Procurement*, http://dx.doi.org/10.1787/9789264056527-en.

Open and inclusive policy making

Citizens expect openness and inclusiveness from government in several areas. One is through a systemic, comprehensive approach to institutionalising a two-way communication with stakeholders, whereby relevant, useable information is provided, and interaction is fostered as a means to improve transparency, accountability and engagement. In addition, access to information and open data policies are key elements for promoting open government. A more open and inclusive policy-making process helps to ensure that policies are better informed and will better match citizens' needs. Facilitating the participation of citizens can enhance representative engagement, build trust in government and harness productive forms of responsibility, including in the delivery of public services. In particular, transparency, accountability and participatory inclusive policy making can be examined from three angles: transparency of national budget, particularly the use of national resources; open government initiatives such as e-government and open data; and participatory/consultative feedback from stakeholders.

Budget transparency has improved, particularly for natural resources

Transparency of the national budget – the disclosure and accessibility of key fiscal and budgetary information – is at the heart of good governance. The economic and social crisis underscored the need for greater budget transparency, and it has become a core component of countries' strategies for open government. The OECD Best Practices for Budget Transparency explicitly recognise the importance of disclosing government budgetary information in a timely and systematic manner, as well as the need to ensure the quality, integrity and, very importantly, the accessibility of this information in order to inform citizens and the legislature and hold government accountable (OECD, 2013).

Kazakhstan has made progress in the transparency of its national budget, particularly the management of its natural resources. The most commendable achievement in this area is Kazakhstan's attainment of the Extractive Industries Transparency Initiative (EITI) status of a "compliant country" in October 2013, in respect of observing the international standard of transparency of revenues from extractive industries. The country now produces EITI Reports that disclose revenues from the extraction of its natural resources. Companies disclose what they have paid in taxes and other payments and the government discloses what it has received. These two sets of figures are compared and reconciled.

The attainment of EITI compliant country status for Kazakhstan is a significant milestone. The government of Kazakhstan had committed itself to implement the EITI since 2005. EITI is the global standard to promote open and accountable management of natural resources. It has a high international, political and anticorruption status as it aims to strengthen government and company systems, inform public debate, and enhance trust. Hence, through EITI, Kazakhstan has laid the foundations to enhance transparency and accountability of the budget. In addition, stakeholders believe that EITI may now be ready to start building bridges and creating synergies with other sustainability initiatives (such as the Green Economy in Kazakhstan) and the new EITI rules may help to make that happen (Ospanova, Ahmadov and Wilson, 2013). Having achieved compliance status in the EITI, the National Stakeholder Council in Kazakhstan is currently undertaking a review process with a view to identifying new activities for EITI implementation. The consultation process will feed in to a revised work plan. There is considerable interest among stakeholders in decentralising the EITI process and establishing regional multi-stakeholder forums, in particular in resource-rich provinces. There may be scope for the inclusion of environmental payments in Kazakhstan's 2014 EITI Report, to be published in late 2015. The achievement of the compliant status put Kazakhstan on the same rank as benchmark countries such as Azerbaijan and Norway.

However, information provided is still limited for greater accountability of budget

Similarly, Kazakhstan has also achieved steady improvement in budget transparency as indicated by the Open Budget Survey conducted by the International Budget Partnership (IBP). Since 2008 Kazakhstan's score on the Open Budget Index (OBI), compiled by the IBP's Open Budget Survey, has consistently improved. According to the latest available OBI in 2012, Kazakhstan scored 48 out of 100 (compared to a score of 35 registered in 2008), which placed the country higher than the average score of 43 for all 100 countries surveyed.

Kazakhstan's OBI score indicates the limited depth of information that is made available. It indicates that the government provides the public with only some information on the national government's budget and financial activities during the course of the budget year. In particular, the ranking implies that it is still a challenge for citizens to hold the government to account for its management of public money (IBP, 2012). Moreover, its OBI score is below most of the benchmark countries (Figure 5.14).

Figure 5.14. **While OBI score has improved, it indicates that only limited information is made available**

Comparison of OBI (Open Budget Index) score across benchmark countries, 2012

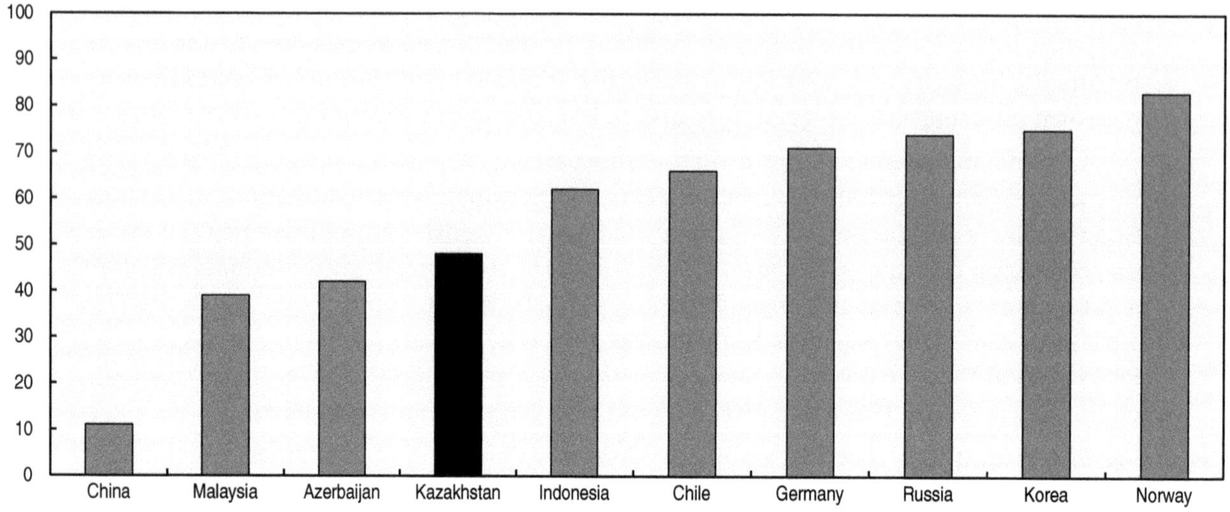

Source: International Budget Partnership (2012), Open Budget Index.

StatLink http://dx.doi.org/10.1787/888933290030

While regular budgetary information is available, there are some areas in which transparency and information gaps need to be addressed. While Kazakhstan has made efforts in making budgetary information accessible to citizens, including through the publication of a semi-annual civic budget and monthly bulletins on budget execution, information gaps remain. For example, Kazakhstan should increase the comprehensiveness of the executive's budget proposal, for example by focusing on providing information on the expenditures presented by economic classification for the budget year, previous years' expenditures classified by administrative, economic, functional domains and programmes, and previous years' revenues. It should also look at areas to improve the comprehensiveness of the year-end report by presenting audited actual expenditures; and by providing extensive explanations for the differences between estimates/forecasts and actual outcomes of macroeconomic variables, non-financial data, performance indicators, and funds intended to target the poor. In addition, there is scope to improve the quality of the audit report by increasing the coverage of annual expenditures audited, publishing audit reports on extra-budgetary funds, and publishing reports listing actions taken (IBP, 2012).

In addition, the Open Budget Survey also examines the extent of effective oversight provided by legislatures and supreme audit institutions (SAIs). These institutions play a critical role – often enshrined in national constitutions – in planning and overseeing the implementation of national budgets. The 2012 Survey suggest that while Kazakhstan has strong legislative strength (with a score of above 66 out of 100), it has weak performance in SAI and public engagement (score below 34). Against this backdrop, the IBP (2012) recommended that Kazakhstan, among other actions, should hold extensive consultations with a wide range of legislators as part of its process of determining budget priorities to improve budget oversight. Kazakhstan should also strengthen the independence of the

SAI, for instance, by requiring the final consent of the legislature or judiciary to remove the head of the SAI, and the budget for the SAI should be determined by the legislature.

Kazakhstan has also made great progress in open government initiatives

The government has set the development of e-government as a key priority and it was the first country in the Central Asian region with an "Open Government" initiative (Kaulanova, 2014). Inspired by successful international experience of e-government development, especially, in the Baltic States and Singapore, Kazakhstan started its e-government project in 2004 by approving a two-year strategic implementation programme. The adoption of the state programme on e-government was the most important step during this period (Kassen, 2010). Several specific modules of the e-government programme are already operational, including "e-licencing" and "electronic state purchases" and several others such as a regional "electronic *akimat*" (regional authority system) and an "e-notariate" (uniform notarial information system) are under development (OECD, 2012b). This could help reduce administrative burdens and control corruption. In addition, the Open Data platform was reflected in the "Information Kazakhstan – 2020" state programme, which was launched in 2013. Specifically, this programme involved analytical work on the country's Open Data readiness assessment (based on World Bank methodological tools), followed by a launch of the beta version[7] of an Open Data portal and a contest among developers for the creation of applications based on Open Data. The Open Data portal (open.e-gov.kz) is operational, but it is still too early to assess its success. One of the most critical factors in the process was the legal framework, which requires regulation for data access in all areas. As a result, there were various amendments to Kazakhstan's information laws. A new legislative framework is being elaborated that aims to underpin the role of e-government in increasing accountability and transparency, and to increase digital literacy among the population. The launch of an Open Government platform is also among the key planned ingredients of reforms to increase the accountability of the state as part of the "100 steps" action plan.

Reflecting the steady progress made in advancing the e-government and open data initiatives, Kazakhstan has made considerable improvement over the years in the global e-government benchmarking survey conducted by the United Nations. In the latest 2014 survey, Kazakhstan was ranked 28th (out of 193 countries) globally in the United Nations e-government development index (EGDI), with a high EGDI score of 0.73 (Figure 5.15). Kazakhstan therefore ranked sixth in Asia and first in Central Asia. This was a vast improvement compared to 2008, when Kazakhstan was ranked 81st in the survey. However, compared to benchmark countries, there is still room for further improvement, especially to close the gap with Korea, Australia and Singapore. In particular, the 2014 United Nations Survey also included findings on open government data (OGD) assessing the development of data publishing globally. The survey highlighted that Kazakhstan, along with most of the benchmark countries such as Australia, Canada, Chile, China, Germany, Korea, Norway, the United Arab Emirates and Singapore, scored higher than 66.6% on data publishing in 2014.

However, more can be done to improve the availability and quality of statistics for better governance. The power of statistics is recognised in their use, which spans the design and implementation stages of country policy frameworks. Good statistics provide the evidence required to develop and monitor effective development policies (OECD, 2007). They highlight where resources are most needed, and provide the means to track progress and assess the impact of different policies. Good statistics also improve the transparency

Figure 5.15. **Kazakhstan has made considerable improvement over the years in e-government and open data initiatives**

United Nations e-government development index (EGDI) and rank, 2014

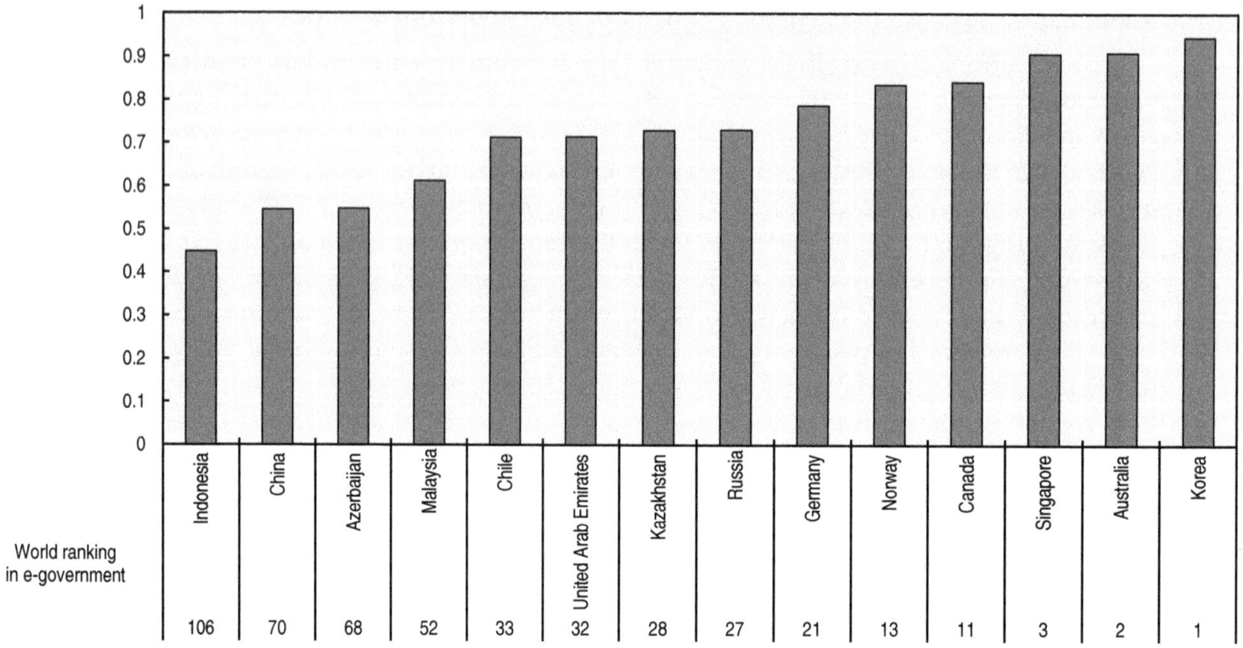

Source: United Nations e-government Survey 2014.

StatLink http://dx.doi.org/10.1787/888933290047

and accountability of policy making, both of which are essential for good governance, by enabling electorates to judge the success of government policies and to hold their governments to account for those policies (Box 5.6).

There are still challenges to promoting inclusive policy making so as to provide greater accountability and responsiveness to the needs of citizens

A government can provide open data and still remain deeply opaque and unaccountable. Inclusive policy making focuses on evaluating the impact of policies on key groups of society that might be disadvantaged by that impact. The World Justice Project's (WJP) newly released Open Government Index 2015, presents the first effort to measure government openness based on the general public's experiences and perceptions gathered from primary survey data.[8] The WJP Open Government Index 2015 showed that Kazakhstan's performance is below most of the comparators. While Kazakhstan has scored relatively better in terms of right to information, it scores poorly for civic participation and complaint mechanisms (Table 5.3). Kazakhstan is taking steps to advance consultation with external stakeholders. Among them, it has established a blog platform for heads of central state bodies to receive directly questions from citizens, which has received over 180 000 requests since its launch in 2012. However, these concern central government authorities only, and not local authorities, and responses are voluntary. Despite these advances in expanding the channels for consultation, limiting public consultation to the formal meetings of expert committees on the one hand and online engagement for the public on the other, does not provide a sufficient opportunity for policy discussions. Furthermore, there are limited arm's length mechanisms to ensure the protection of citizens' rights in a fast and affordable manner (OECD, 2014c).

Box 5.6. **The statistical agenda ahead for Kazakhstan**

The Committee on Statistics of the Republic of Kazakhstan is organised under the leadership of the Ministry of National Economy. The development of official statistics in Kazakhstan has a long history, dating back to 19th century with the first general census of the population being carried out. Following the collapse of the Soviet Union, the Central Statistics Division within the Kazakh Soviet Socialist Republic (SSR) was transformed into the State Committee on statistics and analysis of the Republic of Kazakhstan. The committee is legally regulated by the "State Statistics law" adopted in 1997 and modified in 2010. According to the newly adopted law, the goals of the agency are three-fold: establishing statistical methodology; performing statistical activities in line with the state statistics guidelines; and responding to the needs of society, the state, and the international community for official statistical information.

In 2008, the United Nations Economic Commission for Europe (UNECE) and the UN Economic and Social Commission for Asia and the Pacific (ESCAP) jointly conducted an assessment of the Global Assessment of the statistical system of the Republic of Kazakhstan. This review concluded that the Committee on Statistics of the Republic of Kazakhstan provides an example of good working standards in adherence with the fundamental principles of official statistics and international networking (UNECE and UNESCAP, 2008). They also recommended a revision of the statistical law which took place in 2010. Apart from that, these international organisations suggested some reforms regarding the organisational structure of the committee, a better dissemination of statistics to external users and an increased confidentiality of statistical data (UNECE and UNESCAP, 2008). Based on this assessment, the World Bank supports the country in strengthening the National Statistical System (KASTAT project) to improve the efficiency and effectiveness of the national statistical system to provide relevant, timely and reliable data in line with internationally accepted methodology and best practices (World Bank, 2014). The Committee on Statistics is expecting to conduct a 2016-17 global assessment to assess the work that has been done and further to improve the national statistics of the country (Committee on statistics, 2014).

The OECD Statistics Directorate and the Committee of Statistics of the Republic of Kazakhstan signed a collaboration agreement in April 2014. In addition to the World Bank support, this agreement between the two organisations will result in closer collaboration in areas such as national accounts, environmental economic statistics, and measuring green growth and sustainable development.

Source: Authors' elaboration.

Kazakhstan is implementing reforms to improve access to information. As part of the "100 concrete steps" action plan, Kazakhstan aims to enhance accountability in particular by introducing a freedom of information law. It is also planned to require heads of central executive bodies, local authorities and heads of universities to hold annual reporting meetings with the population.

The experience of OECD countries suggests that sound and inclusive policies require a policy-making process that is transparent, evidence-driven, accessible and responsive to as wide a range of citizens as possible. This calls for inclusion of a diverse number of views in the process of policy design and provision of opportunities for robust public policy debate. To be effective, these elements must be applied at all stages of the design and delivery of public policies and services. Hence, within this context, there is a need to go beyond e-participation to include a more diverse group of citizens, especially those socially vulnerable who might not have access to such e-channels. The potential reach of Open Data and other e-government platforms, such as platforms currently being implemented to encourage discussions on draft legislation (Open Legal acts, currently in beta phase) and Open dialogue (planned) is limited by the level of digital literacy of the population (estimated at 64% by the authorities of Kazakhstan).

Table 5.3. **The WJP Open Government Index 2015 showed that Kazakhstan's performance is below most of the comparators**

	Open Government (OVERALL SCORE)	Dimension 1: Publicised laws and government data	Dimension2: Right to Information	Dimension3: Civic participation	Dimension 4: Complaint mechanisms
Norway	**0.81**	0.73	0.77	0.89	0.86
Canada	**0.75**	0.69	0.68	0.81	0.80
Australia	**0.74**	0.64	0.70	0.80	0.82
Korea	**0.73**	0.71	0.75	0.70	0.75
Germany	**0.72**	0.60	0.68	0.85	0.74
Chile	**0.68**	0.54	0.69	0.73	0.76
Singapore	**0.63**	0.68	0.58	0.55	0.7
Indonesia	**0.58**	0.49	0.56	0.68	0.57
Russia	**0.49**	0.47	0.58	0.42	0.47
United Arab Emirates	**0.48**	0.62	0.47	0.36	0.47
Kazakhstan	**0.44**	0.47	0.56	0.35	0.38
China	**0.43**	0.52	0.53	0.21	0.46
Malaysia	**0.43**	0.51	0.46	0.37	0.37

Source: World Justice Project (2015). Scores range between 0 and 1, with 1 indicating greatest openness. Scoring is based on answers drawn from general population and expert surveys collected for the WJP Rule of Law Index.

Open and inclusive policy making also requires both a greater degree of decentralisation of the management of central public organisations and local governments. Kazakhstan has already introduced various decentralisations of powers to the local level. For example, under the Concept for Development of Local Self-Government (2012), local executive authorities were granted the status of the local self-governance authorities. The new law also delegates additional authorities to *akims* (regional councils) of towns which are subordinate to regional authorities, villages and rural districts to decide on sources of funding, and to approve budget plans for their incomes and expenses after co-ordinating them with the local community. The reorganisation of state functions also led to the devolution of a number of functions to local authorities in 2014. Nevertheless, effective decentralisation requires that these efforts be accompanied by allocation of appropriate resources (OECD, 2014c). Given that devolution increases discretion, central agencies will need to ensure that they have the necessary tools to enable effective vertical and horizontal accountability for results and mechanisms with a greater focus on outcomes, including for ministries within the central government (Aucoin and Heintzman, 2000). This would require striking a balance between the oversight of central agencies of other central government organisations – to ensure accountability and strategic direction, coherence and appropriate administration and financial management across the system – and ministerial empowerment – to achieve higher levels of downstream performance and find new, more effective and efficient ways to ensure accountability for performance, as the command and control systems will no longer be effective. This challenge has already been acknowledged in the new General Approaches for Modernisation of Public Administration by 2020 (OECD, 2014c).

In addition, there should be greater participation of civil society in service delivery. Strengthening relations with citizens is a sound investment in better policy making and a core element of good governance. Besides provision of information, the government would need to create an enabling space for consultation and active citizen participation in policy formulation and the decision-making process (OECD, 2001). Between 2002 and 2011, the government of Kazakhstan directed two programmes towards the development of civil society representation: the "Concept of State Support for Non-Commercial Organisations" (2002-06) and the "Concept of Civil Society Development" (2006-11). The two concepts included formal rules regarding relations between governmental and non-governmental organisations, as well as various forms of support, including through contractual relations. In addition, the "Law of the Republic of Kazakhstan On Public Service" was adopted in 2013, which aims to improve the quality of public services by ensuring the rights and legitimate interests of citizens in this area, and the active involvement of the public in the process of improving the quality of public services. However, across ministries, the prevailing impression is that the changes in the decision-making process have thus far been more formal than actual. Essentially, the problem is linked to the limited room for manoeuvre that the planning system and control from the central administration leave to the ministries. In most cases, the objectives of a regulation are indeed determined before any consultation takes place. In addition, acknowledging that external persons and organisations, including those with dissenting views, should play a role in governmental decision making requires a cultural change in the administration – one that needs to be enforced in practice (OECD, 2014c).

Notes

1. Corruption was selected as the biggest business environment obstacle by 19.3% of firms, followed by the practices of the informal sector (15.0%) (World Bank, 2015).
2. Appropriability is the capacity of the firm to retain the added value it creates for its own benefit.
3. According to the World Justice project (WJP), the rule of law encompasses four universal principles. These are: the government and its officials and agents are accountable under the law; the laws are clear, publicised, stable and fair, and protect fundamental rights, including the security of persons and property; the process by which laws are enacted, administered and enforced is accessible, efficient and fair; justice is delivered by competent, ethical, and independent representatives and neutrals, who are of sufficient number, have adequate resources, and reflect the make-up of the communities they serve. Based on these four principles, WJP developed nine key factors that form the basis of their Rule of Law Index. For the purpose of analysis four of these factors are used as they are considered the most crucial for good governance (OECD, 2013). While there are several interpretations of the rule of law, the indicators developed by the WJP's Rule of Law Index are one of the most comprehensive and systematic approaches (OECD, 2014c).
4. The components include whether people can access and afford civil justice; whether civil justice is free of discrimination; whether civil justice is free of corruption; whether civil justice is free of improper government influence; whether civil justice is not subject to unreasonable delays; whether civil justice is effectively enforced; and whether alternative dispute resolutions are accessible, impartial and effective. Cultural competence acknowledges and responds to the unique views of different people and communities.
5. The Institutional Profiles (Database) IPD project provides a tool quantifying countries' institutional characteristics through indicators built from perception data. By their very nature, institutional phenomena are difficult to observe and therefore to measure. The IPD project aims to quantify countries' institutional characteristics by gathering the perception of experts through a questionnaire. Consequently, those data may not represent the true situation within a country, for example where the experts/respondents are subject to "perception bias". For instance, perceptions may be influenced by the respondent's personality, their scale of values, the professional constraints to which they are subject, the media, the economic and political situation within the country etc. In order to limit the possibility of perception bias and its effects on the results, various precautions were taken when processing the responses to the survey. Systematic checks were carried out to ensure the internal and geographical consistency of the responses and their consistency over time. For this edition, these checking processes have been automated. See *www.cepii.fr/institutions/doc/ipd_2012_cahiers-2013-03_en.pdf*.

6. While the Transparency International Corruption Perceptions Index (CPI) is a composite index that includes data from the World Economic Forum's Executive Opinion Survey, it relies on questions therein related explicitly to undocumented payments and the diversion of public funds and does not include data on meritocracy. The correlation presented in Figure 5.8 remains if the CPI is recalculated excluding the WEF Executive Opinion Survey.
7. Beta versions have gone through alpha testing in-house but precede the final version of the product.
8. The WJP Open Government Index measures the openness of government by looking at the experiences and perceptions of the general public as well as in-country lawyers and public health practitioners, in contrast to efforts that focus on laws on the books or on the implementation of certain laws. At the core of the WJP Open Government Index is the measurement of government openness based on primary data anchored in actual experiences. The Index's scores are built from the assessments of local residents (1 000 respondents per country) and local experts, which ensure the findings reflect the conditions experienced by the population, including marginalised sectors of society.

References

Aucoin. P and Heintzman, R. (2000), "The dialectics of accountability for performance in public management reform", *International Review of Administrative Sciences*, Vol. 66, pp. 45-55.

Azfar, O. and T. Gurgur, (2008), "Does corruption affect health outcomes in the Philippines?", *Economics of Governance*, Volume 9, Issue 3, pp. 197-244, July.

Bertelsmann Stiftung Transformation Index (BTI), (2014), "Kazakhstan Country Report".

Business Anti-Corruption (2015), "Business Corruption in Kazakhstan" *www.business-anti-corruption.com/*.

CEPII (2012), Institutional Profiles Database 2012, Centre d'Études Prospectives et d'Informations Internationales (CEPII), AFD and Directorate General of the Treasury (DG Trésor) of the Ministry of Finance, *www.cepii.fr/institutions/EN/ipd.asp*.

Di Tella R. (2011), "Kazakhstan: Institutions", in "Growth and Competitiveness in Kazakhstan: Issues and Priorities in the Areas of Macroeconomic, Industrial, Trade and Institutional Development Policies", *Working Paper*, Centre for International Development, Harvard University.

EBRD (2014), "Kazakhstan Country Profile", 2012 Regional Self-Assessment, European Bank for Reconstruction and Development, London.

EBRD (2013), "Law in Transition", European Bank for Reconstruction and Development, London.

EBRD (2012), "Regional Public Procurement Legislation Self-Assessment", European Bank for Reconstruction and Development, London.

EBRD (2011), "Life in Transition Survey II", European Bank for Reconstruction and Development, London.

EBRD (2010), "Regional Public Procurement Sector Assessment", European Bank for Reconstruction and Development, London.

EITI (2013), "The 9th National Report on the implementation of the Extractive Industry Transparency Initiative in Kazakhstan 2013" Astana, available at *https://eiti.org/report/kazakhstan/2013*.

Global Integrity (2010), *www.globalintegrity.org/global_year/2010*.

Hatry, H.P. (1999), *Performance Measurement: Getting Results*, Urban Institute Press, Washington, DC.

Hausmann, R., D. Rodrik, and A. Velasco. (2005), "Growth Diagnostics", John F. Kennedy School of Government, Harvard University, Cambridge, MA.

Helliwell, J. F. et al. (2014), "Good governance and national well-being: What are the linkages?", *OECD Working Papers on Public Governance*, No. 25, OECD Publishing. *http://dx.doi.org/10.1787/5jxv9f651hvj-en*.

IBP (2012), *Open Budget Survey 2012: Kazakhstan Country Profile*", International Budget Partnership.

Kassen, M. (2010), "E-Government in Kazakhstan: Realization and prospects", Paper presentation at the 2010 Political Networks Conference Duke University, Durham. N. Carolina.

Kaulanova, A. (2014), "The Rise of Open Data in Kazakhstan", World Bank blog. *http://blogs.worldbank.org/ic4d/rise-open-data-kazakhstan*.

Kenessariyev, U. et al. (2013), "Human Health Cost of Air Pollution in Kazakhstan", *Journal of Environmental Protection*, 2013, 4, 869-876 *http://dx.doi.org/10.4236/jep.2013.48101*. Published Online August 2013 (*www.scirp.org/journal/jep*).

Kline, R., F. Galeotti and R. Orsinil (2014), "When Foul Play Seems Fair: Dishonesty as a Response to Violations of Just Deserts", *Working Paper DSE* N. 920, Department of Economics, University of Bologna, January.

NERA Economic Consulting and Bloomberg New Energy Finance (BNEF) (2011), "The Demand for Greenhouse Gas Emissions Reduction Investments: An Investors' Marginal Abatement Cost Curve for Kazakhstan", Prepared for EBRD, October 2011, London.

OECD (2015a), *Government at a Glance 2015*, OECD Publishing, Paris, *http://dx.doi.org/10.1787/gov_glance-2015-en*.

OECD (2015b), Istanbul Anti-Corruption Action Plan, "Third round monitoring progress update for Kazakhstan", plenary meetings held on 23-24 March 2015.

OECD (2014a), *Regulatory Policy in Kazakhstan: Towards Improved Implementation*, OECD Publishing, Paris, *http://dx.doi.org/10.1787/9789264214255-en*.

OECD (2014b), "Energy Subsidies and Climate Change in Kazakhstan", Final Draft Report, OECD, Paris.

OECD (2014c), *Kazakhstan: Review of the Central Administration*, OECD Public Governance Reviews, OECD Publishing, Paris, *http://dx.doi.org/10.1787/9789264224605-en*.

OECD (2013), *Government at a Glance 2013*, OECD Publishing, Paris, *http://dx.doi.org/10.1787/gov_glance-2013-en*.

OECD (2012), *OECD Investment Policy Reviews: Kazakhstan 2012*, OECD Publishing, Paris, *http://dx.doi.org/10.1787/9789264121812-en*.

OECD (2011), *Towards More Effective and Dynamic Public Management in Mexico*, OECD Public Governance Reviews, OECD Publishing, *http://dx.doi.org/10.1787/9789264116238-en*.

OECD (2009a), *Government at a Glance*, OECD Publishing, Paris, *http://dx.doi.org/10.1787/9789264033177-en*.

OECD (2009b), *OECD Principles for Integrity in Public Procurement*, OECD Publishing, Paris, *http://dx.doi.org/10.1787/9789264056527-en*.

OECD (2007), "Counting Down Poverty: The Role of Statistics in World Development", OECD and Paris 21, OECD, Paris.

OECD (2001), *Citizens as Partners: Information, Consultation and Public Participation in Policy-making*, OECD Publishing, Paris, *http://dx.doi.org/10.1787/9789264195561-en*.

Oman, C. and C. Arndt (2010), "Measuring governance", *OECD Development Centre Policy Brief* No. 39, OECD Publishing, Paris, *http://dx.doi.org/10.1787/5km5z9nnxwxw-en*.

Ospanova, S., I. Ahmadov and E.Wilson (2013), *EITI and Sustainable Development: Lessons and New Challenges for the Caspian Region*, International Institute for Environment and Development. London.

Pollitt, C. and G. Bouckaert (2004), *Public Management Reform: A Comparative Analysis*, Oxford University Press, Oxford.

Rajkumar, A. S. and S.Vinaya. (2008), "Public Spending and Outcomes: Does Governance Matter?", *Journal of Development Economics*, Vol. 86, pp. 96–111.

Rodrik, D (2008), "Thinking about governance", in *Governance, Growth, and Development Decision-Making*, World Bank, Washington DC.

Rothstein, B. and E. Uslaner. (2005), "All for all: Equality and social trust", *LSE Health and Social Care Discussion Paper* No. 15.

Transparency International (2014), *2014 Corruption Perceptions Index*, Transparency International, available at *www.transparency.org/cpi2014* (consulted July 2015).

UNECE (2008), "Environmental Performance Review: Kazakhstan- Second Review", Environmental Performance Reviews Series, United Nations Economic Commission for Europe, New York and Geneva.

UNESCAP (2014), "Governments can use sustainable public procurement to foster inclusive and sustainable development in Asia and the Pacific", *Working Paper*, Macroeconomic and Policy Development Division, United Nations Economic and Social Commission for Asia and the Pacific, Bangkok.

UNECE and UNESCAP (2008), *A Global Assessment of the Statistical System of the Republic of Kazakhstan*, United Nations Economic Commission for Europe and United Nations Economic and Social Commission for Asia and the Pacific, January.

UNPACS (2014), *E-government Survey 2014: E-government for the Future we Want*, United Nations Public Administration Country Studies, New York.

WEF (2014), *Global competitiveness report (2014–2015)*, World Economic Forum, Geneva.

World Bank (2015) Enterprise Surveys, *www.enterprisesurveys.org*, The World Bank, last accessed 28 July 2015.

World Bank (2014), *World Development Indicators* (database), Washington DC, *http://data.worldbank.org*.

W.K. Kellogg Foundation (2004), *Logic Model Development Guide*, W.K. Kellogg Foundation, Michigan.

World Justice Project (2015), *Open Government Index*, WJP, Washington, DC, *http://worldjusticeproject.org/sites/default/files/ogi_2015.pdf*.

World Justice Project (2014), *Rule of Law Index 2014*, WJP, Washington DC, *http://worldjusticeproject.org/sites/default/files/files/wjp_rule_of_law_index_2014_report.pdf*.

ORGANISATION FOR ECONOMIC CO-OPERATION AND DEVELOPMENT

The OECD is a unique forum where governments work together to address the economic, social and environmental challenges of globalisation. The OECD is also at the forefront of efforts to understand and to help governments respond to new developments and concerns, such as corporate governance, the information economy and the challenges of an ageing population. The Organisation provides a setting where governments can compare policy experiences, seek answers to common problems, identify good practice and work to co-ordinate domestic and international policies.

The OECD member countries are: Australia, Austria, Belgium, Canada, Chile, the Czech Republic, Denmark, Finland, France, Germany, Greece, Hungary, Iceland, Ireland, Israel, Italy, Japan, Korea, Luxembourg, Mexico, the Netherlands, New Zealand, Norway, Poland, Portugal, the Slovak Republic, Slovenia, Spain, Sweden, Switzerland, Turkey, the United Kingdom and the United States. The European Commission takes part in the work of the OECD.

OECD Publishing disseminates widely the results of the Organisation's statistics gathering and research on economic, social and environmental issues, as well as the conventions, guidelines and standards agreed by its members.

OECD DEVELOPMENT CENTRE

The Development Centre of the Organisation for Economic Co-operation and Development was established in 1962 and comprises 27 member countries of the OECD: Austria, Belgium, Chile, the Czech Republic, Denmark, Finland, France, Germany, Greece, Iceland, Ireland, Israel, Italy, Korea, Luxembourg, Mexico, the Netherlands, Norway, Poland, Portugal, Slovak Republic, Slovenia, Spain, Sweden, Switzerland, Turkey and the United Kingdom. In addition, 24 non-OECD countries are full members of the Development Centre: Brazil (since March 1994); India (February 2001); Romania (October 2004); Thailand (March 2005); South Africa (May 2006); Egypt and Viet Nam (March 2008); Colombia (July 2008); Indonesia (February 2009); Costa Rica, Mauritius, Morocco and Peru (March 2009); the Dominican Republic (November 2009); Senegal (February 2011); Argentina and Cabo Verde (March 2011); Panama (July 2013); Côte d'Ivoire, Kazakhstan and Tunisia (January 2015); the People's Republic of China (July 2015) and Ghana and Uruguay (October 2015). The European Union also takes part in the work of the Centre.

The Development Centre occupies a unique place within the OECD and in the international community. It provides a platform where developing and emerging economies interact on an equal footing with OECD members to promote knowledge sharing and peer learning on sustainable and inclusive development. The Centre combines multidisciplinary analysis with policy dialogue activities to help governments formulate innovative policy solutions to the global challenges of development. Hence, the Centre plays a key role in the OECD's engagement efforts with non-member countries.

To increase the impact and legitimacy of its work, the Centre adopts an inclusive approach and engages with a variety of governmental and non-governmental stakeholders. It works closely with experts and institutions from its member countries, has established partnerships with key international and regional organisations and hosts networks of private-sector enterprises, think tanks and foundations working for development. The results of its work are discussed in experts' meetings as well as in policy dialogues and high-level meetings, and are published in a range of high-quality publications and papers for the research and policy communities.

For more information on the Centre, please see *www.oecd.org/dev*.

OECD PUBLISHING, 2, rue Andre-Pascal, 75775 PARIS CEDEX 16
(41 2015 09 1P1) ISBN 978-92-64-24675-1 – 2016

www.ingramcontent.com/pod-product-compliance
Ingram Content Group UK Ltd.
Pitfield, Milton Keynes, MK11 3LW, UK
UKHW051501290926
15471UKWH00008B/1337

9 789264 246751